MASTERING SAUCES

MASTERING SAUCES

The Home Cook's Guide to New Techniques

for Fresh Flavors

SUSAN VOLLAND

PHOTOGRAPHY BY ANGIE NORWOOD BROWNE

W. W. Norton & Company
Independent Publishers Since 1923
NEW YORK | LONDON

For information about permission to reproduce selections from this book, write to
Permissions, W. W. Norton & Company, Inc., 500 Fifth Avenue, New York, NY 10110

For information about special discounts for bulk purchases, please contact
W. W. Norton Special Sales at specialsales@wwnorton.com or 800-233-4830

Manufacturing by Courier Kendallville
Book design by Level Inc.
Production manager: Anna Oler

Library of Congress Cataloging-in-Publication Data

Volland, Susan.
Mastering sauces : the home cook's guide to new techniques for fresh flavors / Susan Volland ;
photography by Angie Norwood Browne.—First edition.
pages cm
Includes index.
ISBN 978-0-393-24185-3 (hardcover)
1. Sauces. I. Title.
TX819.A1V65 2015
641.81'4—dc23
                              2015017677

W. W. Norton & Company, Inc., 500 Fifth Avenue, New York, N.Y. 10110
www.wwnorton.com

W. W. Norton & Company Ltd., Castle House, 75/76 Wells Street, London W1T 3QT

1 2 3 4 5 6 7 8 9 0

For Jeff. Thank you for showing me how wonderful life is
when you flavor, texturize, and season it with good friends and family.

CONTENTS

MASTERING SAUCES

INTRODUCTION

Sauces make foods taste "right." Order a piece of chicken or some noodles anywhere in the world, and you're going to get pretty much the same thing. Unembellished ingredients tend to have a global uniformity. Add sauce, and everything changes. Dishes become regional and familial. Turkey gravy is meant to taste like Grandma's. Football gatherings aren't the same without Dave's game day enchiladas. Summer doesn't officially start until Evelyn's famous macaroni salad appears. Even people who may proclaim ambivalence to sauces will customize their sandwiches with light mayo or extra-strong mustard. Lovers of plain steak still choose their favorite salad dressings and baked potato toppings. Sauce is personal. It's everywhere. And it's not always fancy.

Mastering Sauces is about confidence, control, and customization. It's a reminder that the "right" way to make sauce is *your* way. For today's cooks that often means sauces that feature fresh, seasonal produce, international ingredients, and variations for alternative diets and food sensitivities. The first hurdle is to step away from the temptations of jars and packets. Sauces may be uniformly accepted as tasty, but unfortunately, sauce making is often perceived as being a special skill.

I make sauces like a chef. That means I usually make my sauces spontaneously, with drizzles of this, pinches of that, and lots of pan rattling. I have fun with it. When I suggest to other people that they should make their sauces with similar vim, they either nod enthusiastically in agreement or look at me like I've asked them to sprout wings and fly. There isn't a lot of middle ground.

Curious cooks who venture into the world of traditional sauce making often find themselves barraged with French terms, obsessing over cauldrons of simmering bones and subtle color gradations of toasted flour, and awash in seemingly endless quantities of eggs, cream, and butter. Sauce making, like baking or preserving, is often presented as a culinary canon. It is presumed that if you want to get good at it, you need to take it very seriously and start with the classics. That's partially true. Having a solid culinary foundation is what gives me the freedom to make sauces with confidence. But to casual cooks looking for dinner ideas, the old lessons can seem practically prehistoric. Modern cooks want teriyaki and tikka masala, not jugged hare. Tastes have changed. Unfortunately, the lesson plans haven't quite kept up with the times.

Mastering Sauces is meant to be as liberating and lighthearted as sauces themselves. My goal is to get more people to cook. Cooking brings people together. It's creative. No matter how many sets of matching pigments and paintbrushes you distribute, no two people will create the same work of art. Sauces are the same—they just adorn a different kind of blank canvas. I believe that laughing and finger painting with friends is as important as visits to the Louvre. I will forever appreciate the liberty that came with my classical education, but I believe the best way to get more people to cook sauces is to remove a layer of formality and freshen things up. The best sauces are those that fit your lifestyle, not the other way around.

Several years ago, my nephew, Greg, set out to find the perfect combination of warm breadsticks and marinara dipping sauce. He was a ridiculously picky eater. Suddenly, though, instead of just shaking his head and refusing to taste whatever was set before him, he started actively looking for good food experiences. His quest took him to new places. He smelled and saw new things. He compared restaurant A with restaurant B and weighed their merits. We even spent time together making our own breadsticks and sauce from scratch. (Both were judged just "okay.") Best of all, he consciously tasted his food and thought about what he was eating.

Sauces are a part of our daily lives. Sometimes they are best delicately ladled from heirloom china; other times it's all about dipping warm, chewy breadsticks into a marinara that has just the right balance of garlic, oregano, and tomato flavor. If it can be enjoyed while blasting aliens, all the better.

When it comes to cooking, I have strong ties to both the old and the new. I learned my craft from formal women wearing starched caps at the London Cordon Bleu Cookery School. My fellow students were from all over the world and young by decree. We felt a bit ridiculous having to address our peers formally as Mr. this and Miss that. For the first three months, we were not allowed to use any equipment that was plugged in other than the stovetop and oven. In the mornings, we all cooked the same small portions of classic recipes on home-style equipment: omelets with tiny, buttery croutons; timbales of creamy fish mousse; trembling sherry-laced jellies. Each dish was tasted and individually critiqued. In the afternoons, we crowded into a stuffy room for demonstrations and to collectively recite the basic quantities of common recipes by rote. The thought of our formal quarterly exams still makes me shudder with anxiety. Three school directors would loom over your work space with their spoons, picking through your dishes and scribbling notes on their clipboards. You were required to keep all of your trash in a small bin, and after your food was judged, the high priestesses would tip it out to see whether you had peeled your potatoes wastefully or used too many paper towels. Eggshells were to be reserved, because they could be used to help clarify tomorrow's batch of consommé. (That is a technique I have purposely omitted from this book because I never, ever want to do it again.) I hated it, but I now understand how influential that kind of intimacy was. I learned to cook for individuals, not crowds. That's still what I feel most comfortable doing.

When I returned home to Seattle, I had no clue about cooking in a restaurant. Unlike American culinary school graduates, I had never prepared large quantities of food or used professional equipment. But I managed to fake familiarity with steam kettles and huge tilting skillets. I could cook, and that's what really mattered. I catered, baked, and worked in fine-dining restaurants. I saw firsthand why chefs make such great reality TV. When you combine crazy work ethics, perfectionism, heat, noise, knives, artistry, crisis management, and a slightly odd predilection for performance and public service, you have yourself a chef. Cram a team of them into a small high-pressure environment, and you have a rocking restaurant hot line. When it all syncs together, it's a rush unlike any other. The short bursts of unmatched teamwork, pride, and sensory overload manage to offset the long hours, lack of social life, and lousy paychecks—at least for a while. It didn't take long before the hours, the egos, and the impersonality of it all got to me. I didn't want to cook for strangers, so I veered off into food communication and enjoyed spending dinnertime with friends and family again.

I taught, I made pretty food for photographs and TV, I created original recipes for corporations. An editor offered to pay me to write an article, so I started writing.

I traveled, read a lot, and experimented with exotic ingredients and techniques. Twenty-five years after graduating from the Cordon Bleu, I found myself worlds away from that tiny old-fashioned school and part of the *Modernist Cuisine* team.

The founder of *Modernist Cuisine*, Nathan Myhrvold, has one of the world's greatest minds. He was practically a kid when he got his doctorate in theoretical and mathematical physics from Princeton. He also has a master's degree in geophysics and space physics and a bachelor's in mathematics. He did postdoctoral work on quantum theories of gravitation, cosmology, and "curved spacetime" with Dr. Stephen Hawking at Cambridge University before settling in as the chief technology officer at Microsoft. And, all the while, he was cooking. He approached the topic with the curiosity and vigor of any field he studies. He traveled the world to taste and learn. His scientific knowledge and experience drew him toward chefs and innovators who were exploring gastronomy at the molecular level. Eventually his hobby evolved into a branch of his company, Intellectual Ventures. He made room for a kitchen in a lab filled with chemists, physicists, engineers, and expert machinists. And oh, what a kitchen it is.

The Cooking Lab, as it is known today, has some pots and pans hanging from the ventilation hood, and the work stations are set up on the familiar stainless steel tables common to prep kitchens, but that's where the similarities end. There is a rotary evaporator, an industrial homogenizer, an autoclave, and a high-speed centrifuge. Bubbling hot-water circulators are everywhere. The vacuum chamber is in constant use, and the larder is filled with jars labeled "lambda carrageenan," "sucrose esters," and "methocellulose."

I was originally invited to the lab as an editorial assistant to help finish up the giant six-book set *Modernist Cuisine: The Art and Science of Cooking*. (The Cooking Lab, 2011). My job was to clean up spreadsheets and tables, make sense of the data, and add some descriptive, informative text. When I needed clarification, the authors would sit with me and explain the principles so I could summarize things in a few paragraphs. You will find a similar format in this book.

I am by nature a curious cook. I ask a lot of questions. I also consider myself a talented translator of chef talk into "real language." This was my golden opportunity. Chef Maxime Bilet and I would hunch over his computer screen to discuss the recipes, preparations, and theories. Finally, near the end of the project, the staff chefs were sent off for an overdue vacation. I was handed a stack of manuscript pages, a credit card, and instructions to try whatever I wanted. For two weeks, I was given carte blanche in one of the greatest kitchens in the world. Nathan had to show me how to turn the oven on.

I deep-fried thinly sliced starch-infused watermelon chips. I extruded gels into long noodles. I cured fresh squid with salt and lemon and cooked it in a hot-water circulator until it was perfectly al dente. I made inside-out eggs Benedict and spheres of tomato water. And because I am who I am, I complained a lot as I went along: this explanation is confusing, this step should be written here, this amount seems wrong. I tackled the task as I do any recipe testing project: with a focus not on the source, but on the potential for success by readers. In the end, I thoroughly pissed everyone off, but they invited me back.

I tested all of the recipes in *Modernist Cuisine at Home* in my own ramshackle, old-fashioned home kitchen. I cooked slabs of bacon sous vide for 130 hours. I sprayed refried beans out of a whipped-cream siphon and made my own melty "processed" cheese slices out of Greek feta and French Bûcheron. I fell in love all over again with my pressure cooker. Most of all, I was reminded of how much people can do in their own kitchens and how approachable complicated-sounding concepts can be when presented clearly. My old-school education melded with these new ideas and techniques. A modern style of cooking isn't just about expensive toys and exotic ingredients. It's about expanding our options as our understanding of science and materials evolves. Escoffier didn't use xanthan gum, because it wasn't sold at his local supermarket. Your cooking will get better when you have a basic understanding of what is happening to your food at the molecular level, but it isn't necessary to make foams and films or to plate your dinner with tweezers.

When the book was finished, the editorial team celebrated with a feast at Thierry Rautureau's wonderful restaurant Rover's. The woman sitting next to me was vegetarian, so when the rest of us were presented with squab crépinette en jus, she was served an equally impressive arrangement of spring vegetables in a dark broth. She offered me a clandestine sip: it was magnificent—earthy, rich, complex, and as satisfying as any demi-glace. (Since then Rautureau, Seattle's "chef in the hat," has closed Rover's. He now divides his time between his two newer restaurants, Luc and Loulay. He still doesn't get the acclaim he deserves for his brilliant vegetarian dishes.) On the drive home, I started to ponder the dearth of elegant meatless sauces in home kitchens, and *Mastering Sauces* was born.

That said, you won't find the recipe for that vegetable broth anywhere in this book. Yes, I could write out a step-by-step guide for making a very close reproduction of the broth I tasted that day, but it would be exactly the kind of pedantic, intimidating treatise that I want to avoid. The broth itself was very simple. Thierry and his crew collected good, seasonal ingredients and infused their flavors into water. The resulting stock was then concentrated for more flavor intensity and just a hint of syrupy texture. Finally, it was seasoned with a con-

sideration for the ingredients to be sauced, enriched with a touch of butter, and served. Chop, sauté, deglaze, simmer, strain, heat, season, enrich, and finish; that's how that wonderful sauce was made. The ingredients were not exotic or expensive. It was created by chefs who focus on three fundamental principles: maximize flavor, manipulate texture, and season confidently. Rather than fill a book with recipes for very specific sauces, I decided to urge more cooks to practice those same theories.

For many cooks, the concept of "winging it" is accompanied by visions of smoldering pots, wasted ingredients, and a good chance of public humiliation. When my husband first ventured into the kitchen to experiment, I would leave the room so I wouldn't hover. "How much garlic should I add?" he would call out. I would respond, "I don't know, how garlicky do you want it to be?" Growling would ensue. Apparently that wasn't an answer. He didn't want to make those kinds of decisions. If the food flopped when he followed specific instructions, it meant the recipe, not his cooking ability, was bad. After a few tense meals, it became clear to both of us that I would answer specifically when asked, "How much would *you* use?" but vaguely when asked, "How much should *I* use?" Since I didn't know how garlicky he wanted his dish to be, I couldn't tell him precisely how much garlic to add. He eventually understood that the quality of his creations was dependent not on professional dictate but on trusting his own preferences. I'm proud to say that now when my beloved husband cooks, the food that he makes is his own, and it's delicious.

I hope there are many recipes in this book that you will add to your collection. I've done my best to anticipate potential differences in ingredients, equipment, region, and experience. If you like to use recipes as a starting point but tend to customize them, please take a look at the tables and tips for ideas. More than anything, I hope you read and understand the principles behind the concepts and learn to master sauces by trusting your own taste and common sense, and having a cooking adventure now and then. Have fun. When you gather with friends and the talk turns to sauces, you should be able to talk with pride about the sauces you have made and urge others to follow your lead.

THOUGHTS

ON CONTEMPORARY

SAUCES

The first step to bringing a ray of sunshine into the hallowed but dusty halls of sauce making is to redefine what a sauce actually is. For me, it is virtually any moist, full-flavored enhancement to food. Contemporary sauces are those that embrace current preferences in diet, lifestyle, ingredients, and equipment. Never before have I seen so many people divide themselves into dietary tribes: omnivores, locavores, piscivores, nose-to-tail, gluten-free, paleo, vegan. Modern sauces should be equally as diverse. They should be made with fresh local ingredients, a wider selection of texturizers and thickeners, more global flavors, and a healthy respect for busy family schedules.

The recipes in this book lean toward health and diet consciousness but don't dwell there.

There is very little meat, but the book is not vegetarian. Some recipes are designed to make the most of low-impact, local, sustainable ingredients. Others rely on international flavors and imported specialty foods. This dichotomy may seem inconsistent or even wishy-washy, but to my mind, it mirrors modern tastes. I know a vegetarian who can't pass up the occasional bite of roasted duck, avid carnivores who order soy lattes, and cooks at award-winning earth-to-table restaurants who have a fondness for Coke Slurpees and late-night fast-food drive-thrus. I love that!—it seems very human. Sauces, like all things, can be improved when they are approached with respect, an open mind, the acknowledgement of personal tastes and changing preferences, and, wherever possible, a good dose of fun.

INTRODUCTION

17

TOOLS

AND

EQUIPMENT

The most important aspect of a kitchen tool is never the brand name or price, but the comfort and confidence it gives the cook. It is not the wrench that fixes the car, it is the mechanic. If you have a battered favorite saucepan, I'm not going to try to convince you to trade up. Your tools need to get you from point A to point B. The more you understand how they work, the more likely you are to upgrade them.

POTS AND PANS

I pick out cookware like I do a car: I am most interested in reliability, durability, and economy. I'll pay for top-quality equipment like Le Creuset Dutch ovens because I know they last a lifetime. I'm also a fan of inex-pensive, sturdy nonstick frying pans, such as commercial-grade WearEver skillets, from restaurant supply shops, because I developed a feel for them when I worked in restaurants. It's a very personal choice. My only real caveat is that flimsy, poorly made tools are never a bargain.

Lidded Saucepans with Heavy Bases

For pots and pans, "heavy bases" refers to the thickness and sturdiness of the material more than to the actual weight. The pan should rest solidly on the heat source. Thin, unstable, or warped pans have hot spots, react capriciously, and will make your job harder. Some spots may scorch while others remain cool. You may constantly have to chase your ingredients around so they don't settle on one side of the pan, or stir so the sauce at the bottom of the pan is not almost afire while the surface remains cool.

I like my saucepans to have a bright interior, such as stainless steel or white enamel, so I can monitor the color changes of my ingredients. Every cook I've met who complains about having difficulty browning butter or making caramel has cookware with dark interiors. It's also nice to have a gentle rounding where the base of the pan meets the sides so there is no need to dig into sharp corners while whisking.

Nathan Myhrvold, author and founder of *Modernist Cuisine*, is very opinionated about his pots and pans, but not in the way you might anticipate. As he is someone who considers an industrial freeze dryer, a high-speed centrifuge, and a commercial Italian pasta extruder standard cooking equipment, you would expect him to spare no expense in his pots and pans. In fact, at The Cooking Lab, the racks are loaded with inexpensive saucepans from IKEA. Myhrvold is a mathematician, a physicist and an expert in technology, among other things, and he knows that it is the heat source, not the brand name or exterior shine of the pan, that really makes the difference. He and his team use portable induction cookers. These are electric platforms about the size of a cereal box that generate heat through magnetic fields that oscillate at high frequency. This causes any iron-bearing metal that is placed

on the cooker to heat up. It is an energy-efficient method of cooking that offers very precise temperature control. I don't use induction as a rule—in my kitchen, I use an old-fashioned electric coil stove. But, after using those pots and pans in The Cooking Lab, I went to IKEA and loaded my cart full of their 365+ saucepans. They meet all my criteria of heavy bases, bright interiors, comfortable heat-resistant handles, good balance, tight-fitting lids, and a great price.

The pan sizes I use the most for sauce making are 2-quart and 1-quart. A small 2-cup pan is handy for melting butter or making small amounts of sauce reductions.

There are pans marketed specifically as sauce pots. They usually have a wider mouth and sloping walls that release more steam.

Stockpots

A stockpot is designed to hold water. Since there is no risk of burning water, and because water is very heavy, a light stockpot made of thin metal is a reasonable, affordable option. That said, I prefer sturdier stockpots with heavy bases because they can be used for more than just boiling water. I use them to make soup and chili for big crowds, so I want a base that can transfer heat evenly, not just quickly. An 8-quart stockpot with a thick base is a tool few regret purchasing and it may last forever. A big pot of between 12 and 18 quarts can also be handy, not just for big batches of stock, but also for feasts of summer corn or crab boils.

Skillets and Frying Pans

A frying pan is a shallow pan with sloping sides that releases steam well. These are particularly popular with chefs because once you get a feel for it, you can use the rounded sides to flip and toss ingredients without using utensils. Frying pans are also called sauté pans, omelet pans, or skillets.

I have a dozen choices at home, but I tend to reach for the same three most often. A well-seasoned 12-inch/30.5 cm cast-iron skillet can't be beat for searing and browning foods evenly over high heat. For general sautéing, 8-inch/20 cm and 10-inch/25 cm restaurant-style nonstick skillets are great. I buy mine at restaurant supply houses, where they are both heavy-duty and reasonably priced. I can get a thick 12-inch/30.5 cm WearEver aluminum skillet with a sturdy nonstick surface and a heatproof grip for a bargain.

Nonstick surfaces take a beating in my house, so I like coated pans that involve little to no emotional attachment or heavy investment. When the surface inevitably gets scratched or starts to flake after a lot of hard use, I don't fret, because I didn't pay a fortune.

Sauté Pans

While any skillet or frying pan can be used to sauté, a sauté pan is a larger pan with sides that are higher and straighter than those of a frying pan. These pans often have lids and a second C-shaped handle on the side opposite the long handle, to help handle larger, heavier quantities. They are ideal for preparations that first need searing and then gradual simmering in liquid—dishes that tend to have integral sauces. I don't feel these pans benefit from a nonstick coating.

Woks

I would be lost without my traditional carbon steel wok. It is the tool I grab when I want to sear, toss, and shake bite-size ingredients quickly over high heat. It is very responsive to temperature changes, so it will get hot quickly and then cool down when I lift it from the burner. It is durable, so I can clang a metal spoon around in it with no risk of damaging the surface. I use it for deep-frying and steaming. Because a wok is big, needs surface maintenance to prevent rusting, and can be slightly awkward to store, some cooks prefer using smaller pans in a similarly scooped bowl shape with treated surfaces. I am true to my uncoated wok because it gives food stir-fried at high temperatures a slightly steely flavor that becomes a part of the seasoning balance.

Pressure Cookers

Get over your fear and buy yourself a pressure cooker. These work by locking an airtight lid onto the pot. The pressure from the water vapor inside the pot builds as the temperature rises, transmitting heat from the steam to the food more rapidly. The atmospheric pressure increases, thereby raising the temperature. A pressure cooker makes food cook faster, thereby reducing energy use. It is a sealed environment so aromas and flavors that would otherwise escape into the air are trapped in the pot. Pressure can also alter the texture of some foods, making them more succulent and silky. I will forevermore make smaller batches of stock in my pressure cooker. In less than 60 minutes I can have a quart of an intensely flavored chicken stock that otherwise might take hours.

The reason you don't need to be scared of pressure cookers anymore? Modern cookers are built with multiple safety releases—if the pressure or temperature gets too high, these will burst, melt, or release pressure. I use a Fagor stovetop pressure cooker because it is reasonably priced and works well enough, but I covet the lovely high-performance (and expensive) Kuhn Rikon brand because these release almost no steam and respond particularly well to small adjustments in temperature.

Universal Lids

I learned about universal lids from Julia Child's books and television programs. They are flat disks with handles that can cover pots and pans of various sizes. When you have a pot that needs sealing, you can just grab a universal lid and pop it on top without having to search for the matching lid. They are very convenient.

SIEVES AND STRAINERS

Sieves and strainers are in almost constant use when you are making sauces. Buy sieves that have "ears" or lips to keep them balanced, hands free, over a container such as a deep bowl or large liquid measuring cup. If you are straining a heavy pot of hot liquid, the last thing you need to worry about is a wobbly strainer. If you can buy only one, make it a standard 8-inch/20 cm hemispheric sieve with a medium mesh and a long handle. It is a tool that is so practical it hasn't evolved much over the past several centuries. The only real improvement that has been made is the introduction of stainless steel, so the mesh won't rust or discolor foods. This is a workhorse of a sieve, so get a sturdy one. They are easy to find, but the better quality the product, the longer it should last.

I also use a 5- to 6-inch/12.5 to 15 cm fine-mesh sieve for catching any gritty sediment and making sauces silky and smooth. I particularly like a slightly conical 5-inch/12.5 cm version. An even smaller 2- to 3-inch/5 to 7.5 cm sieve is really nice for sifting freshly ground spices and straining small quantities.

A mesh colander is also handy. A colander lined with cheesecloth or a vegetable strainer can get the job done, but a large conical strainer, also called a China cap or chinois, is more commonly used in restaurants. A conical sieve will strain a large amount of liquid without much agitation or any pressing. The sediment collects at the base of the cone, reducing the possibility of clogs. Conical sieves with their own stands will not be as stable over the kind of container you need for straining stock. The more stable the sieve, the less likely you are to have an accident.

Look for good-quality sieves at restaurant supply houses. Today's sieves tend to be made of stainless steel, but I also like to keep a sieve with a flexible nylon mesh on hand to press very pale, creamy, or acidic mixtures without fear of discoloration or of adding a slightly metallic taste. I also like the flexibility of the nylon mesh for sauces with soft pulp and hard bitter seeds, like fresh raspberries. The seeds don't get scraped or grated by the metal. These sieves aren't nearly as sturdy as metal sieves, so don't spend a lot of money on them—you can find them at dollar stores and bargain markets.

Cheesecloth

Try to get in the habit of having cheesecloth on hand. (Maybe even buy two packages the next time you shop.) Every layer of cheesecloth you use to line a sieve or strainer will add refinement to a finished sauce. Historically, in the grand houses of Europe, very elegant sauces were run through fine cloths or sieves, called tamis or tamis cloths, to make them silky smooth and glossy. Cheesecloth can be used similarly. It is also great for making sachets and for bundling up wet ingredients like blanched spinach and squeezing them dry. I buy natural, unbleached cheesecloth.

Baker's or Scientific Sieves

Professional bakers often use flat drum sieves to sift high volumes quickly. Scientists and archeologists who need to sift through specimens tend to like the same thing. You can buy sets of high-quality stainless steel-drum sieves in various meshes from scientific supply houses for a lot less than you might expect. They rest a bit more awkwardly on bowls, but if you have a large quantity of food, like a double batch of vegetable puree, that needs to be pressed through a sieve, these are the best option. Be sure the mesh is nonreactive, preferably stainless steel, so it won't discolor or in any way taint the ingredients.

Food Mills

A food mill is an old-fashioned tool that purees food using a blade, a perforated plate, and a crank. The purees are even, and on some, the texture can be controlled by choosing different plates. I prefer to puree foods in a blender or food processor and press them through a sieve rather than clean a food mill, but if you have one, make the best use of it.

CHOPPING AND CUTTING TOOLS

Knives

Nothing makes a chef shudder more than watching a novice cut with a dull knife. It's not only awkward, it's dangerous. A sharp 8-inch/20 cm French knife or wide rectangular Chinese cleaver/all-purpose tool (called a *tou*) may look menacing, but these can in effect become a responsive extension of your arm. You don't have to buy samurai-quality imported blades. Knives need only to be well balanced, feel good in your hand, keep an edge, and never, ever wobble or bend. A large chef's knife and a sturdy paring knife may be my most commonly used kitchen tools.

Poultry Shears

Poultry shears are the ideal tool for cutting chicken carcasses and fish frames into pieces suitable for the stockpot. Poultry shears are sturdier and stronger than regular kitchen scissors. They are designed for leverage, with sharp tips to negotiate the crevices of chicken carcasses and a notch to help cut through larger bones. Make sure the shears you buy are dishwasher safe or easy to clean to prevent cross-contamination.

Cutting Boards

My sister-in-law prepares all of her ingredients on a small cutting board shaped like a pig. It makes me want to slap my forehead even thinking about it. A small cutting surface means you can only make small cuts and only cut a few items at a time. That means your prep will be very slow. And a cutting board crowded with ingredients is dangerous, because there is a risk of getting bits under the blade and having your knife slip. An unsteady or bouncing cutting

board means that your knife and ingredients will be equally bouncy and unsteady, a very dangerous scenario. I have a dozen or so different cutting boards. When I want to work quickly or I have a lot of chopping or prep to do, I get out big 18-by-24-inch/46 by 61 cm polyethylene restaurant boards. When I'm just making dinner, I use a thick wooden board that is 14 by 17 inches/36 by 43 cm. For raw chicken, meat, or seafood, I often use thin, flexible nylon boards that fit into my dishwasher. I like to have a small 6-by-8-inch/15 by 20 cm wooden or polyethylene board for slicing and chopping garlic or fresh chiles so I don't have to worry about my dessert pineapple having a whiff of raw garlic.

Some people swear that plastic cutting boards are more sanitary, but others cite studies showing that wooden cutting boards are more naturally resistant to bacteria. I have both. I scrub the wooden boards down and scrape them with a butcher's block scraper and plenty of hot, soapy water. I throw the plastic boards into the dishwasher. My oversized boards get a soak in a bathtub of bleach water now and then. Some cooks have color-coded cutting boards to avoid cross-contamination between, for example, chicken or meat and fresh salad greens. I think that is a fine idea, but don't let it lull you into a false sense of security: Color-coded boards don't ensure food safety. Wise decision making and thorough scrubs are better.

ELECTRONICS

A lot of the sauces in this book require chopping, pulverizing, and pureeing. I wish I could recommend a single tool that would do all these things, but I can't. Where I might be indifferent about the brand of your cookware, I urge you to buy only the best countertop machines. You will save yourself endless frustrations, and these will perform and last twice as long. They are a bargain in the end.

Blenders

Get a blender with a heavy base, a sturdy jar that is easy to remove, and good-quality blades. High-speed commercial blenders like the Vitamix are magnificent—they can puree and liquefy so smoothly that the finished sauces need little, if any, straining. Because they also tend to be prohibitively expensive, all of the recipes in this book were tested using a standard countertop blender. Blenders work best with softer, wetter foods that whirl rather than bind or clump.

Very narrow or conical jars can compound the problem of small quantities or thicker mixtures getting mashed under the blades. Whatever comes in contact with the blades will continue to blend while the rest of the food remains static until you stop the machine, scrape the sides and bottom of the jar, and start again. Volume can also be dramatically reduced if you don't scrape the base and blades thoroughly. I also suggest you think about getting a second smaller blender or mini chopper for recipes that make a small amount of sauce, like the Mint Chutney (page 202).

Immersion Blenders

It always surprises me how well these handheld blending sticks work. Once you try the Easy Immersion-Blender Hollandaise (page 388), you will never go back to making this classic sauce with a whisk. You can also plunge an immersion blender into a simmering pot or a drained can of diced or whole tomatoes and blitz everything into a puree. For the Gooey Orange Nacho Cheese Sauce (page 363), there is no better tool. But immersion blenders can miss bits and result in uneven textures unless you are diligent, so passing the sauce through a sieve is always a good idea. They can also splatter the sauce everywhere when used in a shallow container, so for best results, use deep narrow pots or the cylindrical containers that come with these blenders.

Food Processors

Food processors chop drier, bulkier, firmer items like chocolate and nuts more effectively than blenders. The blades are sharp enough to chop herbs, greens, and harder fresh items, such as raw carrots, that a blender might mash, bruise, or grind. They are ideal for pestos, but they do not liquefy ingredients quite as successfully as a blender and are less effective with smaller quantities.

Juicers/Extractors

Several recipes in this book call for freshly extracted fruit or vegetable juice. These are not just liquefied fruits and vegetables, but the natural juices separated from the solids. A juicer is a pricier, more specialized tool than perhaps any other listed here, but extracted juices make vibrant fresh-tasting broths and sauces, and there really isn't a substitution. There are centrifugal juicers and masticating juicers. Both have different attributes that you should consider, such as how much friction they generate and whether they work best with soft or hard items. For me, the most important consideration is how easy the machine is to handle and clean. I have a stainless steel countertop Breville centrifugal juicer/extractor, and I have no complaints.

HAND TOOLS

Salt Cellars

Don't use a salt shaker or salt mill when you are cooking: use a salt cellar filled with kosher salt. You want a sturdy container with an opening large enough that you can reach in with three fingers and pinch up a healthy amount of salt. Sprinkling or shaking salt from a salt shaker will seem like guesswork once you get used to the control you have when salting by feel. Kosher salt is the salt to pinch. It stays quite dry and loose even in humid kitchens and the large flakes are easy to grab and sprinkle but actually add less

sodium by volume than table salt. My salt cellar is a ridiculously ugly, misshapen blob I made at a ceramics class a million years ago.

Pepper Mills

Choose a mill that is easy to grab and use even with slippery hands. You want the fresh perfume of black peppercorns and the ability to add half a grind or twenty. The grinder should be adjustable so you can add large cracked bits or a fine pale powder, depending on the recipe. I like that the spice companies wised up and now build grinders right into the jars. They aren't great, but they mean cooks can have freshly ground pepper at their fingertips.

Whisks

I like a whisk with a thick, comfortable handle and a streamlined shape, rather than a balloon whisk. When making sauces, you are usually whisking to blend rather than to aerate. Whisking also tends to be done in a contained environment, so a big balloon whisk is not the wisest choice. The first whisk I reach for is a narrow 8-inch/20 cm whisk made by Best Manufacturers. This is closely followed by a 12-inch/30.5 cm version of the same. A flat roux/gravy whisk is designed to soften and stir in the brown residue from roasting pans. It also works well to gradually incorporate kneaded butter (see page 344) into bubbling sauces. Some cooks swear by silicone-coated whisks, but I don't find them particularly helpful.

Heatproof Spatulas

I can never have enough flexible heatproof silicone spatulas. They squeegee the bottom and sides of pans, bowls, and blender jars and blades—everything. I have found no better tool for slowly cooked egg-thickened sauces like custards. The width of the blade gives me a good sense of resistance and changes in texture as the egg thickens, the flexibility keeps the sauce in motion from top to bottom, and the sauce clings just enough that I can run my finger through it and check if it "coats the back of a spoon."

Wooden Spoons

Collect them and trade with your friends! I am fond of a basic oval, very lightly concave shape with a long handle, but I am also partial to spoons with a squared-off tip for dislodging the browned bits at the bottom of a pan when deglazing.

Bowl or Pastry Scrapers

Bowl or pastry scrapers are handheld rectangles of flexible nylon. They are used like rubber spatulas to scrape every bit of batter from mixing bowls. They are also perfectly suited for pressing foods through drum sieves. They are available at kitchen shops and restaurant supply stores.

Microplane Graters/Zesters

I consider Microplane kitchen rasps indispensible. The fine zester/grater removes delicate, wispy shavings from dry cheeses. It makes short work of chocolate, ginger, garlic, nutmeg, and citrus. When I look at the knobbly side of the old box grater once relied upon to take craggy bites out of hard cheeses and knuckles, I give a sigh of relief for modern times.

Box Graters

While a Microplane is marvelous for fine, delicate grating, nothing beats a sturdy box grater with big and medium-sized holes for shredding soft cheese or grating carrots.

Garlic Presses

I often just chop my garlic: I have more control of the size, and it can be just as easy to smash and mince a clove of fresh garlic as to locate, use, and then clean a garlic press. But garlic presses are very handy when you have a lot of garlic to process or you want the pieces to be very small or pulpy. I've tried a lot of different brands, and Zyliss is my favorite by far.

Measuring Cups and Spoons

I have loads of different measuring tools. I like sturdy metal measuring spoons and dry measuring cups that are flat and wide and rest solidly on the counter. My favorite liquid measures have nonslip handles and numbers I can read on the inside of the cup as well as the outside.

Mortar and Pestles

There are situations when bashing, breaking up, and pounding ingredients to a paste is the best method of preparation, and nothing works better than a good old mortar and pestle. I am still looking for the perfect set, but I use a 3-inch/7.5 cm-diameter metal cup with a squared-off pestle made in India for pounding and breaking up dry ingredients like whole spices. I use a larger, heavier 6-inch/15 cm-diameter marble set with a more traditional bowl shape for grinding fresh ingredients like basil, shallots, and nuts into pastes or pulp.

MISCELLANEOUS

Fat Mop

This is a somewhat ridiculous looking tangle of synthetic fibers attached to a wand. Fat mops are made from materials similar to those used to clean up ocean oil spills. When you drag the mop over the surface of a sauce, fats cling to it and you can simply lift them out. When you are finished, you simply wash the mop in the dishwasher. You won't get every drop of fat, but it is more efficient than spooning it off.

Kitchen Scale

The rest of the world weighs their dry goods. We Americans should too. I suggest buying a digital scale that will measure from as little as a fraction of a gram all the way up to 5 or 7 pounds. As an experiment, have a few friends or family members each measure a cup of flour, then weigh each one and see for yourself how "precise" dry measuring cups are. Now do grated cheese.

Blowtorch

The little torches sold at gourmet stores for making crème brûlée are pretty cute, but I much prefer a full-sized hardware-store BernzOmatic MAP-Pro gas torch with a trigger ignition. I use it to char onions and garlic before adding them to an infusion or stock. If my compound butter is too cold or not melting well, I hit it with a bit of direct flame. A few careful swipes over cheesy sauces makes them bubbly and brown. I once found myself in a pinch when I was doing some promotions for a local radio station. I was meant to grill some brand-name chicken pieces on location. Unfortunately, someone had lost a part on the gas grill at a previous event. I clandestinely simmered the chicken pieces in sauce and then blasted them with a blowtorch until they were evenly glazed and lightly charred at the edges. I presented the platter of "barbecued" chicken next to the idle grill. One taster sidled up to me and said, "I know my barbecue. You sure know how to do it right!" Never underestimate what kind of kitchen magic you might pull off with a decent blowtorch.

A NOTE

ABOUT

INGREDIENTS

I live in Seattle, so I have a wealth of diverse, top-notch ingredients within a few miles of my home. I hope you are so lucky. Most of the ingredients in this book are available at good supermarkets. Specialty items can be found at ethnic and gourmet markets or online.

For the recipes in this book:

- Salt is always kosher. If you use regular table salt, you will need to reduce the quantity (measured by volume) by 50 percent and then season to taste from there. I use Diamond Crystal kosher salt.

- Herbs, including bay leaves, are fresh unless otherwise specified.

- Peeled is implied for ingredients peeled before using: onions, garlic, shallots, carrots, and ginger.

METRICS AND MEASUREMENTS

I am convinced that weights and the metric system are superior for precision in the kitchen, but I'm always going to feel most comfortable with a cup of this and tablespoon of that. I've compared international standards of measurements and worried over the subject for years. Finally, I spelled out my concerns to esteemed New Zealand cookbook author and food writer Lauraine Jacobs. Her advice? "Get over it!" For this book, I suggest the following:

- Buy a scale.

- Metric conversions are included for weights, lengths, and temperatures, for a global audience. Cups and tablespoons are still used for volume because cooks tend to have their own preferred conversions. I understand that technically one cup is 236 ml and 7 ounces is 198 grams, but very few people measure with that kind of precision, so I've rounded off the numbers for convenience.

- Try to be consistent. Mince, slice, chop, and sliver as evenly as possible. Fill dry measuring cups to the rim and level your measuring spoons.

- Unless otherwise stated, the most common North American fruits and vegetables found at the supermarket are used as the standard for size and shape. I recognize that there are regional differences, but there are too many variables to include them all, and in a book that urges customization, specificity like this seemed counterproductive.

Volume

¼ teaspoon	1.25 ml
½ teaspoon	2.5 ml
1 teaspoon	5 ml
1 tablespoon	15 ml
1 cup	240 ml
1 quart	1 liter

Weight

1 oz	28 g	8 oz	225 g	15 oz	425 g
2 oz	60 g	9 oz	250 g	16 oz	450 g
3 oz	85 g	10 oz	285 g	1.5 lb	675 g
4 oz	115 g	11 oz	312 g	2 lbs	900 g
5 oz	140 g	12 oz	340 g	2.2 lbs	1 kg
6 oz	170 g	13 oz	370 g	3 lbs	1.4 kg
7 oz	200 g	14 oz	400 g	5 lbs	2.3 kg

HOW MUCH IS A PINCH?

Most cookbooks equate a pinch with an amount that is less than ⅛ teaspoon, but I think that, in truth, a pinch is better described as "just enough." This lack of specificity may be frustrating for some cooks, but a pinch tends to be more about control and distribution than a precise measurement. Chefs grab or "pinch" ingredients so they can feel exactly how much they are adding. They will sprinkle on the ingredient until it seems the like right amount, often stopping before they use all that they pinched up. Perhaps the most helpful tip is that a pinch is a three-fingered action. Pinch up a dry ingredient between your thumb and first two fingers and then sprinkle from up high so it is evenly dispersed. As a rule, the stronger the flavor, the smaller the pinch. Out of curiosity, I measured what I call "a good pinch" of kosher salt several times, and I consistently came up with about ⅓ teaspoon. A "small pinch" of cayenne or ground cloves can be as little as ⅛₂ teaspoon. I urge you to pinch, sprinkle, and taste again and again until you get a feel for how much your own measurements can change flavors.

HOW MUCH TO SERVE

These recipes were developed for households of four to six people. I suggest the following general serving sizes:

- **2 tablespoons of sauce per person is a good average. Increase or decrease that amount depending on the intensity, consistency, and preparation.**

- **1 to 2 teaspoons per person is often enough for very intense or concentrated sauces like the Cream Sherry Reduction (see the table on page 151) and Harissa (page 307).**

- **½ cup of sauce per person is a good estimate for fresh salsas and sauces that are featured as an integral part of a dish, such as Tikka Masala Sauce (page 222), Tomatillo and Pumpkin Seed Sauce (page 214), and the Cheese Sauces (pages 355–65).**

- **½ to ¾ cup of sauce per person is appropriate for broths and noodles sauces such as Tamarind Coriander Broth (page 130) and Eggplant and Spinach Tomato Sauce (see the table on page 185).**

- **Consider making double the amount of Holiday Gravy (page 330) you think you need.**

- **The better your sauces are, the more quickly they will disappear. Remind yourself that while it's never a good thing if guests leave your table hungry, it never hurts to have them wanting just a little more.**

A FEW WORDS ON FOOD SAFETY

I highly recommend that you educate yourself on how food can become tainted and how to prevent that. It isn't something that can be covered in a short paragraph.

I have offered suggestions on how and how long to store recipes. These tend to be reliant on when quality starts to suffer more than the potential for health risk. I am a bit of a fanatic about purging leftovers and prefer to make something fresh rather than warm up food from the fridge—even sauces.

Here are my rules to cook by:

- **Educate yourself on the basics of safe food handling.**

- **Keep your work surfaces and tools clean.**

- **Be vigilant about the possibility of cross-contamination.**

- **Use good-quality fresh ingredients.**

- **If you or someone you are cooking for has medical concerns, don't use potentially high-risk foods like raw or undercooked eggs.**

- **Don't underestimate the severity of food allergies.**

- **Use your food instead of storing it.**

THE THREE FUNDAMENTALS OF SAUCE MAKING

No matter what the global origins, level of refinement, or historical relevance of your recipe, the same three principles apply: maximize flavor, manipulate texture, and season confidently. It doesn't matter if you feel more comfortable following recipes like doctrine or building your own grand creations spontaneously. If you approach every preparation with an attitude of control and thoughtfulness and keep these three fundamental considerations in the forefront of your mind, you will become a more confident and skilled cook.

MAXIMIZE FLAVOR

Try to describe a particularly flavorful sauce in detail. It's tough—kind of like describing the artistry of a piece of sculpture or music. A certain memory may come instantly to mind. You can practically taste it. Maybe it's a spectacular dish you were once served at an elegant restaurant. Perhaps you immediately think of your grandmother's specialty. What is it about the combination of ingredients that makes the flavor just right? Does the sauce capture the essence of a season or a particular ingredient? Does it stimulate your palate with a bold *kapow* or tickle it with a delicate, fresh purity? Is it rich with butter, bright and tangy, or complexly spiced and deep? When you are able to define the flavor you are looking for in your final dish,

you can think beyond the recipe steps and toward the end goal.

Flavor is different from taste. There are only five true tastes: salty, sweet, sour, bitter, and a savory taste called umami. Taste is the body's response to stimulation of certain sensors on the tongue and palate. Flavor is more ethereal and complicated. It's what wine drinkers are trying to convey when they describe their Chardonnay as "flinty, with a hint of apricot jam." If flavor were simple, winemakers would make their wines taste exactly like their best vintage every year. But flavor is fleeting and ever changing. It is sun-warmed strawberries enjoyed alongside blooming lilacs or fiery curries near salty seas.

I think of flavor as the natural components, baselines, and aromas of an ingredient. You make a great cup of coffee by creating a bold infusion of fresh dark-roast coffee beans. Coffee that is weak or insipid can be made more drinkable by adding a lot of cream and sugar, but isn't it preferable to just make a good strong brew in the first place? The same is true for sauces. You can stir elemental seasonings like salt and sugar into a bland sauce to stimulate your taste buds, but it's a rather industrial approach. You're not going to get a complex, fresh-tasting, or ethereal preparation simply by wielding a salt shaker and pepper mill. You need to start with good ingredients and prepare them mindfully.

Flavor is reliant on solubility and volatility. Food is carried into your body by liquids. It's why we chew and have saliva. Flavor is also inextricably linked to scent. People who have lost their sense of smell tend to have little interest in food. They recognize that a pickle is briny, tart, and crisp because it stimulates the mouth, but the cucumber and dill have no hint of the garden. The nose tingle from cloves and mustard seeds does not evoke memories of spice bazaars. Taste buds are just one way we experience foods. The nose, sinuses, and soft palate are stimulated by vaporized flavor molecules. Sizzling bacon, hot buttered popcorn, cookies fresh from the oven—how tempting would they be without their tantalizing aromas? A hard green peach has very few of the volatile oils, aromas, and accessible flavors of ripe sun-kissed fruit, so it has virtually no flavor.

Fresh herbs are a perfect example of the power of moisture and volatility. Rosemary grows prolifically in Seattle. It's almost impossible for me to walk by a bush without fondling a twig. Even a gentle touch will cause cell walls to break down and release fragrant vapors and oils from the leaves, scenting both the air and my fingertips. Dried rosemary doesn't have quite the same magic. There is still a peppery, citrus-tinged forest smell, but it is less lively and there is a back note of twigs. Instead of a light touch, the dried herb needs a proper crumble to release trapped oils and aromas. Old or powdered herbs can be devoid of any of their original essence. If your herbs smell like autumn leaves or dust, those are the flavors you will be adding to your recipe. It is often best to omit a miserable herb altogether than to sprinkle in something that smells and tastes like old hay.

More flavor isn't always better. Burnt toast has more flavor and aroma than fresh bread, but it isn't an improvement. You're never going to crunch on a cinnamon stick, suck on a dried chipotle, or enjoy tea leaves by the spoonful. Quality is preferable to quantity. You need to make wise choices.

USE GOOD INGREDIENTS

Buy fresh, seasonal, local ingredients. Make your own stock. Chop fresh onions and garlic. Shop for less, more often, and buy the right foods at the right stores. You will find better dried chiles at a Latin market than at a German deli. Use ingredients expediently. Get rid of items that taste bad. Spend a few extra bucks on really good oils, butter, and cheeses when you can. But remember that expensive doesn't always equate with good. Braised free-range squab with fresh truffle butter sounds well and good—but a badly frozen bird overloaded with rancid or suffocating riches? I'd rather have a plate of well-spiced chickpeas.

CONSIDER EVERY DROP OF LIQUID—YOU CAN'T PICK OUT THE BAD ONES

Each drop of liquid will disperse and blend with every other drop. Since you can't pick out the bad ones from the good, it's best to make every bit count. I'm not suggesting that you boil your pasta in artesian spring water. But I do believe that your food will instantly improve when you remember that it's not a single step or ingredient that creates a great sauce—it is respect for every element.

Fresh lemons are filled with water, acidity, and aromatic oils. So are some plastic squeeze bottles. Which do you want in your food? When added to a sauce, both liquids will behave similarly. Both the fresh and reconstituted lemon juices are acidic, so they will change the pH of the sauce and stimulate sensors on the palate that recognize sour. If it's just acidity you are looking for, you might try a pinch of powdered citric acid or a splash of vinegar. If it's aroma and

perfume you want, maybe you should use only the zest of the lemon or perhaps a bit of pure lemon oil. No matter what option you choose, you will be adding that essence to every drop of the sauce. Now consider what happens when that flavor is not fresh lemon but scorched garlic or some fusty wine. Unpleasant flavors are distributed at the same molecular level as good ones. You can dilute and mask them, but they are still there—in every drop.

TREAT FLAVORFUL FATS LIKE PRECIOUS MATERIALS

You hear it from chefs all the time: "Fat is flavor." Fat is pleasing. It has a nice texture. Also, most flavor molecules are fat soluble, so to enjoy those flavors, there must be some fat in a dish. That said, I personally don't believe that *more* fat adds *more* flavor in sauce making. A tablespoon or two of butter, cream, or good oil can elevate a sauce more than sloshing in a whole cup. It's the care and handling of rich ingredients that makes a difference.

Fats are very perishable. They degrade, spoil, and burn more easily than you may think. Foods that are high in fat, like oils, nuts, cheese, cream, and butter, should be as pure and fresh as possible. They must be stored well, handled respectfully, and used expediently. A jug of cheap vegetable or canola oil from the wholesale store may seem indestructible and everlasting, but it's definitely not. If you compare the smell and taste of rancid and fresh oils, you will be shocked at the difference. The stale taste in your salad or whiff of acrid fumes wafting from your hot skillet will no longer be something you consider "normal." You can do better. You know how much oil you go through in a month—buy the appropriate size container. Always store specialty oils in the refrigerator. Use more-heat-tolerant oils like vegetable, canola, rice bran, coconut, and peanut oil to fry and sear at high temperatures. Use flavorful heat-sensitive fats like butter and extra-virgin olive oil at lower temperatures. Extra-special oils should be featured or used as a flavorful finish.

Volatiles are tiny aerated droplets of moisture and essential oils that give foods aroma. They are what give fresh sage, ripe blackberries, and cinnamon sticks their fragrance and therefore their flavor. Treasure and nurture these aromatics. Keep them safe until you are ready to release them. Toast and grind your own spices. Grate your own aged Parmesan. Warmth aerates these droplets and makes them more accessible to the nose. A sprinkle of freshly chopped parsley on lemony sole fillets, a drizzle of fine olive oil over warm pasta—these are aromatic finishes that bring dishes alive. Carelessness can destroy volatiles. High heat or long cooking will kill their magic. Exposure to air will vaporize essential oils. Herbs that were finely chopped the day before will not be as verdant as those minced shortly before you use them.

WHEN NECESSARY, CHANGE THE RATIO OF FLAVORFUL AND FLAVORLESS COMPONENTS

This may seems ridiculously oversimplified, but I know several cooks who believe more in tricks and kitchen secrets than in their own common sense. If your sauce is bland, just add something flavorful. If it seems jarringly intense, tone it down. Instead of gazing with disappointment into a bowl of wet, flavorless salsa or, worse yet, apologizing for it, take action! Change the balance of flavorful and flavorless components. Since you can't will more sunshine into hard tomatoes, come up with an alternative. Drain off any watery brine and replace it with some spicy tomato juice, Bloody Mary mix, or chile sauce. Add some minced chipotles in adobo, a pinch of cumin, a heap of fresh cilantro, or sliced scallions. The salsa will taste different from what you set out to make, but if you like it, where's the harm?

DON'T PANIC, THINK!

Overly dramatic chefs may swear, shout, and throw pots, but they rarely panic. When something goes wrong, they figure out a way to fix it. Don't give up on your food—try to reimagine it. Different isn't bad. Now and then you will make mistakes. That's okay: The best chefs in the world do too. They just don't broadcast it. They think of alternative ways to get good food on the table.

MANIPULATE TEXTURE

Texture matters. A sauce can be innovative, well matched, and perfectly seasoned, but if the consistency is off, it can detract from the food it is meant to enhance. Stir-fried vegetables are best glazed with a shimmering soy-scented gloss, not smothered in congealed gray goo. Dollops are tempting. Blobs are worrisome. Pureed sauces should be velvety and smooth, not weepy, grainy, or paste-like.

A "napping" consistency was considered the textural ideal when I studied sauce making. Roux-thickened sauces were meant to be draped evenly over the food, thinned just enough to show the contours of the fish fillet or lamb chop. They could pool neatly on the plate, but not so much that there was a sense of chaos or flooding. Times have changed. Sauces are now more likely to be served under or alongside your entrée than over. Restaurants have traded in cozy sauce blankets for shimmering broths, glossy smears, and Pollock-esque drips and splatters.

This expanded appreciation for texture means that there is more room for flexibility and adaptation. Where once a sauce was meant to hold and cling evenly as platters were formally passed at the table, today sauces can be more lively and interactive. Drizzling, mopping, dipping, and spreading sauces at the table should be encouraged.

Aroma and sight are the first senses stimulated when food appears. If it looks good, a taste can't come soon enough. A plate of asparagus topped with a trembling butter-enriched sauce will garner a much different response than one served with knobby, greasy curds.

TEXTURE VOCABULARY

There is no question that texture can be tricky. I think the best place to start is with vocabulary. What's the difference between thin and brothy? Liquid and pouring? Cohesive and binding? An elementary understanding of how different core ingredients can alter the movement of water will give you a better idea of how to anticipate and control sauce texture. When you have the confidence to skillfully manipulate the texture of your sauces, you will have reached an important benchmark in cooking.

Binding	Having a texture that will pull other ingredients together. Thick, cohesive, and usually made with starch or eggs.
Body	Substance, density, and structure.
Brothy	Having just a bit more body and viscosity than water.
Chunky	Having large bits and recognizable pieces.
Clinging	Having enough viscosity or body to adhere to a spoon or food.
Coarse	Rough, gritty, fibrous, rustic, unrefined.
Coats the Back of a Spoon	When you stir a sauce, turn the spoon over, and draw your finger through the liquid a clear channel should remain.
Cohesive	Unified and pulled together.
Congealed	Solidified or seized up, often unpleasantly.
Coulis	Usually refers to a tomato or fruit puree that is liquid and even but not silky smooth.
Curdled/Broken/ Shattered	An emulsion that has separated back into fat and water; often used in context with protein-rich sauces such as mayonnaise and hollandaise. The term used tends to depend on the size, shape, and consistency of the divided particles.

continues

Emulsified	Having oil and water molecules mixed together rather than separated.
Even	Consistent in texture, containing well-mixed ingredients that are similarly sized.
Glaze	Highly concentrated and sticky. *Glace* is the French term.
Liquid	Able to run relatively quickly and evenly in a stream when poured.
Mucilaginous	Slippery, gooey, and slightly sticky.
Napping	Adhesive and coating but still slightly fluid. To nap foods with sauce means to blanket them.
Paste/Pasty	Very thick and often starchy and gluey, spreadable, not always perfectly smooth. Can often leave a bland, flat coating in the mouth.
Pouring	Able to run quickly and evenly in a stream but still thick enough to cling to foods and loosely pool on the plate.
Pureed	Moist and evenly blended.
Reduced	Concentrated through evaporation.
Saucy	Pulled-together, cohesive, and gently thickened but still fluid.
Separated	Divided into parts with similar characteristics, such as solids and liquids, oil and water.
Silken	Smooth, refined, and melting, often with a sheen.
Slippery	Having a slick, liquid viscosity that may not melt or disappear immediately on the palate.
Smooth	Without apparent lumps, grit, or fibers; often blended, pulverized, or sieved until the individual particles are small and even.
Spreadable	Thick enough to be scooped and smeared.
Sticky	Adhesive.

Stringy	Seeming as though there are fibers or threads running through the sauce; falls from the spoon in long unevenly thickened streams.
Suspended	Blended, cohesive, and lightly thickened but unstable. Most often used to describe the state of butter when it is warmed enough to be melted but the emulsion remains intact. Creamy but not oily.
Syrupy	Viscous, slightly sticky, shiny and liquid; often clear or translucent.
Thin	Fluid enough to be poured in a quick stream from a spoon but still able to cling in a light film.

INTERFERING WITH THE MOVEMENT OF WATER— HOW ELEMENTARY INGREDIENTS ALTER TEXTURE

Thinking about food at a molecular level sounds much more technical and complicated than it actually is. Thinking about what ingredients are made of helps to predict how a sauce will cook and what the final texture might be. When water molecules bash into other molecules, their movement is disrupted. The final consistency of a sauce depends on what gets in the way of the movement of those water molecules. Every ingredient is a complicated mixture of many different components, but there are a few particularly common textural elements that you will most often deal with when making sauces.

Sugars

Sugar-rich ingredients include honey, syrups, fruits, vegetables, juices, wines and liqueurs, and, of course, processed and raw sugars. Sugars can make sauces syrupy, viscous, sticky, shiny, crystallized, jam-like, and/or caramelized. Sugar can draw the juices from fresh fruits. Artificial sweeteners should be avoided—they won't make sauces syrupy and they don't taste good.

Starches

Starch-rich ingredients include grains, flours, tuberous vegetables, plantains, and winter squash. When dispersed evenly throughout sauces, starches can make them smooth, filmy, velvety, clinging, stretchy, gooey, gummy, doughy, and/or pasty. Starches can also mask flavors, especially salt, so starch-rich sauces require extra salt and seasoning.

Fats

Fat-rich ingredients include oils, butter, cream, nuts, egg yolks, cheeses, and chocolate. Fats are smooth, melting, silky, creamy, mouth-coating, rich, oily, greasy, and/or sometimes congealed. Oil is liquefied fat. Fat and water molecules don't mix, so technique is important when combining them. Fats tend to be particularly temperature sensitive.

Proteins

Proteins are one of the reasons that traditional sauce-making lessons can be so formal and complicated. Proteins are diverse and temperature sensitive, and they call for caveats and extra explanations. Since this book is relatively protein light, rather than delve into all of the variables, I will explain a few key principles here. Meaty, viscous sauces like reduced meat and poultry stocks get much of their texture from gelatin. Gelatin comes from collagen. Collagen is a key structural protein and is very prevalent in connective tissues and bones. Chicken wings, cartilage-rich knuckle bones, and pork skin make much more gelatin-rich stocks than lean meat, but meat has more flavor, so both components are important in making stocks and sauces. Depending on the concentration, sauces rich in natural gelatin can be silky, viscous, clinging, glossy, syrupy, jiggly, set, springy, congealed, and/or rubbery. Natural gelatin is particularly good for texturizing sauces because it is clear and basically tasteless, and it can be repeatedly melted, solidified, boiled, and blended with little change in structure.

Other protein-rich ingredients, such as eggs, cream, and cheese, will also alter sauce texture. Eggs are technically gels and thus contain natural gelling agents. They can thicken warm sauces by trapping water in a mesh of proteins that develops with heat and time. Eggs and dairy products are also naturally occurring emulsions. That means that the water and fat droplets within them are evenly interspersed, and they will remain that way until something, like overheating, interferes with the structure or balance. When an emulsion fails, the oil and water will separate, usually unpleasantly. But when these protein-rich emulsions are correctly used in sauces, they can make textures that are custardy, creamy, elastic, jiggly, and/or foamy. When an emulsion breaks, the sauce can become greasy, curdled, wet, beady, and/or uneven.

Enzymes are also proteins. In this book, they are referred to only in regards to how increased enzymatic activity in fresh ingredients, like tomatoes and some salsas, can help release more aromas. Enzymatic activity increases with warmth. That's why a ripe strawberry, picked and eaten in the morning sunshine is such a delight. Put that same berry in the fridge, and the magic is soon lost.

Solids Such as Cellulose, Fibers, Pulp, and Particulates

When it comes to texture, these are the ingredients I tend to refer to as "everything else." While a carrot contains natural sugar and starch, its other components, like cellulose, are also texturizers. The same is true of leafy greens, the pulp of apricots and chiles, nut butters, bread crumbs, and ground spices. Solids bulk up sauces, giving them textures that can be pulpy, pureed, coarse, thick, gritty, crunchy, mealy, dense, meaty, and/or even. Fibers and particulates tend to be quite stable and easy to manipulate through movement, such as stirring, straining, sieving, and blending, or diluting or concentrating a sauce.

COMMON TECHNIQUES FOR CHANGING TEXTURE

A handful of basic techniques can be used to alter the texture of most sauces. Detailed instructions and reminders are scattered throughout the relevant chapters.

Thin

To stir in more liquid to make the sauce more fluid and free running. Try to use a liquid with a similar or complimentary flavor so the sauce doesn't taste diluted.

Reduce

To thicken and concentrate flavors by removing water through evaporation. Use this technique only with heat-tolerant sauces. Simmer, uncovered or partially covered, stirring or agitating regularly to prevent burning, until the sauce has reached the desired consistency and intensity. Yield is always diminished of course, and sauces that are already very salty or spicy will become more so.

Blend/Puree/Chop

To change the particle size and distribution. A salsa or fresh green sauce that seems to be lacking cohesion can often be united with another pulse or two in the food processor. Unstable emulsions can often be pulled together in a blender.

Sieve/Strain

To remove excess moisture; strain out unwanted coarse, fibrous, or large particles; or refine sauces by passing them through various sieves, layers of cheesecloth, or even coffee filters.

Emulsify

To interrupt the movement of water molecules with oil droplets. When fat and water droplets are evenly distributed, a sauce becomes cohesive and thickened. When they break and separate, they will return to their original textures (or worse, depending on what caused the break). Fat and water must be carefully and gradually mixed. (See Simple Emulsions—Getting Oil and Vinegar to Play Nice, page 253.)

Add a Thickener

To bulk up a thin sauce with a thickener like roux or slurry. Consider adding a thick puree, paste, or sauce base. (Refer to the Texturizers table on page 33.)

Enrich

To thicken and fortify a sauce by carefully adding fat, such as butter, egg yolks, or a few tablespoons of cream. (See Final Flair— Finishing and Enriching Sauces, page 431.)

Change the Temperature

As a rule, stable sauces will become thinner if they are warmed and thicker as they cool. Sauces made with eggs or lots of butter or dairy products and emulsified sauces should never be exposed to extremes in temperatures. Sauces with a high proportion of ground seeds and nut butters can sometimes seize up when heated.

PRESENTATION

How you serve a sauce can alter the perception of its texture

All Sauces

Universally, sauces should be fresh and served at the appropriate temperature. It's often best to sauce your foods just before you serve them. Give sauces a stir before you serve them to even the texture, add a bit of life, and boost the aromas.

Broths and Very Thin Sauces

Serve food with broths and very thin sauces in bowls or shallow dishes. Or consider passing the sauce separately in a bowl, pitcher, or cruet. Serve in individual ramekins if dunking is intended. Feature the main ingredients and embellish them with broth, rather than the other way around, or it can be perceived as soup. Combine foods with very thin sauces at the last minute, or even tableside, to prevent them from absorbing too much broth and becoming waterlogged. Examples are Fresh Mushroom Jus (page 138), Carrot Caraway Broth (page 132), and Tentsuyu— Tempura Dipping Sauce (page 280).

Stable Smooth Sauces That Are Clinging, Fluid, or of Pouring or Napping Consistency

These textures are very adaptable and easy to work with. You can serve the sauces over, under, or alongside your foods. Ratio is perhaps the biggest consideration. Try not to skimp on sauces or drown foods. Examples are Holiday Gravy (page 330), Roasted Cauliflower–Parmesan Sauce (page 172), and Pranee's Thai Peanut Sauce (page 209).

Chunky Sauces

Texture plays a big part in chunky sauces, so it should be highlighted. Make sure the elements are well mixed and distributed and then spoon, dollop, or heap the sauce on or alongside foods. Examples are Grilled Artichoke Salsa (page 237), Creole Sauce Made with Dark Brown Roux (page 341), and White Sauce with Radicchio, Bresaola, and Parmesan (see the table on page 324).

Intense Condiments and Very Concentrated Sauces

Think small and decorative: drips, dots, and drizzles. Very concentrated sauces like the Pink Grapefruit and Hibiscus Reduction (page 154) are often best portioned by the cook, but very spicy or intense sauces like Hara Masala (page 206) are sometimes best served separately or passed so diners can help themselves to as much or as little as they like.

Temperature-Sensitive Sauces

Heat or chill the food and serving dishes appropriately. When you pour an absolutely perfect egg-based or suspended butter sauce onto a scorching-hot plate or over a sizzling steak straight off the grill, it will instantly break and all your effort will have been for naught. In that same vein, if you pour a warm, flowing cheese sauce or demi onto plates or foods that are too cold, it can congeal. Gravy boats can be warmed with hot water, but don't heat the whole thing, or the handle will be too hot to pass. You can maintain the perfect temperature of delicate sauces such as White Wine Butter Sauce (page 403) and Easy Immersion-Blender Hollandaise (page 388) by holding them in a thermos or warm-water bath. If a sauce seems to be prone to forming a skin, place a butter wrapper or piece of heat-safe plastic wrap directly on the surface.

Mix It Up!

Serve multiple sauces and various textures on the same plate: mix and match and make it striking. Serve a grilled chicken breast in a shallow bowl with some hot Sweet Corn and Green Chile Broth (page 137) and top it with a spoonful of Butternut Squash and Piquillo Pepper Salsa (page 239) or Quick Diced Guacamole (see the table on page 245), and maybe a squiggle of Lime and Cotija Cheese Mayo (see the table on page 387). Serve grilled beef ribs glazed with Korean Pear Bulgogi Sauce (page 293) and a smear of Grilled Scallion and Dashi Puree (see the table on page 178) or scattering of Cucumber and Sweet Onion Relish (see the table on page 245).

TEXTURIZERS

Please use the following table as a starting point for building texture in sauces. Suggested amounts are given for 1 cup of sauce intended to reach a fluid, slightly syrupy, and clinging consistency.

Texturizer	Ratio and best method for thickening 1 cup of liquid
Traditional White Roux (made with all-purpose flour)	Stir 1 tablespoon flour into 1 tablespoon hot oil, drippings, or melted butter until smooth. Cook until the roux is bubbly and the raw flour taste is gone but the roux is still pale. For thicker, binding sauces, double the quantities of fat and flour. Simmer the sauce for at least 5 minutes. See Demystifying Roux (page 317).
Traditional Golden Roux (made with all-purpose flour)	Stir 1 tablespoon flour into 1 tablespoon hot oil, drippings, or melted butter until smooth. Cook until the roux is golden brown and smells toasted. Simmer the sauce for at least 10 minutes. See Demystifying Roux (page 317).

Best for	Attributes	Drawbacks
White sauces, gravies, and soups. This roux is the foundation for the French béchamel family of sauces. See White Sauce Done Right (page 321) and Holiday Gravy (page 330).	Silky, mild flavored, very simple and quick to make. Easily adapted. Can be used to make much thicker and even binding sauces. Stable. Holds and stores well. The added fat can also be considered a flavor enhancement.	Can be lumpy, pasty, and bland when not made properly. Starch masks flavor, so careful seasoning and maximizing flavor are important. Makes clear liquids opaque. Not suitable for many special diets.
Gravies, sauces, and soups made with light stocks. A golden roux is the foundation for the French velouté family of sauces. See Holiday Gravy (page 330) and Shelley's Lemon Sauce for Fish (page 337).	Silky, very simple, and quick to make. Can add an appealing slightly toasted flavor redolent of baked bread. Stable. Holds and stores well. The added fat can also be considered a flavor enhancement.	Can be lumpy, pasty, and bland when not made properly. Starch masks flavor, so careful seasoning and maximizing flavor are important. Makes sauce opaque. Not suitable for many special diets.

continues

Texturizer	Ratio and best method for thickening 1 cup of liquid
Traditional Brown Roux (made with all-purpose flour)	Stir 2 tablespoons flour into 2 tablespoons hot drippings or oil until smooth. Cook over medium-low heat until the roux is brown. The darker the color, the more assertive the taste. See Demystifying Roux (page 317).
Dairy-Free Roux (made with oil, coconut oil, margarine, or other butter substitutes)	The same ratios and techniques apply as for traditional roux. See Expanding on Roux (page 344).

Best for	Attributes	Drawbacks
Dark and savory sauces with bold flavors. Cajun or Creole sauces. This roux is the foundation for the old-fashioned French espagnole family of sauces and an ingredient in demi-glace. Often used for flavor rather than just thickening. See New Mexican Red Chile Sauce (page 339) and Creole Sauce made with Dark Brown Roux (page 341).	Silky. Adds a distinct nutty flavor. The roux can be made ahead of time and reheated if necessary.	Can take 20 to 40 minutes of stirring and constant attention; the starch granules can seem grainy when not cooked for at least 20 minutes. Prone to burning. The thickening potential is a fraction of that of paler roux.
Traditionally made sauces that aren't enhanced with butter, such as kosher, vegan, or allergy-sensitive dishes. See Holiday Gravy (page 330), and New Mexican Red Chile Sauce (page 339).	A very simple adaptation of a butter-based roux. Excellent way to use a traditional thickening technique for special diets such as kosher, dairy-free, vegan, and reduced-cholesterol.	The flour can sometimes seem grainy and the fat slightly greasier than with a butter-based roux. Some fats, like coconut oil, add a distinctive flavor. Many butter substitutes contain a lot of water and salt, which can unpleasantly alter flavor and texture.

continues

Texturizer	Ratio and best method for thickening 1 cup of liquid
Gluten-Free Roux (made with nonwheat flour, such as rice flour)	As a rule, the same ratios and techniques apply as for traditional roux. Use 1 tablespoon of fat and 1 tablespoon of flour. Serve the sauces soon after preparation, as they don't store as well. See Expanding on Roux (page 344).
Cold Roux	Make a large batch of roux and refrigerate until ready to use. Gradually whisk a few teaspoonfuls of cold roux into a simmering sauce until the right consistency has been reached, about 1½ tablespoons of pale roux or 3 tablespoons of brown roux for each cup of liquid. See Expanding on Roux (page 344).
Kneaded Butter/Beurre Manié	Blend equal quantities of flour and butter by volume until smooth. Gradually whisk the kneaded butter into simmering sauce. The amount needed will depend on consistency and makeup of the sauce. See Expanding on Roux (page 344).

Best for	Attributes	Drawbacks
Traditionally made gravies and sauces for people with allergies and food sensitivities. See Gluten-Free Casserole Cream (page 327).	Very simple way to make gluten-free versions of favorite gravies and sauces.	No flour substitute will have the same properties of wheat flour. Some flours can be slightly gritty and don't stay cohesive when chilled. Some need a bit of extra simmering to start to thicken and get smooth. Some have very distinct flavors. Darker flours can discolor very light sauces and gravies.
Recipes that need a quick fix or for high-volume situations. Prepared dark brown roux can be purchased online and at some specialty stores.	A cold roux can be added gradually to a simmering liquid, rather than adding liquid to a pan of freshly made roux. Can be stored and used as needed. A big batch of dark brown roux can be made ahead to greatly reduce the cooking time of your next batch of gumbo or sauce.	In home kitchens, making a roux from scratch or adding kneaded butter may actually be more efficient. Can become rancid and pick up unpleasant flavors when not used expediently.
Gradually thickening sauces that are already simmering, where butter and flour are appropriate flavors. Especially good in French stews and braised dishes with large, integral pieces.	Quick to make and use. Thickens and enriches a sauce with a finish of butter as well as starch. Excellent way to quickly add a bit of mild-flavored silkiness to simmering chunky mixtures. Offers control: once the texture seems just right, you stop adding it.	Only suitable for sauces that are enhanced with butter. Can make sauces pale, opaque, and slightly cloudy. Can taste slightly of raw flour. The addition of starch will mask flavor slightly. Often more is made than is used, so there tends to be waste.

continues

Texturizer	Ratio and best method for thickening 1 cup of liquid
Wondra	Stir together 2 tablespoons Wondra with ¼ cup cold liquid until smooth. Pour into warm sauce, stir, and bring to a simmer. I have also been known to simply shake and whisk a bit of Wondra directly into a sauce; it is less likely to clump than plain flour because of the manufacturing process. See Expanding on Roux (page 344).
Cornstarch Slurry (in several countries, cornstarch is called corn flour)	Stir together 1 teaspoon cornstarch and 1 tablespoon cold liquid until smooth. The starch will settle quickly, so stir again before adding to the pot. Cornstarch must reach the boiling point to thicken. See Slurries—Pourable Starch Thickeners (page 367).

Best for	Attributes	Drawbacks
An "emergency" remedy to quickly thicken sauces that are already simmering. Can also be used to bind and pull together wet vegetable or cheese fillings.	A good last-minute fix. Wondra is shelf stable, so it can kept be on hand for whenever you need it. There is little raw starch or flour taste that needs to be cooked out.	The increased volume can dramatically mute flavors. Last-minute additions can result in a slightly less refined and glossy texture than roux or other slurries (see below). Makes sauces very opaque. There are many quick alternatives that are superior in texture and flavor.
Thickening simmering liquids very quickly. Fat-free sauces and international sauces like stir-fry sauces that are made without butter or wheat flour. Gluten-free and special-diet gravies and sauces. See Endlessly Adaptable Stir-Fry Sauce (page 369).	Inexpensive, quick, gluten-free, dairy-free, fat-free. Very responsive. Can be added gradually so that when the texture seems just right, you stop adding it.	Distinctive flavor and texture that can seem oddly commercial when used in excess. Thickening properties are reduced with extended cooking. Can get unpleasantly sticky and gummy. Masks natural flavors.

continues

Texturizer	Ratio and best method for thickening 1 cup of liquid
Potato Starch Slurry (use powdered pure starch from potatoes, not flour made from dried potatoes)	Stir 1 teaspoon potato starch into 1 tablespoon cold liquid until smooth. The starch will settle quickly, so stir again before adding to the pot. Potato starch must reach the boiling point to thicken. See Slurries—Pourable Starch Thickeners (page 367).
Arrowroot Slurry	Stir together 1 tablespoon arrowroot and 2 tablespoons cold liquid until smooth. The starch will settle quickly, so stir again before adding to the pot. Pour into sauces and heat; boiling is not necessary.

Best for	Attributes	Drawbacks
Thickening simmering liquids quickly. Fat-free sauces that are best made without butter or wheat flour. Gluten-free and special-diet gravies and sauces. Often used in Scandinavian sauces. See Endlessly Adaptable Stir-Fry Sauce (page 369).	As easy to use as cornstarch, but with a milder, slightly less distinct flavor and perceived gooeyness. It's inexpensive, quick, gluten-free, dairy-free, fat-free, and more appropriate than roux in many international sauces. Very responsive. Can be added gradually so that when the texture seems just right, you stop adding it.	Potato starch is not as widely available as cornstarch. Thickening properties are reduced with high heat and extended cooking. Can get unpleasantly sticky and gooey when used in excess. Masks natural flavors.
For sauces made without butter or wheat flour. For adding a bit of relatively flavorless starch to increase stability. See Vegan Corn "Hollandaise" (page 389) and English Pouring Custard (page 422).	Has a relatively unassuming flavor that is easily masked with other ingredients. Gluten-free, fat-free, dairy-free. Quick and responsive. Makes clear and glossy sauces. Thickens and stabilizes sauces before they reach the boiling point, without a raw starch taste.	Slightly more temperamental and ingredient sensitive than many other thickeners. Can have a creamy, slightly pudding-like texture and taste when made carelessly. Can seem slimy, especially when used with dairy products. Sauces can be boiled briefly, but if they are, they tend to go slack again when they cool, so avoid overheating or boiling them.

continues

Texturizer	Ratio and best method for thickening 1 cup of liquid
Kudzu (Kudzu Root) Slurry	Stir together 2 teaspoons kudzu root nuggets or 1½ teaspoons powdered kudzu root and 2 tablespoons cold liquid until smooth. The starch will settle quickly, so stir again before adding to the pot. Pour into warm or cool sauces and simmer until thickened.
Tapioca Starch Slurry	Stir together 1 teaspoon tapioca starch with 1 tablespoon cold liquid until smooth. The starch will settle quickly, so stir again before adding to the pot. Tapioca starch will thicken almost immediately when it is introduced to hot liquids and does not need to reach the boiling point. See Slurries—Pourable Starch Thickeners (page 367).
All-Purpose Flour Slurry	Stir together 1 tablespoon all-purpose flour with 2 tablespoons cold liquid until smooth. The starch will quickly settle, so stir again before adding to the pot. Simmer for at least 10 minutes to cook out the raw taste of the flour. See Slurries—Pourable Starch Thickeners (page 367).

Best for	Attributes	Drawbacks
Very similar to arrowroot. Traditional Japanese ingredient used extensively in health and whole-food cooking. See Kudzu-Thickened Vegan Japanese Curry Sauce (page 229).	Similar to arrowroot, but even more unassuming and slightly more stable. Very smooth with a mild, clean taste. Not as sticky or gluey as cornstarch or tapioca starch. Gluten-free, fat-free, and dairy-free. Considered a whole-food product because it is made with minimal processing.	Expensive; can be difficult to find. Can be slightly bitter. Can develop a strange wobbly, stringy consistency when used in excess and when cooled, but that tends to melt away when sauces are reheated.
Fruit sauces and fillings. Sauces that are best heated rather than boiled. See Cherry Wine Sauce (page 374).	Very quick and responsive. Thickens and clears before the boiling point is reached. Clear and shiny sauces. Has a perception of sweetness, perhaps because tapioca is most commonly used in desserts.	Too much will quickly make sauces sticky and gooey and seem oddly processed (like canned pie filling). Adds a mild starchy sweetness. The starch can create clear beads if it is not thoroughly blended before adding. Can lose thickening power and scorch with long cooking and high temperatures.
Thickening simmering sauces or soups, especially those that started with a white roux but require a touch more flour. Best reserved for long-cooking dishes so the raw flour taste will cook out.	An easy way to add a bit more flour to sauces, soups, and gravies that aren't quite thick enough. Fat-free.	Can add a pasty taste and texture, especially if not cooked for long enough. There are thickening alternatives that may be superior, such as reduction or adding a vegetable puree.

continues

Texturizer	Ratio and best method for thickening 1 cup of liquid
Masa Harina Slurry	Stir together 1½ tablespoons masa harina and 3 tablespoons cold liquid until well blended. Pour into sauces, soups, or stews and simmer until they are thick and the gritty texture of the corn softens. Thickening will be slow and gradual.
Reduction	Simmer or boil sauces until some or all of the water evaporates and they reach the preferred consistency. Volume and time is completely dependent on the integral ingredients in the sauce. See Reductions (page 145).

Best for	Attributes	Drawbacks
Texture-rich, boldly flavored Southwestern or Mexican soups, sauces, and stews that are complemented by a distinctive corn tortilla flavor. I use a bit of masa harina slurry in tortilla soup and chili.	Adds an appealing flavor and unique texture to Southwestern and Mexican preparations.	Has a very distinctive flavor and texture, making it inappropriate for many sauces. Tends to be very gritty because of the large particle size. Takes quite a bit to thicken a sauce. Thickening will continue as it simmers. Can congeal slightly when cooled and will not reheat as smoothly as sauces made with some other flours.
Heat-tolerant sauces that need to be concentrated in flavor or texture.	An almost universally appropriate technique for heat-tolerant sauces. No added ingredients are necessary. Flavors will be increased rather than diminished.	Only appropriate for heat-tolerant sauces. Can make fresh-tasting sauces taste overcooked or jammy. Takes time and attention. Volume is diminished, sometimes greatly. Basic tastes will be concentrated so sauces that are already salty, bitter, or spicy will become more so.

continues

Texturizer	Ratio and best method for thickening 1 cup of liquid
Egg Yolks (for cold or warm emulsions)	1 large egg yolk can emulsify as much as 1 cup oil when the ingredients are very skillfully introduced. I prefer to use 2 to 3 yolks for added richness and stability. Very slowly and gradually introduce the fat into the eggs while whisking or blending constantly. See Adding Emulsifiers (page 260).
Egg Yolks (for thickening warm sauces)	Gradually stir a few tablespoons of warm sauce into a large egg yolk, then reintroduce the mixture into the sauce and gradually heat until the sauce has thickened slightly. Do not overheat. See Finishing and Enriching Sauces with Egg Yolks (page 433).
Egg Whites	Fold 1 egg white, beaten to soft peaks, into cool sauces for a light, moussey consistency

Best for	Attributes	Drawbacks
Emulsified sauces such as vinaigrettes, dressings, mayo, and hollandaise. See Emulsified Egg Sauces and Their Modern Alternatives (page 380), Classic Caesar Salad Dressing (page 261), and Easy Immersion-Blender Hollandaise (page 388).	Makes dressings creamy and rich. Makes simple oil-and-vinegar emulsions more stable. Has a very natural, appealing texture and flavor.	Raw or lightly cooked eggs can be a health risk. Requires good technique and patience. Sauces will be heat sensitive.
Custards and to finish and enrich sauces. See English Pouring Custard (page 422).	Adds unmatched richness, creaminess, and viscosity. An all-natural, traditional, and historic technique. Adds the unique texture of gelled proteins rather than starch. Flavors are enhanced rather than diminished.	Needs to be carefully added to sauce and gently warmed. Makes sauces heat sensitive. Sauce can turn grainy and shattered, or broken, when heated over. Sauces can seem stodgy, cloying, and old-fashioned.
Mousse-like texture. Adds foaminess to traditional French sauces like Easy Immersion-Blender Hollandaise (page 388) and Creamy Dressings (see the table on page 266).	Lightens and adds a fluffy, light consistency, especially to rich or creamy sauces.	Raw eggs can be a health risk. Egg whites can result in a slightly weepy consistency, especially when the sauce isn't served expediently. There are limited applications where the texture is an enhancement rather than a distraction. Sauces become very heat sensitive and less stable.

continues

Texturizer	Ratio and best method for thickening 1 cup of liquid
Butter	Gradually whisk 1 to 3 tablespoons cold butter, cut into small pieces, into barely simmering sauce until the butter is liquid but not completely melted. Do not boil once the butter has been added. See Finishing and Enriching Sauces with Suspended Melted Butter (page 431).
Heavy Cream or Crème Fraîche	Very gradually stir 2 tablespoons heavy cream or well-stirred crème fraîche into sauces of virtually any temperature. For best results, temper the creams with a tablespoon or two of the warm sauce before adding it. Do not substitute lighter cream or sour cream in hot sauces; these do not have the same structure or thickening power. See Finishing and Enriching Sauces with Dairy Products (page 432).
Sugars (granulated, palm, and brown sugars; evaporated cane juice)	As little as 1 tablespoon sugar can add a slight syrupy viscosity to 1 cup sauce, especially fruit- or vegetable-based sauces.

Best for	Attributes	Drawbacks
Finishing, enriching, and adding gloss to warm sauces. See White Wine Butter Sauce (page 403).	Often a crowd-pleaser. Kind of like adding a flavorful sauce to another flavorful sauce. Easy to use. No added starch, so flavor is enhanced rather than diminished. Also adds sheen. The addition of a touch of fat increases flavor solubility.	High-fat. Unstable; very temperature sensitive, so the sauces do not hold well, chill, or reheat cohesively. Butter can make sauces look unappealingly greasy if the natural emulsion breaks. Not suitable for all diets.
Finishing and enriching sauces. Balancing flavors. See Paprika and Sour Cream Tomato Sauce (see the table on page 186) and Green Peppercorns and Cream Demi-Glace (see the table on page 351).	Often a crowd-pleaser. Easy to use. Enhances rather than diminishes flavor. Can add a fresh flavor and balance to very intense sauces. Can also add visual appeal. The addition of a touch of fat increases flavor solubility.	High-fat. Can "shatter," or break, if subjected to extreme heat changes or high acidity. Too much can overwhelm and swamp flavors rather than enhance them. Not suitable for all diets.
Sauces enhanced by sweetness and a syrupy consistency, such as purees, some tomato sauces, dressings, condiments, and dessert sauces. See Mint Chutney (page 202), BBQ Sauce Base (page 288), and Seasonal Dessert Sauces (see the table on page 415).	Easy way to add shine, gloss, and fluidity. Sweet is a basic taste, so in addition to altering texture, it can be used to balance and enhance the other basic tastes. Can make raw fruit sauces and salsas juicier and slightly more aromatic. Easily manipulated through concentration and reduction.	Will quickly alter the taste balance. Can thin sauces, especially cold sauces. Can go from syrupy to sticky quickly, especially when cooled. There is a risk of crystallization when sugar granules are added carelessly and in very large amounts. Can be tricky to fix when too much sugar is added.

continues

Texturizer	Ratio and best method for thickening 1 cup of liquid
Xanthan Gum	As little as 1/16 teaspoon can pull together "weepy" sauces or make thin sauces slightly syrupy. If possible, mix thoroughly with other dry ingredients before blending into a sauce. Or sprinkle the tiniest pinch, just the amount that can be held on the very tip of a sharp knife, over a sauce and stir, whisk, or blend in very well. See Xanthan Gum (page 180).
Agar-Agar	1½ teaspoons flakes will set 1 cup liquid. The agar-agar must be completely melted. The cold set gel is then blended back into a liquid syrupy sauce.
Nuts and Seeds (pulverized or as pastes such as tahini, and butters such as peanut butter, almond butter, and sunflower kernel butter)	Blend as much as ¼ cup finely ground nuts or 2 tablespoons nut butter into sauce. Thickening potential can double in some cases if the sauce is warmed.

Best for	Attributes	Drawbacks
Pulling together "weepy" uncooked sauces. Adding viscosity and stability. See Fresh Melon-tini Sauce (page 377) and Eggless Mayo (page 384).	Adds stability and gently pulls together sauces that are weeping water or juices. Does not need to be heated or cooked. Gluten free.	Challenging to get the quantity right. Can become "beady" if not sprinkled and whisked carefully. Can get very slimy. Difficult to correct when used in excess.
Intriguing uncooked or very minimally cooked liquids or sauces. See Fresh Citrus Sauce Thickened with Agar-Agar (page 378).	Vegan gelling agent that can turn very fresh lightly cooked liquids into inventive viscous, clinging sauces. Colors can be brilliant. Meatless, fat-free, gluten-free. All-natural.	Agar-agar has a distinctive flavor that some people find unpleasant. Can be slightly tricky to source. Slightly fussy and time-consuming to use. The gel must set and then be liquefied again. Agar-agar can be hard to melt completely. If it is not fully melted, the texture will be beady. Blending traps air bubbles, so sauces are not always clear.
Cool sauces, dressings, vinaigrettes, and dips that are enhanced by the taste and richness of nuts or seeds. Some international savory and spicy sauces. Sauces for some specialty diets. See Power Pesto (page 198), Stir-Together Peanut Butter–Hoisin Dipping Sauce (page 211), and Almond Tahini Sauce (page 212).	Very flavorful natural product. Vegan, gluten-free, whole food. Can make sauces seem creamy without the addition of dairy. Large variations in textures and flavors.	Allergy risk. High in fat, so the oil can separate out (but it can usually be stirred back into sauces that don't have a lot of other fats). Can seize up when heated. Can add a gritty or mealy texture. Distinctive flavors. Nuts that were once crisp will gradually soften.

continues

Texturizer	Ratio and best method for thickening 1 cup of liquid
Soaked Pureed Raw Nuts or Seeds (such as raw cashews, almonds, and sesame seeds)	About ¼ cup nuts soaked in water until very soft, then drained and pureed until smooth, will add a creamy consistency when blended into a liquid. Can become thick when heated.
Chia Seeds	1 tablespoon dried chia seeds can be soaked in a liquid or thin sauce overnight, or presoaked and stirred or blended into a sauce.
Purees Made from Cooked Starchy Vegetables (such as potatoes, plantains, and winter squash)	Varies according to the ingredients in the sauce. ⅓ cup very smooth potato puree will gradually thicken a sauce if simmered for at least 5 minutes.

Best for	Attributes	Drawbacks
Sauces that need to be dairy-free but are enhanced by fat and creaminess. Cool sauces, dressings, vinaigrettes, and dips. Some international savory and spicy sauces. See Vegan Cashew Sour Cream (page 273) and Vegan Cashew "Cheese" Sauce (page 365).	Add flavorful fat and creaminess without animal products. Gluten-free, vegan, and good for many special diets. Enhances flavor as well as texture.	Allergy risk. Can take planning ahead, since the nuts are best pureed after soaking overnight. A high-speed blender is the preferred tool for very smooth blends. Weaker blenders can leave grit and result in uneven sauces. More heat sensitive than dairy creams. Can seize up, become pasty, and/or separate when heated or chilled.
Texture-rich chilled fruit and vegetable juices, purees, puddings, and salsas.	Adds a very specific slippery and bead-like texture. Can be hydrated in flavorful liquids. High in fiber and nutrients. Vegan, gluten-free, fat-free. Adds texture to sauces without heat.	Can take planning ahead, since the seeds are best soaked overnight. There will be some discoloration. When seeds are left whole, the "fish egg" texture can be unappealing. There are many superior thickening techniques.
All-vegetable gravies, purees, and sauces with body that benefit from natural flavors and textures. Overly intense mixtures that need a bit of taming.	Adds body and flavor. Vegan, dairy-free, and a good choice for many specialty diets. A good way to add bulk to mellow overly intense, salty, or spicy sauces.	Not especially refined, delicate, or precise. Solids can separate, settle, or make a sauce look slightly wet. Adds very specific flavors, and often sweetness, as well as thickening properties. Sauces can seem pasty or soupy.

continues

Texturizer	Ratio and best method for thickening 1 cup of liquid
Purees of Pulpy or Pectin-Rich Fruits or Vegetables (such as onions, roasted garlic, eggplant, apples, pears, or stone fruits)	Varies according to the ingredients in the sauce. Stir in about ⅓ cup roasted onion puree, applesauce, or eggplant puree or as little as 1 teaspoon of tomato paste.
Dried Bean and Legume Flours (such as garbanzo bean, chana flour, or finely ground toasted lentils)	Varies according to the product used. Stir together 2 to 3 tablespoons very finely ground bean or legume flour and ¼ cup cold liquid until smooth. The solids may settle quickly, so stir again before adding to the pot. Pour into a simmering sauce and cook for a minimum of 30 minutes, preferably longer, to remove any raw taste.
Tofu	Puree 2 to 4 oz/60 to 115 g drained soft tofu into cold sauces or dressings.

Best for	Attributes	Drawbacks
All vegetable gravies, purees, and sauces that benefit from natural flavors and textures. See Savory Meatless Gravy Thickened with Roasted Onion and Garlic Puree (page 174) and Easy Onionless Tomato and Apple Curry Sauce (page 232).	Adds body and flavor. Can be customized as needed. Vegan, dairy-free, and a good choice for many specialty diets. Depending on the fruit or vegetable, sauces can be made jammy, viscous, creamy, binding, or paste-like.	Not especially refined, delicate, or precise. Solids can separate or settle or make a sauce look slightly wet. Add very specific flavors. Tends to make sauces sweet.
Long-cooking sauces and some curries. Full-flavored, opaque, hearty sauces.	Authentic and ancient thickening ingredients with a distinct earthy flavor. Vegan, gluten-free, and suitable for many special diets.	Tricky to use as a thickener rather than a basic ingredient. Better suited for stews and slow-cooked dishes. High risk of lumpiness when sauce is not stirred until perfectly smooth. Must cook for an extended time to remove the harsh raw bean or legume flavor. Can make sauces very thick and pasty, more like porridge than sauce.
Creamy sauces, dressings, and purees. See Eggless Mayo (page 384) and Vegan Soy Cream Sauce (page 328).	Inexpensive, accessible, and adaptable. Mild flavor. Vegan, gluten-free, and suitable for many special diets. Adds a bright, fresh, and "clean" creaminess.	Allergy risk. Variety and quality of tofu can vary dramatically. Water content will alter the final texture and can make sauces unstable. Must be very smoothly blended, or the sauces can get grainy or seem weepy or broken.

SEASON CONFIDENTLY

Taste can't be shared—it's yours alone. I've got a friend who swears by peanut butter and raw onion sandwiches. Another who puts pickles on her tacos. Whoever prepares the food gets to decide how it should taste. When cooks stop trusting their own preferences and try to guess what others might like, there's a chance no one will be satisfied.

Taste is the stimulation of certain receptors in your mouth. True tastes include salt, sour, sweet, and bitter, but sensory scientists have also confirmed that there are cells stimulated by a fifth savory component they call umami. To adjust the balance of these elemental tastes in your food is to season it. Since no two people have the exact same distribution or level of stimulation of taste receptors, no two people will season their food the same way. That's why restaurants have salt and pepper shakers on the tables and garnish plates with fresh lemon wedges. Chefs carefully season their food to their own high standards but send their plates out knowing that not everyone will agree. You will be amazed at how much better your food is when you grant yourself the same permission.

There are scientists, researchers, and scholars devoted to studying taste and flavor at subatomic levels. They can pinpoint neurons that turn certain tastes on and off and can re-create remarkably accurate natural flavors from drops and potions mixed in test tubes. Cooking does have a lot to do with math, chemistry, and physics, but it is also creative and artistic. Brilliant musicians first learn scales, theory, and rhythm. Painters understand the roles of color, tint, and line. There are some chefs who can dial in the seasoning and flavor of their dishes like wizards, but few people are born with such a gift. Instead of getting frustrated because your sauce doesn't taste like something you enjoyed at a fancy restaurant, give yourself a break, back up to an elementary level, and let yourself grow from there. I wish there were a simple algorithm or multistep process that would make a sauce taste perfect every time, but since every ingredient and situation is different, and flavors evolve and change, I can only suggest ways to teach yourself how to taste critically. When you taste mindfully and consider what exactly is going on in your mouth, you are better equipped to find satisfying solutions.

YOUR SENSE OF TASTE CAN BE IMPROVED THROUGH CONSCIOUSNESS AND EXERCISE

Seasoning has always been something I've had to work at. Whenever I think I've mastered it and stop actively trying to get the flavor balance right, I find myself serving meals that are flat and uninspired. Seasoning is a skill that needs to be continually practiced, honed, and experimented with. I have battled allergies and chronic sinus problems all my life. When you're a food professional and your sense of smell is out of commission, you can't rely on the complicated nuances of flavor. I often "feel" for taste balance.

Think about what happens when you bite into a tart green apple. There is a crackle from the skin and the bursting of water-rich cells. When the juices mingle with your saliva, the sides of your tongue almost cringe and curl, and the feeling expands deep inside your mouth and under your tongue. Your salivary glands gush and tissues become agitated and electric, sometimes causing your cheeks to contract and brows to scrunch into that "sour lemon face." You didn't just *taste* sour—you *felt* it.

Many children are taught about taste with the aid of a tongue map. These maps illustrate how tastes can be perceived in different regions of the mouth: sweet at the tip of the tongue, sour at the sides, salty on the front edges, and bitter at the back. Umami was slow to be acknowledged as a fundamental taste in part because it lit up so many regions in the mouth. The tongue map has come under a lot of fire recently. Experts discredit it because taste receptors are actually distributed all over the palate, not just in patches. But I stand by it. It works for me. Yes, the tongue map is an oversimplification of what is a very complicated sense, but as a starting point for learning how to season, it can't be beat.

To experience how your palate "feels" when different tastes are stimulated, I urge you to try this simple experiment: Set out 4 cups with ¼ cup warm water in each, then make single taste samples by adding a definitive ingredient to each cup. For sweet, stir in 1 teaspoon sugar. For salty, stir in ¼ teaspoon kosher salt. For an acid or sour taste, add 1½ teaspoons distilled white vinegar or ¼ teaspoon powdered citric acid (also sold as sour salt). For umami, add ¼ teaspoon MSG or ½ teaspoon low-sodium soy sauce. Bitter is a tricky taste to isolate for a test like this. I hear that powdered chicory root and ground caffeine tablets work well, but I don't keep those on hand. You can create a fifth sample using cocktail bitters, or extra-strong, unflavored black tea. There is another taste test that follows this one that also illustrates the "feel" of bitter.

Taste a sip of one sample. Think about what you feel rather than just what it tastes like. Take another taste of the same sample and swirl the solution around in your mouth. Feel how it stimulates the tissues in and around your tongue. Even though taste map skeptics may say otherwise, salt will be perceived right away at the front and sides of the tongue. Sweet is a quick fix, right at the tip and then throughout your mouth. It has you wanting more. Sour is a jolt. The first perception may be in your nose if you used vinegar, because of its volatility. Recognize that. Acknowledge that a lot of what you are experiencing as taste does not exclusively rely on your tongue and taste buds. Sour tastes will quickly make the sides of

your tongue and mouth seem electric: your mouth will literally water. Umami is a revelation. You may first perceive it as simply salty, but when you compare it to the pure salt solution, you will feel that it's deeper and more widespread. It's savory. Bitter is a late taste, or a lingering "aftertaste" that settles in the back of the tongue and mouth.

Combine small amounts of the different solutions to see how they interact. Then, finally, mix 1 tablespoon of each solution together in another cup. Note how remarkably balanced and somehow satisfying it is, and yet it's just well-seasoned water. Imagine what it would taste like with flavor! Every time I repeat this exercise, I am reminded of how heavily processed mass-produced sauces rely on the stimulation of these taste receptors. Add a touch of chicken fat, some powdered onion, a drop of coloring, and a touch of thickener, and you have the root of a remarkable number of cheap sauces.

With practice, you may start to recognize your palate's hot spots and what taste expert Barb Stuckey refers to as "taste deserts"— areas where taste buds may be damaged or sparse and so are less sensitive. Do this exercise with others, and each one of you will have both similar and unique experiences. My father swears he doesn't "feel" taste reactions in the same places I do. But he likes my food because the balance of seasonings is pleasing to both of us, no matter where the taste buds happen to fire.

Another way to experience how different tastes "feel" and move in the mouth is with a relatively unassertive ground spice like mild paprika. (Ground cumin also works.) Start with 2 teaspoons of the plain spice: Put 1 teaspoon in a dish and set it aside. Lightly toast the second sample in a dry skillet over medium-low heat for about 1 minute, until it darkens slightly and becomes aromatic. Put it in a second dish. Taste a tiny bit of the first untoasted sample. It will be pretty much what you expect and similar to what you smell in the bottle—slightly pungent and quite bright, maybe with a peppery bite. The stimuli will primarily be in the front and sides of your tongue, but it will likely leave a slightly harsh aftertaste deep in your throat. Now rinse your mouth and taste the toasted sample. The taste stimuli have moved. There is less action up front, less zip. More of your mouth is involved. There seems to be more depth and balance. The bitterness is not as late, abrasive, or malingering, but more central, finishing, and balanced. This is a lesson on how it is possible to manipulate what you experience on your palate. It also shows how cooking can alter taste.

Taste sensitivity tends to dim as we age. Pregnancy can rewire the senses. There are many medical conditions that alter the sense of taste. Alzheimer's and cancer treatment can leave patients complaining that their food tastes like cardboard. While she was recovering from some injuries, my mother swore salt was being added to her

food by the cupful. Understanding your own physiology can help you taste, judge, and alter the balance of the dishes you create in a pleasing way.

The next time you find yourself wondering what to add to a sauce, consider those single-item taste samples. How does the sauce stimulate your tongue map? Does just one region fire early and then disappear? Is there nothing up front, but then a late or lingering aftertaste? When one flavor map region is overpowering another, or an element seems to be missing, the finished dish will be less satisfying. Balance these out with more salt, more acid, or a savory undertone. If it is simply flat and lifeless, it probably needs added intensity and flavor, not just seasoning.

HOW PROFESSIONALS APPROACH SEASONING

Chefs have the experience necessary to create a good base of seasoning without much thought. Some pinch, sprinkle, and scatter ingredients so confidently that it seems they must get it right every time. I used to try and mimic this professional flair and nonchalance, assuming that the right amount of seasoning would eventually just spring from my fingertips.

It took me a while before I realized that the very best dishes were made by cooks who were slow and deliberate when seasoning their preparations. They would taste, think, take careful action, and then taste again.

Great chefs also taste the individual ingredients before they ever reach the pot. Are the berries sweet or tart? Is the basil peppery or floral? Is the olive oil fruity or acidic? They adapt their approach to the various preparations before things ever start to sizzle. Chefs aren't afraid to ask for a second opinion, but they tend to make such requests specific in nature. They don't just say, "Do you think it tastes good?" They ask, "Does it need more acidity? Does it have enough bite? Would you add more salt?" If they are stumped, they may spoon small amounts of a sauce into a dish and experiment with seasoning adjustments and additions until they find their answer. That way, the entire pot doesn't become a laboratory. Since taste and flavors evolve and change, sauces are always tasted again and adjusted before service. Skillful seasoning is not magic—it is methodical and attentive.

RECOGNIZE TASTE BURNOUT

There can be a point when you have tasted and tweaked a sauce so many times you just can't taste it anymore. Give yourself a break. Give the sauce a break. Eat a cracker or a tuft of bread. Rinse your mouth out with water. Go outside for a breath of fresh air. If you keep just adding more and more seasoning, there is a risk you will end up with a highly seasoned but not very good sauce. If possible, taste the sauce with a bit of the food it is meant to be served with. Sometimes, when your sauce is "not quite there" and you leave

it alone, you can return to it and appreciate all that is good and real rather than an indefinable component you perceive as missing.

SIMPLE VERSUS BOLD SEASONING

There are warring factions on flavor and seasoning. One camp believes that food should taste like itself. I'm a big follower of this philosophy. Well-prepared fresh, seasonal ingredients need little embellishment. A leaf of lettuce should taste of lettuce, not a complicated spiced or rich cream dressing. A lovely fillet of white fish or oyster should taste of the water it lived in. I am fully devoted to simple, natural flavors until I taste something that absolutely explodes with intensity. With one bite I'm a convert. My alliance flip-flops and I vow that good food must be spicy and complicated. I trade in my simple stir-fried pea shoots for mouth-numbing Sichuan eggplant. I replace my minimally seasoned fresh tomato sauce with a puttanesca loaded with cured olives, anchovies, and chile flakes. And just as I am utterly convinced that the only way for food to be really good is when it's in-your-face, I have a bite of pear or a perfectly boiled new potato and I'm right back where I started. There is no right answer. Some dishes should be seasoned with a very light hand, others are elevated by ramping things up to extremes. But if everything you prepare lingers somewhere in the middle—*almost* simple or *almost* bold—you can do better. You are in for some really fun meals when you decide to mix things up.

THE FIVE BASIC TASTES

Sweet

Sugar is nature's way of telling you everything's going to be okay. Mother's milk is naturally sweet. Seeds are wrapped in ripe, sweet fruits inviting consumption (and distribution). A tiny bit of sweetness can round out sharp, bitter, or salty sauces. Unlike many other tastes, sugar can be a strong and complementary counter to another single intense taste: sweet and sour, sweet and spicy, sweet and salty.

Salt

People are salty. Human beings require salt for survival. The most common reason a sauce "doesn't taste right" is because it needs more salt. Too little salt can make a dish seem off-kilter, unfinished, and out of balance. Rely on your taste buds, not your eyes, when you are adding salt. Consider how you might salt each of the ingredients rather than the whole pot. Kosher salt crystals require about twice the volume to reach the sodium content of table salt, so amounts can seem alarming if you haven't used it before. Salt is not inherently unhealthy except for those who have been instructed by their doctors to follow a low-sodium diet. The first instruction doctors tend to give people who are staring on a low-sodium diet is to make their own food. Homemade sauces usually have dramatically less sodium than their commercial counterparts.

Sour

Adding a sour element is not the same as making a tart sauce. Acidity is the taste most linked to freshness. A few drops of vinegar, a pinch of citric acid, or a spoonful of diced tangy tomatoes can make a flat sauce start to sing. Acids make the mouth water, which is perceived as tantalizing. Acidity can also "widen" a sauce by stimulating the sides of the tongue, the cheeks, and salivary glands.

Bitter

Unlike the other basic tastes, bitter has a negative connotation. Bitter is an alarm stimulus that can signal that foods have gone bad or that plants might be poisonous. But it is also one of the basic tastes, so when there is no bitter stimulation, it seems as if something is missing. Bitter tastes are pronounced in many of our most treasured foods: coffee, red wine, mustard, spices, greens, fermented items, and roasted or grilled foods. Bengali feasts often start with a bitter dish in the belief that it will ready the tongue and stomach for the rest of the meal. Bitter tends to be a late taste, stimulating the back of the tongue and palate; it is associated with aftertaste. If bitterness is too prevalent, try to move the tastes toward the front of the palate with salty, sweet, and sour elements.

Umami

Huh? That's usually the reaction I get when I use the word *umami* around most people. Sometimes called "the fifth taste," umami can be a difficult flavor to describe, but then think about how hard it would be to describe salt or sour without examples. The simplest description of the term is "savory." The official definition from The Umami Information Center (www.umamiinfo.com) is:

. . . a pleasant savoury taste imparted by glutamate, a type of amino acid, and ribonucleotides, including inosinate and guanylate, which occur naturally in many foods including meat, fish, vegetables, and dairy products. As the taste of umami itself is subtle and blends well with other tastes to expand and round out flavors, most people don't recognize umami when they encounter it, but it plays an important role [in] making food taste delicious.

Some naturally umami-rich ingredients are Parmesan and other aged cheeses, roasted meats, cooked or dried tomatoes, mushrooms, anchovies, yeast concentrates, and sauces like soy, tamari, fish sauce, and Worcestershire. Think of an intense savory ingredient or dish, and chances are good it is loaded with free glutamates. Have you ever run into a tiny, salty crystal when you are eating Parmesan cheese? That's pure glutamate—pure umami.

Umami stimulates sensors throughout your mouth. It fills things out. Adding an umami-rich ingredient can make vegan and vegetarian items taste meatier. Umami makes a sauce taste like . . . more. When salt, sweet, sour, and bitter aren't cutting it, add something rich in umami, like soy sauce or a dash of Worcestershire, and you will be amazed at the difference it makes. When I first heard the term, it was described as a certain earthy, slightly complicated freshness. It conjured up thoughts of farmers' market asparagus and young cucumber skins. I still think of it in those terms. It remains a much more romantic, albeit slightly less scientific definition.

WHEN FIVE TASTES AREN'T ENOUGH

Taste may technically mean the stimulation of certain cells, but there is more to it than that. The influence of flavor is crucial. Intensity, texture, how flavors linger, even color and sound will make a difference in how foods are perceived. How would you describe a peanut, an onion, or an oyster if you were to use only the five tastes? What about foods with metallic, peppery, earthy, refreshing, or creamy characteristics? Sometimes five tastes just don't seem like enough.

The ingredient that makes a chile hot, capsaicin, is not a taste, but the stimulation of tiny pain receptors on the palate. Astringency, like that of persimmons, pomegranate seeds, and unripe bananas, involves a tiny bit of bonding and temporary paralysis of tissues. And then there are regional disagreements about taste. Chinese chefs consider the five basic tastes to be salt, sweet, sour, bitter, and pungent. Indian Aryurvedic cooking includes sweet, salty, sour, bitter, pungent, and astringent. There are scientists pushing to have fat recognized as a taste and others who are determined to eradicate the concept of fundamental tastes altogether. They believe there are hundreds of tastes, not just five. Jean Anthelme Brillat-Savarin, the early nineteenth century gastronome and food documentarian, suggested that love was a sensory consideration in food. I'm not going to argue. I think homemade is an especially desirable taste. The point is that good food should taste right to you, not just to a panel of sensory scientists.

Want to Learn More?

There are some brilliant books on the subject of taste, flavor, and seasoning, including *Taste What You're Missing: The Passionate Eater's Guide to Why Good Food Tastes Good* by Barb Stuckey (Free Press, 2012); *The Elements of Taste* by Peter Kaminsky and Gray Kunz (Little, Brown, 2008); and *The Flavor Bible: The Essential Guide to Culinary Creativity, Based on the Wisdom of America's Most Imaginative Chefs* by Karen Page and Andrew Dornenburg (Little, Brown, 2008). Scientists are constantly exploring the mechanics of taste, breaking it down to cellular receptors and neurons, so there is always new information available.

SEASONING ALTERNATIVES

The following table suggests seasoning ideas that can add interest as well as boost the basic tastes. Instead of kosher salt, a pinch of smoked salt or truffle salt might be even better. Many of the ingredients have multiple characteristics. Mix and match them. Just because you add chile powder doesn't mean black pepper should be omitted. In addition to the five basic tastes, also consider boosting the flavors or enhancing them with creaminess, brightness, pungency, astringency, and/or aroma.

Salty

Specialty salts such as Himalayan pink salt, smoked salt, truffle salt, or Maldon sea salt

Soy sauce or tamari

Fish sauce

Salty cheeses such as feta, Parmesan, or myzithra

Concentrated commercial stocks or soup bases

Bragg liquid amino acids or Maggi liquid seasoning

Marmite, Vegemite, or nutritional yeast flakes

Salty pickles or pickling brines

Seasoning powders such as Goya Sazón, Vegeta, and instant dashi

Salt-cured anchovies, anchovy paste, or dried salted fish

Capers

Olives or olive brines

Salted plum products, such as li hing powder, Japanese ume paste, or umeboshi vinegar

Clam nectar

Salt-cured ham or other salty meats

Sweet

Sugars such as granulated, brown, Demerera,
   turbinado, or evaporated cane juice

Palm sugar

Honey or honey powder

Molasses

Syrups such as maple, agave, barley malt, or
   flavored syrups

Syrups or juices from preserved or canned fruit

Concentrated apple or grape juice sweeteners

Mirin, sweet wines, or liqueurs

Jellies, jams, marmalades, or chutneys

Caramelized onions or sweet vegetables like
   winter squash or sweet potatoes

Powdered milk, powdered cream, or malted
   milk powder

Fruit purees

Reduced fruit juice

Dates, raisins, or dried fruits

Caramel

Sweetened condensed milk

Frozen juice concentrates

Sour/Tangy

Citrus juices such as lemon, lime, grapefruit,
   pomelo, or calamansi

Vinegars

Powdered citric acid (sour salt) or powdered
   food-grade malic acid

Verjus

Tabasco sauce

Vinegary pickle juices

Tamarind

Unripe fruits

Cultured dairy products such as yogurt, sour
   cream, buttermilk, or kefir

Tomatillos

Frozen juice concentrates such as lemonade,
   limeade, or cranberry juice

Amchoor (ground dried green mango)

Hibiscus or rose hip infusions

Chopped or grated raw tomatoes

Umami/Savory

MSG or seasoning blends made with MSG

Parmesan or similar aged cheese

Dried, roasted, or browned mushrooms

Tomato paste or other concentrated tomatoes,
   such as dried, roasted, or seared tomatoes

Worcestershire sauce

Marmite, Vegemite, or nutritional yeast flakes

Fermented bean pastes such as miso,
   doengang, shoyu koji, gochujang, or Sichuan
   bean paste

Soy sauce or tamari

Fish sauce

Anchovies or anchovy paste

Browned flavors and glace from roasting or
   searing meats, poultry, or vegetables

Bragg liquid amino acids

Prepared Chinese sauces such as oyster sauce,
   hoisin sauce, or XO sauce

Maggi, Jugo, or Jumbo seasoning

Bacon

Seasoning salts with MSG, such as Accent,
   Vegetal, or Goya Sazón

Dried kelp (kombu) infusion

Bitter/Peppery

Peppers such as black, white, green, pink, or
Sichuan

Mustard, dry or prepared

Cocktail bitters such as Angostura or
Peychaud

Fresh ginger

Chiles, chile sauces, or chile powders

Liquors or liqueurs such as pastis, absinthe,
amaro, and Campari

Wasabi or horseradish

Dark bitter greens or herbs

Citrus zest

Coffee or espresso

Strongly brewed tannic teas such as black tea,
green tea, or rooibos (red bush)

Tannic red wines

Unsweetened cocoa powder or dark chocolate

Spices such as cumin, cinnamon, juniper,
coriander, or licorice root

Tonic water

TURNING WATER INTO SAUCE

onsider plain water to be an empty vehicle. It picks up soluble components, transports them, and, when necessary, can even be urged to leave through evaporation.

Dissolving flavorful particles in water can be as simple as brewing a cup of tea or stirring cocoa powder and sugar into warm milk. To infuse flavors, you need to mix the wet with the dry. The technique is so utterly simple and familiar it tends to be done almost unconsciously, but effort and intention will improve infusion. I know how to make a good cup of tea because centuries of tea drinkers before me figured out the specifics. They cultivated the proper plants and established a pleasing ratio of leaves to water and the best amount of time to let them steep.

I'm a huge advocate of creating your own original dishes and combining new flavors. I also think the best place to start is with the fundamentals. That is why, instead of rushing right into stock, we start with simply getting a feel for how to transfer the elements of a solid ingredient into a liquid and how much this simple act can improve your food. Infusions evolve into stocks, broths, and very thin sauces. These are manipulated, concentrated, and enriched and soon enough that simple infused water becomes an intense and refined sauce.

INFUSIONS

DON'T FEEL LIKE MAKING STOCK? HOW ABOUT BREWING SOME INGREDIENTS IN HOT WATER, LIKE A CUP OF TEA?

At the start of a sauce cookbook, the author is expected to expound on the virtues of making fresh stock and urge you to spend your evenings and weekends simmering bones, vegetables, and herbs into clear nectar. I'll get to that. Chefs make fresh stocks every day because they spend their days and nights in well-equipped kitchens and their livelihoods depend on their ability to make good food. Tired home cooks peering into the fridge for midweek sustenance don't have the same motivation. What if, though, instead of adding plain water to your dishes or relying on a commercially prepared product there were another alternative? What if you brewed something resembling a quick savory tea? The flavors are fresh, it can be customized to suit your meal, and the ingredient list is your own. And because every drop counts, it will make a difference.

Once you get in the habit, you will find all sorts of ways to naturally infuse flavors into water. The next time you make stir-fried chicken, simmer some chopped chicken scraps in a cup of water while the rice cooks. Strain this quick stock and use it as a base for your stir-fry sauce, and each bite will have more chicken flavor. Imagine what a quick infusion of dried mushrooms, tamarind pulp, or dried shrimp would add. Simmer a dried chile, a corncob, or an apple peel in water and use the strained liquid to deglaze a pan, to make risotto, or to steam fish. Don't worry too much if what you end up with is weak. These "mock stocks" and simple brews will never have the complexity or body of long-simmered stocks. They are not meant to be straight-across substitutions for broths, but convenient, fresh alternatives that will also give you a better idea of the roles of infusion and flavor.

It was once common for recipes to call for using the cooking water from boiling pasta, potatoes, and beans. Some still do. Not only does this liquid add flavor, it adds thickening potential. M. F. K. Fisher, one of the first great American food writers, made the juices from canned fruits and vegetables sound almost tantalizing in her book *How to Cook a Wolf*. She clearly illustrated how water was measly in comparison, especially during hard times.

As with tea, intensity will vary according to ingredient quality, preparation, ratios, temperatures, and steeping time. You may wonder, if it's more flavor I'm looking for, why don't I just add more minced onion, ground spices, or grated cheese? Go ahead! Look around your kitchen. You probably have spices, chutney, dried chiles, bits of cheese, and produce staples that you never considered as potential sauce ingredients. Whenever you are reluctant to add a particular ingredient because of the texture or concentration of it, consider how else you might add it. Infuse it in the liquid destined for the sauce pot—not just water, but also milk, stock, melted butter, oil, even alcohol. In some cases, like the Rose-Scented Almond Milk (page 98) or Strong Red Bush (Rooibos) Tea with Honey (page 129), a quick infusion can be a sauce in itself.

DRIED MUSHROOM WATER

This is an especially easy and flavorful infusion and a quick meatless alternative to stock. You are hydrating the mushrooms while you make the infusion, so you can use both the liquid and the reconstituted mushrooms. The mushrooms can be chopped and added to pasta sauces, cream sauces, or stir-fries.

YIELD: ABOUT ¾ CUP

2 or 3 dried shiitake or forest mushrooms, or 5 or 6 dried porcini pieces, or 3 or 4 dried morels

1 cup boiling water

> Put the mushrooms in a small bowl and cover with the water. Leave to infuse for at least 5 minutes, but preferably 15 minutes or longer.

> Lift out the mushrooms and squeeze out any liquid. Strain the liquid through a fine sieve or cheesecloth before using to remove any grit or sand.

DRIED TOMATO WATER

This has become a new favorite of mine because it adds a hint of complex tomato flavors and umami tastes without adding the bulk of fresh tomatoes or canned tomato products. You can chop the reconstituted tomatoes and use them in your sauce or save them for another recipe.

YIELD: ABOUT ¾ CUP

2 or 3 dried tomatoes (not packed in oil), chopped or crumbled

1 thin slice onion (any kind)

1 clove garlic

1 cup boiling water

> Combine the tomatoes, onion, and garlic in a bowl. Cover with the water, stir, and leave to infuse for at least 5 minutes.

> Strain the liquid; reserve the tomatoes.

TAMARIND WATER AND TAMARIND PULP

Tamarind is a tropical pod with a sticky brown flesh that is both tangy and sweet. Dissolved in varying concentrations, it can be used to make a thin, tart water or a thick, pulpy puree. Both are used as an ingredient in Latin American and Asian cuisines. Tamarind comes in several forms. Whole pods can sometimes be found with fresh produce. When the shells, seeds, and fibers are removed, they can be eaten like candy. I always keep a block of lump tamarind on hand. Sticky cakes of tamarind pulp often contain some seeds and fibers that can easily be removed as the cake softens. Thai lump tamarind has a particularly appealing tangy taste. You can also buy prepared tamarind purees and syrups, but they tend to be quite dull or so concentrated they seem like molasses.

TAMARIND WATER

This is an excellent tangy, fruity, alcohol-free alternative to wine.

> Pour ¾ cup boiling water over 1 heaping tablespoon (1 oz/28 g) lump tamarind. Leave to soften for a minute, then stir and mash the tamarind. Let steep for 3 to 4 minutes longer, then stir again or, if the water is cool enough, use your fingers to loosen the pulp from the seeds and fibers. Strain the liquid, pressing as much pulp as possible through the sieve. Discard the seeds and fibers.

TAMARIND PULP

Use as a tangy ingredient in curries and peanut sauce.

> Break up 3 tablespoons (3 oz/85 g) lump tamarind and combine it with 1 cup water in a saucepan. Simmer for 1 to 2 minutes, stirring often, until the tamarind is soft and and the mixture has thickened. Press the pulp through a sieve and discard the fibers and seeds.

CHEESE WATER

The flavors in cheese are water soluble. That means you can infuse hot water with aged cheese and use it like stock. Simmer fresh vegetables like broccoli and cauliflower in cheese water. Splash it into pasta sauces or use it in place of milk to make unusual white sauces or gravies. There is no goo, stringiness, or excess calories. Of course, there are caveats. It takes a lot of cheese to make flavorful water, and neither the water nor the spent cheese has the appeal of the original. I only make this when I have a collection of dry bits, odd chunks, and rinds that keep getting passed over at dinnertime but are too good to waste.

YIELD: ABOUT 2½ CUPS

1 cup (3 oz/85 g) finely grated cheeses, such as aged Gouda, Gruyère, and/or Manchego (the sharper and drier the cheese, the better)

3 cups boiling water

Pinch of kosher salt (optional)

Pinch of sugar (optional)

Pinch of dry mustard (optional)

Pinch of cayenne pepper or dash of Tabasco (optional)

> Put the grated cheese in a large bowl and gradually pour the boiling water over it, stirring with a spoon or silicone spatula. Resist the urge to use a blender, food processor, or whisk, or you will end up with an impossible mess of melted cheese glued to the blades. Continue to stir for an entire minute so the cheese is thoroughly infused into the water. Cover and let steep for 5 minutes. The cheese solids will sink.

> Carefully decant the top liquid, without disturbing the settled cheese solids—you can strain it through a few layers of dampened cheesecloth, but do not use an unlined sieve, or you will have a terrible time cleaning the sticky cheese from the mesh. Any remaining warm melted cheese is very tempting and it can be scooped up with chunks of bread or vegetables like an impromptu fondue, but it won't have the flavor of regular melted cheese. As with the spent bones and vegetables in stock, it's usually best to just throw it out.

> Season the cheese water with a pinch of salt if it tastes flat. Add a little sugar if it's bitter. Or add a bit of dried mustard or cayenne for more pizzazz.

> If storing, cover and refrigerate for up to 1 week or freeze for up to 3 months.

MOCK STOCKS AND SIMPLE INFUSIONS

A quick-brewed infusion doesn't require the investment of stock, and it is a great improvement over plain water. Most of these suggestions start with a single cup of water. Some ingredients, like nutritional yeast flakes and miso, can just be stirred into warm water. Others, like chicken and fish scraps, need to be simmered until they are cooked through. Use these "mock stocks" as a base for slurries, to liquefy purees, to moisten salsas, or to deglaze roasting pans or skillets.

Veggie Trimmings	Combine equal quantities of cold water and chopped vegetable scraps from the meal you are preparing—such as cauliflower or celery leaves, broccoli, chard or mushroom stems, parsley stems, carrot tops, tomato skins and seeds, pea pods, and/or clean potato peels—in a saucepan. Add a pinch of salt, bring to a boil, cover, and simmer for at least 5 minutes. Strain.
Onion and Garlic	Pour 1 cup boiling water over ½ cup chopped or thinly sliced onion, shallot, leek greens, and/or sliced scallions, and 2 sliced garlic cloves. Cover and leave to steep for 5 minutes. Or combine the ingredients in a saucepan and simmer for 5 minutes; strain. For a sweeter flavor, sauté the vegetables in a bit of oil until tender before adding cold water. For a slightly smoky taste, char the raw onions and garlic directly on a burner or with a blowtorch before combining with the water. You can also add onions, shallots, and/or garlic to virtually any savory infusion.
Mock Beef	Pour 1 cup boiling water over ½ cup chopped or thinly sliced onion or shallots, 2 sliced garlic cloves, and ½ teaspoon Marmite. Stir and leave to steep for 5 minutes. Or combine the ingredients in a saucepan and simmer for 5 minutes. Strain. For a sweeter flavor, sauté the onions and garlic in a bit of oil until golden brown before adding the Marmite and water.
Tomato	Pour 1 cup boiling water over 2 or 3 chopped dried tomatoes (not packed in oil) or 2 teaspoons tomato paste and 1 slice of onion and 1 sliced garlic clove. Cover and leave to steep for at least 5 minutes. Or combine the ingredients in a saucepan and simmer for 5 minutes. Strain.

continues

Carrot	Pour 1 cup boiling water over ½ cup grated carrots, 1 slice of onion, 1 sliced garlic clove, and 1 teaspoon tomato paste or 1 tablespoon ketchup (optional). Stir well, cover, and leave to steep for 5 minutes. Or combine the ingredients in a saucepan and simmer for 5 minutes. Strain.
Ginger, Honey, and Citrus	Pour 1 cup boiling water over 2 coins fresh ginger, 2 or 3 wide strips of lemon, orange, or grapefruit zest, and 1 tablespoon honey. Cover and leave to steep for 5 minutes: Strain. Depending on the menu, you can add a dried chile, piece of star anise, or bruised herb stems for variation.
Chicken	Combine ½ cup chopped raw chicken scraps, such as bits of meat, bones, and/or skin, and 2 cups cold water in a saucepan. Bring to a boil over high heat, then reduce the heat to a simmer and cook, covered, for about 10 minutes. Strain.
Mock Chicken	Stir 1 tablespoon nutritional yeast flakes and a pinch of poultry seasoning (optional) into 1 cup water.
Miso	Stir 1 tablespoon miso into 1 cup water.
Black, Green, or Herbal Tea	Steep 2 tablespoons loose leaf tea or 2 tea bags in 1 cup boiling water for 3 minutes; strain. Try licorice, mint, chamomile, Turkish apple, rooibos (red bush), dried hibiscus (*flor de jamaica*), rose hips, ginger, or sage. Black teas can add bitter tannins, a slight smokiness, and astringency. Green teas can add a floral, vegetal, or slightly citrusy element.
Umami	Pour 1 cup boiling water over ⅓ cup grated Parmesan cheese, 1 tablespoon ketchup, 1 anchovy or ¼ teaspoon anchovy paste (optional), and 2 teaspoons Worcestershire sauce. Stir well and let steep for 5 minutes. Strain.
Corncob	Cut a corncob into 1-inch/2½ cm pieces. Put in a saucepan with enough cold water to cover and simmer, covered, for 5 to 7 minutes. Strain. Use raw, cooked, or even lightly roasted cobs.

Cured or Dried Meat	Combine ¼ to ⅓ cup finely chopped very lean bacon, prosciutto ends, ham, and/or salami scraps with 1 cup water in a saucepan, cover, and simmer for at least 5 minutes. Remove from the heat and leave to infuse until you are ready to strain and use. It will be cloudy.
Dried Fruits	Combine ¼ cup chopped dried fruit, such as raisins, golden raisins, dates, figs, apricots, prunes, and/or dried pears with 1 cup water in a saucepan and simmer for 5 to 7 minutes. Strain. This can mimic the fruitiness of sweet wines without the alcohol.
Roasted Barley Tea	Simmer 1 tablespoon roasted barley (Korean barley tea) in 1 cup water for 5 minutes. Strain. It may be tempting to increase the quantity of grain, but it can give the liquid a more acrid, almost burnt flavor and is not recommended.
Fresh Herbs	Pour 1 cup boiling water over 3 to 5 sprigs dense or hearty herbs, like rosemary or thyme; 3 to 5 bay leaves; or up to ½ cup bruised tender herbs such as chervil, chives, or cilantro. Cover and leave to steep for 5 minutes. Strain.
Shrimp Shells or Fish Trimmings	Combine very fresh or frozen shrimp shells or fish trimmings such as heads, frames, or collars and enough cold water to cover in a pot. Simmer for 10 minutes. Strain through a fine sieve or two layers of dampened cheesecloth.
Apple or Pear Peelings and Cores	Cover the scrubbed peelings and core from 1 apple or pear with water in a small saucepan and bring to a boil, cover, and simmer for 5 minutes. Strain.
Anchovies or Dried Shrimp	Pour 1 cup boiling water over 6 to 8 cleaned, preserved anchovies (dried, canned, or salted) or 2 tablespoons dried shrimp and simmer or leave to infuse for 5 minutes. Strain. For the best flavor, toast the shrimp in a dry pan for 1 minute before adding the water.

DASHI

Dashi is a clear savory infusion that is an indispensable part of Japanese cooking. It has a marvelous salty smokiness and gentle aroma of the seashore. It can be used as stock, as a base for broths, or to moisten vegetables destined to become intriguing sauce purees, like the Grilled Scallion and Dashi Puree (see the table on page 178). Dashi is the ingredient that makes a simple soy dipping sauce like Tentsuyu—Tempura Dipping Sauce (page 280) taste so quintessentially Japanese. It is sometimes referred to as stock, but that's only because it is a simple clear liquid that adds complexity and intensity. In practice, it is merely two ingredients steeped in hot water. Japanese bonito flakes, katsuobushi, are shaved from dried, smoked skipjack tuna. Kombu is dried kelp. Both are available in some supermarkets and many health food stores, as well as Asian markets. Bonito flakes should be dry and fluffy and have a fresh, nonoffensive aroma. The ingredients store well, and once you have them on hand, you can brew a batch of dashi in minutes. Even though it is quick to make, I often make extra so I can have tubs in the freezer for even more convenience.

YIELD: 3½ CUPS

1 to 2 postcard-sized pieces kombu (dried kelp)

4½ cups cold water

1 cup (1 to 1½ oz/28 to 45 g) loosely packed dried bonito flakes (katsuobushi)

> Wipe the kombu with a damp paper towel to remove any white salty film. Combine the water and kombu in a saucepan. If you have the time, let the seaweed soak for 15 to 20 minutes to soften it and make more flavors available.

> Bring the water and seaweed to a boil. Shake the bonito flakes over the surface of the water and return the water to a boil so the fish flakes are agitated and moistened. Remove the pan from the burner, cover, and leave to steep until the fish flakes hydrate enough to sink to the bottom of the pan, about 12 minutes.

> Set a sieve over a deep container and strain the dashi, without pressing on the solids; discard the solids. (It is possible to make a second stock from the drained bonito flakes, but it won't have the same depth or delicacy.)

> If storing, cover and refrigerate for up to 2 days or freeze for up to 3 months.

DRIED-ANCHOVY DASHI

> Omit the bonito flakes. Soak ⅓ cup small dried anchovies (niboshi) with the kombu in the cold water for at least 15 to 20 minutes and, preferably, up to 4 hours, for a stronger flavor. Bring the mixture to a boil, reduce the heat, and simmer, covered, for 5 minutes. Remove the pan from the heat and leave to steep for another 5 minutes, then strain as above. The flavor is stronger and slightly "fishier" than that of dashi, but certainly not overwhelming. This is especially good with winter dishes and noodles.

VEGAN SHIITAKE DASHI

> Omit the bonito flakes. Soak 6 to 8 crumbled dried shiitake mushrooms with the kombu in the cold water for at least 30 minutes, and, preferably, up to 4 hours, for a stronger flavor. Bring the mixture to a boil, reduce the heat, and simmer, covered, for 5 minutes. Remove the pan from the heat and leave to steep for an additional 5 minutes, then strain, pressing gently on the solids to extract as much liquid as you can.

ROSE-SCENTED ALMOND MILK

We have an ancient rosebush in our yard that produces the most aromatic blossoms I have ever encountered. One sniff, and people start to brainstorm about ways to capture their essence. They were the impetus for this lovely almond milk. It is rich but still delicate, romantic, and slightly celebratory. Serve it as a thin sauce with cold poached chicken garnished with pomegranate seeds, or on rice pudding with sliced strawberries. Almond milk is available in many supermarkets. Use a fragrant local honey like wildflower if you can.

YIELD: 2 CUPS

2 cups plain unsweetened almond milk

About 1 cup loosely packed unsprayed organic rose petals (use more if your roses are lightly scented, or substitute ½ oz/14 g food-grade dried rose petals)

2 tablespoons honey, or to taste

> Stir the ingredients together in a medium saucepan. Heat gently over medium heat until there is steam rising from the milk, but do not boil. Remove the pan from the heat, stir the mix again, cover, and leave it to steep for 5 to 7 minutes.

> Set a sieve over a deep bowl and strain the milk, pressing gently on the petals; discard the solids. Taste and adjust the sweetness with more honey if you like.

> Serve warm or cold.

> If storing, cover and refrigerate for up to 3 days. If the milk separates, just give it a shake or stir.

LEMONGRASS AND LIME LEAF EXTRACT

Some flavor molecules are dissolved with alcohol. Vanilla beans are one example of an ingredient that is particularly good infused into alcohol. I love the exotic taste and perfume that lemongrass, fresh lime leaves, and galangal add to Southeast Asian soups and sauces, but I don't cook Thai or Vietnamese food often enough to keep the fresh ingredients on hand. This recipe was created with a few leftover bits I couldn't quite part with. Stir a tablespoon of this infusion into a hot broth or sauce just before serving for a tempting, exotic aroma. I am not above doctoring up instant ramen noodles with coconut milk and spice pastes. A splash of this extract makes them seem much fancier than they are. A few drops are not unwelcome in original cocktails either.

Galangal is a rhizome similar to ginger but with a scent of camphor. It is available fresh at Asian markets.

YIELD: ½ CUP

1 stalk lemongrass

8 to 10 fresh lime leaves (makrud), sliced into ribbons

2 tablespoons minced fresh galangal or ginger

¾ cup vodka or white rum

> Remove the hard, dry outer leaves from the lemongrass and discard. Cut off the root end and thinly slice the lemongrass, starting at the thick, tender end and stopping when it becomes tough and difficult to slice.

> Combine the sliced lemongrass, lime leaves, and galangal in a clean, dry pint jar. Pour in the vodka. Seal and shake. Leave to infuse for 2 weeks.

> Line a sieve with two layers of cheesecloth and strain the extract into a clean container; discard the solids.

> Store in a tightly sealed container in a cool, dark place for up to 6 months.

TIPS

for Creating Your Own Innovative Infusions and Mock Stocks

- Heat increases solubility: hot or warm liquids dissolve flavors more quickly than cold. Very light infusions can be made by simply pouring boiling water over ingredients, stirring, and leaving them to steep. You can also mix ingredients in cold water and zap them in the microwave for a minute on high, then leave them to steep until you are ready for the liquid. For the best flavor, I suggest combining the ingredients in a saucepan, bringing the water to a boil, and simmering everything for a few minutes, then leaving the liquid to steep until you are ready to strain it.

- Freshly exposed surfaces increase flavor accessibility. A chopped shallot will infuse more flavor into a cup of water than a whole shallot. Smash cloves of garlic with the side of a knife. Bend and bruise fresh herbs. Crack whole spices. One small freshly peeled and grated carrot can add more flavor than an entire bag of whole waterlogged "baby" carrots.

- Flavors can be infused into water, fat, or alcohol—or, in more tempting terms, juice, milk, cream, butter, or vodka.

STOCKS

t's time for the stock talk. I'm often asked, "What should I do next to get *really* good?" by people who have just discovered a love of cooking. Many are looking for a nudge toward culinary school or a justification for buying some really fancy cookware. They are rarely thrilled with my standard answer: *Make stock!*

Lessons in stock making include many of the basic concepts you need to know to become a good cook: ingredient familiarity, basic knife skills, sautéing, roasting, browning, deglazing, infusing, temperature control, straining, manipulating flavor and texture through concentration, and the rudiments of food safety and storage. But I understand the disappointment that accompanies my answer. After all that time chopping, roasting, simmering, and skimming, you end up with flavored water. *Yawn.* Why not just buy the stock and spend your energy creating a feast? You can. But your finished dishes will be influenced by the choices of a commercial processor, not the flavors and soluble elements of the fresh ingredients you have selected. They won't be as good.

Add water to a dish, and you dilute it. Add stock, and you enhance it with the natural sweetness of root vegetables, the aroma of herbs and spices, and the savory complexity of roasted meats or poultry. Stock isn't meant to be soup. It is a foundation or building block, not a highly seasoned finished preparation. In fact, many of the ingredients most commonly used in stock—mild root vegetables, chicken, white fish, and veal are valued because they are quite indistinct. A stock made with intentionally nonspecific flavors is not the same thing as a weak stock. It's fine to add more distinctive and assertive flavors now and then. I don't hesitate to add turnips or lamb bones to my stockpot, though these stocks will not be suitable for as many recipes. But when they are right, they are spot on.

The basic principles of infusion apply to stock making. You want to dissolve the flavors and properties of solid ingredients into water. Bones are added to stock not just for their heightened savory flavor, but also for the body they add to a sauce. Proteins like collagen from bones and connective tissues melt into the water. It's what commercial gelatin is made from, and why meat, poultry, and fish juices can turn to jelly in the fridge. When skillfully made, pots of water infused with bones and root vegetables can become glossy syrups of pure, concentrated meat flavor. It is a remarkable transformation, and it explains the zealotry with which many cooks approach the subject of stock and sauce making.

The best stocks are clear. It is more a point of pride than a scientific necessity. If a stock is cloudy, it has more floating particulates and fat droplets mixed in. It may taste just fine, but dishes made with such a stock will have a similar murk. Many of the tips for making stock are meant to improve clarity. To simmer a pot of diverse components for hours and in the end pour off a shining, clear liquid is quite a challenge, and chefs *love* a challenge.

It is a marvelous feeling to be able to reach into the freezer and grab some of your own homemade stock to add to a preparation. You know that every part of your dish is made with wholesome, flavorful ingredients that meet your quality standards.

THE BOUQUET GARNI

Bouquet garni is a very pretty name for bundle of aromatic herbs used to infuse a fresh herbal perfume into long-cooking preparations like soups, stocks, stews, and sauces. It is most often made with a healthy sprig of fresh thyme, a bay leaf, and 3 or 4 bruised sprigs of parsley or parsley stems. Sometimes you will see it bound with a bit of leek green. It is meant to add a relatively generic depth of flavor that most people tend to define simply as "herbs." I am so in love with the bouquet garni that I have huge thyme and bay leaf plants in my yard that I can pluck and trim with abandon. (I would fill my beds with parsley too, if I could figure out how to keep the plants alive.) Tying the herbs with twine makes it much easier to fish them out, especially if you tie a loose end to the pot handle. If they will be strained out, I skip the bundling step altogether and just toss the herbs into the pot. I have seen jars of tied herbs labeled "bouquet garni" on supermarket store shelves. They're kind of cute, but fresh is always best.

AROMATICS

You will see the term "aromatics" throughout this book. It doesn't just mean ingredients that smell good. It is an umbrella term that refers to a base of ingredients that infuse a depth of flavor into every bite of a sauce. It almost always involves oil. When you take an extra minute or two at the very beginning of a preparation to build a good base of flavors, you will end up with a more multifaceted finished sauce. Sautéing shallots, garlic, onions, ginger, and/or chiles in oil is basically the same thing as making a savory tea, but rather than flavoring water, you are flavoring fat. The heat also cooks the ingredients, transforming their structures and flavors. The infused oil carries flavor to every drop of the sauce, and adds layers of complexity that are impossible to just stir in at the end, or add with a shaker.

The technique is global. Two very common aromatic bases are mirepoix and sofrito. Even if the terms seem foreign, there is a good chance you're familiar with the technique. *Mirepoix* is a French term that refers to a mix of vegetables, usually onion, carrots, and celery, cooked in butter or oil until translucent or just tender. *Sofrito* has more Latin roots and refers to a mix of sautéed onions, garlic, and peppers. Cajun dishes often start with the "holy trinity" of sautéed celery, bell peppers, and onions (although there are dissenting opinions about the inclusion of celery and the omission of garlic). One of the measuring sticks in Chinese cooking is how skilled a chef is at adding fragrance to the cooking oil. If there is even a hint of scorched garlic or flabby scallions hidden in an otherwise perfect preparation, the dish is a disappointment. Many Indian recipes start by frying whole spices in butter or oil "until they pop." In Thai kitchens, curry pastes are simmered with coconut milk "until the fat shows" and pools of spiced oil appear. When this flavored oil dots the surface of a finished dish, it shows diners that the cook cares about flavor.

In the Three Fundamentals of Sauce Making (page 33), I suggest that to maximize flavor you should consider fat to be a precious material. That's because most flavors are fat soluble. When you start your sauce by infusing even a little bit of cooking oil with onions, garlic, chiles, and/or ginger, you are making sure that every bite carries that complexity. So take care when you soften, sauté, sizzle, or cook these aromatics. It matters more than you may think.

USING A PRESSURE COOKER TO MAKE STOCK

Today's pressure cookers are a far cry from the scary old metal tankers with bolted lids and big dials that looked like they belonged on a submarine. Modern pressure cookers have multiple safety mechanisms built in so that if the interior temperature or pressure increases to threatening levels, the seals and vents melt or break to safely release pressure.

I used my pressure cooker mainly for making silky tender beans and quickly softening tough ingredients like artichokes and ham hocks before I learned how spectacular stock made in a pressure cooker can be. Flavors and aromas don't escape with the steam as they do in an open kettle. Because there is no moisture lost from long hours of simmering and evaporation, you can use less water. Pressure-cooked stocks often end up crystal clear because there is little agitation or temptation to stir.

Carefully follow the instructions for your particular pressure cooker regarding volume, timing, pressure levels, and depressurizing. Sauté ingredients right in the base as you would in a stockpot, or combine roasted or prepped ingredients. Cover the solids with cold water, making sure you don't surpass the "fill" line. Bring the water just to a boil over high heat. Seal the cooker. The moment the gauge shows that full pressure has been reached, reduce the temperature to low and continue to cook under pressure for the time suggested—start timing once full pressure has been reached. When the stock is ready, remove the cooker from the stove and leave it to cool and depressurize naturally. You can also rinse the edges of the lid with cold water to depressurize. Then strain and proceed as usual.

EASY, ADAPTABLE VEGETABLE STOCK

Freshly made vegetable stock is quick, inexpensive, and very adaptable. Homemade vegetable stock has a simple, sweet earthiness that adds complexity and depth of flavor to sauces. For darker, sweeter stock, roast the vegetables until they are browned. Resist the urge to stir the stock as it simmers—tiny particles of cooked vegetables will break off and make the stock cloudy. The table on page 108 suggests many ways you can customize vegetable stock to add even more flavor to your sauces. The yield for this recipe is smaller than the other stock recipes because it is so quick to fix you shouldn't hesitate to make it as you need it.

YIELD: 4 CUPS

1 tablespoon vegetable oil or light olive oil

1 medium yellow onion, sliced

2 medium carrots, sliced

1 stalk celery, sliced (optional)

1 clove garlic

⅓ cup white wine (or substitute Tamarind Water, page 91, as an alcohol-free alternative)

1 bouquet garni (1 large sprig fresh thyme, 1 bay leaf, and 3 or 4 sprigs of bruised parsley, tied in a bundle; see page 103)

6 to 8 black peppercorns

Pinch of kosher salt

4 to 5 cups cold water

> Heat the oil in a stockpot over medium-high heat. Add the onion, carrots, celery, and garlic and cook, stirring occasionally, until the vegetables have softened slightly, 5 to 7 minutes. Try to move the vegetables only enough for them to cook evenly, not so much that they break up. Pour in the wine and reduce by half to boil off the alcohol and concentrate the flavor.

> Add the bouquet garni, peppercorns, salt, and just enough cold water to cover all of the vegetables. Bring to a boil, then partially cover, reduce the heat to a simmer, and cook at a trembling simmer for 30 to 45 minutes.

> Set a sieve over a container and strain the stock without pressing on the solids. Discard the solids.

> Putting pots of piping-hot stock in the refrigerator can raise the internal temperature to unsafe levels, so cool the stock before refrigerating.

> Cover and refrigerate for up to 5 days or freeze for up to 6 months.

PRESSURE-COOKER VEGETABLE STOCK

> Seal the components in a pressure cooker and cook, following manufacturer's recommendations, for about 20 minutes.

CUSTOMIZE YOUR VEGETABLE STOCK

Use the Easy, Adaptable Vegetable Stock (page 106) as a starting point to create original, seasonal variations. Sometimes a vegetable stock made with scallions, ginger, and a splash of soy is more appropriate as a broth or stir-fry sauce base than the French standard. Add a few corncobs and use the stock in sauces with Southwestern flavors. If you have summer garden vegetables that are getting away from you, or a CSA membership that is beginning to seem overly ambitious, turn your bounty into stock. Freeze it, and you can reminisce about those ingredients over midwinter pasta or soup.

Sometimes I infuse more flavor into a vegetable stock base by adding the bones from rotisserie chicken, some meat scraps, or a ham bone. You can add a bit of seafood flavor by stirring in half a cup of dried bonito flakes or a few toasted dried shrimp into finished stock and leaving them to infuse for 5 to 7 minutes before straining.

Remember that stock is meant to be a building block, not a fully seasoned soup or broth. If you want to make these stocks more concentrated, reduce them for intensity and season them creatively. The tomato variations, The Sweet Autumn Stock, and The Brewer's Stock make excellent sauce reductions when simmered all the way down to a syrupy glaze. (See Reductions, page 145.)

Light Tomato	Stir in 2 tablespoons tomato paste with the vegetables during the sautéing step, or substitute up to 1 cup tomato juice for some of the water. Omit the wine. Add a teaspoon of cumin seeds, dried basil, oregano, or marjoram, if desired.
Taste of Spring	Substitute 1 cup sliced scallions for half of the onion. Add 1 to 2 cups chopped asparagus stems at the sautéing step. If you are lucky enough to have morel mushrooms on hand, add a few. You can also add a handful of chopped fresh pea shoots or pea pods 5 minutes before the stock is finished.
Summer Garden	Add up to 2 cups mature garden vegetables, such as diced eggplant, sliced zucchini, chopped green beans, chard stems, and/or cherry tomatoes at the sautéing step.
Sweet Autumn	Omit the celery. Add 1 cup diced squash or pumpkin and the peel from an apple. Stir in 1 tablespoon tomato paste with the vegetables during the sautéing step. Substitute hard dry cider or ale for the wine.

Taste of Winter	Add 1 cup fresh well-scrubbed potato peels, 3 or 4 dried shiitake or forest mushrooms, or up to 1 cup chopped fresh mushrooms at the sautéing step. The starch from potato peels will make the stock slightly cloudy. When the stock is done, stir in 1 teaspoon Marmite, if desired.
Sofrito	Add 1 cup diced tomato and ¾ cup chopped Anaheim or green bell pepper at the sautéing step. For extra flavor, blister and char the skins of the tomato and pepper first by rolling them on a hot burner. For more Latin American flavor, add ¼ teaspoon cumin seeds and several fresh cilantro sprigs or a teaspoon of dried oregano.
Soy Sauce	Substitute 1½ cups sliced scallions, negi (giant green onions), or leek greens for the onion. Use 2 coins of fresh ginger in place of the bouquet garni. Optionally, add 2 or 3 dried shiitake or forest mushrooms and a square of rinsed kombu (dried kelp) with the water. Substitute sake for the wine. Add 1 to 2 tablespoons soy sauce after straining the stock.
Brewer's	Substitute ale for the wine. Add 1 tablespoon roasted barley (Korean barley tea) with the water. Before the stock is strained, stir in 2 tablespoons nutritional yeast flakes. The stock will be slightly cloudy.
Corn	Add 2 corncobs cut into 1- to 2-inch/2.5 to 5 cm rounds when you add the water. Roast the cobs to a golden brown before cutting them if you prefer a toastier flavor.
Tomato Fennel	Replace the celery with 1 sliced fennel bulb. Stir in 2 tablespoons tomato paste during the sautéing step or substitute 1 cup tomato juice for some of the water. Add 2 to 3 strips of orange zest, if desired.
Red Pepper and Paprika	Add 1 diced red bell pepper, 2 tablespoons mild paprika, and 1½ teaspoons caraway seeds at the sautéing step.
Coconut	Add 1 sliced jalapeño pepper during the sautéing step. Use Tamarind Water (page 91) in place of the wine. Substitute 1 can (14 oz/414 ml) light coconut milk for 1½ cups of the water or add 1 cup raw or toasted unsweetened coconut flakes.

continues

Chinese Herbal	Substitute 2 cups sliced scallions for half of the onion. Omit the bouquet garni. Substitute Shaoxing wine or medium-dry sherry for the white wine. Add 3 coins of fresh ginger, 2 crumbled dried shiitake or forest mushrooms, and if desired 6 or 7 dried red dates (jujubes) or 2 tablespoons goji berries with the water. Some Asian markets sell blends of dried specialty herbs for herbal stocks and broths.
Korean Radish	Peel and slice a 2-inch/5 cm piece of Korean radish or daikon. Substitute it, along with 1 cup of sliced scallions or negi (giant green onions), for half of the onion. Substitute sake for the white wine. Omit the bouquet garni. Add a piece of kombu seaweed, 4 garlic cloves, a coin of fresh ginger, and, if desired, a pinch of Korean chile powder to the water.

THE MAILLARD REACTION— BROWN IS A FLAVOR AS WELL AS A COLOR

I used to refer to everything that gradually turned brown as "caramelizing". Now I understand that caramelization is the correct term only when sugars melt and turn brown. When meat browns, it is due to the Maillard reaction, a complex chemical transformation involving amino acids, sugars, and heat. It turns baked bread brown and French fries golden. The Maillard reaction creates savory flavors and aromas as well as color. Many umami tastes are created or increased by the reaction. Browned pigments and flavors from both the Maillard reaction and from caramelization are water soluble, so stocks and sauces made with browned ingredients will not just be darker in color, they will have a more intense "browned" flavor. As with caramelization, foods will only brown at temperatures higher than that of boiling water. The Maillard reaction will not begin until the surface water in the food has evaporated and the temperature rises to the browning point, about 275°F/135°C. Deglazing (see page 111) is an excellent way to capture and rehydrate these concentrated savory flavors.

DEGLAZING A PAN

To deglaze a pan is to splash some liquid into it to dissolve and capture the brown, concentrated juices and flavorful cooking residues that stick to the pan when you sear, fry, or roast foods. To relegate those yummy tidbits to the kitchen drain would be a crying shame.

Since solubility increases with heat and reduction concentrates liquid, the pan should be warm enough to sizzle and simmer when the liquid is added. This is easy enough with a hot skillet after searing a chicken breast, but if you are deglazing a roasting or baking pan, it's best to place it over medium heat on a burner, or two burners if the pan is very large.

Add enough liquid to swirl around and liquefy those brown particles. Water works; wine, stock, juice, simple infusions, or broths are better. If you add too much, simmer it to evaporate and concentrate the liquid. Different liquids add different thickening and texturizing potentials. Wine is particularly good for deglazing because the natural acidity works as a solvent and the high temperature quickly cooks off the harsh alcohol taste. The resulting deglazing liquid, depending on how much you have, can be used as a sauce, an ingredient in a sauce, or a sauce foundation.

If there are stubborn bits in the pan, gently rub them with the back of a spoon so they loosen without having to scrape at the surface of the pan. Be warned—if the pan residue smells burnt, looks black, or is dry or crumbly rather than dark and sticky, the only flavor you will be saving is carbon. It is best to skip the deglazing step and maximize flavors another way.

RICH AND SAVORY MEATLESS (VEGAN) BROWN STOCK

Brown meat stock is a core ingredient in French sauce making, but there is no reason that only meat eaters should enjoy a savory brown stock. This recipe has layers of flavor from browned root vegetables, dried mushrooms, and roasted barley. Only half of the onions are roasted to prevent the finished stock from being too sweet. The stock is brightened with wine and herbs and then finished with umami-rich Marmite to mimic meaty flavors. It makes a marvelous soup broth and gravy base and can even be reduced into a remarkably intense savory vegetarian syrup. Because it is all-vegetable, it will never be as viscous and sticky as reduced stocks made from protein-rich bones.

Roasted barley is sold as tea in Korean markets. It adds a toasted, smoky taste. Marmite is a concentrated yeast paste from England that can be found in the spice or condiment aisle of a good supermarket or specialty store. To make a gluten-free variation of this stock, substitute roasted corn for the barley and omit the Marmite.

YIELD: 4 CUPS

2 tablespoons vegetable oil or light olive oil

2 tablespoons tomato paste

3 medium yellow onions, cut into wedges

4 or 5 large carrots, peeled and cut into medium slices

1 whole head garlic, cut in half horizontally so the cloves are exposed

½ cup red wine (for an alcohol-free alternative, substitute Tamarind Water, page 91, or a dried fruit infusion—see the table on page 95)

> Preheat the oven to 425°F/215°C.

> Stir together the oil and tomato paste in a large bowl. Add half of the onions, the carrots, and garlic and toss to coat well. Scatter the vegetables in a single layer in a large roasting pan or on a baking sheet with sides; use two pans if necessary to keep the vegetables from being too crowded.

> Roast until the vegetables start to just color, about 15 minutes. Carefully flip the vegetables and return them to the oven. Continue roasting, flipping the vegetables every 6 to 8 minutes until they are evenly brown, about 30 to 35 minutes total. The vegetable tips and the cooking juices at the bottom of the pan should be dark brown and sticky but not at all burnt.

> Scoop the roasted vegetables into a stockpot. Pour the wine into the hot roasting pan and use a wooden spoon to gently loosen and dissolve the sticky brown bits into the wine. Pour the deglaz-

1 oz/28 g dried shiitake or forest mushrooms (about 8 shiitakes), broken into pieces

¼ cup roasted barley (Korean barley tea)

1 bouquet garni (1 large sprig fresh thyme, 1 bay leaf, and 3 or 4 sprigs bruised parsley, tied in a bundle; see page 103)

5 or 6 black peppercorns

Pinch of kosher salt

About 8 cups cold water

½ teaspoon Marmite (optional)

ing liquid into the stockpot and add the remaining onions, the mushrooms, roasted barley, bouquet garni, peppercorns, and salt. Add enough cold water to cover the ingredients.

> Bring to a boil, then half-cover the pot with a lid, reduce the heat, and cook at a trembling simmer for 45 minutes; do not stir.

> Set a sieve over a deep container. Line the sieve with a few layers of dampened cheesecloth to catch smaller particulates. Strain the stock, without pressing on the solids; discard the solids.

> Stir the Marmite, if using, into the hot stock.

> Putting pots of piping-hot stock in the refrigerator can raise the internal temperature to unsafe levels, so cool the stock before refrigerating.

> Cover and refrigerate for up to 5 days or freeze for up to 6 months.

PRESSURE-COOKER RICH AND SAVORY MEATLESS BROWN STOCK

> Combine the browned and fresh ingredients in a pressure cooker, seal, and cook, following the manufacturer's directions, for about 25 minutes.

REALLY GOOD CHICKEN STOCK

Chicken is perhaps the most familiar and universal of stocks. It is savory and flavorful but still quite neutral. It is light colored. Made from scratch, it has enough natural collagen to become viscous and syrupy when concentrated. The best chicken stocks are made with stewing hen. They taste intensely of chicken. Farm-fresh stewing hens are mature birds that have lost all their tenderness. In Seattle, I can find small, wiry, tough-as-nails birds in the freezer section of Asian markets and sometimes Latin groceries. If stewing hens are not available, substitute chicken wings. The cartilage and connective tissues add more gelatin and body to stock than meatier pieces. Use turkey wings to make Really Good Turkey Stock. Use a cleaver and poultry shears to cut through the bones.

I highly recommend using a pressure cooker for maximum flavor and infusion; instructions are below.

YIELD: ABOUT 8 CUPS

2 small stewing hens or 2 to 3 lbs/ 1 to 1.4 kg chicken wings, all pieces cut into 2-inch/5 cm chunks

1 large yellow onion, cut into medium slices

1 carrot, peeled and cut into medium slices

1 stalk celery, sliced (optional)

1 bouquet garni (1 large sprig fresh thyme, 1 bay leaf, and 3 or 4 sprigs bruised parsley, tied in a bundle; see page 103)

5 to 7 black peppercorns

Pinch of kosher salt

½ cup white wine (optional)

About 10 cups cold water

> Combine the chicken chunks, vegetables, bouquet garni, peppercorns, salt, and wine, if using, in a stockpot. Add enough cold water to cover everything by no more than 1 inch/2.5 cm. Bring the water to the boil over high heat, then partially cover with a lid, reduce the heat, and cook at a trembling simmer for 1½ hours. You can poke down ingredients that bob to the top now and then, but do not stir, or the stock will be cloudy.

> Set a large sieve or colander over a container. For clearer stock, line it with a few layers of dampened cheesecloth to catch smaller particulates. Strain the stock, without pressing on the solids; discard the solids.

> Putting pots of piping-hot stock in the refrigerator can raise the internal temperature to unsafe levels, so cool the stock before refrigerating.

> Cover and refrigerate for up to 5 days or freeze for up to 6 months.

> Note: *If you have the time, blanch the chicken pieces before starting. Put them in a pot with enough cold water to cover and bring it to a boil over high heat, then drain, discarding the water, and proceed. You may think the blanching step would drain off flavor, but it actually makes a clearer, more cleanly flavored end product.*

ROASTED CHICKEN STOCK

> Preheat the oven to 400°F/205°C. Toss the chicken chunks and vegetables in vegetable oil and arrange them in two roasting pans or rimmed baking sheets. Roast, flipping the pieces every 10 to 15 minutes, until they are an even dark brown, about 45 minutes. Transfer the chicken and vegetables to a stockpot. Deglaze the roasting pans with the wine, using the back of a spoon to gently dissolve the flavorful bits on the bottom of the pans. Add the deglazing liquid and the remaining ingredients to the stockpot and proceed. The yield will be reduced to 6 to 7 cups.

PRESSURE-COOKER CHICKEN STOCK

> Halve the recipe and put the ingredients in a pressure cooker. Seal and cook according to manufacturer's directions for 40 to 45 minutes.

SLOW-COOKER CHICKEN STOCK

> Halve the recipe. Combine all of the ingredients in a slow cooker and cook on low for 6 to 8 hours or on high for 4 hours.

LEFTOVER CHICKEN, TURKEY, OR HAM BONE STOCK

> Substitute the bones, meat, and cartilage from leftover roasted chicken or turkey. (I suggest you freeze leftover rotisserie chicken carcasses and scraps until you have enough to make a full pot of stock.) Or use a large ham bone. There will not be as much intense flavor or dissolved collagen as from fresh poultry, but this makes a great base for soup.

AFTER THE STOCK IS MADE—YOU REALLY WANT ME TO THROW ALL THIS STUFF AWAY?

If you made the stock properly, the solid ingredients will have little, if any, flavor left in them. Taste a carrot. Taste a scrap of chicken meat. The texture might seem satisfying and homey, but the flavor is negligible because it dissolved into the water. Throw them out. You haven't wasted the ingredients, just transformed them. This was always a challenge for my mom. She would see chunks of tender vegetables and succulent, meaty bones and start to holler as I headed toward the bin. After a heavy sigh and a few snatched tastes, she would agree and surrender. You can pick through the stock ingredients and rescue bits that can be used as bulk or filler, but that's all they will add—volume and texture. Even for soup, it's better to chop up new vegetables or fresh chicken and cook them to perfection.

BROWN BONE STOCK

Bones are used to make stock because connective tissues and cartilage are rich in collagen. Collagen makes gelatin, which adds body. Concentrated stocks that have lots of natural gelatin will reduce into the syrupy, gravy-like consistency so prized in meat sauces. Traditionally veal knuckle bones are used, but they often need to be special-ordered from a butcher. I usually use beef bones. For a browner, more highly flavored stock, I add a few meaty, connective tissue–rich bones like neck bones, oxtails, shanks, or ribs. It is best to have bones that are in about 2-inch/5 cm pieces, but some butchers are reluctant to cut them. Adjust the initial roasting time as needed depending on the bones you get. If you have bones of varied sizes, pull out the smaller pieces as they become dark brown. You can roast the vegetables too, but I think that makes the final stock a bit too sweet.

YIELD: 6 TO 8 CUPS

5 lbs/2.3 kg beef bones or veal knuckles, with a few meaty pieces of neck bones, beef shanks, oxtails, or ribs thrown in for flavor

2 tablespoons vegetable oil or light olive oil

1 tablespoon tomato paste

½ cup red wine (or substitute Tamarind Water, page 91, or a dried fruit infusion—see the table on page 95)

1 large yellow onion, cut into 6 wedges or thickly sliced

1 large carrot, peeled and quartered or thickly sliced

> Preheat the oven to 425°F/215°C

> For a clear, clean-tasting stock, blanch the bones before you roast them: Put the bones in a stockpot, cover them with plenty of cold water, and bring just to a boil over high heat. Drain; discard the blanching water. Cool the bones slightly.

> Combine the oil and tomato paste in a small bowl. Put the bones in a large roasting pan and brush the tomato paste and olive oil mix evenly all over the bones, then spread them out in the pan.

> Roast the bones for 30 minutes. Turn the pieces over and continue roasting for another 15 to 20 minutes, until the meat, bones, and cooking juices at the bottom of the pan are dark brown but not at all burnt.

> Scoop the bones into a large stockpot. Pour off the fat from the roasting pan, pour the wine into the hot pan, and use a wooden spoon to gently loosen and dissolve the sticky brown juices into the wine.

continues

2 stalks celery (optional), quartered

Pinch of kosher salt

8 black peppercorns

1 bouquet garni (1 large sprig fresh thyme, 1 bay leaf, and 3 or 4 sprigs bruised parsley, tied in a bundle; see page 103)

About 1 gallon cold water

Pour the deglazing liquid into the stockpot. Add the remaining ingredients and add just enough cold water to cover the ingredients completely.

> Bring the water to a boil over high heat, then partially cover the pot with a lid, reduce the heat, and cook at a trembling simmer for 6 to 8 hours. You can poke the bones or ingredients down into the pot now and then, but do not stir, or the stock will become cloudy.

> Set a large sieve or colander over a container. For clearer stock, line it with a few layers of dampened cheesecloth to catch smaller particulates. Carefully pour the stock into the strainer, without agitating the pieces much. Stop pouring when the sediment runs. Strain, without pressing on the solids. Discard the solids.

> Putting pots of piping-hot stock in the refrigerator can raise the internal temperature to unsafe levels, so cool the stock before refrigerating.

> Cover and refrigerate for up to 5 days or freeze for up to 6 months.

> Note: *After you make the stock, there will still be plenty of collagen and gelatin left in the bones. If you like, return the bones to the clean stockpot and add fresh vegetables and water. Bring to a boil and simmer for 4 to 12 hours. Strain as above. This clearer, lighter stock is called a* remouillage. *It has plenty of gelatin, but not a lot of flavor.*

PRESSURE-COOKER BROWN BONE STOCK

> Halve the recipe. Put the roasted bones, deglazing liquid, and the remaining ingredients in a pressure cooker. Seal and cook according to the manufacturer's directions for 2 hours.

LAMB OR GAME BIRD STOCK

> Substitute meaty lamb or game bird bones for all or half of the beef bones. Simmer for only 4 to 5 hours.

THE CELERY DEBATE— WHY A CLASSIC STOCK INGREDIENT IS LOSING FAVOR

Celery has fallen out of favor as a stock ingredient. For a very long time it was considered an essential ingredient for any stock, broth, or soup base. Now more and more chefs seem to be shunning celery and making stocks with only carrots, onions, and perhaps the occasional leek, claiming that celery adds nothing more than a slight bitterness and lots of extra sodium. A medium stalk of fresh celery has about 30 mg of sodium, but there are lots of vegetables, including carrots, that are equally high in sodium. Personally, I like the astringency and slight bitterness of celery so I always include it. If you are not a fan, leave it out.

QUICK SHRIMP SHELL STOCK

The shells are the most flavorful part of a crustacean, and once you know how easy it is to make stock from them, you will never again be so cavalier as to discard such a precious ingredient. They are also quick-cooking, so you can make a full-flavored stock in 30 minutes or less. Shells should always smell fresh and clean, never old or overly pungent. Use the stock for pureeing vegetable sauces or as a base for pan sauces, or reduce it to a concentrated syrup to stir into mayo or butter sauces.

YIELD: 2½ CUPS

2 teaspoons vegetable oil

½ cup chopped yellow onion

¼ cup chopped carrot

Shells from 1 lb/450 g shrimp (about 2 cups loosely packed shells)

1 teaspoon tomato paste

¼ cup white wine

1 bouquet garni (1 large sprig fresh thyme, 1 bay leaf, and 3 or 4 sprigs bruised parsley, tied in a bundle; see page 103)

Pinch of kosher salt

5 or 6 black peppercorns

About 3 cups cold water

> Heat a medium saucepan over medium heat. Add the oil. Stir in the onions and carrot and cook, stirring often, until tender and aromatic but not browned, about 3 minutes. Stir in the shrimp shells and cook for about 2 minutes, until the shells are pink. Add the tomato paste and stir until the shells are lightly coated, being careful that the mixture doesn't burn.

> Add the wine and reduce it by half. Add the bouquet garni, salt, peppercorns, and enough cold water to just cover the ingredients. Bring the water to a boil over high heat, then cover, reduce the heat, and simmer for 12 to 15 minutes.

> Set a strainer over a container and line it with a few layers of dampened cheesecloth. Strain the stock; discard the solids.

> Putting pots of piping-hot stock in the refrigerator can raise the internal temperature to unsafe levels, so cool the stock before refrigerating.

> Cover and refrigerate for up to 3 days or freeze for up to 3 months.

WHOLE SHRIMP OR SHRIMP HEAD STOCK

> Use 8 to 10 oz/225 to 285 g coarsely chopped shrimp heads or whole (shell-on) small shrimp and double all the remaining ingredients. Simmer for 30 minutes.

LOBSTER, CRAB, OR CRAWFISH SHELL STOCK

> Use 8 to 10 oz/225 to 285 g lobster bodies and shells, crab shells, or crawfish heads and double all the remaining ingredients. To crush and crack the shells before using them, put them in a sturdy zip-top bag, cover with a kitchen towel, and pound with a mallet or the bottom of a skillet. Simmer the stock for 30 minutes.

FISH STOCK

Good fish stock should taste bright, clean, and fresh. Think of it as a quick hot rinse rather than a long, slow simmer. The best fish stock is made from fish frames, heads, and scraps. These may be slightly disconcerting for some, but they add more flavor and gelatin than steaks or fillets. Only use scraps that are as fresh and sweet smelling as fish you would serve for dinner. I use mild white fish frames, like cod, snapper, and tilapia for my stock. Here in Seattle, there is no shortage of salmon frames, but fattier fish tend to make stronger, cloudier stocks. Salmon stock has a place, but the distinctive flavor really makes it appropriate for salmon dishes alone.

Fish stocks are high in gelatin, but unlike gelatin-rich meat and poultry stocks, their taste isn't improved by extensive concentration and reduction. Light fish stocks are particularly good in broths and simple roux-thickened sauces like Shelley's Lemon Sauce for Fish (page 337). Because I always use saltwater fish, I don't add salt; consider it optional.

YIELD: 8 CUPS

1½ lbs/675 g fish frames, heads, and/or scraps from mild white fish such as flounder, sole, snapper, cod, and/or tilapia

1 medium yellow onion, sliced

1 carrot, sliced

1 stalk celery, sliced

1 small leek, tender white and light green parts only, sliced

1 bouquet garni (1 large sprig fresh thyme, 1 bay leaf, and 3 or 4 sprigs bruised parsley, tied in a bundle; see page 103)

2 strips lemon zest (optional)

> Rinse the fish skeletons. Cut the heads lengthwise in half. Remove and discard any gills and remaining organs.

> Combine the fish, vegetables, bouquet garni, lemon zest, if using, peppercorns, and wine, if using, in a stockpot and add enough cold water to cover. Bring to a boil over high heat, then half-cover the pot and reduce the temperature to maintain a trembling simmer; do not stir. Small, thin fish frames may be fully infused in as little as 10 to 12 minutes; larger fish heads may take 25 to 30 minutes.

> Set a sieve over a container. Line the sieve with a few layers of dampened cheesecloth to catch smaller particulates. Strain the stock, without pressing on the solids; discard the solids.

> Putting pots of piping-hot stock in the refrigerator can raise the internal temperature to unsafe levels, so cool the stock before refrigerating.

5 or 6 black peppercorns

½ cup white wine or dry vermouth (optional)

About 9 cups cold water

> Cover and refrigerate for up to 3 days or freeze for up to 3 months.

TIPS
for Creating Your Own Stocks

- Stock is a great place to use mature, slightly unattractive ingredients, but always follow the chef's mantra: "When in doubt, throw it out!" If your holiday turkey carcass has dried up and tastes like stale refrigerator, what makes you think it will make an appealing infusion? I advocate the use of mature carrots, fresh potato peelings, apple cores, chard stems, corncobs, and shrimp shells, but I urge you to only use ingredients that are lively and fresh smelling.

- The smaller you cut the vegetables, the more surface area will be exposed and the more flavor will be extracted. But the smaller the vegetable pieces are, the more quickly they will soften and break up, possibly making the stock cloudy. For quick-cooking fish and vegetable stocks, vegetables can be in pieces as small as a grape. For very-long-cooking stocks like brown bone stock, they should be about 2-in/5 cm pieces.

- If you are cooking some of the ingredients before you add water, try to keep stirring to a minimum to prevent bits from breaking off and making the stock cloudy.

- Browned flavors and pigments are water soluble (see The Maillard Reaction, page 110). Ingredients that are roasted to a dark brown will make dark, savory stocks. Chicken bones that are browned will make a stock that tastes more like roasted chicken. When vegetables such as onions and carrots are caramelized, they will be much sweeter. I often combine raw, lightly cooked, and browned vegetables for balance.

- Starting with cold water helps to make a clearer stock. Cold fats congeal and float to the surface rather than mixing into the hot water, and that makes them easier to skim off later, if you choose to do so. Also, the vegetables have a chance to start cooking gradually so the exteriors don't break down as much.

- Use only enough cold water to cover the ingredients by about 1 inch/2.5 cm. It is tempting to add more, but try to resist—in the end, you are likely to spend more time reducing that extra water out of your soups and sauces to get more flavor.

- Don't boil stock. Boiling agitates and breaks up the ingredients, making the stock cloudy. When you add the cold water, turn the heat up to high, but as soon as the water just starts to boil, reduce the heat to maintain a trembling simmer.

- Don't stir stock. It will get cloudy from the particulates breaking up, the fat mixing into the water, and the sediment rising. Keep agitation to a minimum.

- Skimming the surface is optional. Some chefs swear by it, others claim that a foamy "raft" adds flavor. I tend to skim only when the surface looks particularly unappealing or when company is over. When I skim, I find myself fussing over a stock that would be better left alone.

- Stock is done when the ingredients have released their flavor into the water. This can take as little as 20 minutes for skeletons of small white fish and chopped tender vegetables and up to 12 hours or more for beef knuckle bones.

- Strain stock carefully. After all the effort you put into making a clear stock, you don't want to stir up a bunch of sediment. Set a large fine-mesh strainer or cheesecloth-lined colander over a deep container and slowly pour the stock into it—don't just dump the contents into the strainer. Stop pouring once the sediment starts to flow. Do not press on the solids, just let the stock drain completely.

- Throw away the solids and then use, refrigerate, or freeze the stock. The legend of a pot of stock perpetually simmering on the back of the stove can be dated to an era long before refrigeration. It is about as currently relevant and romantic an idea as tuberculosis. Stocks are perishable. They should be used immediately or properly stored.

- Big pots of piping-hot stock do not belong in the refrigerator. They can warm the ambient temperature to levels that breed bacteria in other foods. It is also not a good idea to leave a pot of stock to slowly cool at room temperature. The best solution is to refrigerate stock in a wide, shallow container, at a depth of no more than 4 inches/10 cm. Or chill the stock quickly over an ice bath and then refrigerate.

- Freeze stock in handy quantities. Some organized cooks use ice cube trays. I like to scoop cold stock into zip-top freezer bags in 1-cup, 2-cup, and 4-cup quantities.

COMMERCIAL ALTERNATIVES TO HOMEMADE STOCK

Homemade stock is infinitely superior to commercial products, but as much as I would dearly love to stand on a pulpit of righteousness and warn you against the evils of store-bought stocks and broths, the truth is, I use them myself. I justify it this way—freshly baked cookies are heavenly, but in a pinch, an Oreo does the trick.

I usually buy only chicken stocks and broths. I find most meat stocks to be insipid brown or overly salty water with none of the natural gelatin I want in bone stock. And since homemade vegetable stocks and infusions are so quick to make, I rarely bother with their lesser ready-made alternatives.

Be discriminating: Read labels. Choose brands made with ingredients you would put in your own stockpot. Frozen stocks tend to be the best. They have good fresh flavors and a simple list of ingredients. Cans and boxes vary greatly in quality. Since they tend to be highly seasoned, they are often labeled as broths and should be used accordingly.

I also collect specialty products from international markets. I love Italian porcini stock cubes. Knorr makes some intriguing bouillon cubes like tomato, shrimp, and garlic that I find only at specialty stores. Japanese instant dashi powder is salty and full of MSG, but that's not always unwelcome. Surprisingly, matzo ball soup base is usually vegan. It's not my first choice, because of the crazy amount of sodium it has, but it can make comforting, "chickeny" gravy for those who don't eat meat.

Stirring ready-made stock and soup bases into simmering pots of sauces to add depth, salt, and umami is a "trick" used in more restaurants than you might imagine. It's not ideal, but it's a quick fix for boosting savory flavors. Although there are some decent wholesale products, I figure that if the "chicken-flavored" base you are using is actually a poultry-free blend of fat, salt, yeast, and garlic powder, why not just add butter, salt, nutritional yeast flakes, and garlic to your sauce?

There's a lot of MSG in many commercial stocks, broths, and concentrated bases. That's because people like it. Many of the world's most popular brand name seasonings include MSG: Goya Sazón, Vegeta, and many American all-purpose seasoning mixes. Adding them to your sauces is perhaps the easiest way to increase one of the five basic tastes, umami (see page 77). I'm fine with it, but if you prefer not to consume MSG, read the labels and buy brands that leave it out.

If you've become so accustomed to the intensity of commercial products, homemade can sometimes seem oddly simple. It's meant to. It's *good* when food tastes homemade.

BROTHS, JUS, AND VERY THIN SAUCES

For a long time, the terms "stock" and "broth" were used interchangeably, but there is now a pretty well established delineation. Stock is an ingredient meant to be a building block, with little seasoning and few assertive flavors. A broth can stand alone. For example, chicken stock is used to make a well-seasoned chicken broth. Many store-bought varieties are labeled as broth because they are already highly seasoned.

Sometimes a well-made broth is all the sauce you need. By expanding your definition of sauce, you instantly increase your repertoire. Take away any preconceived notions that a sauce should be thick, sticky, or binding, and you can rethink how dishes are seasoned, embellished, plated, and presented. It's a whole new world. Handmade ravioli that might seem smothered in a heavy tomato or cream sauce is brought to life with a drizzle of intense Fresh Mushroom Jus (page 138) or Red Pepper and Onion Broth (page 133). Grilled summer vegetables and a scattering of chickpeas are enlivened with a spicy Harissa Broth (page 142).

Seasoning balance is crucial. Just because a sauce is thin doesn't mean it can be watery or bland. Thin sauces must have depth of flavor and intensity, or they can come across as a mistake. Go ahead and really blow up the flavors. If, in the end, the broth is too strong, you can always dilute it with water with no worry about altering the texture.

Presentation of thin sauces and broths is slightly different from that of many other sauces. They don't stay in place. They are easily absorbed, so they can waterlog otherwise carefully prepared ingredients if not served immediately. Broths are best introduced to their accompaniments right before service or at the table. Another reason to love broths? It's a great excuse to expand your collection of interesting bowls and dishes.

Assorted texturizers (clockwise from top left: all-purpose flour, potato, garlic, agar-agar flakes, potato starch, xanthan gum, cream, sesame seeds and raw cashews, brown sugar, butter, miso), page 48.

Tomato Infusion, with ingredients for Mushroom Water,
Roasted Barley Tea, and Fresh Herbs Infusions, from *Turning
Water into Sauce*, pages 93, 89, and 95.

Potato and onion pierogi with Carrot Caraway Broth, from *Turning Water into Sauce*, page 132.

Salmon fillet with Chinese Crackling Scallion and Garlic Sauce, from *Turning Whole Foods into Sauces*, page 203.

Blue cheese and Seckel pears with Port Reduction,
from *Turning Water into Sauce*, page 149.

Puttanesca Sauce on fiorentini pasta, from *Sauces That Start with a Can of Diced Tomatoes*, page 185.

Almond Tahini Sauce (foreground) with Pistachio
and Preserved Lemon Gremolata (background), from
Turning Whole Foods into Sauces, pages 212 and 216.

Salsas, Relishes, and Fresh Chopped Sauces (clockwise from top left: Fresh Pear, Cranberry, and Kumquat Relish; Charred Tomatoes with Hatch Green Chiles Salsa; White Cabbage Pico de Gallo; Butternut Squash and Piquillo Pepper Salsa; Kimchee and Scallion Relish; Last-Minute Cherry Tomato and Olive-Bar Antipasto Relish), from *Turning Whole Foods into Sauces*, starting on page 236.

STRONG RED BUSH (ROOIBOS) TEA
WITH HONEY

This recipe is truly minimalist. It is one of my favorite examples of how you can make innovative and elegant sauces just by redefining what a sauce should be. Red bush, also known as *rooibos*, is an earthy, tannic tisane popular in South Africa. The tea makes a lovely sienna-colored brew. It is available in gourmet supermarkets and tea shops. Pour the cooled sweet tea over orange slices for a perfect dessert after a spicy meal.

Support your local bee populations and buy some really good honey.

YIELD: 1½ CUPS

3 tablespoons loose red bush (rooibos) tea or 4 tea bags

1 or 2 whole cloves (optional)

2 cups boiling water

1 tablespoon honey

> Combine the tea and cloves in a teapot or heatproof bowl. Pour over the boiling water and stir well to combine. Cover and let cool to room temperature.

> Strain the tea through a very fine sieve and stir in the honey. Serve as a sweet broth at room temperature or cover and chill before serving.

SWEET GREEN TEA WITH FRESH MINT AND GINGER

> Substitute 2 tablespoons aromatic green tea leaves or 3 bags of green tea for the rooibos. Replace the cloves with 2 or 3 bruised fresh mint leaves and 1 coin fresh ginger. Infuse in the hot water for only 4 minutes, then strain and stir in sugar or honey to taste. Cover and chill. Use as a sauce for tropical fruit or tapioca.

TAMARIND CORIANDER BROTH

This is a tart, sweet, and savory tropical broth. It can be refreshing when served cool or exotic and warming when paired with spicy flavors. I like it, warm or cold, with rice noodles, perhaps topped with shrimp, bean sprouts, and sliced cucumbers. Add some corn or potato starch, and you have an intriguing stir-fry sauce.

YIELD: 2 CUPS

1 tablespoon coriander seeds

¼ cup (2 to 3 oz/60 to 85 g) lump tamarind

2 tablespoons grated palm sugar or granulated sugar, or to taste

1 or 2 small dried chiles (optional)

½ teaspoon kosher salt, or to taste

2 cups boiling water

4 or 5 sprigs fresh cilantro and/or 1 or 2 sprigs fresh mint (optional)

1 tablespoon fish sauce (optional)

> Put the coriander seeds in a small dry skillet and toast over medium heat until they are golden brown and aromatic, about 2 minutes. Cool slightly and crack in a mortar. Or crack the seeds by pressing on them with a skillet.

> Break up the tamarind and put it into a medium bowl, along with the coriander, sugar, chiles, if using, and salt. Pour in 1 cup of the boiling water and mash the tamarind pulp with the back of a wooden spoon until the sticky bits dissolve into the water; there will be some hard tamarind seeds and fibers that will not dissolve. If you are using cilantro or mint, add it. Pour in the remaining water. Stir and leave to infuse for 5 minutes.

> Set a sieve over a container and strain, pressing on the solids to extract as much liquid and pulp as you can. Taste the broth and season it with the fish sauce, if using, and additional sugar to taste.

> Serve hot, or cover and refrigerate for up to 1 week.

USING A JUICER TO MAKE SAUCES

Anyone who is interested in making vibrant, colorful sauces from fruits and vegetables should consider buying a juicer. It is on my list of "must have" countertop appliances and one of my favorite tools for creating intriguing sauces with garden-fresh flavors and dazzling color.

The first question most people ask me is, "what's the difference between a juicer and a high-speed blender?" Juicers extract the juice from the skin and fibers. You certainly can liquefy foods in a blender, but to get juice, you need a juicer. I have a remanufactured Breville juicer that was reasonably priced and cleans up easily. I'm really happy with it. It may generate more friction than many "juice-your-way-to-optimal-health" fans approve of, but I don't mind. I juice to make tasty beverages and to access flavorful ingredients.

You can make breathtakingly elegant starters and light entrées by simply arranging fresh ingredients in pretty bowls and serving them with a well-seasoned juice as sauce. Broths made from fresh juices are best served lightly chilled, at room temperature, or just heated through so they keep their pure flavors. Boiling can cause separation of solids and liquids, but I don't mind it. I actually like the gradient color changes of broths that settle naturally. They stir together in an instant. If that is not what you are aiming for, simply warm the juice gently or, if your broth seems oddly grainy, pass it through a fine sieve or a couple of layers of dampened cheesecloth.

Fresh juices also make innovative sauce reductions (see the table on page 150). Boil the juice until the liquid becomes super-concentrated. For the best juice reductions, choose produce that is heat tolerant and rich in natural sugars and pectins, such as tree fruits. Vegetables that are high in sugar, like carrots, beets, and onions, also make good reductions. Very starchy ingredients like sweet potatoes aren't good options because the juice thickens before the flavors are concentrated.

Combining juices with different attributes is often a good idea. Adding a bit of apple juice to a pepper extraction or the juice from a small potato to celery juice will add viscosity. Vegetables such as cauliflower and zucchini are mostly cellulose and water, so the juices will never develop body. Green juices can become gray and lifeless when they are overcooked, so they should be served as fresh as possible.

If you don't have access to a juicer, buy freshly extracted juices from your local juice bar.

CARROT CARAWAY BROTH

This is one of the simplest recipes in the book. A touch of warmth and hint of spice and salt turn a plain juice into carrot sauce. It is particularly good with potato and onion pierogi or buckwheat noodles. It is also nice with salmon or braised beef short ribs. Stir in a bit of yogurt or sour cream for variation. I tend to leave the caraway seeds in the sauce because I like the crunch, but you may prefer to strain it before serving.

YIELD: 1½ CUPS

1½ cups freshly extracted carrot juice

½ teaspoon caraway seeds

¼ teaspoon kosher salt (optional)

Pinch of smoked paprika or cayenne pepper

> Combine the carrot juice and caraway seeds in a small saucepan and heat over medium-high to just under a boil. Remove the pan from the heat, cover, and leave to infuse for 5 minutes.

> Strain the sauce if you don't want to serve it with the seeds. Gently reheat if desired. Season to taste with salt, if using, and the paprika and serve.

> If storing, cover and refrigerate for up to 3 days. The broth may separate, but it will come together with a stir or shake.

RED PEPPER AND ONION BROTH

You need a juicer to make this recipe because you're not likely to find a juice bar that sells these juices. Enjoy this bright red, savory broth as a complement to legumes, green vegetables, oily fish like mackerel or bluefish, and small stuffed pasta, such as tortellini.

YIELD: 2 CUPS

1 cup freshly extracted red bell pepper juice

½ cup freshly extracted onion juice

1 clove garlic, sliced

¼ teaspoon kosher salt

> Combine the juices and garlic in a medium saucepan and heat over medium-high to just under a boil. Remove the pan from the heat, cover, and leave to infuse for 2 to 3 minutes.

> Strain the broth through a few layers of dampened cheesecloth. Reheat if desired. Season to taste with salt and serve.

> If storing, cover and refrigerate for up to 3 days. The broth may separate, but it will come together with a stir or shake.

BEEFY BEET BROTH

This sauce is kind of like a very thin, delicate borscht. The color is brilliant purple and the flavor is salty, slightly tart, and very earthy. Serve it with sauerkraut-filled piroshky, tender braised beef, or hearty garlic sausage. You can also soak peeled hard-boiled eggs in the broth overnight to give them an intriguing look and flavor.

YIELD: 1½ CUPS

1½ cups Brown Bone Stock (page 117)

½ cup freshly extracted beet juice

2 or 3 sprigs fresh dill, bruised and torn

1 teaspoon apple cider vinegar, or to taste

½ teaspoon kosher salt

> Combine the beet juice and stock in a medium saucepan and heat over medium-high to just under a boil. Add the dill, remove the pan from the heat, cover, and leave to infuse for at least 5 minutes.

> Strain the broth. Reheat if desired. Season with the vinegar and salt. Serve warm or cold.

> If storing, cover and refrigerate for up to 3 days.

COLD KALE AND CUCUMBER BROTH

When it is first extracted and blended, this is a vibrant green juice. After it rests for a while, the solids begin to rise and separate and can be scooped away so the juice can be served as clear, flavorful "water." A bit of yogurt can turn it into a creamy sauce. In any form, it is a lovely unexpected addition to tomato and fresh mozzarella salad, cold poached fish, whole grains, or raw summer vegetables.

YIELD: 1½ CUPS

¾ cup freshly extracted kale juice

½ cup freshly extracted cucumber juice

½ cup freshly extracted green apple juice

1 tablespoon freshly squeezed lime juice

Dash of Tabasco sauce (optional)

Finely ground black pepper (optional)

¼ cup plain yogurt (optional)

> Combine the juices in a bowl and season with the Tabasco and black pepper, if using. Serve immediately as a fresh green broth, or refrigerate until the solids separate, then spoon off the solids that have risen to the top and carefully decant the clear juice, or strain it through several layers of dampened cheesecloth.

> If the broth looks muddy, stir a few tablespoons of it into the yogurt until smooth, then return the yogurt mix to the remaining broth to make a creamy pale green broth. Serve chilled.

KNOW A COOK WHO HAS EVERYTHING? HOW ABOUT A CENTRIFUGE?

Laboratory centrifuges are a favorite kitchen toy of the modernist movement. Capsules are filled with liquids like freshly extracted tomato juice or pureed fresh blueberries. They are loaded into the machine at an angle, with the bottoms pointed away from the center, and spun at superhigh speeds. The densest parts of the liquid are flung to the bottom of the container and compacted beneath a layer of clear, flavorful "water," which is actually an undiluted natural juice. Both of these layers make intriguing ingredients in their own right. The clear juice is particularly nice as a surprising light broth or flavoring and the concentrated solids can be used to add flavor, color, and texture.

I don't have a culinary centrifuge myself, but I've seen them used. The best results come from very large, super-high-speed laboratory centrifuges, but those, obviously, are not a practical option for home kitchens. You can find a small tabletop model online for about the same price as a really good espresso machine. The volume is small and clarity may not be pristine, but it can still be a lot of fun. There are always safety considerations when using machines like these. Buy only a new machine, preferably one meant for organic materials, and follow every safety precaution.

SWEET CORN AND GREEN CHILE BROTH

You can make simple broths by whizzing a few flavorful ingredients in a blender with a liquid and then straining the juice. This corn broth is slightly sweet and spicy and can be served hot or chilled. Use it in a new take on a Low Country Boil with red-skinned potatoes and grilled shrimp. It's also great with fish, crab, and tomatoes. I've even tossed this broth with pasta and Parmesan cheese to appease picky young eaters. I like the zip from pickled jalapeños or "nacho" slices. Fresh green chiles are also good, but canned green chiles tend to make the sauce a little gray. A few teaspoons of tomato paste can brighten the color. If you just can't bear to throw away the solids you have strained out, stir them into a corn bread batter to add moistness and texture.

YIELD: 2 CUPS

2 cups fresh or thawed frozen corn kernels

¼ cup diced pickled jalapeños or nacho slices

3 cups water or a Mock Stock, such as Onion and Garlic or Mock Chicken (see the table on page 93)

Kosher salt

Pinch of cayenne pepper or chipotle pepper powder (optional)

> Combine the corn kernels, green chiles, and water in a blender and puree on high for a full minute. Set a sieve over a saucepan and strain the broth into the pan, pressing on the solids to extract as much liquid as possible.

> Bring the broth to a boil over medium-high heat and simmer for a minute or two, just to cook the raw taste out and marry the flavors. Season with salt to taste and the cayenne, if using. The broth may separate, but it comes together with just a stir. Serve warm.

> If storing, cover and refrigerate for up to 3 days.

MINTY GREEN PEA BROTH

> Replace the corn with 2 cups of thawed frozen green peas. Omit the jalapeños and add ¼ cup loosely packed fresh mint leaves. Use chilled or warm for risotto, salmon, or scallops.

FRESH MUSHROOM JUS

When you cook mushrooms slowly in a tightly covered pan, they exude a dark earthy jus. It takes quite a few mushrooms to get much of this precious liquor, but if you can keep yourself from slurping the stuff straight from the measuring cup, a little goes quite a long way. Splash the jus over ravioli, sautéed greens, or miso-glazed tofu. Put a grilled portobello mushroom between two slices of garlic bread and serve a ramekin of this jus alongside, and you have a vegetarian version of a French Dip. Meat lovers will also find this to be a great improvement over the salty commercial beef bouillons used to stretch the natural juices collected from roast beef or London broil.

The mushrooms must be fresh, heavy, and full of natural water. Shriveled, winkled, light-as-a-feather mushrooms will give up very little jus. Plain white button or cremini mushrooms work well. Adding a few extra chopped shiitake, portobello, chanterelle, king trumpet, or maitake mushrooms will enhance the color and flavor. The added water and salt help extract more liquid from the cell walls.

YIELD: ¾ TO 1 CUP

1 lb/450 g mushrooms, rinsed and chopped, including all stems, skins, and gills

½ cup water

½ teaspoon kosher salt, plus more to taste

> Stir together all of the ingredients in a pot with a tight-fitting lid. Cook, covered, over medium heat until you see the first signs of steam coming from the pot, about 3 minutes. Stir well, cover again, reduce the heat to medium-low so the mushrooms will gradually weep their natural juice, and cook for 20 to 25 minutes, stirring once or twice to check the progress. Try to peek as little as possible, to reduce evaporation. (If you prefer, you can combine the ingredients in a pressure cooker and cook at full pressure for 10 minutes.)

> Set a fine-mesh strainer over a container. Pour the mushrooms and juice into the strainer and press on the solids to remove as much jus as possible. Alternatively, pour the mixture into a strainer lined with cheesecloth, gather up the sides of the cheesecloth to form a parcel, and squeeze the mushrooms as dry as possible. Add more salt to taste and serve.

> If storing, cover and refrigerate for up to a week or freeze for up to 6 months.

> Note: *After they are cooked and drained, the mushrooms will not have a lot of flavor left. The taste and texture most closely resembles that of old-fashioned canned mushrooms, so they make a great addition to the Thick Mushroom Casserole Cream (page 325). They can also be used to bulk up pasta dishes, fillings, soups, or stews.*

CLAM NECTAR

Clam nectar is the natural juice that is released when clams are cooked. I live in the Pacific Northwest, so it's both easy and economical for me to make my own ocean-fresh nectar rather than buying the overly salty commercial varieties, but I always run into a quandary. When you steam clams just until they are cooked, there isn't a lot of juice. If you increase the amount of water and continue to simmer it until the broth tastes really good, the clams get overcooked. My answer is to add extra aromatics as well as some water, cook the mix just until the clams open, and then remove the clam meats, return the shells to the pot, and simmer the broth for an extra 5 to 7 minutes. You can then use the tender cooked clams in chowder or a pasta sauce and still have enough flavorful clam nectar to use as an interesting sauce with seared fish or rice noodles, or drizzle over sautéed greens or asparagus. I use Manila clams, but any type will do.

YIELD: ABOUT 1½ CUPS

1 tablespoon butter or vegetable oil

¼ cup minced yellow onion

2 tablespoons minced carrot

2 tablespoons minced leek

1 clove garlic, sliced

Pinch of red chile flakes

1 lb/450 g clams (any variety), scrubbed

¼ cup white wine or light beer (optional)

1 cup water

1 sprig fresh thyme or parsley, or a sprig of each

> Heat a large saucepan over medium high heat and add the butter. Stir in the onion, carrot, leek, garlic, and chile flakes and cook until the vegetables have started to soften but not brown, about 3 minutes. Add the clams and stir to mix well. Add the wine and simmer for about 1 minute, uncovered. Add the water, herbs, and peppercorns, cover, and simmer until the clams open, 3 minutes or so depending on the size of the clams.

> Remove the clam meats from the shells. (Save them for another use.) Return the empty shells to the pot, cover, and simmer for another 5 to 7 minutes so the broth picks up more clam flavor.

> Strain the nectar through a sieve lined with several layers of dampened cheesecloth to ensure it is free of grit, sand, or bits of shell. The clam nectar will be naturally salty, but taste it and adjust the seasoning if needed.

5 or 6 black peppercorns

Kosher salt (optional)

> If storing, cover and refrigerate for up to 3 days or freeze for up to 6 months.

MEATY CLAM NECTAR

> Fry 2 oz/60 g chopped bacon, ham, pancetta, or chorizo with the vegetables before adding the clams. Serve with seafood and summer vegetables.

TOMATO AND OLD BAY CLAM NECTAR

> Add ½ cup diced fresh tomatoes or drained canned diced tomatoes after the vegetables have softened. Stir in 1 tablespoon Old Bay Seasoning. Use beer instead of wine. Serve with lobster, sausages, polenta, or steamed red potatoes.

HARISSA BROTH

One of my favorite things about highly seasoned broths is that they can mimic the flavors of elaborate slow-cooked dishes without the investment of time or money. A traditional North African couscous can take all day. Heaps of the fluffy grain are served with tender stewed meats and vegetables. Often a bowl of the cooking liquid is served alongside. This recipe is a nod to that side of flavorful broth. In minutes, you can have a spicy mix to spoon over instant couscous, chickpeas, or sautéed vegetables. Or serve it in bowls with grilled fish, lamb skewers and warm flatbread for dunking.

Harissa is a Tunisian hot pepper paste that is widely used as a condiment and seasoning. There is a recipe for it on page 307 if you want to try making your own. I particularly like this broth made with fish or lamb stock, but a good vegetable stock like the Summer Garden (see the table on page 108) is also very good. The saffron adds a lovely perfume and color, but if you don't have it, it can be omitted.

YIELD: 2½ CUPS

1 tablespoon olive oil or butter

¼ cup chopped yellow onion

2 cloves garlic, chopped

1 cup diced fresh tomatoes or canned diced tomatoes, drained

2 teaspoons Harissa (page 307) or store bought harissa to taste

½ teaspoon ground cumin

2½ cups Fish Stock (page 122), Lamb Stock (page 119), Really Good Chicken Stock (page 114), or Vegetable Stock (page 106, or see the table on page 108)

> Heat a medium saucepan over medium-high heat. Add the oil, then stir in the onion and garlic and cook, stirring often, until softened but not browned, about 2 minutes. Add the tomatoes and cook until they are soft and juicy, about 2 minutes. Stir in the harissa and cumin. Add the stock, cinnamon stick, saffron threads and salt and bring to a boil. Half-cover the pan, reduce the heat to a simmer, and cook until the flavors have married and the liquid has reduced and concentrated, about 30 minutes. Remove the pieces of cinnamon stick.

> Add the lemon juice. Taste and season with additional harissa, salt, and/or lemon juice, if desired. Straining is optional. Serve hot.

> If storing, cover and refrigerate for up to 3 days or freeze for up to 3 months.

1 cinnamon stick, broken in half

6 to 8 saffron threads (optional)

½ teaspoon kosher salt, or to taste

2 tablespoons freshly squeezed
   lemon juice, or to taste

TIPS

for Creating Your Own Broths, Jus, and Thin Sauces

- Sauces that are thin in texture shouldn't be thin in flavor. Each spoonful should enhance the food it is served with, not dilute it.

- Thin sauces should be aromatic. Fragrant vapors wafting from your dish are a big part of the appeal, so do what you can to emphasize volatile compounds. Finish dishes with fresh herbs or a citrus garnish.

- Serve enough broth so each bite can be enjoyed with a slurp of sauce, but not so much that the ingredients are drowning: ½ to ¾ cup per person is a good range for an entrée.

- Thin sauces should look like an accompaniment to the other ingredients; if they become the main feature, you have veered into the realm of soup.

- Broths and thin sauces tend to be more elegant when they are sparkling clear. To remove unwanted fat droplets or sediment, strain a broth or thin sauce through several layers of dampened cheesecloth or even a coffee filter. (The yield will be diminished.) Beating egg whites into a boiling stock is part of the classic technique for clarifying consommé. When it comes to cooking at home, I'd rather serve a slightly cloudy broth than go to all of that trouble.

- If there is a hint of oily rainbow on top of the broth or sauce and you find it unappealing, mask it by adding a few droplets of really good, flavorful oil right before serving to make it look intentional.

- Dishes served with broth can be complemented with another texture-rich sauce, such as dollop of thick puree, salsa, pesto, or chile sauce.

REDUCTIONS

Remove excess water, and sauces become more concentrated. Flavors intensify. Textures change. Watery tomato sauces can become thick and rich. Curries marry. Juices can be reduced into robust and supple glazes. And stock? Oh, my. A well-made stock can be reduced into a pure, savory syrup with more meaty intensity than any steak, roast, or chop.

Reduction as a technique is simple enough. If your sauce seems weak or dilute, simmer it for a bit, and the taste will become more concentrated. The increased ratios of pectin, sugar, starch, and dissolved proteins will make reduced sauces seem "saucier."

In addition to describing a cooking technique, the word "reduction" also refers to a particular type of sauce. A sauce, syrup, or glaze that is created by the simple act of attentive simmering is a sauce reduction. Reductions are high-end restaurant favorites because they are flavor packed, glossy, and often colorful. They can be combined and artistically featured with various smears, drizzles, and dots. Because reductions tend to be seen in pricy restaurants and look so artistic, they are sometimes perceived as being fancy. But simmering a liquid into sauce doesn't take a masterful hand—just patience, good timing, and a basic understanding of ingredients.

To make good sauce reductions, you need to choose liquids that will boil into appealing concentrations and know when to pull them off the stove. The higher the ratio of potential thickeners—sugar, pectin, starch, and dissolved proteins like collagen and gelatin—the more likely the reduction will become sauce-like. Black coffee isn't going to reduce down into a sauce when you boil out the water, but fresh apple cider makes a great reduction because it has a lot of natural sugar and pectin and boils down into a sauce with body.

To many sauce lovers, the zenith is an intense, glossy gravy made from reduced meat stock. Some are so packed with natural gelatin they can be as solid and bouncy as a Super Ball when chilled. A traditional French demi-glace is made by combining equal quantities of concentrated meat stock (glace de viande) and roux-thickened brown sauce (sauce espagnole). (See What's the Difference Between a Demi-Glace, a "Demi," and a Meat Reduction?, page 347.) In addition to being elegant, meat stock reductions are expensive and time-consuming to make, so they are best reserved for special events.

I tend to prefer fruit, vegetable, and dessert wine reductions. They have a similar intensity but they use fewer resources and take minutes rather than days to make. A great place to start when you are experimenting with reductions is balsamic vinegar. The aged dark vinegar cooks down into a sweet, tangy, complex syrup. Balsamic reductions have so much appeal that retailers bottle them up in pretty containers and sell them as an expensive specialty item. You can spend about ten minutes simmering a mediocre bottle of balsamic vinegar into your own glaze for a fraction of the price. Put it in your own fancy bottle.

To reduce a sauce, you bring a liquid to a boil and simmer it until enough of the water has evaporated to reach the texture and flavor you are looking for. There is no magic formula, because reduction depends on the ingredient, the quantity, and the size and shape of the pan. The more uncovered surface area, the more quickly the sauce will reduce. Splash some wine or broth into a sizzling-hot shallow skillet, and it will instantly become concentrated. Make a tomato sauce in a tall narrow pot with the lid just tilted, and it can simmer on low for hours, gradually concentrating into a thick, rich ragù. If you are a collector of cooking gear, you can buy pots with heavy bases and sloped sides that are specifically designed for reduction. I have a few LeCreuset saucepans with white enameled interiors. These are my favorites for reductions, caramel, and browned butter, because it is easy to see the changes in color and texture.

It takes a bit of practice before you feel confident. Chances are good that you will burn a batch at first, so start by trying the cheap stuff like cola and apple juice before you reduce a bottle of vintage port. The table of Intriguing Meatless Reductions (page 150) offers some suggestions and starting points.

SIMMERING VERSUS BOILING

While the term "boil" is bandied about quite a lot, the actual technique is rarely used. A true boil is reached when there are rolling waves of large bubbles. It is a raucous and violent cooking technique that can bash and bruise foods and will often overcook the outside of a food before the interior reaches tenderness. "An angry boil" is best reserved for quickly blanching green vegetables, keeping dry pasta from sticking to itself when it is added to the pot, and making a proper pot of English tea. Most sauces are warmed, simmered, or gently boiled.

- **Warm:** Heated until the liquid is an even low temperature. Wafts of steam may start to rise, but the sauce or liquid should not be so hot it bubbles.

- **Scalding:** Heated until very small bubbles start to rise and pop at the edges of the pan but there is little or no movement on the surface other than wafts of steam.

- **Trembling:** This is a rather poetic word that describes a very low simmer, where the steam rises evenly in wisps and the small, regular bubbles at the edges of the pan have just enough force to make the surface quiver. "Trembling" is often used to describe the best temperature for cooking stocks for an extended time—as hot as possible with very little or no agitation.

- **Simmering:** Having small, widely distributed, but regular even bubbles. Rather than gradually bringing a liquid to a simmer, you have a lot more control when you turn the heat to high at first, until the sauce just boils, then turn it down to a controlled simmer.

- **Gentle, even boil:** A step up from simmer, where small to medium bubbles are distributed over the entire surface of the liquid and there is clear agitation of the ingredients but no aggressive rolling or churning.

- **Boiling:** Having many bubbles over the entire surface. Thinner sauces will start to churn, thicker sauces will splatter slightly. If a very thick liquid forms big, slow, random bubbles that burst like lava, it means the liquid at the bottom of the pan is getting hotter than the liquid at the top and may quickly burn. Give the sauce a good stir and reduce the temperature slightly.

- **Angry or Rolling Boil:** Having many fast, aggressive bubbles that churn and stir up the liquid. If you drop something light into the liquid, you will actually be able to see it roll from the top to the bottom in the currents. There can be a lot of splatter and the pan can clatter on the burner from the action inside.

COVERED POTS—WHY YOU SHOULDN'T ADJUST LIDS IN ANOTHER PERSON'S KITCHEN

Tilting pot lids can control the rate of evaporation. Sometimes I tilt a lid to speed it up, sometimes I half-cover a pot to slow it down. Every once in a while, I just want a window so I can take a quick peek into the pot now and then. Since the kitchen is the busiest room in the house, guests are inevitably drawn toward the stove. Some see the disorder on the stovetop and feel the need to tidy things up. They figure I'm too busy or distracted to see that the lids are all wonky. My mother was a lid straightener. She'd be enticed by the sounds and smells, sidle up to a simmering pot, give things a stir, and then seal everything up tight. It took several reminders (mostly daughterly shrieks, heavy sighs, and eye rolls) before she understood that while it might have looked sloppy to have the pot lids balanced like that, it was intentional. Eventually she started policing my lids herself, reprimanding any who came near. I'm as guilty as anyone of sneaking a peek and a stir, but I do my best to replace the lid at exactly at the angle I found it. I suggest you do too.

ONE-INGREDIENT SAUCE REDUCTIONS

Balsamic Vinegar Reduction

Balsamic vinegars vary a lot. The best, super-expensive ones are mellow and slightly syrupy right out of the bottle. Treasure those. Cheap, harsh vinegars can be smoothed and sweetened by reducing them by about half, until they become clinging. Try not to inhale the fumes at the start, or you are likely to cough. Because balsamic vinegar is so dark, you can easily overcook or even burn it without seeing any color change. You need to keep lifting the pan and swirling the vinegar—and stop the cooking as soon as it clings to the back of a spoon. Use the finished reduction as an intense, tangy drizzle alongside grilled or roasted meats and vegetables or as a dipping sauce for fresh strawberries.

Port Reduction

Port generally becomes concentrated and saucy when reduced to about one-quarter of its original volume. Of course, the better the port, the better-tasting the reduction, but it is almost criminal to waste a good port by boiling it. I usually use affordable ruby port. A port reduction often accompanies seared foie gras, but it is also spectacular alongside poached pears, blue cheese, nut tarts, or even an elegant sweet potato preparation like a soufflé or galette.

Pomegranate Reduction

Pomegranate juice becomes a tangy ruby syrup when it is reduced. Start with fresh or bottled pomegranate juice. Juice blends like pomegranate and cherry or blueberry are fine if you like the added flavors. Pomegranate molasses is a darker, more concentrated pomegranate reduction used in Middle Eastern preparations. Use this reduction as an ingredient or as accompaniment to grilled lamb or chicken kebabs or goat cheese, or drizzle over ice cream or chocolate desserts. It is also very nice stirred into dressings and fruit relishes.

INTRIGUING MEATLESS REDUCTIONS

Once you get a feel for how easy, intense, colorful, and elegant reductions can be, you may find yourself boiling up liquids with almost reckless abandon. I heartily encourage this. Some of these variations require fresh juice, but others are made with ingredients right off store shelves.

Foods that are cooked in a slow, moist environment tend to create juices that can be reduced into complicated sauces. Make the most of them. The variations in this table are options for dishes that are cooked quickly and may need a touch of intensity, contrast, or color. On average, these reductions take about 25 minutes of simmering and yield about ¼ cup sauce.

Red Cabbage and Vinegar	Combine the freshly extracted juice from 1 head red cabbage and 1 yellow onion. Simmer the juice until syrupy. Finish with 1 to 2 tablespoons apple cider vinegar, a pinch of brown sugar, and plenty of salt. Nice with corned beef, schnitzel, roasted chicken, and potato dumplings. Stir in a bit of sour cream for a richer, slightly fresher-tasting sauce.
Tomatillo and Green Chile	Combine 1½ cups freshly extracted tomatillo or green tomato juice (from about 1 lb/450 g tomatillos, husked and rinsed), or green tomatoes and ½ cup green chile juice (from approximately 8 oz/225 g jalapeño, Anaheim, and/or poblano chiles), with the juice of 1 yellow onion. Simmer until it is the consistency of thin ketchup. Season with salt and a pinch of sugar. Nice as a dipping sauce for taquitos, drizzled on tamales, or served as a condiment for whole grilled fish.
Onion and Ale	Simmer 4 cups strained, freshly extracted onion juice (from approximately 6 large yellow onions) until it is a thick, caramel colored, slightly bitter syrup. Add a good pinch of salt and 3 to 4 tablespoons of amber ale or stout. Goes well with bratwurst, Cheddar cheese, and steaks.
Carrot with Sriracha	Reduce 3 cups carrot juice until it is the consistency of thin ketchup; stir the juice as it reduces to mix in the solids. Add 2 tablespoons sriracha or your favorite red chile paste, such as sambal oelek, to taste. Use as a dip for satays, a sauce for tofu, or a topping for rice.
Spicy Thai Pineapple	Combine 4 cups pineapple juice, 1 halved Thai bird chile, 1 garlic clove, and 2 lime leaves (makrud) and simmer until syrupy. If desired, stir in 1 tablespoon top-quality fish sauce. Serve with fish or shrimp or as a dipping sauce for fresh spring rolls.

Cherry Juice	Simmer 3 cups bottled unsweetened cherry juice until syrupy. Serve with duck or pork chops, ice cream, or chocolate desserts. Stir in a few tablespoons of almond milk to make a creamy sauce.
Bloody Mary	Simmer 2 cups tomato juice until it is the consistency of ketchup. Stir in 1 tablespoon prepared horseradish, ¼ teaspoon celery salt, and plenty of black pepper. Finish with a good dash of Tabasco and another of Worcestershire sauce. Reduced tomato juice has a fresher flavor than canned tomato sauce. Serve like cocktail sauce.
Holiday Cranberry	Simmer 4 cups cranberry-apple juice until reduced to a syrup. Remove from the heat and add 1 broken cinnamon stick, 4 or 5 whole cloves, a thin slice of fresh ginger, and (optional) a blade of mace. Cover, cool to room temperature, and strain through a fine-mesh sieve. If desired, add a tablespoon of apple schnapps or brandy before serving. Serve with roasted turkey or duck, soufflés, or steamed puddings.
Apple and Ginger	Combine 4 cups fresh apple cider and 5 or 6 coins of fresh ginger and simmer until syrupy. Strain, or simply fish out the pieces of ginger. Serve with roasted squash, sweet potatoes, turkey, or vanilla ice cream.
Pear, Chardonnay, and Cardamom	Combine 1½ cups freshly extracted or bottled pear juice with 1 cup Chardonnay and 5 or 6 crushed cardamom pods and simmer until syrupy. Strain, or pick out the cardamom pods. Serve with Brie, crepes, or almond cakes.
Cream Sherry	Simmer 2 cups cream sherry until syrupy. Use as a slightly sophisticated alternative to caramel sauce alongside sharp cheeses, nut cakes, or fruit desserts.
Black Currant and Pastis	Simmer sweetened black currant juice until syrupy. Let cool, then add 1 tablespoon pastis, such as Ricard, or other anise-flavored spirit like Pernod or ouzo. Serve with seared chicken livers, quail, chocolate desserts, or vanilla ice cream.

continues

Condensed Coffee Cream	Combine 2 cups heavy cream and ⅓ cup cracked dark-roast coffee beans in a large saucepan (so there is less risk of the pan boiling over) and simmer until reduced by half. Strain through a fine-mesh sieve and stir in 2 tablespoons sugar. Use with tortes or nut or chocolate desserts.
Ginger Ale, Cola, or Other Sodas	Simmer 2 cups soda until thick and syrupy. Cola and ginger ale reductions can be used as a barbecue or ham glaze or a dessert syrup with strawberries or coconut custard. Brightly colored fruity sodas make fun drizzles and dots on plated desserts. Do not use sugar-free soda.

CELERY JUICE REDUCTION WITH HORSERADISH

Fresh juices often condense into sweet syrups, but celery has a good amount of natural sodium and a certain astringency, so it remains savory when you boil it down. I add the juice of a small waxy potato to add some starch and help to thicken and bind the sauce so it doesn't need to be reduced quite as far. This helps it retain a better color, but the starch increases the potential for scorching— so stir or whisk the sauce often as it cooks. The plain celery reduction is very good and can be used as a simple sauce or ingredient, but the added pungency of horseradish and extra seasoning turns it into a stand-alone sauce. This is particularly good with roast beef or steaks. If you don't use fish sauce, it can serve as an intriguing vegetarian alternative.

YIELD: ABOUT ½ CUP

3 cups freshly extracted celery juice (from about 1 large mature head)

2 tablespoons freshly extracted potato juice (from a small waxy peeled potato, such as Red Bliss or Yukon Gold; optional)

1 to 2 tablespoons prepared horseradish

1 tablespoon freshly squeezed lime juice (optional)

1 tablespoon fish sauce (optional)

> Combine the celery juice and potato juice, if using, in a medium heavy saucepan and bring to a boil over high heat. Reduce the heat slightly and cook at a gentle boil, stirring in any residue, until the sauce becomes syrupy. As the sauce thickens, check the consistency regularly by lifting the pan from the stove and swirling the reduction in the pan. When it clings to the sides and bottom of the pan like warm honey, it is done. If you're not sure, remove the pan from the heat and drizzle a few drops of the reduction onto a cold plate. If it runs like water, it needs more time; if it collects in dots, it is done. It will thicken further as it cools. Reducing the juice should take about 20 minutes total.

> Stir in the horseradish and the lime juice and the fish sauce, if using. Serve warm or at room temperature.

> If storing, cover and refrigerate for up to 5 days or freeze for up to 3 months.

PINK GRAPEFRUIT AND HIBISCUS REDUCTION

When citrus juice is boiled and reduced, you lose most of the volatile fresh perfumes, but it's still got a certain charm. I particularly like reduced grapefruit juice. Adding dried hibiscus blossoms gives it more tang as well as a wonderful color. Like Campari, this sauce is an acquired taste. The inviting candy color is countered with a clear and complicated bitterness. That's part of the appeal. Serve this with rich dishes like fatty salmon. It's also nice with poached pears and I like it on vanilla ice cream, especially with coconut cookies alongside.

Dried hibiscus blossoms (*flor de jamaica*) can be found at Latin markets and tea shops.

YIELD: ABOUT ½ CUP

4 cups unsweetened pink grapefruit juice

3 or 4 dried hibiscus blossoms (*flor de jamaica*), crumbled

Pinch of kosher salt (optional)

> Combine the grapefruit juice and hibiscus in a medium heavy saucepan and bring to a boil over high heat. Reduce the heat slightly and cook at a gentle boil until the juice is reduced to about ½ cup. Turn down the heat and watch it more closely until the juice is reduced to a syrup. As the sauce thickens, check the consistency regularly by lifting the pan from the stove and swirling the reduction in the pan. When it clings to the sides and bottom of the pan like warm honey, it is done. If you're not sure, remove the pan from the heat and drizzle a few drops of the reduction on a cold plate. If it runs like water, it needs more time; if it collects in dots, it is done. It will thicken further as it cools. Reducing the juice should take about 30 minutes total.

> If storing, cover and refrigerate for up to 2 weeks.

APPLE AND ONION REDEYE GRAVY

As I understand it, true redeye gravy is just a splash of coffee poured into a hot skillet that has been used to fry up some country ham, bacon, or sausage. It's more of a deglazing liquid than an actual gravy. I should probably try that someday, but as a native Seattleite, I have an unnatural compulsion to take any perfectly good, simple coffee preparation and make it all fancy. Real coffee aficionados may gasp at the idea of boiling coffee, but in this case, it's all about the sauce, not the beverage. The thin finished sauce should be salty and a little bitter, with a taste that is rounded out by the sweetness of the onion and apple cider. Pour it generously over fried ham, eggs, and/or creamy grits.

YIELD: ABOUT ½ CUP

1 tablespoon drippings and residue left in a skillet used to fry bacon or ham

2 tablespoons minced yellow onion

½ cup freshly brewed coffee

½ cup fresh apple cider or apple juice

¼ teaspoon kosher salt

Freshly ground black pepper

> Heat the pan of drippings and frying residue over medium-high heat. Add the onion and cook, stirring often, until golden brown and tender, about 2 minutes. Add the coffee and apple cider and use the back of the spoon to dissolve any flavorful brown bits in the bottom of the pan, then bring the liquid to a boil over high heat. Reduce the heat to medium and simmer until the liquid has reduced to a light syrup, 3 to 4 minutes. Season with the salt and plenty of black pepper.

> Serve hot, with whatever you cooked in the skillet.

VEGETARIAN APPLE AND ONION REDEYE GRAVY

> Omit the drippings and meat residue and start with a clean skillet heated over medium heat. Add 1 tablespoon butter or light olive or vegetable oil, then add ¾ cup thinly sliced onions and cook, stirring often, until tender and caramelized to an even brown, about 10 minutes. Add the coffee and apple cider and simmer until the liquid has reduced by half, 3 to 4 minutes. Taste and season generously with salt and black pepper. Serve with grits or savory French toast.

DATE GASTRIQUE

Gastrique is a French sauce-making term for a base of dark caramelized sugar deglazed with vinegar. It is traditionally added to sticky meat or poultry glaces to create piquant, elegant meat sauces. This isn't technically a gastrique, but it is a sticky brown sweet-and-sour glaze that has a similar appeal. It can be blended into brown sauces or stand alone as a dipping sauce for appetizers like papadums or pakoras. It is also nice with fish or goat cheese, or as a dessert sauce. Try brushing it on grilled meats like barbecue sauce. I've even got a friend who shakes it up into a cocktail with vodka and ice.

The strained date pulp is not used in this recipe, as it no longer has the flavor of fresh dates, but it can be saved to be used in muffin batters or smoothies. The flavor of fresh lime juice is especially complementary, but if I don't want the syrup to be thinned, I use powdered citric acid, also known as sour salt.

YIELD: ½ CUP

8 oz/225 g soft, meaty dates, such as Medjool, pitted and chopped

4 cups water

3 tablespoons freshly squeezed lime juice (or substitute ½ teaspoon citric acid for a thicker syrup)

Pinch of kosher salt (optional)

> Combine the chopped dates and water in a medium saucepan, stir well, and bring to a boil over high heat. Reduce the heat to medium and simmer for 5 minutes.

> Set a sieve over a container and strain the liquid. Press on the date solids gently to remove as much liquid as possible but very little pulp; too much pulp, and the sauce will become cloudy and thick rather than syrupy.

> Discard the solids, and return the liquid to the saucepan and boil until it is the consistency of warm honey, about 12 minutes.

> Stir in the lime juice and salt if using. Serve warm or cold.

> If storing, cover and refrigerate for up to a week.

WHY REDUCED MEAT JUICES ARE SO REVERED

Glace de viande is the French term for meat juice or stock that is reduced until sticky and super-intense. Start to finish, the process can take days. Bones are roasted until brown and then simmered with vegetables and herbs to make great stock. That stock is then used in place of water to simmer still more roasted bones and vegetables. In some restaurant kitchens, this may be repeated again and again, unlocking an almost primal level of liquid, meaty intensity. As the water in the stock is gradually simmered away, what remains is the essence of pure, roasted meat, scented perhaps with a bit of vegetables, wine, and herbs. In other words, it's nirvana for meat lovers.

Veal bones are commonly used, not just because of the mild flavor and adaptability of the finished product, but because they have loads of connective tissues and collagen that gradually melt into gelatin. These dissolved proteins thicken and bind sauces unlike anything else. Sauces made with meat reductions have a clarity, gloss, and silky texture that can't be mimicked with fat or starch. Chicken stock can also be reduced down to a savory sauce, but it must be made with very high-collagen pieces, like wings and feet. Pork skin is loaded with natural gelatin and pieces of it can be added to a stockpot, but both pork and lamb tend to be quite fatty and the flavors can be quite strong and distinctive when they are reduced.

Vegetable essences can be roasted and concentrated, but because there is no collagen, they will never have the texture of meaty syrups. The Rich and Savory Meatless (Vegan) Brown Stock (page 112) and some of the vegetable stock variations (see the table on page 108), like the Tomato Fennel, Sweet Autumn, and Brewer's, will reduce down into lovely concentrations. But they must be reduced to practically nothing.

MEAT GLACE (GLACE DE VIANDE)

Not exactly a sauce, this is more of a treasured sauce-making ingredient. It is a fundamental ingredient in both classic and contemporary sauces. If you are an enthusiastic cook, I highly recommend that you try making this at least once. Spending two or three days sourcing, roasting, and simmering bones into stock and then cooking them down into a cup of intense meat glace is a culinary experience, not just gravy. You will learn firsthand what it takes to make those intense, glossy demi-glace sauces and meat reductions you might have tasted in elegant restaurants. You will also have a better appreciation of why they can be so expensive. Roasted bone stock is used in place of water to make an even darker, meatier stock. This is strained and simmered into a superconcentrated meat glace. (*Glace* is the French spelling. The word "glaze" is also used, but I find that it sounds more like something you would brush on meat rather than a concentrated sauce, so I prefer the French term.) Be sure to watch the reduction process closely. If you overreduce the stock to the point where there is even a hint of burnt flavor, the entire batch can be ruined and all that work and expense is for naught. Stop when the stock is just syrupy. It will get thicker as it cools, and you can always reduce it a bit more if necessary. Traditional demi-glace is made with a 1:1 ratio of meat glace and brown roux-thickened meat sauce. These days, it isn't unusual for the reduction itself to be served as a sauce.

Note: Make the Brown Bone Stock at least 1 day ahead.

YIELD: 1 TO 1½ CUPS

5 lbs/2.3 kg beef bones or veal knuckles, with a few meaty, cartilage-rich neck bones, oxtails, shanks, or ribs thrown in for flavor

2 tablespoons vegetable oil

1 tablespoon tomato paste

½ cup red wine

1 large yellow onion, thickly sliced

1 carrot, peeled and thickly sliced

> Preheat the oven to 425°F/220°C.

> For a clear, clean–tasting stock, blanch the bones: Put them in a stockpot, cover with plenty of cold water, and bring just to a boil over high heat. Drain; discard the blanching water. Cool the bones slightly.

> Combine the oil and tomato paste in a small bowl. Put the bones in a large roasting pan and brush the tomato paste and oil mix evenly all over the bones, then spread them out in the pan.

> Roast the bones for 30 minutes. Turn the pieces over and continue roasting for another 15 to 20 minutes, until the meat, bones, and cooking juices at the bottom of the pan are dark brown but not at all burnt.

2 stalks celery, thickly sliced (optional)

1 recipe Brown Bone Stock (page 117), cold

Pinch of kosher salt

1 bouquet garni (1 large sprig fresh thyme, 1 bay leaf, and 3 or 4 sprigs bruised fresh parsley, tied in a bundle; see page 103)

> Scoop the bones into a large stockpot. Pour off the fat from the roasting pan and deglaze the pan by pouring in the wine and using a wooden spoon to gently loosen and dissolve the sticky brown bits and concentrated juices into the wine. Pour the liquid into the stockpot. Add the onions, carrot, and celery, if using.

> Pour the cold stock over the bones and vegetables. Add additional cold water if needed to just cover the bones. Add the salt and bouquet garni. Bring the stock to the boil; do not stir. Half-cover, reduce the heat, and cook at a trembling simmer for 6 to 8 hours.

> Set a strainer or a colander lined with a few layers of dampened cheesecloth over a container. Carefully pour the stock into the strainer, without agitating it, so it remains clear. Try not to pour in any sediment.

> Transfer the stock to a large saucepan and bring to a boil. Reduce the heat to a simmer and cook until the stock has reduced to about 2 cups. Then turn down the heat and watch it more closely until the stock has reduced to a thin syrup. As the sauce thickens, check the consistency regularly by lifting the pan from the stove and swirling the reduction in the pan. When it clings to the sides and bottom of the pan like warm honey, it is done. If you're not sure, remove the pan from the heat and drizzle a few drops of the reduction onto a cold plate. If it runs like water, it needs more time; if it collects in dots, it is ready. It will thicken further as it cools. (The glace is very dark, so you can't judge it by color.)

> Cool.

> For convenience, cut the cold glace into 1-inch/2.5 cm squares. Cover and refrigerate for up to a week or freeze for up to 6 months.

TIPS
for Creating Your Own Sauce Reductions

- Some ingredients work better than others. To make a saucy reduction, you need to start with a liquid that has natural thickening potential, such as sugar, pectin, starch, or proteins like gelatin. Teas and infusions will reduce down to nothing because they are little more than water.

- Liquids that are high in sugar quickly reduce into syrups. It is especially easy to make reductions from dessert wines and juices. I figure that if a fruit bakes up well in a pie or jelly, the juice should make a good reduction—think apples, peaches, cherries, blueberries, and cranberries. (Sadly, rhubarb juice doesn't have enough natural sugar or pectin to reduce well.)

- Bottled fruit juices, both sweetened and unsweetened, work very well. I love reductions made with black currant, cranberry, and pomegranate juice blends.

- Fruits and vegetables that don't have a lot of thickening potential, like cauliflower, or those with a very high amount of starch, like sweet potatoes, are best made into purees rather than reductions.

- Stocks made with ingredients with a lot of connective tissues make great reductions because the dissolved collagen adds body and viscosity.

- After the liquid is reduced, you can brighten and balance the reduction with acidic seasonings like citric acid, citrus juice, or even a tablespoon of yogurt or sour cream. Reductions that seem one-dimensional can be given depth with a touch of umami-rich fish sauce, a drop of Worcestershire, or a pinch of chile powder. Stirring in minced fresh herbs just before serving adds freshness and color.

CAN A SAUCE BE OVERREDUCED?

YES! Overreduction is not just possible, it is far too easy, and the results are always terribly disappointing. The sauce may not look burnt, but the flavors seem dead. It might seem as if you could just reconstitute the sauce by adding water, as with frozen orange juice concentrate, but it doesn't work that way. (Juice concentrates are made by a cold-evaporation method so the orange juice remains fresh tasting.) When a sauce is overcooked, caramelized, or burnt, no amount of water will revive the flavor. It's a bit like willing your well-done steak to taste medium-rare or an overcooked broccoli floret to taste bright and fresh again.

Because some of the best meaty sauces are made by incorporating the superconcentrated residue left in a roasting pan or skillet, you might wonder how you can possibly overconcentrate a meaty liquid through reduction. You have already roasted the bones, deglazed the pan, and rehydrated the concentrated juices, why go through all of that effort to just end up with another sauce base rather than an actual sauce? A good meat stock reduction should taste more like the dark, crispy end slices of a prime rib roast than like licking the roasting pan. Err on the side of caution.

THE QUANTITY QUESTION—IS THAT REALLY GOING TO BE ENOUGH?

The tiny amount of sauce left after extensive reduction can be alarming. You may start with 3 or 4 cups of liquid and end up with little more than a few tablespoons of sauce. But a little goes a long way. These superconcentrated sauces are meant to be served by the teaspoon, not by the boatful. And if you pair an artful drizzle of a fruit or wine reduction with another complementary sauce, even half a teaspoon may be enough. It can be helpful to plate dishes in the kitchen so everyone gets enough. You can also serve sauce reductions in small bowls with tiny spoons rather than anything with a spout. And always beware of kitchen visitors wielding tufts of bread.

TURNING WHOLE FOODS INTO SAUCES WITHOUT ADDING THICKENERS

A trip to the farmers' market can really energize culinary creativity. There is potential everywhere you look. This section is chock-full of suggestions on how to turn produce into sauces by making the most of natural textures. In fact, part of my original motivation for this book was to show how seasonal, low-impact foods can be made into elegant and flavorful sauces without relying on animal products or traditional thickeners such as roux.

FRESH VEGETABLE AND FRUIT SAUCE PUREES

iquefying fruits and vegetables is easy: all you need is a juicer or blender. But it takes an artful hand to turn a puree into a sauce that really soars. Roasted cauliflower, garlic, anchovies, and aged cheese can be whizzed into a sort of sauce, but you will only knock it out of the park with careful finishing.

The technique is simple. If the produce needs softening, cook it in a way that will maximize flavor, such as simmering it in a liquid other than plain water, roasting, or even cooking it sous vide. (See Sous Vide and Sauce Making, page 390.) Once the ingredients are tender, you simply whiz them up with a combination of intriguing embellishments. The fun part is choosing which delectable blend will enhance your dish the most. Consider how the natural texturizers in the ingredients you add, like water content, starch, sugar, pectin, pulp, and fiber, might affect the final consistency. Purees are easy to manipulate. Anything that seems uneven, coarse, or wet can be blended, sieved, simmered, or enriched to help it come together.

Silky liquid sauce purees are lovely, but very thick purees also have their place. They can be used as texturizers to thicken other sauces. Caramelized onions and roasted garlic are particularly good savory thickeners for gluten-free and vegan gravies. Thick purees of fruit, vegetables, or greens can be stirred into dressings, cream sauces, and pan sauces to add body and flavor. They can help to bind fillings or be used as a layer in vegetable lasagna. They also make innovative spreads, condiments, and dips. Try the Thick Pea Spread (page 170) in a BLT, as a dip with pita bread, or as an intriguing dollop for guests to stir into pasta primavera.

PRESSING FOODS THROUGH A SIEVE

Pressing foods through a sieve means forcing ingredients through the mesh, not just giving them a quick shake or stir in the strainer. It is a methodical, mechanical task. The terms "strain" and "sieve" tend to be used interchangeably and can get confusing. Even more troublesome is that the tool for straining food might be called a sieve, a strainer, or a colander.

I use the term "strain" to refer to the simple act of draining liquids from solids. Sometimes the liquid should just drain naturally, with no agitation. Other times, I suggest pressing on the solids gently to extract as much liquid as possible. To press a sauce or ingredient *through* a sieve, you smear or mash the food into the mesh, then scrape it up and do it again. I often do a large spoonful at a time so I have plenty of surface area to work with. Keep spreading, pressing, and scraping until all that is left in the sieve is a completely dry mixture of oversized, tough, or fibrous bits. The finer the mesh, the more time it will take to press the solids through, but the silkier the texture will be.

Many times, some of the pulp will not fall but will cling to the outside of the sieve. Rinse off your spoon or spatula before you scrape this into the bowl—you don't want to absently reintroduce bits and pieces into the mix after you have worked so hard to remove them.

GREEN PEA AND THAI BASIL SAUCE

After a long, gray winter, Seattleites see sunshine and become ravenous for tender, flavorful greens. After months of root vegetables, coarse dark greens, and canned tomato sauces, this vibrant green pea sauce is like nectar. Because it is particularly good with seafood, I like to use dashi as the liquid. Instant dashi is very salty, so adjust the seasoning carefully. I love this with the season's first wild salmon, seared scallops, or cheese-filled ravioli scattered with Dungeness crab or crisp fried pancetta. If you want a more decadent or creamy sauce, melt a few pats of cold butter into the warm sauce just before serving. A tablespoon of buttermilk or plain yogurt can be added if the sauce is served cold.

YIELD: 2½ CUPS

2 cups fresh or thawed frozen green peas

2 tablespoons chopped fresh Thai basil or fresh sweet basil

1½ cups Dashi (page 96) or Vegetable Stock (page 106, or see the table on page 108), plus more as needed

½ teaspoon kosher salt, or to taste

1 tablespoon fish sauce (optional)

> If you are using fresh peas, blanch them in boiling water until they are just warmed through and vibrant green, about 1 minute. Drain and plunge peas into an ice water bath to stop the cooking immediately. Frozen peas can simply be thawed and drained.

> Combine the peas, basil, and dashi in a blender and puree until smooth. Press the sauce through a sieve and add additional dashi as needed to make a thin, pourable sauce. Season with the salt and fish sauce, if using. Warm gently and serve.

> If storing, cover and refrigerate for up to 3 days.

DELICATE HERBAL PEA SAUCE

> Replace the dashi with an extra-strong brew (3 to 4 times the recommended tea-to-water ratio) of herbal tea such as Sleepytime or chamomile. Omit the basil and fish sauce.

FRESH FAVA BEAN SAUCE

> Substitute blanched and peeled fava beans for the peas and chopped mint for the basil. Omit the fish sauce. Serve with new potatoes, poached fish, or cold sliced lamb.

continues

THICK PEA SPREAD

> Reduce the amount of liquid by half. Scrape down the sides of the blender often when pureeing to ensure a smooth paste. Season well. Use in BLTs, on smoked salmon bagels, or as a dip.

SWEET POTATO AND KOREAN CHILE PASTE SAUCE

This unusual combination is smooth, sweet, salty, and spicy. I like it with grilled marinated beef, salmon, or meaty mushrooms like maitake and king boletus (porcini). It's also great spooned over a bowl of steamed rice, with a few wilted greens. Gochujang is a sweet-and-spicy fermented Korean chile paste that is sold in tubs or tubes. It is becoming increasingly available at good supermarkets. You can substitute carrots or kabocha squash for the sweet potatoes.

YIELD: 3 CUPS

2 cups diced peeled sweet potato (about 12 oz/340 g)

2 cloves garlic

About 3 cups Really Good Chicken Stock (page 114), Vegetable Stock (page 106, or see the table on page 108), or Roasted Barley Tea Mock Stock (see the table on page 95)

2 tablespoons Korean chile paste (gochujang), or to taste

½ teaspoon kosher salt, or to taste

1 tablespoon unseasoned rice vinegar (optional)

> Combine the sweet potatoes, garlic, and just enough stock to cover in a medium saucepan. Bring to a boil over high heat; cover and reduce the heat to maintain a simmer. Cook until the sweet potatoes are soft, about 20 minutes.

> Put the contents of the pan into a blender and add the chile paste. Puree to a smooth paste, scraping the sides of the bowl as needed. Gradually add more stock to thin the sauce to the desired consistency. Season with the salt and a touch of extra chile paste if you like. The puree should be intensely flavored to stand up to the entrée it is to be served with; it should not just be a tasty soup. Add the rice vinegar if you prefer a bit more tanginesss, and season with additional salt if needed.

> Warm gently and serve.

> If storing, cover and refrigerate for up to 3 days.

ROASTED CAULIFLOWER–PARMESAN SAUCE

This may be slightly more complicated than other creamy cauliflower sauces, but the extra steps give it a nice flavor and textural appeal without relying on cream or butter. The finished sauce is packed with savory umami flavors. A thicker, more rustic sauce can be spooned alongside roasted chicken or into fluffy baked potatoes. When sieved and thinned, it becomes velvety and refined and goes well with salmon, sliced rare beef, or vegetable timbales. I've even used it as an alternative to white sauce in macaroni and cheese.

If you prefer a richer sauce, use some cream or half-and-half in place of some of the stock, or stir in a tablespoon of cold butter just before serving. The cheese needs to be finely shaved to melt smoothly. If the sauce seems grainy, strain it after it is blended.

YIELD: 2 CUPS

10 oz/285 g cauliflower florets (about ½ large head of cauliflower)

8 cloves garlic

2 tablespoons vegetable oil or olive oil

1½ to 2 cups Really Good Chicken Stock (page 114), Brown Bone Stock (page 117), or Cheese Water (page 92)

2 or 3 anchovy fillets or 1 teaspoon anchovy paste (optional but highly recommended)

> Preheat the oven to 450°F/175°C.

> Toss the cauliflower and garlic cloves with the oil until evenly coated. Scatter the vegetables on a rimmed baking sheet and roast for 15 minutes, or until dark brown but not burnt.

> Transfer the cauliflower and garlic to a medium saucepan. Add 1 cup of the stock, bring to a boil, cover, and until the cauliflower is very soft, about 10 minutes.

> Transfer the mixture to a blender. Add the anchovies, cheese, and ½ cup stock and puree until the sauce is smooth and fluid. For a more refined puree, press the puree through a sieve. Season with the salt and Worcestershire.

> Return the puree to the saucepan and reheat over low heat. Adjust the texture if needed with additional stock. Serve warm.

1 oz/28 g Parmesan or Pecorino
  Romano cheese, finely grated
  (about ⅓ cup)

¼ teaspoon kosher salt

Dash of Worcestershire sauce

> If storing, cover and refrigerate for up to 3 days.

SAVORY MEATLESS GRAVY THICKENED WITH ROASTED ONION AND GARLIC PUREE

Gravy should be available to all who crave it. This variation is appropriate for many specialty diets that may have considered gravy a thing of the past. Roasted onions and garlic add caramel sweetness and an added layer of umami flavor. The darker you cook the onions, the sweeter the finished sauce will be. Marmite is an English yeast concentrate that has a very strong savory, salty flavor, almost like meat glace. It is a vegetarian ingredient that adds a meaty-tasting depth or flavor as well as a darker color; it is not gluten free.

This gravy is also good made with beef or turkey stock.

YIELD: 2 CUPS

1 head garlic

1 large yellow onion, cut into 8 wedges

1 tablespoon vegetable oil

2 cups Rich and Savory Meatless (Vegan) Brown Stock (page 112); heated

½ teaspoon Marmite (optional)

¼ teaspoon kosher salt, or to taste

Freshly ground black pepper

> Preheat the oven to 350°F/175°C.

> Cut the top off the garlic so the cloves are just exposed. Toss the onion wedges and garlic with the oil to coat.

> Put the onion and garlic in a small baking dish or a loaf pan and roast for 40 minutes, or until the onion pieces are soft and dark brown on the edges. Cool until you can comfortably handle the head of garlic.

> Scoop the onions into a blender or food processor. Squeeze the softened garlic cloves out of their skins and add to the onions. Puree until smooth.

> Gradually blend in the warm stock until the gravy reaches the desired consistency. A thicker sauce will hold together better than a very thin sauce. Press the sauce through a sieve if there are any unappealing lumps or the texture is coarse. Season well with the salt and pepper. Serve warm.

> This gravy tends to separate, with the solids sinking to the bottom. Just give it a stir before you pass the gravy boat. It will also settle if chilled. Simply whisk it again while reheating.

> If storing, cover and refrigerate for up to 3 days.

COFFEE-BANANA RUM SAUCE

This sauce tastes a lot fancier and more complicated than it is. You simply caramelize a banana in brown sugar and butter and add some rum, coffee, and a bit of yogurt for tang, then blend it up. Serve it with brownies à la mode, coconut cake, or crepes.

This is one of those sauces that you want to just eat by the spoonful. If you leave it thick, you can serve it as a pudding.

YIELD: 1 CUP

1 tablespoon butter

3 tablespoons brown sugar

1 ripe banana, sliced

¼ cup dark rum (substitute strong black coffee or orange juice if you prefer an alcohol-free sauce), or as needed

½ cup very strong coffee or espresso, or as needed

¼ cup plain yogurt, stirred until smooth

A few drops of vanilla extract

Pinch of kosher salt

> Melt the butter in a medium sauté pan over medium heat. Add the brown sugar and stir until bubbly. Add the banana slices and cook until they are soft and coated with caramel, about 2 minutes.

> Add the rum, being careful to avert your face and protect your hands from the steam if the pan is very hot, and stir to mix. Simmer to cook off some of the alcohol and reduce to a syrupy sauce.

> Transfer the banana mixture to a blender, add coffee, and puree until smooth. Add the yogurt, vanilla extract, and salt and puree to blend. Thin to the desired consistency with more coffee or another splash of rum. Serve warm or cold.

> If storing, cover and refrigerate for up to 3 days.

TANGY BANANA RUM SAUCE
> Omit the coffee. Add 2 tablespoons freshly squeezed lime juice and increase the yogurt to ⅓ cup. Thin with additional rum or orange juice.

SEASONAL VEGETABLE AND FRUIT SAUCE PUREES

The three sauce-making fundamentals—maximize flavor, manipulate texture, and season confidently—are particularly important when it comes to making successful pureed sauces. Make the most of natural flavors by choosing excellent ingredients and doing your best to elevate and enhance their tastes, rather than dilute them. When a sauce needs to be especially assertive, I sometimes use double-strength stock. To do this, simply double the amount of stock called for and simmer it until it is reduced to the appropriate amount. Wherever you might think of adding plain water, consider a quick-brewed savory "tea" to add a bit more flavor (see the table on page 93).

Texture is key in sauce purees. You never want to serve a sauce that seems better suited for a nursery. Thinner tends to be preferable to thicker. Remember to season generously: these are sauces, not side dishes or soups, and they won't be served alone. A touch of acidity can add a sense of freshness, and a splash of an umami-rich liquid seasoning, like soy, Maggi, or fish sauce, can broaden and fill out thin-tasting savory purees.

Celeriac, Shallot, and Mustard	Combine 2 cups diced peeled celeriac and ⅓ cup sliced shallots with 1½ cups beef stock or double-strength chicken or vegetable stock in a saucepan. Cover and simmer until the celeriac is soft, about 25 minutes. Puree the mixture until smooth. Press through a fine sieve and add additional stock as necessary to thin to the desired consistency. Stir in 2 tablespoons whole-grain or Dijon mustard and season with plenty of salt and black pepper. Serve with halibut, wild salmon fillets, ham, or corned beef.
Spicy Charred Eggplant	Cut ½ large eggplant lengthwise into slabs. Halve, core, and seed 1 red bell pepper. Brush the vegetables with a bit of oil and grill or broil, turning once, until tender and charred on both sides, 4 to 5 minutes. Chop and transfer the vegetables to a blender and add 1 diced tomato, 2 to 3 cloves garlic, and 1 teaspoon harissa, or a good pinch of red chile flakes. Puree until smooth. Add enough Dried Tomato Water (page 90) or vegetable stock to thin to the desired consistency. Season well with salt and black pepper. Finish with a few tablespoons of extra-virgin olive oil.

continues

Sunchoke and Dried Tomato	Combine 2 cups diced peeled sunchokes (Jerusalem artichokes), 3 to 4 sliced dried tomatoes, 2 cloves garlic, and 1 cup double-strength vegetable or chicken stock in a saucepan. Cover and simmer until the sunchokes are soft, about 15 minutes. Puree to a smooth paste. Press though a fine sieve. Thin to the desired consistency with additional stock or tomato juice. Season well with salt, black pepper, and a pinch of cayenne. Serve with grilled fish, polenta, or chicken.
Parsnip and Parsley	Combine 1½ cups diced peeled parsnips with 1½ cups double-strength vegetable stock or chicken stock in a saucepan, cover, and simmer until soft, about 20 minutes. Puree until smooth. Press through sieve. Thin to the desired consistency with additional stock. Season well with salt and black pepper. Just before serving, stir in 2 tablespoons very finely minced parsley and if desired, a tablespoon of butter. Serve with roast pork, turkey, pheasant, or Arctic char.
Grilled Scallion and Dashi	Trim 3 or 4 bunches of scallions or spring onions and lightly coat with vegetable oil. Grill over hot coals or broil until charred and tender, 2 to 3 minutes. Chop. Combine in a blender with 1 cup warm dashi and pulse until evenly blended but still coarse, adding additional dashi or a bit of sake to reach the consistency you like. Add a few drops of toasted sesame oil. Serve with black cod or tofu or on cold noodles.
Carrot and Crab Stock	Combine 2 cups diced peeled carrots and 1½ cups double-strength Crab Shell Stock (page 121) in a saucepan, cover, and simmer until the carrots are soft, about 20 minutes. Puree with 1 teaspoon tomato paste. Press through a sieve and thin with additional stock or carrot juice as needed. Season well with salt, a pinch of cayenne, and a little freshly squeezed lemon juice. If desired, finish with a tablespoon of butter and a teaspoon of chopped fresh tarragon. Serve with lobster, risotto, crab cakes, or pot stickers.

Pear and Campari	Combine 1½ cup diced peeled pears with ¾ cup pink grapefruit juice in a saucepan, cover, and simmer until soft, about 8 minutes. Puree until smooth. Thin with additional grapefruit juice if needed. Add 2 to 3 tablespoons Campari. Serve with fresh sweet cheese, almond cakes, or white chocolate mousse.
Maple Squash	Combine 1½ cups diced peeled butternut squash or pumpkin with 1 cup apple cider and 3 tablespoons pure maple syrup in a saucepan, cover, and simmer until soft, about 20 minutes. Puree until smooth. Thin with additional apple juice if needed. Season with a pinch of salt and plenty of freshly grated nutmeg. Serve with smoked turkey, cheese ravioli, spice cake, or waffles.
Rhubarb and Red Currant	Combine 2 cups sliced rhubarb with ½ cup red currant jelly in a saucepan. Cover and simmer until soft, about 6 minutes. For a savory sauce, add ¼ cup sautéed onions. Puree until smooth. Add a tablespoon of cream if the color seems muddy. Serve with pork tenderloin or as a dessert sauce with sliced strawberries and ice cream.
Holiday Persimmon	Combine 2 chopped persimmons (you can use either the flatter, firm Fuyu type or extremely ripe acorn-shaped hachiyas), 1 cup apple juice, ¼ cup golden raisins, 1 cinnamon stick, ½ teaspoon ground ginger, ⅛ teaspoon ground cloves, and a few gratings of nutmeg in a saucepan. Cover and simmer until the raisins are soft and plump, about 20 minutes. Remove the cinnamon stick and blend until smooth. Press through a sieve. Thin with a bit of brandy or additional apple juice if needed. Serve with roasted pork, baked apples, bread pudding, or butter cakes.
Cranberry Apple	Combine 1 cup cranberries, ½ cup chopped peeled apple, and 1 cup apple or cranberry-apple juice in a saucepan, cover, and simmer until the cranberries burst and soften, about 8 minutes. Puree until smooth. Press through a sieve to remove any seeds. Thin with additional juice and sweeten to taste with sugar or honey. Serve with turkey, with Swedish meatballs, on pancakes, or with chocolate or spice cakes.

XANTHAN GUM

Xanthan gum can alter the texture of sauces without interfering with flavor or freshness. Brassicas like cabbage and broccoli are the natural host for the bacteria from which xanthan is derived. The commercially available product is produced in bulk by the fermentation of a similar strain of bacteria with natural sugars. Some of the sticky bits that are produced are collected, dried, and processed into a fine powder. It's one of those ingredients that people used to shriek about as a food additive but is now sold in bulk at health food stores and organic markets. Xanthan gum is commonly used in gluten-free baking, but I use it to manipulate sauce texture. I first learned about it when I was a food stylist. A touch added to spaghetti sauce or soups would prevent them from separating and looking "weepy" on set. A tiny, and I mean TINY, bit of xanthan gum—no more that what you can collect on the very tip of a sharp knife can slightly alter the texture and stability of a cup of sauce (from 0.1 to 0.4% by weight). A bit more can make sauces thicker and slightly slippery, like the Fresh Melon-tini Sauce (page 377). I use the natural viscosity to advantage in the Eggless Mayo (page 384) to make the tofu mixture binding, glossy, and slick, like real mayo. Too much xanthan gum can make a sauce slimy.

Xanthan gum needs to be well blended with the other ingredients to work. Ideally you will mix it into another dry ingredient like salt or sugar and add them at the same time. It's easier to evenly disperse that way. If that isn't an option, use your fingertips to sprinkle a fine dusting over the surface and mix, whisk, or blend thoroughly. Some sources suggest leaving the xanthan gum on the surface of the sauce for a moment to soak up moisture before it is whisked in. That is fine, but only if there are no tiny clumps of powder. Xanthan gum does not need heat to thicken. If it doesn't seem to be working, stir or blend the sauce longer before adding more.

As a side note: if for some reason a puppy gets hold of an open package of xanthan gum and spreads it all over your kitchen floor, I suggest you sweep up absolutely as much of the dry powder as possible before you start to mop. Trust me.

TIPS
for Creating Your Own Sauce Purees

- Consider what natural texturizers, like water content, starch, sugar, pectin, pulp, and fiber, the raw ingredients have. It will help to predict the consistency of the finished sauce. See Interfering with the Movement of Water—How Elementary Ingredients Alter Texture (page 43).

- Starch tends to make purees very smooth, binding, and quick to thicken when heated. Sauces made with starchy vegetables like sweet potatoes, fava beans, or squash will be velvety but need a higher percentage of added liquid.

- Fruits and vegetables like cauliflower, rhubarb, zucchini, or rutabaga are predominantly water and cellulose and therefore will not become sauces that are smooth or creamy unless you add ingredients with those textural characteristics.

- Juicy fruits like berries are high in sugar and pectin and will make syrupy, jam-like sauces. Pulpy fruits like plums, tomatoes, or persimmons will cook into thicker pastes.

- Acidity is the taste most often linked to freshness. If your puree is lackluster, add a bit of lemon juice or vinegar or a pinch of powdered citric acid. Finely chopped fresh herbs stirred in just before service can also add vibrancy.

- Sometimes purees and puree-thickened sauces can start to separate. Particles will fall to the bottom or solids will float to the top. If a sauce that you are happy with starts to separate or looks weepy at the last minute, give it a whisk or whiz it up with an immersion blender and serve it proudly. No one is going to complain if it tastes good.

- Fresh ingredients are not your only option for sauce purees. I have made quick last-minute sauces out of pureed and embellished pickled beets, olives, pimentos, or marinated artichoke bottoms. Canned fruits like apricots in light syrup or crushed pineapple can be made into sauces that work with both savory and sweet preparations.

- Avoid any hint of Pablum. Sauce purees must tantalize your guests, not have them wondering if they have been served a side dish or soup gone wrong.

- Purees must be intensely flavored to be used as sauces. See Seasoning Alternatives (page 79) for creative ideas on how to boost the taste.

SAUCES THAT START WITH A CAN OF DICED TOMATOES

Open a can of tomatoes, add a few interesting ingredients from the fridge or cupboard, and in minutes you will have a wholesome, satisfying sauce. The recipes here start with a single can of diced or pureed tomatoes because these are one of the most diverse and adaptable ingredients in a sauce-making larder. It is also because the Puget Sound is a veritable wasteland for ripe, garden fresh tomatoes except for about three weeks in early September, when everything ripens at once. I don't live in one of those magical regions where sweet sun-ripened tomatoes are available most of the year, so I have learned to love canned tomatoes.

I buy reduced-sodium organic diced tomatoes in juice. They can make chunky sauces or be whizzed up into a smooth, fresh-tasting puree with an immersion blender. I think pureed diced tomatoes taste fresher than canned tomato sauces.

Tomatoes are complicated—that's part of the appeal. There is the natural sweetness and acidity of the fruit, as well as deep and savory umami elements when they are cooked down, concentrated, or dried. Scientists have isolated hundreds of different flavor components in tomatoes. Handled in different ways, a can of tomatoes can be raw and fruity, thick and binding, even syrupy and jam-like. The tomatoes can stand alone or be used to enhance and texturize other sauces. They will continue to evolve and change in the pot as they marry with other ingredients, and even as they rest overnight and are reheated. Tomatoes carry herbs and spices well. Cooked down into a thick paste, they can be a flavorful thickener. They enhance the color and brightness of a drab sauce. In other words, canned tomatoes are sauce magic.

QUICK FRESH-TASTING TOMATO SAUCE

Sometimes a tomato sauce should just taste like tomatoes. I used to mask the fresh tomato flavor with loads of garlic, wine, and herbs, cooking the sauces for hours until they were concentrated and naturally sweet. While there is a time and a place for that kind of sauce, I've found that a very fresh tasting, lightly seasoned tomato sauce has more adaptability. This bright, aromatic sauce can stand alone or be a starting point for the table of International Tomato Sauces on page 185.

YIELD: ABOUT 1½ CUPS, ENOUGH TO SERVE WITH 4 ENTRÉES; A DOUBLE BATCH WILL COAT 1 LB/450 G PASTA

1 tablespoon olive oil or vegetable oil

¼ cup minced yellow onion

1 clove garlic, chopped

Pinch of red chile flakes (optional)

One 14½ oz/411 g can diced tomatoes

¼ teaspoon kosher salt, or to taste

Freshly ground black pepper

> Heat a medium saucepan over medium heat. Add the oil, then stir in the onion, garlic, and red chile flakes and cook, stirring often, until the vegetables are very soft but not browned, about 6 minutes. (I prefer meltingly soft onions to crisp bits in tomato sauces.)

> Stir in the tomatoes and juice, salt, and pepper to taste. Bring the sauce to a boil, then reduce the heat, half-cover the pan, and simmer, stirring often, until the tomatoes have softened but the flavor is still bright and fresh, 4 to 5 minutes. Check the seasoning and add more salt and pepper to taste as needed. If you prefer a smoother sauce, puree with an immersion blender.

> Serve hot or cold.

> If storing, refrigerate in a nonreactive container for up to 5 days or freeze for up to 4 months.

INTERNATIONAL TOMATO SAUCES

The recipes in the table below are variations of the Quick Fresh-Tasting Tomato Sauce (page 184). Part of the reason why tomatoes are such a globally popular sauce ingredient is their adaptability and ability to carry and enhance other flavors.

These recipes make about 2 cups of sauce each; a double batch should thoroughly coat 1 lb/450 g of pasta.

Garlic and Basil	Increase the garlic to 4 cloves. Stir in 3 tablespoons chopped fresh basil just before serving.
Puttanesca	Do not cook the sauce—simply stir the ingredients together in a bowl. Increase the olive oil to ¼ cup and the garlic to 2 cloves. Add ⅓ cup chopped black or green olives, 2 tablespoons drained capers, 2 mashed anchovies, and 2 tablespoons chopped fresh parsley. Leave the sauce to infuse for 20 minutes before tossing with hot pasta.
Arrabbiata	Increase the chile flakes to 1 teaspoon, or to taste. Simmer the sauce, covered, for 20 minutes. Finish with 2 tablespoons chopped fresh parsley.
Eggplant and Spinach	Add 1½ cups diced eggplant along with the onions and garlic and cook until all the vegetables are browned and soft, about 5 minutes. Deglaze the pan with ¼ cup red wine and reduce it by half. Add the tomatoes and seasonings and simmer, covered, for 15 to 20 minutes. Stir in ½ cup blanched, drained, and chopped spinach and cook until just warmed through. Finish with 2 tablespoons extra-virgin olive oil and a few drops of truffle oil (optional). Toss with hot pasta or serve on bruschetta or with sausages.
Quick Mole	Omit the chile flakes. After the onions and garlic are tender, stir in about ⅓ cup ready-made mole paste, then add ½ cup chicken or vegetable stock and stir until thoroughly mixed before adding the tomatoes. Simmer, covered, for at least 20 minutes, and up to 1 hour. Add a pinch of sugar along with the other seasonings and finish with a squeeze of lime juice. Puree the sauce until smooth.

continues

African Spicy Peanut	Double the onions and omit the garlic. Add 1 minced jalapeño, serrano, or habanero pepper with the onions. Stir in ¼ cup all-natural peanut butter and 1 teaspoon curry powder, then add ¾ cup chicken or vegetable stock and stir until evenly mixed. Add the tomatoes and simmer, uncovered, for 25 minutes, stirring often to prevent scorching. Serve with chicken or assorted vegetables, like potatoes, carrots, winter squash, and hearty greens.
Paprika and Sour Cream	Use 1 cup sliced onions. Omit the chile flakes. Cook the onions until soft and brown, about 10 minutes. Stir in 2 tablespoons paprika (sweet or smoked, or use hot paprika if you like a spicy sauce). Add the tomatoes and seasoning and simmer, covered, for 20 minutes. Puree the sauce if you want. Stir a few tablespoons of the warm sauce into ½ cup sour cream, adding more as needed until the sour cream is warm and smooth, then pour the warm sour cream mixture into the sauce; do not boil the sauce after the cream has been added. Finish with 1 tablespoon chopped fresh dill or parsley. Serve over egg noodles with chicken, sautéed mushrooms, and/or green beans.
Ranchero	Seed, stem, and toast 2 or 3 dried New Mexican red or pasilla chiles. Break the toasted chiles into pieces, cover with 1½ cups boiling water, and leave to steep while you prepare the sauce ingredients. Add 1½ teaspoons ground cumin and 1 teaspoon dried oregano to the sautéed onions and garlic, then add the chiles and soaking water along with the tomatoes and simmer for at least 30 minutes, until the chiles are very soft. Puree the sauce; press it through a sieve if you want a very smooth sauce. Season with plenty of salt.
Sausage	Brown 8 oz/225 g crumbled sausage meat, such as spicy Italian, chorizo, merguez, or even vegetarian Field Roast in a skillet. Add the onions and garlic and continue with the recipe.

5-INGREDIENT PIZZA SAUCE

I believe that really stellar pizzas are made with a dough that is chewy and flavorful, a very simple sauce, minimal toppings, and an extremely hot, even heat source. I will never meet the strict Neapolitan pizza standards, but my homemade pizzas are mighty good, in part because of this sauce. True Neapolitan pizzas are made with San Marzano tomatoes. They are available in cans and can be worth the added expense here.

YIELD: 1½ CUPS; ENOUGH FOR TWO 14-INCH/36 CM PIZZAS

¼ cup olive oil

1 tablespoon chopped garlic

Pinch of red chile flakes

One 14½ oz/411 g can diced or crushed tomatoes

Kosher salt

> Heat a heavy bottomed saucepan over medium heat. Add the oil, garlic, and chile flakes and cook, stirring often, until the garlic is tender and aromatic but not browned, about 1 minute. Stir in the tomatoes and a small pinch of salt and bring to a boil. Reduce the heat and simmer, uncovered, until the sauce is very thick, about 25 minutes. Stir regularly to make sure the sauce doesn't scorch.

> Taste and season with more salt as needed.

> If storing, cover and refrigerate for up to 5 days or freeze for up to 6 months.

DAN'S "INSTANT" CANNED TOMATO SALSA

Our dear friend Dan Richardson introduced us to this almost-instant salsa. A can of tomatoes, a few fresh ingredients, a touch of a button, and you have a salsa you can proudly serve to drop-in guests. It's become a staple in our house. Unfortunately, the fresh flavors are lost when the sauce is heated, so I don't recommend it for cooking.

YIELD: 2 CUPS

One 14½ oz/411 g can diced or whole tomatoes

½ cup coarsely chopped yellow onion

1 jalapeño pepper, sliced (add a second jalapeño or substitute a hotter chile if you like your salsa very spicy)

3 to 5 sprigs fresh cilantro

Juice of 1 lime

Kosher salt

Pinch of sugar (optional)

A few dashes of hot sauce, such as Tabasco or Tapatío

> Put the tomatoes, onion, jalapeño, and cilantro in a blender or food processor and pulse a few times until coarsely but evenly chopped. Add the lime juice and season to taste with salt. Add a pinch of sugar if the salsa seems too acidic and a few dashes of hot sauce for more chile flavor.

> If storing, cover and refrigerate for up to 3 days.

FOOD AND POLITICS

Tomatoes are a polarizing and political food. Some nutrition gurus claim that tomatoes promote longevity and that the higher lycopene levels in canned and concentrated tomatoes make them even healthier than fresh. Other factions say that even organic canned tomatoes are unsafe due to the risk of BPA (bisphenol A) leaching from the cans. I've also read that the source of tomatoes in any form should be carefully researched or there is a chance you may be supporting a system of modern-day slavery for poorly treated and compensated pickers. Add the GMO/big agro issues to the list of concerns, and tomatoes become one very hot sauce ingredient.

I think it's important to address this issue of politics and dissenting opinions about "good" and "bad" foods. Several years ago, I sat down and tried to list all of the potential political tribulations and hot-button health issues in a simple peanut butter and jelly sandwich. Just a few minutes into it, and a food that seems innocent and child-like had turned into a poison that no caring, forward-thinking adult would ever subject their child to. It was an eye-opening exercise.

I realized that there is no way to clearly separate food from politics. Food is both social and personal. I can state my preferences, but to insist that someone eat as I do is akin to telling them how to worship or to vote. I try to make informed choices, and understand that I can make a difference with my dollars. But I also know that some people's dollars can only go so far. Many people don't have access to the ingredients I do. That doesn't make them irresponsible. Food is meant to bring people together, to nourish them, not antagonize. No matter where you stand on a political food issue, please try to keep things friendly.

TIPS
for Creating Your Own Tomato Sauces

- A 14½ oz/411 g can of diced tomatoes holds about 1¾ cups.

- Whole or diced tomatoes in juice can easily be blended to make tomato puree or a fresh-tasting unseasoned tomato sauce.

- Consider draining the tomatoes and then adding the juice and solids at different times. Sauté the drained tomatoes with the aromatics until they soften, thicken, and sweeten, then add the juice when you add the other liquids.

- Tomatoes are very acidic. Dairy products can "shatter" when they are stirred haphazardly into hot tomato mixtures. Warm the creamy ingredient slightly first and add it gradually.

- The taste and texture of tomatoes change dramatically the longer they cook. Tomatoes will not only thicken, but also become darker and more savory. The Quick Fresh-Tasting Tomato Sauce on page 184 takes just minutes to soften and cohere slightly. If you puree that same sauce and simmer it very slowly until it is nearly dry, you will have a thick, dark, umami-rich tomato paste.

- Because tomatoes are high in natural sugar, tomato sauces can be quick to burn if left unattended. Use a pot with a heavy base and stir the sauce regularly. The longer a tomato sauce cooks and reduces, the sweeter it becomes—and the more likely it is to scorch. Adjust the lid of your pot to control the amount of steam that evaporates.

- If you are stumped about how to get your tomato sauce to taste better, it might just be a matter of leaving it to simmer a while longer so the flavors infuse and concentrate.

- Adding sugar to tomato sauces is the subject of contentious debate. Tomatoes are a fruit, but they are used most often in savory preparations. They vary in sweetness, even the canned ones. A piquant Italian red sauce rich with herbs and aromatics is not enhanced much with sugar unless you have developed a taste for sweet commercial sauces. But a bit of sugar can really round out a tomato-based Quick Mole or African Spicy Peanut Sauce (see the table on page 185).

- Tomato sauces that seem wet or weepy can be pulled together with a tiny bit of xanthan gum (see page 180). Don't use too much, or it can get oddly slippery. Start with just enough that will fit on the very tip of a sharp knife, sprinkle it over the surface, and whisk or blend it well to thoroughly distribute it.

- Many tomato sauces taste better the following day.

BEYOND PESTO

GREEN SAUCES, PASTES, AND BASES

Greens, herbs, and chiles of all kinds are used globally to make sauces, pastes, and bases that are rarely matched in vibrancy and freshness. Basil pesto is perhaps the most familiar in North America. Sadly, I was working as a caterer when pesto reached maximum menu saturation in the late 1980s. It took me more than a decade to recover from pesto burnout. I understand now that the green, cheesy spread I grew to loathe bore little resemblance to the aromatic, very perishable paste from Genoa it was fashioned after. To pound summer basil leaves in a mortar with garlic and a drizzle of olive oil, as the sauce was meant to be made, was a revelation. The fragrance is dizzying: floral and slightly peppery. The color is shamrock green. Make pesto at the very last minute and then dollop it by the spoonful onto steaming pasta so it can be stirred in at the table. The heat aerates the essential oils and it becomes a treat for the eyes and nose as well as the taste buds. But basil isn't the only green herb that makes amazing sauces. Cilantro, spinach, arugula, and even lettuce can be turned into a fresh sauce.

Green sauces made with heartier herbs and robust flavors, like Gaucho Chimichurri (page 201) and Trinidad Green Seasoning (page 204), have an appealing freshness but will keep and become pleasantly infused when refrigerated overnight. In addition to being served as a condiment, they can be used as marinades or enhancements to other sauces. Hara Masala (page 206) stirred into plain yogurt makes an excellent dip or dressing.

MORTAR-AND-PESTLE PESTO GENOVESE

I debated about putting a basic basil pesto in this book. In the end, I decided that the best thing to do was not just blend up more basil, nuts, and cheese, but to remind home cooks about the traditional way to make the sauce, using a mortar and pestle. A mortar and pestle may seem hopelessly prehistoric, but it still has a place in contemporary sauce making. Yes, it takes more effort than whizzing everything up electrically, but there is a marvelous sense of accomplishment and a sort of bonding that happens when you work with the ingredients manually. And once you taste a tangle of piping-hot pasta topped with a dollop of this essence of summer, you will never again consider buying the khaki-green stuff sold in jars. If your time is precious, you can make this sauce in a food processor, but I urge you to try it at least once the old-fashioned way.

YIELD: ABOUT ¾ CUP

3 cloves garlic

4 cups lightly packed fresh basil leaves, preferably more floral than peppery or minty

2 tablespoons pine nuts

½ teaspoon kosher salt, or to taste

¼ cup best quality extra-virgin olive oil

3 tablespoons finely grated top-quality Parmesan cheese, such as Parmigiano-Reggiano

> Combine the garlic and a few basil leaves in a large mortar and pound and grind the mixture to a paste with the pestle. Gradually add more basil leaves and continue to mash. If the mixture doesn't seem as if it is progressing, add some of the pine nuts or salt to help with the grinding. Once the garlic, basil, pine nuts, and salt have all been evenly pulverized together, gradually drip and drizzle in the olive oil while blending and mashing. Stir in the cheese and serve immediately.

FOOD-PROCESSOR PESTO GENOVESE

> Turn the food processor on and drop the garlic cloves into it. Add the pine nuts and finely chop. Scrape the sides of the bowl. Add the basil and salt and pulse until finely and evenly chopped. Scrape the sides of the bowl again. Turn the food processor on and gradually pour the olive oil in a thin stream to form a paste. Pulse in the cheese and serve immediately.

WHY A GOOD MORTAR AND PESTLE REMAINS RELEVANT

The first time I stepped into Nathan Myhrvold's famous Cooking Lab to test recipes, one of the first tools I needed was a mortar and pestle. It had me giggling. There I was, alone and granted unlimited access to the most high-tech cooking equipment available, and what I wanted was a bowl and a stick. I was too embarrassed to ask for one for fear of being mocked as hopelessly Stone-Aged, but I shouldn't have hesitated. Even in a kitchen that can turn olive oil into a powder and make "espresso" from mushrooms, the mortar and pestle is considered a vital cooking tool. There were, in fact, several choices. I just didn't know where to look.

There are times when spices need to be cracked, not powdered. Garlic, lemongrass, and shallots pounded to a paste taste and smell different than when they are sheared with a blade. To mash and pulverize ingredients is to break up cells, release aroma, and mingle oils and juices in a manner no blender can match.

I suggest that you pass over the small ornamental sets for something big and sturdy. The bowl should be quite deep and slightly gritty. The pestle should be long enough that you can get a good grip. If you want to pound out half a cup of pesto, you need something with enough volume to hold the handfuls of fresh basil leaves. I am still searching for the perfect all-purpose set. Until I find it, I have several so I can choose the right tool for the job at hand.

BEYOND BASIL PESTO

Basil pesto is best made when giant, floral bouquets of the herb fill the market stalls. Hothouse basil may be available all year round, but there are many other seasonal alternatives. Cilantro, arugula, parsley, and romaine lettuce are always readily available. Whatever mix of greens and aromatics you choose, start with a slightly pungent base of garlic, shallots, chiles, and/or scallions in a food processor or blender. When they are chopped, add a heap of greens and pulse the machine until the mixture is coarse but even. Add any ingredients that may add bulk, like nuts or cheese, then gradually add a flavorful oil to pull it all together and infuse the flavors. Since pestos are best lightly warmed rather than hot, this is a good place to use really top-notch oils. The sauces are meant to be intense, almost too strong and salty to enjoy off a spoon. That helps them to stand up to heaping bowls of hot starchy pasta.

Cilantro and Cotija Cheese	Chop ¼ cup diced red onion, 1 stemmed and seeded jalapeño pepper, and 2 garlic cloves in a food processor. Add 3 cups lightly packed fresh cilantro leaves with tender stems and pulse until evenly mixed. Add ½ cup crumbled Cotija cheese and ½ teaspoon dried oregano. Blend to a paste, gradually adding ¼ cup vegetable oil or peanut oil. Season to taste with plenty of kosher salt. Serve with grilled steak or roasted chicken, as a spread on tortas, or stirred into salsas and dressings.
Arugula, Walnut, and Asiago	Chop 2 cloves garlic with a pinch of red chile flakes in a food processor. Add 3 cups lightly packed arugula leaves and 3 tablespoons walnut pieces and pulse until evenly mixed. Add ½ cup finely grated Asiago cheese. Blend to a paste, gradually adding ¼ cup extra-virgin olive oil or walnut oil. Season to taste with a squeeze of fresh lemon juice and plenty of kosher salt. Toss with pasta and spring vegetables, serve as a condiment with steaks, or stir into vinaigrettes.
Spinach, Pistachio, and Porcini	Grind enough dried porcini mushrooms in a spice mill or clean coffee grinder to make 1 tablespoon fine powder. Chop ½ cup unsalted roasted pistachios, 2 cloves garlic, and 1 teaspoon finely grated lemon zest in a food processor. Add the porcini powder. Add 4 cups loosely packed baby spinach leaves and pulse until evenly mixed. Blend to a paste while gradually adding ¼ cup extra-virgin olive oil. Season to taste with plenty of kosher salt. Add a tablespoon of pistachio oil or a few drops of truffle oil, if you like. Toss with cheese-stuffed pasta, serve as a condiment with salmon, or spread on panini or canapés.

Warm Parsley and Bacon	Chop ¼ cup diced onion with 3 garlic cloves in a food processor. Add 2 cups lightly packed fresh parsley leaves with tender stems, 2 tablespoons apple cider vinegar, and 1 tablespoon coarse mustard and pulse until evenly blended but not smooth. Stir in ¼ cup olive oil and 3 tablespoons crumbled crisp bacon. Season with kosher salt and freshly ground black pepper to taste. Warm gently and serve over boiled potatoes or with smoked sausages.
Romaine, Green Pea, and Wasabi	Puree ½ cup blanched fresh or thawed frozen green peas and ½ cup sliced scallions in a food processor or blender. Add 2 cups chopped romaine lettuce leaves and pulse to chop evenly. Add 1 tablespoon prepared wasabi, or more if you like it especially pungent. Blend to a paste while gradually adding 3 tablespoons vegetable oil or light olive oil. Season to taste with kosher salt. Use to top cold buckwheat noodles, shrimp, fish, or tofu.
Nettle and Avocado	Chop 2 tablespoons minced shallots and 2 cloves garlic in a food processor. Add 1 cup blanched fresh nettles, squeezed dry, and 2 tablespoons minced fresh chives and pulse until evenly blended. Add 1 avocado, halved, pitted, and peeled, 1 teaspoon finely grated lemon zest, 2 tablespoons freshly squeezed lemon juice, and plenty of kosher salt and freshly ground black pepper. Blend to a paste while gradually adding 2 tablespoons avocado oil or light olive oil. Serve with salmon, toss with pasta, or stir into sautéed mushrooms; or use as a dip for flatbreads. The avocado will gradually darken the pesto.

POWER PESTO

Fresh sauces can revive and energize your body as well as your palate. Almost any health and diet-focused organization has a list of power foods for optimum nutrients, energy, and well being. Blend up a batch of this raw pesto, and you can practically hear the party of antioxidants mingling with omega-3 fatty acids. Now and then, when I need a break from rich foods, I will serve this as part of a raw meal, tossed with zucchini sliced into long, thin "noodles" on a mandoline or spiral slicer. It also works well as a dip or a spread, swirled into a salad dressing, or tossed with whole grains.

YIELD: 1¼ CUPS

3 cloves garlic

3 tablespoons walnut halves and pieces

1 tablespoon ground flaxseeds

2 cups lightly packed baby spinach leaves

2 cups lightly packed torn kale (tough stems removed)

2 teaspoons powdered spirulina, chlorella, blue green algae, or unsweetened dry "green juice" mix (optional)

½ teaspoon finely grated lemon zest

2 tablespoons freshly squeezed lemon juice

2 teaspoons honey (optional)

> Turn a food processor on and drop in the garlic cloves. Add the walnuts and flaxseeds and pulse until evenly chopped. Add the spinach, kale, spirulina, if using, and lemon zest and pulse until the mixture is finely and evenly chopped. Scrape down the sides of the bowl. Add the lemon juice, honey, salt, and cayenne, then turn the food processor on and gradually add the oil in a thin stream to blend.

> Serve at room temperature or lightly warmed.

> If storing, refrigerate for up to 2 days with a piece of plastic wrap pressed against the surface of the sauce or a thin layer of olive oil poured on top to prevent oxidation.

½ teaspoon kosher salt

¼ teaspoon cayenne pepper

½ cup grape seed or extra-virgin
olive oil

BAGNET VERD—PIEDMONTESE GREEN SAUCE

Elisabeth Giacon Castleman is a cookbook translator, historian, and genuinely charming woman. When I was looking for a more authentic version of Italian green sauce than the simple parsley and garlic blend I typically made, I thought of her. She sent me instructions on how to make this Piedmontese bagnet verd, as well as a wonderful recipe from a Northern Italian Renaissance author, Christoforo di Messisbugo, which was first published in 1567. His recipe for green sauce called for mixed herbs, bread, strong vinegar, and, as a sweet option, some apples or sugar. It was tempting to re-create that ancient version, but in the end my love of this simple, tangy parsley sauce won out. Bagnet verd is traditionally served with meat, but it seems to go with almost anything. My go-to potluck dish is a heap of roasted new potatoes served at room temperature with this garlicky green sauce as a dip.

YIELD: 1½ CUPS

½ cup torn bits of rustic white bread (crusts removed)

3 tablespoons red or white wine vinegar

1 cup lightly packed fresh parsley leaves with tender stems (from about 1 large bunch)

1 clove garlic

1 hard-boiled egg yolk

2 oil- or salt-packed anchovy fillets

1 teaspoon capers

1 cup extra-virgin olive oil

½ teaspoon kosher salt

> Soak the bread in the vinegar while you prepare the remaining ingredients.

> Combine the soaked bread, parsley, garlic, egg yolk, anchovies, and capers in a food processor and pulse to a coarse, even paste. Transfer to a bowl and stir in the olive oil and salt for a rustic version; or if you prefer a more emusified, smooth sauce, with the processor running, gradually pour the olive oil in a thin stream until it is completely blended and then season with the salt.

> Serve at room temperature.

> If storing, cover and refrigerate for up to 2 days. The color will not be as vibrant.

GAUCHO CHIMICHURRI

This is a popular Argentinean parsley sauce. I was not a big fan at first. I thought it was pretty, but not terribly interesting. After reading *Culinary Intelligence* by Peter Kaminsky I realized what the problem was—chimichurri is a rule breaker. It's a fresh herb sauce that actually improves with a bit of age. Oddly, the versions I had tried were almost too fresh, too much like oily coarse parsley instead of what the gauchos of the pampas once carried in their saddlebags. The original sauces were not made from herbs delivered daily from the greengrocer, but from foraged greens and dried herbs. Kaminsky has spent a lot of time cooking alongside one of Argentina's great chefs, Francis Mallmann. He makes his chimichurri by soaking chopped fresh herbs and aromatics in a saltwater solution seasoned with vinegar and chiles. I don't presume to have such expertise, but I no longer worry about keeping the mix a brilliant fresh green, as with fresh pesto or mint sauce. I stir together a blend of fresh parsley, garlic, and dried oregano. I like the peppery depth this has even more after a day or two. It is great with virtually any simply prepared ingredient like fish, potatoes, or even parsnips, but it soars to great heights when served with flame-seared beef and plenty of fresh air.

YIELD: ¾ CUP

½ cup finely chopped fresh parsley

6 cloves garlic, minced

¼ cup water

2 tablespoons dried oregano

2 tablespoons olive oil

2 tablespoons apple cider vinegar
   or white wine vinegar

1 teaspoon kosher salt

¼ teaspoon red chile flakes

> Stir together all of the ingredients in a container. Seal and leave to infuse for at least 4 hours, or for best flavor, overnight.

> Serve at room temperature.

> If storing, cover and refrigerate for up to 5 days.

MINT CHUTNEY

Mint chutney is a bright green fresh sauce traditionally served alongside South Indian breads like dosas or with fried snacks like papadums, samosas, or pakoras. The combination of ingredients makes it lively, with a refreshing aroma and sweet, sour, salty, and hot tastes. It can be stirred into plain yogurt, used as a dip, drizzled onto flatbreads, or served as topping for plain rice. It is a welcome alternative to the overly sweet mint sauces often served with roast lamb. Substitute a few sprigs of cilantro for some of the mint for variation.

This sauce is made in a blender, but because of the small volume, you need to regularly scrape the sides and then scrape every tidbit from the blades when it is finished. Use a mini chopper if you have one.

YIELD: ABOUT ½ CUP

1 cup lightly packed fresh mint leaves

¼ cup freshly squeezed lemon juice

2 tablespoons grated palm sugar or brown sugar

1 to 2 tablespoons minced serrano chile (for a milder sauce, use a jalapeño)

2 teaspoons minced fresh ginger

½ teaspoon kosher salt

About 1 tablespoon water if needed

> Combine the mint, lemon juice, sugar, chile, ginger, and salt in a blender or mini chopper and pulse to chop and blend. The small volume of sauce can make it a little fussy to blend, so stop the blender and scrape down the sides often. Add a teaspoon or two of water if necessary to make a more liquid sauce.

> Serve at room temperature.

> If storing, refrigerate for up to 3 days with a piece of plastic wrap pressed directly against the surface of the sauce. The chutney will gradually darken as it oxidizes.

CHINESE CRACKLING SCALLION AND GARLIC SAUCE

In some ways, this recipe epitomizes my passion for simple, fresh sauces. It's just hot oil infused with garlic and chiles and loaded with sliced scallions. It's served crackling hot, poured straight from a wok onto whole fish, grilled steaks, roasted potatoes, or even bowls of plain rice. I call it "Chinese" because it reminds me of some of my favorite dishes. It's part sauce, part condiment, and part stir-fry. The steely perfume of a hot wok or cast-iron skillet is an important ingredient in this preparation. I've made this with just about any greens I've had on hand. Try it with chopped ramps, kale, bok choy greens, arugula, or garlic chives. Chopped romaine lettuce works too.

Make sure all of the ingredients are ready before you start. This is a last-minute preparation that is best made and served immediately.

YIELD: ABOUT 1 CUP

¼ cup peanut oil

2 or 3 cloves garlic, thickly sliced

¼ teaspoon red chile flakes

Greens from 3 or 4 scallions, thickly sliced (about ¾ cup loosely packed)

½ teaspoon kosher salt

Freshly ground black pepper

> Heat a wok or a cast-iron skillet over high heat. When heat waves can just be seen rising from the pan, swirl in the oil. Add the garlic and chile flakes and sizzle to infuse the flavor into the oil, about 15 seconds. (If the garlic burns, throw it all out and start over.) Add the scallions and quickly stir to mix—they should sizzle and crackle. Season generously with salt and pepper, immediately pour over the dish to be sauced, and serve.

TRINIDAD GREEN SEASONING

This is a fluid mixture of fresh herbs, chiles, and garlic used in the Caribbean, especially Trinidad. Serve it alongside grilled meat. Slather it over chicken or fish before cooking. Add it as a secret ingredient to dressings, soups, or sauces. I've never been to the region, I have only read about green seasoning and experimented with various blends, but as I understand it, the less precise the recipe is, the more authentic. There are a few ingredients that should always be included—thyme, scallions, chiles, and garlic. Cilantro, parsley, celery, and oregano make regular appearances, but the rest of the "green" can vary according to what you might be growing or what inspires you at the produce stand. You can use more celery and celery leaves, some basil, dill, a little sage, or a sprig of mint or lemon balm.

YIELD: ABOUT 1½ CUPS

1½ cups sliced scallions (about 1 large bunch, both green and white parts)

1 cup loosely packed fresh long-leaf cilantro (also known as recao, culantro, chado beni, or ngo gai) or loosely packed cilantro leaves with tender stems

½ cup loosely packed fresh parsley leaves with tender stems

1 stalk celery, chopped

3 ají dulce peppers, seeded and chopped, or about ⅓ cup minced other mild flavorful chiles (you can use hot chiles if you prefer)

> Combine all of the ingredients in a food processor and pulse to a slightly coarse paste. Add additional water if necessary to make a flowing, more liquid consistency.

> Use immediately, or cover and leave to age and mellow in the refrigerator for up to a week.

3 tablespoons chopped fresh
thyme (from about 1 bunch,
including any tender stems)

2 to 3 sprigs fresh basil, preferably
Thai, tough stems removed

3 to 4 sprigs fresh oregano, tough
stems removed

3 cloves garlic

1 teaspoon kosher salt

2 to 3 tablespoons freshly
squeezed lime juice

½ cup water, or as needed

HARA MASALA—
INDIAN GREEN SPICE BASE

This is a pungent, intense fresh green sauce. It can be served as a condiment, but it is more tradi-tionally used as a base for aromatic green curries. Stir it into yogurt, coconut milk, or Vegan Cashew Sour Cream (page 273). Rub it on chicken or fish before grilling, or add it to dressings or vegetable purees to make dips and spreads.

YIELD: 1 CUP

2 cups lightly packed fresh cilantro leaves with tender stems (from about 2 bunches)

1 cup lightly packed fresh mint leaves (from about 1 large bunch)

¾ cup chopped shallots

1 or 2 hot green chiles, seeded and sliced, such as serrano, or 4 to 6 stemmed green Thai bird chiles

8 cloves garlic

1 tablespoon grated or minced fresh ginger

1½ teaspoons kosher salt

¼ teaspoon ground turmeric

¼ teaspoon ground cloves

¼ teaspoon ground cardamom

3 tablespoons vegetable oil

> Combine the cilantro, mint, shallots, chiles, garlic, and ginger in a food processor and pulse to an even coarse paste. Add the salt, turmeric, cloves, and cardamom and pulse to mix well. Gradually pour in the oil and blend to a paste.

> Use immediately, or transfer to a sealed container and refrigerate overnight to infuse and mellow. You can pour a thin layer of oil over the top to help seal and preserve the color.

> The sauce can be refrigerated for up to 5 days.

NUT SAUCES

TURNING WHOLE FOODS INTO SAUCES WITHOUT ADDING THICKENERS

Nuts and seeds have been used to texturize and enrich sauces since the dawn of cooking. They can mimic the rich, smooth properties of cream and butter or be binding, pasty, or crunchy. Nut sauces are so intriguing that I often find myself featuring the sauces even more than the foods they accompany. Pranee's Thai Peanut Sauce (page 209), made with freshly roasted, pounded peanuts, needs little more than some rice and maybe a bit of wilted spinach to be a satisfying meal.

The Georgian Walnut Sauce (page 213) and Pistachio and Preserved Lemon Gremolata (page 216), resemble pesto and can similarly be used as intriguing flavor and textural additions to other sauces like vinaigrettes and dressings.

Nuts and seeds must be as fresh as possible. Many years ago, I taught an absolutely disastrous cooking class. Anything that could have gone wrong did. Perhaps most humiliating was my preparation of an elegant pumpkin seed butter sauce with rancid pepitas. I'd bought the seeds that very day, but obviously from the wrong store. I urge you to learn from my mistakes and always taste nuts and seeds before you use them.

PRANEE'S THAI PEANUT SAUCE

In addition to operating the I Love Thai Cooking School in Seattle, Pranee Khruasanit Halvorsen works as a consultant and leads culinary tours of Thailand. She invited me into her kitchen when she heard I was looking for an authentic Thai peanut sauce. Like all good teachers and sauce makers, she explained that there is no one perfect way to make a recipe. You need to customize every dish for the people you are cooking for, using the best of the materials you have on hand. I asked her for fresh peanut flavor, so she created this version made with freshly roasted peanuts pounded in a mortar. Use this thick peanut sauce as a dip for grilled tofu or chicken skewers or spoon it over stir-fried green vegetables and rice.

YIELD: 1 CUP

½ cup (3 oz/85 g) raw peanuts, preferably Spanish or a similar small, intense red-skinned peanut

2 shallots, thinly sliced

1 tablespoon very very thinly sliced fresh lemongrass

1 tablespoon chopped fresh ginger

1 clove garlic, chopped

1 cup unsweetened coconut milk

2 teaspoons Thai red or Penang curry paste

2 or 3 fresh lime leaves (makrud)

2 tablespoons grated palm sugar or brown sugar, or to taste

> Preheat the oven to 350°F/175°C.

> Put the peanuts on a small baking sheet and bake until they have darkened and have a deep roasted peanut aroma, about 12 minutes. When they are just cool enough to handle, rub the nuts together in your hands or a dry towel to remove as much of the skin as possible.

> Combine the shallots, lemongrass, ginger, and garlic in a mortar and pound to a paste. Remove and set aside. Pound the skinned peanuts in the mortar until they are quite smooth and starting to get sticky. Set aside. (You can use a small electric food chopper to finely chop the shallot and lemongrass mixture and/or a spice mill or coffee grinder to pulverize the peanuts if you prefer.)

> Combine ½ cup of the coconut milk with the curry paste and lime leaves in a saucepan and bring to a simmer over medium-high heat, then reduce the heat and simmer, stirring often, until the water evaporates and the oil in the coconut milk "starts to show," about 5 minutes. Add the pounded shallot

continues

2 tablespoons Tamarind Pulp (page 91), or to taste

1 tablespoon fish sauce, or to taste

and ginger mixture and cook over medium-low heat, stirring often, until the shallots and ginger have softened and the ingredients have a sweet perfume but have not browned, about 5 minutes.

> Stir in the pulverized peanuts, the remaining ½ cup coconut milk, the sugar, tamarind pulp, and fish sauce. Simmer until the sauce has thickened and the flavors have married, about 5 minutes. Remove the lime leaves and adjust the seasoning with additional sugar, tamarind pulp, and/or fish sauce to taste.

> Serve warm.

> If storing, cover and refrigerate for up to 3 days.

STIR-TOGETHER PEANUT BUTTER–HOISIN DIPPING SAUCE

This sauce is nutty, sweet, and slightly exotic, and, it can be whipped up in less time than the quick-cooking dishes I like to dunk in it: grilled chicken skewers, Vietnamese spring rolls, or pot stickers. Double or triple the recipe, and you can use it to simmer chicken or as a sauce for chewy stir-fried noodles. It keeps well.

YIELD: ½ CUP

¼ cup hoisin sauce

¼ cup water, coconut water or Really Good Chicken Stock (page 114)

2 tablespoons all-natural peanut butter (smooth or chunky)

1 tablespoon fish sauce (or substitute 2 teaspoons light soy sauce or tamari)

2 teaspoons sambal oelek or Sriracha (page 302), or to taste

1 tablespoon freshly squeezed lime juice, Tamarind Water (page 91), or rice vinegar

> Whisk together all of the ingredients in a small bowl. Taste and adjust the seasoning. Serve the sauce at room temperature or lightly warmed.

> If storing, cover and refrigerate for up to 2 weeks.

ALMOND TAHINI SAUCE

This is a creamy, dairy-free condiment with Mediterranean roots. I particularly like it drizzled over grilled eggplant and peppers. It can also be used as a dip for vegetables or spread in pita bread sandwiches. I suggest that you blanch the almonds yourself. It takes only a few minutes, but the taste is much better and the moisture content is higher than with preblanched (skinned) almonds. Substitute blanched almonds and skip the first step if you prefer.

YIELD: 2 CUPS

¾ cup whole raw almonds

½ cup tahini

2 cloves garlic, mashed or pressed

¾ cup cold water, or more as
    needed

⅓ cup freshly squeezed lemon
    juice

½ teaspoon kosher salt

Pinch of sugar (optional)

> Cover the almonds with boiling water and let them soak for at least 5 minutes. When the water is cool, lift out one almond at a time and give it a pinch to slip it out of the softened skin.

> Combine the blanched almonds, tahini, and garlic in a blender and puree to a thick paste, scraping down the sides of the jar as needed. With the blender on high, gradually add the cold water and lemon juice to make a smooth, light-colored sauce. Season with the salt and sugar, if using. The sauce will thicken slightly as it stands. Thin it with additional water to reach a pouring consistency if you prefer.

> If storing, cover and refrigerate for up to 1 week.

GARLIC TAHINI SAUCE

> Omit the almonds, increase the garlic to 3 cloves, and reduce the water to ⅓ cup. Stir in 2 tablespoons very finely chopped fresh parsley for added color and freshness.

GEORGIAN WALNUT SAUCE

I first tasted this sauce on a cold January evening in St. Petersburg. Rich with garlic and herbs, it was slathered over a lovely plate of broiled eggplant. I've seen many recipes in Russian cookbooks for Georgian walnut sauce, but this version is as close as I've been able to come to matching that particular taste memory. It is meant to be slightly coarse, not a smooth paste. Sometimes I just chop the ingredients by hand and stir them together. In addition to eggplant, this goes well with roasted chicken, salmon, and braised lamb. Stuff baby bell peppers with it and served them as appetizers.

YIELD: 1 CUP

¼ cup minced yellow onion or shallots

3 cloves garlic, chopped

1 cup loosely packed fresh parsley leaves with tender stems

1 cup (4 oz/115 g) walnut halves and pieces

¼ teaspoon red chile flakes or hot paprika

½ cup olive oil

½ teaspoon kosher salt, or to taste

Freshly ground black pepper

> Combine the onion and garlic in a food processor and pulse until evenly chopped but not pulverized. Scrape down the sides of the bowl. Add the parsley, walnuts, and chile flakes and pulse until blended but still quite coarse. Transfer to a bowl, stir in the olive oil, and season with the salt and pepper to taste. Alternatively, finely chop all of the ingredients by hand and stir them together.

> Serve at room temperature or very gently warmed.

> If storing, cover and refrigerate for up to 3 days. The sauce will solidify when it is cold, and the nuts will soften after a day, but it is still nice when it is warmed to room temperature.

TOMATILLO AND PUMPKIN SEED SAUCE

I learned a lot from this sauce. *Pipián verde* is a lovely green stew/sauce served in Guatemala and Mexico. I'd attempted to make the authentic dish multiple times, but they all seemed to go wrong at some point. Halfway through each batch, I inevitably ended up feeling as if someone, somewhere, was rolling their eyes at my technique. Finally I decided to start practicing what I preach, stop stressing out about authenticity, and just make the sauce I wanted for dinner. It was a great decision. My version is slightly coarse, green, and tangy with tomatillos. It's loaded with fresh cilantro and made nutty with freshly toasted pumpkin seeds. Smother mahi mahi fillets with the sauce and simmer them in a skillet until just tender. Use it over enchiladas. Stir it together with grilled vegetables and shrimp. Or just serve it as a dipping sauce for chips. If you are pressed for time, you can skip the charring steps and substitute canned tomatillos and roasted green chiles, but the flavors can be slightly briny and wan.

YIELD: ABOUT 2 CUPS

8 oz/225 g tomatillos (about 6), husked (or substitute canned)

2 Anaheim or Hatch green chiles

1 tablespoon olive oil

½ cup chopped yellow onion

2 cloves garlic, chopped

1 teaspoon ground cumin

About 1 cup Vegetable Stock (page 106, or see the table on page 108) or Really Good Chicken Stock (page 114)

1 teaspoon kosher salt or to taste

½ cup (3 oz/85 g) hulled raw pumpkin seeds (pepitas)

> Char the tomatillo skins by holding them with tongs over a gas flame, rolling them on a very hot grill or electric burner, or using a blowtorch. (If you are using canned tomatillos, omit this step.) Put the hot tomatillos in a bowl and cover it with a clean dish towel or plastic wrap so they can steam for a few minutes. This will loosen the skins even more. Char the chiles the same way and add to the bowl.

> When the tomatillos and chiles are cool enough to handle, wipe and rub off the charred skins with a paper towel. Don't worry about getting every last dark fleck—they will add flavor. Chop the tomatillos. Core, seed, and chop the chiles.

> Heat a medium saucepan over medium-high heat. Add the oil, then add the onion and garlic, and cook, stirring often, until golden brown and tender, about 3 minutes. Stir in the cumin and cook for 30 seconds. Add the chopped tomatillos and green chiles, moisten with about ¾ cup of the stock, and season with a pinch of the salt. Simmer, half-

1 cup lightly packed fresh cilantro leaves with tender stems

A few dashes of hot chile sauce, like Tapatío or Tabasco (optional)

covered, stirring occasionally, until the tomatillos have broken down and the sauce resembles a thick puree, about 20 minutes.

> While the tomatillos are cooking, toast the pumpkin seeds: Heat them in a dry skillet over medium heat; shake the pan often, tossing the seeds so they don't burn. When they have all darkened and popped, transfer them to a bowl or plate to stop the cooking. Set aside to cool.

> Combine the warm tomatillo mixture, toasted pumpkin seeds, and cilantro in a blender or food processor and blend to a coarse paste. Transfer to a saucepan and stir in enough additional stock to thin the sauce to the desired consistency. Taste and season with the remaining salt and the chile sauce.

> Reheat the sauce before serving. It can be served immediately, but it will taste even better the following day.

> If storing, cover and refrigerate for up to 4 days or freeze for up to 4 months.

PISTACHIO AND PRESERVED LEMON GREMOLATA

A classic gremolata is more garnish than sauce: it is a blend of chopped fresh parsley, minced garlic, and citrus zest that is a traditional topping for osso buco. This recipe starts with a similar base of parsley but morphs into a sauce with the addition of chopped nuts, olive oil, shallots, and salty preserved lemon. It is a Mediterranean sauce mash-up that flirts with pesto. It can be used in the traditional style as a topping that offers contrasting taste and texture over velvety braised meats, tender fish fillets, or mixed vegetables. It can also be used as a spread. Swirl it into yogurt or mayonnaise or add a dollop to tomato or pan sauces.

Preserved lemons are very salty, and many pistachios are heavily salted, so I don't add any extra salt. The fresh sauce has a nice crunch and brightness if you serve it right away, but it will marry and soften in an appealing way as it stands. Preserved lemons are sold at gourmet stores and Mediterranean markets.

YIELD: ¾ CUP

½ cup (4 oz/115 g) chopped
   roasted pistachio

¼ cup chopped fresh parsley

2 tablespoons minced preserved
   lemon

2 tablespoons minced shallots

1 clove garlic, minced or pressed

3 tablespoons extra-virgin olive oil
   or pistachio oil

Freshly ground black pepper to
   taste

> Stir together all the ingredients in a bowl. Or, for a finer paste, pulse the ingredients a few times in a food processor or blender. Serve at room temperature.

> If storing, cover and refrigerate for up to 3 days.

TIPS
for Creating Your Own Nut Sauces

- Use only very fresh nuts, seeds, and nut butters. These all degrade quickly and few things can ruin a sauce faster than rancid oils. Store them in the refrigerator or freezer, and smell and taste them before you use them.

- Buy all-natural nut-butters. Additives are unnecessary and can make sauces seem gummy and uneven.

- The taste is always improved when you process your own ingredients. If you have a source for fresh nuts, crack and collect your own nut meats. Buy whole raw almonds and blanch or sliver them yourself. Roast raw peanuts.

- Less can be more. Adding too much nut butter is often more problematic than adding too little. A tablespoon or two can add a more accessible nut flavor and appealing texture than half a cup.

- Recipes made with a very high ratio of nuts or seeds are more likely to seize up. If you find yourself with a nearly solid, grainy sauce, add stock or water and blend until it becomes smooth again.

- Tender raw nuts and seeds like cashews, blanched almonds, and sesame seeds that are soaked overnight in water can be ground into smooth, silky creams. Use them as dairy replacements, thickeners, flavor enhancements, and for enrichment. See Vegan Cashew Sour Cream (page 273) and Vegan Cashew "Cheese" Sauce (page 365).

- Whole or large pieces of toasted nuts can add crunch and texture but will soften quickly when they are wet. If you want a toasty crunch, add them just before serving.

THE ALLERGY ISSUE

Please don't minimize food allergies and intolerances. They don't just make people sneeze, itch, or bloat—they can kill. Do you really want to risk it? I welcome guests with special dietary needs, but when it comes to potentially lethal reactions, I urge them to bring along an emergency remedy (like an EpiPen) and even their own food. If you have made a peanut sauce in your blender or food processor, it can cross-contaminate whatever goes in next. When I worked at a restaurant, a patron with a black pepper sensitivity reacted to his food because his steak had picked up some residual pepper from the grill. For some people with celiac disease, the gluten in a single crumb of bread is enough to damage their gut for weeks.

Talk to your guests. Find out exactly what they can tolerate and what they are most comfortable with. The people I know with food sensitivities are thrilled just to be invited and welcomed graciously—even if all they can eat is individually wrapped cheese sticks on paper plates.

CURRY SAUCES

urry is not a single spice or standardized spice blend but a preparation. In Western terms, it is most similar to sautéed and simmered dishes or perhaps something braised on the stovetop. Curries are often richly spiced and thickened with integral components like softened vegetables, nuts, and legumes. The sauce itself tends to be the main feature, enhanced with a bit of meat or vegetables, rather than the other way around. Because true curries are complete dishes that are built in the pan, not just served as an accompaniment, the recipes that follow are inherently inauthentic. But, judging by the number of prepared curry sauces now available on grocery shelves, I'm guessing that's not much of a problem for many people. Homemade curries can be a remarkable improvement over store-bought, and they are especially rewarding—make a good curry from scratch, and you will be proud of yourself. I promise.

Curry powders and pastes can contain dozens of different ingredients. The blends are customized according to taste, region, local traditions, ingredient availability, and the preference of individual households. Ground turmeric is the yellow component in curry powder. It is relatively flavorless and is traditionally used more for its color, antiseptic, ceremonial, and health-giving properties than for taste. I've found that curry powders

that are a darker ocher rely less on turmeric and so tend to be more complex than those that are a bright canary yellow.

Chicken tikka masala has been declared one of the national dishes of Britain. An amber gravy-like curry has achieved a similar status in Japan. Fiery curries are a staple in Jamaica. Curry, both the spice blends and the preparations, rate right up near the top when it comes to favorite global dishes. If a generic yellow grocery store spice stirred into chicken salad is the only curry flavor you know, you are in for a very pleasant surprise.

Curry sauces are very diverse, but there are a few consistent techniques. First, a base is created. Aromatics like onions, shallots, ginger, and garlic are cooked in fat—oil, butter, or sometimes reduced coconut milk. They tend to be cooked slowly, over medium heat rather than high, so they become meltingly tender and golden brown. In many curried dishes, the spice mixes are added early and cooked a bit before the liquids are added. This gives the spices a rounder, mellower flavor. Err on the side of too many spices rather than too few, but don't consider the prevalence of spices to be a substitution for careful seasoning. A curry that includes fish sauce may also need a pinch of salt. Just because it has chiles doesn't mean a bit of black or white pepper is unwelcome. I've repeatedly learned from example that authentic curries taste best when they are made with more oil and salt than I would instinctively add. Because they tend to be long-cooked, most curries are finished with bright fresh flavors like cilantro sprigs, sliced scallions, and lime wedges. The more slowly the curry cooks, the better it tends to be the next day.

I often toast and grind my own spices. Because ours is a curry-loving household, I also keep Madras and S&B brand curry powders, as well as a tub of Thai red curry paste, on hand at all times. If you can only choose one, make it a good quality all-purpose curry powder.

Because I am such a curry fan, it was tough to choose which curries to include here. I included recipes for several international favorites in order to illustrate some of the differences in technique and ingredients.

TIKKA MASALA SAUCE

This may be the most beloved curry sauce in the West. The gentle complexity of sweet spices paired with a tomato tang and decadent creaminess makes it almost universally appealing. It's one of the only sauces in this book that include heavy cream. To make chicken tikka masala, simply add chunks of cooked chicken to the sauce and simmer until warm. While the sauce has many traditional Indian elements, it was actually created in England as a handy way to use leftover cooked tidbits of tandoori chicken. You can also simmer shrimp, vegetables, tofu, or paneer—a mild fresh Indian cheese—in it. Mop it up with warm naan.

YIELD: 2½ CUPS

1 teaspoon coriander seeds

1 teaspoon cumin seeds

1 teaspoon kosher salt, or to taste

½ teaspoon chile powder (mild or fiery hot, according to your taste)

½ teaspoon ground cardamom

¼ teaspoon ground turmeric

¼ cup (4 tablespoons) ghee (see page 394), butter, or vegetable oil

2 cups finely chopped shallots or yellow onions

1½ tablespoons finely chopped fresh ginger

2 cloves garlic, finely chopped

> Toast the coriander and cumin seeds in a small dry skillet over medium heat until they start to color and smell very aromatic, 2 to 3 minutes. Transfer the seeds to a spice mill or coffee grinder, add the salt, and grind to a fine powder. Mix this with the chile powder, cardamom, and turmeric.

> Heat the ghee in a large saucepan over medium heat. Add the onions, ginger, and garlic and sauté until the onions are very tender and golden brown, about 8 minutes. Add the mixed ground spices and cook 30 seconds. Stir in the tomatoes, water, sugar, and cinnamon and simmer, half-covered, until the tomatoes have softened and the sauce has thickened slightly, about 20 minutes.

> Gradually stir in the cream. Remove and discard the cinnamon stick. Season with additional sugar and salt to taste. If you prefer a smooth sauce, blend with an immersion blender or puree in a blender or food processor.

> If you want to make this an entrée, add chicken, shrimp, paneer, or vegetables and simmer until cooked through. Serve warm.

1 cup diced peeled tomatoes
(canned are fine)

1 cup water

1 tablespoon light or dark brown
sugar, or to taste

½ cinnamon stick

¾ cup heavy cream, warmed

> If storing, cover and refrigerate for up to 5 days. The flavor will improve overnight.

THAI COCONUT CURRY SAUCE

This elementary Thai curry sauce is meant to demonstrate a few basic techniques and flavors, not encapsulate the vast array of intricate Southeast Asian curries. The ingredient list is manageable and accessible—I can buy everything at my local supermarket. Like tikka masala, this is a Western favorite. It is quite thin, but still creamy, and it is particularly good simmered with relatively quick-cooking ingredients, like diced kabocha squash and shrimp, or tofu, peppers, and straw mushrooms. Substitute Thai yellow, green, or Penang curry paste for variation. The lime leaves and pieces of ginger and lemongrass can be left in and avoided, or fished out and discarded.

YIELD: 1½ CUPS

3 tablespoons vegetable oil

2 tablespoons Thai red curry paste

1 cup unsweetened coconut milk

½ cup Really Good Chicken Stock (page 114), Vegetable Stock (page 106, or see the table on page 108), Quick Shrimp Shell Stock (page 120), or an appropriate Mock Stock (see the table on page 93)

3 coins fresh ginger or galangal

One 2-inch/5 cm piece lemongrass, tender part only, cut lengthwise in half and smashed with the side of a knife

2 fresh lime leaves (makrud)

2 teaspoons grated palm sugar or brown sugar

> Heat a medium saucepan over medium heat. Add the oil, then stir in the curry paste and fry, stirring constantly, until the paste darkens slightly and loses its raw aroma, about 1 minute. Whisk in half the coconut milk and bring to a boil, then simmer until the coconut milk is reduced to a thick cream and "the oil shows," separating out into colorful pools.

> Stir in the remaining coconut milk, the stock, ginger, lemongrass, lime leaves, and sugar and simmer, stirring occasionally, until the sauce has thickened slightly and the flavors have infused, 10 to 15 minutes.

> If you want to add vegetables, meat, or seafood to make this an entrée, add now and simmer just until cooked through.

> Stir in the basil. Season with the fish sauce and lime juice and serve warm.

> If storing, cover and refrigerate for up to 2 days.

2 sprigs fresh Thai basil, tough
stems removed (about 15 leaves)

1 tablespoon fish sauce

1 tablespoon freshly squeezed lime
juice

FIERY ISLAND CURRY SAUCE

Caribbean curries have roots in India and Pakistan, but the dishes have evolved and been adapted into unique preparations. Often they are slow-simmered meaty stews spiced with a basic curry powder and then given more oomph with local flavors like chiles, allspice, thyme, and pungent herbs. This sauce can easily be turned into a traditional entrée by simply searing some pieces of raw meat or poultry in hot oil before you start the sauce. Chicken and goat meat are especially good. Here the ground spices are toasted for just a moment in the dry pan before the oil is added. This is a slightly different method for treating toasted spices than you may see elsewhere, but it has the same function of removing the raw harshness and giving the spices a rounder, more mellow taste.

This sauce will taste even better the next day, so make it ahead if you can.

YIELD: 2 CUPS

2 tablespoons hot curry powder

1 teaspoon ground cumin

¼ cup vegetable oil

1 cup chopped yellow onion

1 cup chopped carrots

4 cloves garlic, chopped

2 or 3 Scotch Bonnet chiles, seeded and diced (see Tips for Handling Chiles, page 298), or more to taste

1 cup diced tomatoes (drained canned tomatoes are fine)

1 teaspoon ground allspice

> Heat a large saucepan over medium heat. Add the curry powder and cumin and toast, stirring constantly, until the curry has darkened slightly but is not burnt, about 20 seconds. Stir in the oil and leave to bubble and cook the spices for about 30 seconds more. Stir in the onion, carrots, garlic, and minced chiles and cook, stirring often, until the onions are tender, about 5 minutes.

> Add the tomatoes and allspice and cook for 1 minute. Stir in the stock, thyme, and salt and simmer, half-covered, until the ingredients are fully infused and the sauce is rich and thick, at least 30 minutes.

> If you want to add other vegetables to make this an entrée, add them now and simmer until cooked through.

> Season with additional salt if needed. Add the long-leaf cilantro and scallions. Serve hot.

> If storing, cover and refrigerate for up to 5 days or freeze for up to 6 months.

1 cup Vegetable Stock (page 106,
or see the table on page 108),
Really Good Chicken Stock
(page 114), Brown Bone Stock
(page 117), or water

2 sprigs fresh thyme or ½ teaspoon
dried thyme

1 teaspoon kosher salt, or to taste

3 or 4 leaves long-leaf cilantro
(also known as recao, culantro,
chado beni, or ngo gai),
chopped, or 3 to 4 sprigs fresh
cilantro

3 tablespoons sliced scallions
(white and green parts)

JAPANESE CURRY SAUCE, TWO WAYS

Japanese curry is a lot like gravy. It is smooth, comforting, and good slathered over almost anything: chicken, meat, shrimp, vegetables, even noodles. It can also be served like a stew by adding chunks of potatoes and carrots. It is a very popular family dish in Japan, and there are curry restaurants that ladle the sauce over many different food combinations. I have included two different recipes here. The first is a traditional roux-thickened version made with chicken stock. In the interest of illustrating how recipes can be adapted for modern tastes, I also created a vegan sauce thickened with kudzu root. It is certainly not traditional, but it's always good to have a few recipes for comforting sauces with no fat, no gluten, and no animal proteins for guests with special diets.

I often use apple juice in place of stock because I really like the combination of apples and curry. S&B brand curry powder will add the most authentic flavor. It is available in small cans in the Asian food section of many supermarkets.

TRADITIONAL JAPANESE CURRY SAUCE

YIELD: 2 CUPS

2 tablespoons vegetable oil

2 tablespoons all-purpose flour

1½ tablespoons curry powder (preferably S&B brand)

2 cups Really Good Chicken Stock (page 114), Vegetable Stock (page 106, or see the table on page 108), or Quick Shrimp Shell Stock (page 120), heated

1 teaspoon kosher salt, or to taste

1 teaspoon sugar (optional)

> Heat the oil in a saucepan. Remove the pan from the heat, stir in the flour until a smooth paste forms, then return the pan to the heat and cook, stirring, until the flour has a mild, toasty aroma, about 2 minutes. Stir in the curry powder and cook for about 15 seconds. Whisk in the stock, season with salt, and sugar, if using, bring to a boil over high heat. Reduce the heat and simmer, stirring often, until the sauce is the consistency of gravy and the flavors have infused, about 10 minutes.

> If you are using the sauce as a stew base, add any additional ingredients and simmer until they are cooked through. Season with additional salt and sugar to taste and serve.

> If storing, cover and refrigerate for up to 3 days.

KUDZU-THICKENED VEGAN JAPANESE CURRY SAUCE

YIELD: 2 CUPS

1½ tablespoons curry powder (preferably S&B brand)

4 teaspoons kudzu nuggets or 1 tablespoon kudzu powder

1 cup cold Vegetable Stock (page 106, or see the table on page 108)

1 cup apple juice (or use all stock if you prefer)

1 teaspoon kosher salt, or to taste

> Stir together the curry powder and kudzu in a small bowl. Stir in ¼ cup of the cold vegetable stock until smooth.

> Bring the remaining ¾ cup stock and the apple juice to a boil in a medium saucepan. Pour the curry and kudzu mixture into the boiling stock and stir well. Add the salt and simmer for about 5 minutes, until the sauce is thick and the flavors have infused.

> If you are using the sauce as a stew base, add any additional ingredients and simmer until they are cooked through. Season with additional salt to taste if necessary and serve.

> If storing, cover and refrigerate for up to 3 days. The chilled sauce will have an odd texture, but that will melt away when it is reheated.

LENTIL AND TAMARIND CURRY SAUCE

One of my all-time favorite curries is sambar. It is a thin, soup-like, spicy lentil curry that is a South Indian staple. Many authentic recipes call for twenty or more exotic ingredients. This is a very simple homage to the real deal. A ladleful over rice with maybe a little salty pickle or papadum alongside is all the food you need . . . ever. Sambar is also good served in a cup alongside the fermented-batter breads *dosa* and *idli*.

Toor dal are soft, yellow legumes sometimes called yellow pigeon peas. They are available at specialty markets. To add a bit more authentic flavor to this recipe, crush two or three peppercorn-sized nuggets of asafoetida and sizzle it in the hot oil with the chiles.

The flavor of this sauce will improve overnight, so make it a day ahead if you have the time.

YIELD: 3 CUPS

½ cup red lentils, toor dal (yellow pigeon peas), or yellow split peas

2 tablespoons coconut oil or vegetable oil

1 teaspoon black mustard seeds

1 teaspoon cumin seeds

1 or 2 dried hot red chiles, such as long Indian chiles or chiles de árbol (or substitute ½ teaspoon red chile flakes)

⅓ cup minced red onion or shallots

½ teaspoon ground coriander

¼ teaspoon ground turmeric

½ cup Tamarind Water (page 91)

> Cook the lentils in plenty of simmering water until very soft, about 25 minutes.

> Drain the lentils well and mash them with a fork to a thick paste. The mixture shouldn't be perfectly smooth—a few recognizable pieces of legume are fine. Set aside.

> Heat a large saucepan over medium-high heat. Add the coconut oil, stir in the mustard seeds, cumin seeds, and whole chiles, and cook until the mustard seeds pop and crackle, about 1 minute. Reduce the heat to medium, add the onion, and sauté until very tender and golden brown, 3 to 4 minutes. Stir in the coriander and turmeric and cook for a few seconds more.

> Add the mashed lentils, tamarind water, and stock and simmer until the sauce is slightly thickened and the flavors have married, 20 to 30 minutes. Discard the chiles

1 cup Vegetable Stock (page 106, or see the table on page 108)

1½ teaspoons kosher salt

> If you want to add additional vegetables, like carrots, cauliflower, potatoes, okra, or peppers, add them now and simmer them until tender. Serve warm.

> If storing, cover and refrigerate for up to 5 days or freeze for up to 6 months.

EASY ONIONLESS TOMATO AND APPLE CURRY SAUCE

My friend Susan is burdened with several medical issues that are linked to food. In addition to being gluten-intolerant, she is allergic to sulfites, so she has to avoid onions, garlic, shallots, leeks, and almost anything derived from corn. As a result, her sauce choices are limited. I threw this recipe together when Susan and her curry-loving husband, Wayt, came to dinner. It was a thrill to see her enjoying flavors that she had long missed.

Because of her food sensitivities, I also made my own curry powder, but a good commercial blend works fine. This sauce is particularly good simmered with florets of cauliflower.

YIELD: 2½ CUPS

2 tablespoons olive oil or ghee (see page 394)

1 tablespoon minced fresh ginger

2 tablespoons hot curry powder

One 14½ oz/411 g can diced tomatoes

1 cup diced peeled apple (1 medium apple)

1 cup apple juice

½ teaspoon kosher salt, or to taste

> Heat a medium saucepan over medium heat. Add the oil, then add the ginger and sauté until tender and aromatic, about 2 minutes. Stir in the curry powder and cook for 15 seconds. Add the tomatoes and simmer until the liquid has reduced by about half, 3 to 4 minutes.

> Stir in the apple, apple juice, and salt, half-cover the pot, and simmer, stirring occasionally, until the apples are tender, about 12 minutes.

> Use an immersion blender or food processor to coarsely puree the sauce. The finished texture should be more like marinara than applesauce. Thin with water or additional apple juice if necessary and add salt to taste.

> Serve hot.

> If storing, cover and refrigerate for up to 5 days or freeze for up to 3 months.

TIPS
for Creating Your Own Curry Sauces

- All-purpose curry powders are usually a mix of turmeric, cumin, coriander, varying levels of heat from chiles, and a few sweet spices like cloves and cinnamon. Madras-style curry powders and S&B Japanese curry powders are pretty good blends that aren't hard to find.

- Because spices are dried, not cooked, it is prudent to take a moment to toast or sizzle them for a few seconds before you add more ingredients. This will help to mellow and deepen their flavors, turning the raw sharpness into a more rounded complexity. Be careful that ground spices don't burn.

- Curry pastes are made with fresh ingredients like chiles and herbs in addition to dried spices. These also benefit from a bit of cooking before the liquid ingredients are added.

- Curries tend to derive their texture from a mix of ingredients and techniques, not one single method. Some Indian curries call for aromatic foundation ingredients like onions, ginger, and garlic, and sometimes chiles and tomatoes, to be pureed into a paste before they are sautéed. Raw nuts like cashews and almonds are soaked and then blended. Coconut cream is reduced until it thickens. Legumes are ground into flours to add flavor and texture.

- Curries don't have to be perfectly emulsified. That doesn't mean that it's okay if a curry looks greasy or curd-like, but pools of colorful spiced oil dotting the surface of the sauce are not unwelcome. "Cook until the oil shows" is a common instruction. The pools can indicate that a free-flowing well-spiced oil flavors the entire dish.

- Curries will be slightly tamed by starchy accompaniments like plain rice or flatbreads. Underseasoned and underspiced curries that tasted all right in the pot will seem bland on the plate.

SALSAS, RELISHES, AND FRESH CHOPPED SAUCES

auces made from minced or chopped fresh seasonal ingredients add zest and life to almost any plate. The only limitation may be your imagination. "Salsa" can be an umbrella term that describes sauces that are raw or cooked, mild or spicy, chopped, diced, or coarsely pureed. In the United States, salsa is usually the spicy, slightly chunky tomato mixture that overtook ketchup as our national condiment back in the early 1990s, but it is more accurately defined as the word for sauce in Spanish and Italian. If I were pressed for a contemporary definition, I would describe salsa as a fresh-tasting sauce with a savory element like onions or chile. Relishes tend to be slightly more erudite mixtures that are sometimes complexly spiced or sweetened. And when I can't quite figure out what to call a mix of fresh ingredients, I just call it sauce. Few people worry about semantics when their mouths are full.

After flavor, I think the most important consideration in a fresh salsa, relish, or chopped sauce is cohesion. The mixture must be a united community of ingredients rather than a bunch of stuff awkwardly clustered as if at a middle-school dance. I vividly remember being reprimanded by a director at my cooking school because my composed salad "fell apart into unappetizing lumps on the plate." It made me acutely aware of not just how ingredients look, but how they might transfer to the plate, fork, and mouth. Cohesion in a fresh chopped sauce can come from texture, shape, and moisture content. Flavor and seasoning intensity will also help turn a basic mélange of chopped ingredients into a recognizable sauce.

HOW SALT CAN MAKE FRESH INGREDIENTS SAUCY

Salt craves water. It draws water from whatever source it can, even through cell membranes. That's why when you salt a fruit or vegetable, it will gradually become soft or flabby, resting in a salty pool of its own juices. Cells that were once tight, crunchy water balloons have seeped water and lost their explosiveness. That can be a good thing when making salsas. Drawing the water out of fresh fruits and vegetables can create a natural briny juiciness that becomes part of the sauce. The slightly more flexible texture of the fresh ingredients can help them become better integrated. Unless sodium is a concern, salt your salsas generously. The more contact the salt has with the ingredients, the more quickly the water will be drawn out. A very chunky salsa will take longer to get saucy from salt than a finely chopped or pureed preparation. The more moisture the ingredients have, the juicier the salsa will be. You may need to let some salsas rest for quite a while before serving them. It can take several hours, or even overnight, for a dry mixture like the White Cabbage Pico de Gallo (page 236) to become tender and saucy without added liquid.

WHITE CABBAGE PICO DE GALLO

I tend to forget about this salsa until I'm at a restaurant and a bowl of it appears before me with a big basket of chips. I instantly do the hungry-person-at-a-Tex-Mex-restaurant thing and wolf down so many chips that I have little room for dinner. The last time I found myself scraping desperately at the empty bowl, I decided to start making it at home. It's easy, cheap, and keeps really well. Serve some alongside a more traditional tomato salsa, and you may be surprised by which bowl empties the fastest. Chop the pieces quite small, about the size of a lentil or pea, so the mix can be easily scooped up with chips. It's also great on fish tacos.

YIELD: 2½ CUPS

1½ cups minced white cabbage

1 cup minced tomato

½ cup minced yellow onion

1 jalapeño or serrano chile, seeded and minced, or to taste

2 tablespoons chopped fresh cilantro

1 tablespoon freshly squeezed lime juice

½ to ¾ teaspoon kosher salt

Pinch of sugar (optional)

About ⅓ cup tomato or mixed vegetable juice (optional)

> Stir together all of the ingredients except the optional juice in a bowl. Add the juice if you need to serve the salsa right away, or leave the salsa to soften for at least 4 hours at room temperature, and as long as overnight in the refrigerator.

> If storing, cover and refrigerate for up to 3 days.

GRILLED ARTICHOKE SALSA

In Moss Landing, California, you can paddle a kayak beside sea otters or meander through the beautiful Elkhorn Slough Reserve with a pair of binoculars at the ready for spotting members of the vast bird community. It has become one of our favorite stops on road trips through California. Last time we were there, it was April and the artichoke fields were in their prime. I had my first taste of artichoke salsa served warm atop a pile of tortilla chips. That version was a bit rough around the edges, so I created my own. Use it in *chilaquiles*, on tacos, or as a sauce over tamales.

I love the taste of the grilled artichokes and onions, but plain steamed artichokes, and even canned artichoke bottoms will work.

YIELD: 3 CUPS

2 globe artichokes

1 medium yellow onion

3 tablespoons olive oil

2 cloves garlic, chopped

2 cups diced fresh tomatoes or one (14.5 oz/114 g) can diced tomatoes

1 canned chipotle pepper in adobo, minced

1 teaspoon kosher salt, or to taste

2 tablespoons chopped fresh cilantro (optional)

> Steam, boil, or pressure-cook the artichokes until they are just tender: this will take about 25 minutes in a steamer or boiling water or about 10 minutes in a pressure cooker. Drain the artichokes and set aside until they are cool enough to handle.

> Cut the artichokes in half from stem to tip. Scoop out and discard the bristly chokes. Remove and discard the tough outer leaves (or enjoy the more tender ones dipped in melted butter). Trim and peel the stems. You will have 4 artichoke halves with the chokes removed, stems that are tender enough to eat, and enough leaves to help pick up some charred grilled flavor as they brown.

> Prepare a bed of hot coals in a charcoal grill or preheat a gas grill to high. Lightly oil the clean grilling surface.

> Cut the onion into thick rounds. Brush the onions and artichokes lightly with some of the oil. Grill the vegetables until they are evenly charred a dark

continues

brown but still moist and tender inside, about 4 minutes. Cool until they can be comfortably handled.

> Remove and discard any remaining artichoke leaves. Chop the artichokes and onion.

> Heat a large saucepan over medium-high heat. Add the remaining oil, then add the garlic and cook until tender and aromatic but not browned, about 30 seconds. Stir in the tomatoes and cook, stirring often, until they are tender and the liquid has thickened slightly, 5 to 6 minutes. Add the chopped artichokes, onions, chipotle pepper, and salt and simmer, half-covered, until the mixture has come together as a cohesive and even sauce, about 8 minutes. Remove from the heat, add the chopped cilantro if using, and adjust the seasoning.

> Serve warm or cold.

> If storing, cover and refrigerate for up to 3 days or freeze for up to 3 months.

BUTTERNUT SQUASH AND PIQUILLO PEPPER SALSA

You don't have to use exclusively raw ingredients to make an appealing seasonal salsa or relish. Cook the squash until it is al dente—just long enough for it to lose the raw taste but still have a firm bite. This is particularly good with autumn foods like turkey, pork, and sausages. Or use it as a topping for cheese omelets or bowls of steaming farro or barley. You can also use it as a dip with thick-cut potato chips. For a more complex flavor, grill or char the scallions. This is a good place to use a top-notch olive or nut oil. Piquillo peppers are sold in jars at many supermarkets and specialty stores.

YIELD: 2 CUPS

1 cup finely diced butternut squash

¾ cup chopped piquillo peppers or roasted red peppers

½ cup sliced scallion greens

2 tablespoons extra-virgin olive oil, nut oil, or pumpkin seed oil

1 tablespoon minced canned chipotle pepper in adobo

1 clove garlic, minced or pressed

1 tablespoon apple cider vinegar

½ teaspoon kosher salt

¼ cup salted roasted pumpkin seeds (pepitas; optional)

> Put the butternut squash in a saucepan and cover with cold water. Bring the water to a boil over high heat and simmer just until the squash loses its hard raw quality but is still firm, about 2 minutes. Drain in a sieve and rinse under cold water to stop the cooking.

> Stir together the blanched squash, piquillo peppers, scallions, oil, chipotle, garlic, vinegar, and salt in a bowl. The flavor will improve as the salsa sits. Stir in the pepitas just before serving for added crunch.

> If storing, cover and refrigerate for up to 3 days.

FRESH PEAR, CRANBERRY, AND KUMQUAT RELISH

Use this as a crunchy alternative to a standard holiday cranberry sauce. It can also be tossed into a spinach salad, warmed as part of a pan sauce, even spooned onto crackers and ripe cheese as an appetizer or savory finish to a meal. If kumquats are unavailable, substitute 2 teaspoons finely chopped orange zest.

YIELD: 2 CUPS

1½ cups diced peeled pear, such as Bosc or Red Bartlett

¾ cup coarsely chopped fresh cranberries

4 or 5 kumquats, halved, seeded, and chopped

3 tablespoons minced candied ginger

3 tablespoons orange juice or cranberry juice

1 tablespoon sugar

Pinch of kosher salt

> Stir together all of the ingredients in a bowl. Cover and leave to rest until ready to serve. The relish become softer and juicier as it rests; it can even be made the night before and refrigerated, but the pears will start to discolor.

LAST-MINUTE CHERRY TOMATO AND OLIVE-BAR ANTIPASTO RELISH

Everyone needs at least one go-to recipe that can be thrown together at the very last minute. It seems like every supermarket has an olive bar these days, and that is very handy when time is precious. Each one will have a different assortment of ingredients, but there are few olive-bar components that don't work well with tomatoes: select whatever seems appealing, chop it up, and stir it together with an equal quantity of halved or quartered cherry tomatoes. The saucy mix can be scooped up with pita chips or served as a condiment alongside sliced meats or cheeses, rotisserie chicken, or frittatas. Warm it and toss with fresh pasta. If you like, stir in some chopped basil at the end for additional freshness and perfume.

YIELD: 1½ CUPS

1 cup assorted items from a grocery or specialty store olive-bar, such as assorted brined and stuffed olives, roasted peppers, peperoncini or Peppadew peppers, marinated artichoke hearts, pickled onions, roasted garlic, capers, and/or pickled mushrooms

1 cup (about 6 oz/170 g) cherry tomatoes, halved or quartered

2 tablespoons extra-virgin olive oil

> Pit any olives that still have stones. Chop the olive-bar ingredients.

> Stir them and the tomatoes together with the olive oil. Leave the salsa to infuse while you prepare whatever else you might be serving it with.

> Serve at room temperature.

PEAK-OF-SUMMER
RAW TOMATO–BASIL SAUCE

During those brief few weeks in late summer when the tomatoes finally ripen in Seattle, we eat them at practically every meal. This is one of our favorites, especially when it is tossed with home-made pasta. If the tomato skins are tough, take the time to peel them before slicing (see Tomato Concassé, page 243). Use a mix of whatever tomatoes happen to be on hand. Prepare the sauce before putting the pasta water on, and the salt and natural enzymes will make the mix juicier and more aromatic.

YIELD: 3⅓ CUPS, ENOUGH TO THOROUGHLY COAT 1 LB/450G FRESH PASTA

1 lb/450 g ripe tomatoes, chopped, or, for very small tomatoes, simply halved

1½ teaspoons kosher salt

3 or 4 cloves garlic, minced

½ cup extra-virgin olive oil, or to taste

¼ cup lightly packed torn fresh basil leave

Freshly ground black pepper

> Toss the tomatoes with the salt in a bowl and leave them to rest while you prepare the remaining ingredients.

> Stir the garlic into the tomatoes and moisten with the olive oil.

> Just before serving, toss the tomato mixture with the basil and plenty of black pepper.

> Serve at room temperature.

TOMATO CONCASSÉ—PEELED, SEEDED, AND DICED TOMATOES

Tomato skins and seeds may not seem nefarious, but few tomato sauces are enhanced by random curled bits of tough tomato skin or dots of slippery seeds. I'm not an especially delicate person, but once you get accustomed to the refinement of a well-prepared tomato sauce, the alternative can seem almost unbearably coarse. *Concassé* is the term chefs use for peeled, seeded, and diced tomatoes.

To peel and seed tomatoes, bring a pot of water to a boil. There must be at least enough water to thoroughly cover one or two tomatoes. Set a bowl of ice water next to the stove. Remove the cores from the tomatoes. This is easy to do with sharp paring knife, but if you are coring a lot of tomatoes, consider buying a great little tool that chefs call a "tomato shark": it is a small concave spoon with wicked serrated teeth that will scoop out cores with a simple flick of the wrist. After the cores have been removed, make an X in the skin at the other end of each tomato.

Drop a tomato or two into the boiling water and give them a gentle stir. Lift them out after about 5 seconds and plunge into the ice water bath. The exterior of the tomatoes should cook just enough so the skin slides off but not so much that the flesh of the tomato is much altered. The riper the tomato, the more quickly the skin will loosen. If the skin is reluctant to come off a tomato, blanch it for 5 seconds more. When you have bright red tomatoes that just won't release their skins, you are experiencing the tragedy of off-season tomatoes; color is not the indicator of ripeness it once was. Repeat with any remaining tomatoes.

Lift the tomatoes from the ice water and peel off the skins. The tabs from the Xs you cut will help with this. Cut the tomatoes in half and gently squeeze and nudge the seeds out. The jelly that holds the seeds is a gelatinous membrane, often called the placenta, and it has more tomato flavor than any other part of the fruit—save as much as you can. If you like, you can collect the seeds and jelly in a sieve, press the juice through, and discard the dry seeds. Dice the tomatoes.

Tomato concassé can theoretically be stored for a day or two, but tomatoes are never enhanced by refrigeration.

SEASONAL SALSA, RELISH, AND FRESH CHOPPED SAUCE IDEAS

The sky's the limit when it comes to mixing and matching fresh seasonal ingredients. Here are just a few of the spontaneous salsas I've enjoyed. Remember that the salt will draw out the natural moisture and make dense ingredients more flexible, but it takes time. If you want a saucy dish in a hurry, add a little oil or flavorful liquid. If your salsa seems too wet, simply pour off some of the liquid.

Pico de Gallo	Stir together 2 cups minced tomatoes, ½ cup minced yellow onion, 1 minced jalapeño or serrano chile, 2 tablespoons chopped fresh cilantro, 1 tablespoon freshly squeezed lime juice, and plenty of kosher salt.
Charred Tomatoes with Hatch Green Chiles	Char 3 medium tomatoes on a hot grill, directly on a burner, or with a blowtorch. Core and chop. Stir the juicy tomatoes and charred bits of skin with ½ cup diced roasted Hatch or similar New Mexican or Anaheim green chiles, ½ cup minced yellow onion, 2 tablespoons freshly squeezed lime juice, ¼ teaspoon chile powder, such as cayenne or chipotle, ¼ teaspoon ground cumin, and plenty of kosher salt.
Tomato, Corn, and Pickled Jalapeños	Stir together 1½ cups diced tomatoes, ½ cup blanched fresh or thawed frozen corn kernels, ⅓ cup minced yellow onion, and ¼ cup minced canned jalapeños in escabeche (mince and add some of the pickled onions and carrots too if you like). Add kosher salt and a few dashes of pepper sauce like Tapatío or Tabasco, to taste.
Carrot Habanero	Stir together 2 cups very finely minced carrots with ½ cup minced red bell pepper, ¼ cup minced yellow onion, 2 tablespoons chopped fresh cilantro, ½ teaspoon kosher salt, and 1 finely minced habanero chile. Leave to infuse for at least 4 hours so the carrots soften and the salsa gets juicy.
Mild Jicama, Orange, and Tomato	Stir together 1 cup diced jicama, 1 cup diced tomatoes, ½ cup chopped orange segments, all membranes removed, 2 tablespoons sliced scallions, ½ teaspoon kosher salt, and ¼ teaspoon finely grated orange zest. Add 1 tablespoon freshly squeezed lime juice and a pinch of chile powder for more zing if you like.

Spicy Pineapple	Stir together 1½ cups finely chopped fresh pineapple, ½ cup minced red onion, ½ cup sliced scallions, 1 minced jalapeño or habanero pepper, 1 minced red serrano or Fresno pepper, 2 tablespoons chopped fresh cilantro, and ½ teaspoon kosher salt.
Mango and Peppadew Peppers	Stir together 1½ cups diced fresh mango (about 1 large), ¼ cup chopped Peppadew peppers (4 to 6 peppers), 3 tablespoons sliced scallions, 2 tablespoons freshly squeezed lime juice, 1 tablespoon minced pimentos or roasted red peppers, ¼ teaspoon cayenne, ancho, or chipotle chile powder, and ¼ teaspoon kosher salt.
Green Mango, Pear, Chile, and Thai Basil	Stir together 1 cup finely julienned peeled unripe (green) mango, ½ cup finely julienned peeled Asian pear, 1 tablespoon freshly squeezed lime juice, 1 tablespoon grated palm sugar or granulated sugar, ½ teaspoon kosher salt, 1 tablespoon very thinly sliced or julienned red jalapeño, serrano or Fresno chile pepper, and (optional) 1 teaspoon fish sauce. Leave to infuse for at least 30 minutes. Stir in 2 tablespoons finely sliced fresh Thai basil leaves before serving.
Apricot Fennel	Stir together 1½ cups diced apricots, ½ cup minced fennel, 2 tablespoons minced sweet onion, such as Walla Walla Sweet, 1 tablespoon sherry vinegar or freshly squeezed lemon juice, 1 tablespoon honey, ¼ teaspoon kosher salt, and freshly ground black pepper to taste.
Quick Diced Guacamole	Gently stir 2 diced ripe but firm avocados (about 2 cups) together with ¼ cup minced tomato, 2 tablespoons minced yellow onion, 1 tablespoon chopped fresh cilantro (optional), 1 tablespoon freshly squeezed lime juice, plenty of kosher salt, and a good dash of pepper sauce, like Tapatío or Cholula. (Mash with a fork if you prefer a more traditional texture.)
Cucumber and Sweet Onion	Stir together 1 cup diced English (hothouse) or Persian cucumber, 1 cup diced sweet onion, such as Walla Walla Sweet, 2 tablespoons unseasoned rice vinegar, 1 teaspoon yellow mustard seeds, 1 teaspoon fish sauce (optional), kosher salt to taste, and plenty of freshly ground black pepper.

continues

TURNING WHOLE FOODS INTO SAUCES WITHOUT ADDING THICKENERS

Grated Summer Squash and Herb	Stir together 2 cups grated zucchini and/or crookneck squash, 1 tablespoon chopped fresh oregano, 1 tablespoon chopped fresh basil, 1 tablespoon chopped fresh parsley, 1 minced or pressed garlic clove, 1 teaspoon finely grated lemon zest, ½ teaspoon kosher salt, plenty of freshly ground black pepper, and a pinch of cayenne or Aleppo chile powder. If desired, add 1 to 2 tablespoons extra virgin olive oil just before serving.
Raw Kohlrabi, Kale, and Mushroom	Stir together 1 cup minced peeled kohlrabi, 1 cup finely chopped kale, 1 cup chopped or diced button or cremini mushrooms, 2 tablespoons olive oil (optional), 2 minced garlic cloves, 1 tablespoon freshly squeezed lemon juice, ½ teaspoon kosher salt, and plenty of freshly ground black pepper. Leave to soften and infuse for at least 2 hours.
Kimchee and Scallion	Stir together 1 cup chopped cabbage kimchee, with its juices, ½ cup sliced scallions, ½ cup minced daikon radish, and 1 teaspoon sesame oil.
Garlic Scape and Radish	Stir together ⅓ cup sliced garlic scapes, 2 cups minced red radishes, 1 tablespoon freshly squeezed lemon juice, 1 tablespoon minced fresh basil, ½ teaspoon kosher salt, and plenty of black pepper. Leave to infuse for at least 2 hours. Finish with a few drops of truffle oil, if desired. For a milder flavor, blanch the garlic scapes.
Pea, Baby Turnip, and Chive	Stir together 1 cup blanched fresh or thawed frozen green peas, ½ cup minced baby turnips, 3 tablespoons minced fresh chives, 2 tablespoons olive oil or walnut oil, 1 teaspoon finely grated lemon zest, ¼ teaspoon kosher salt, and plenty of freshly ground black pepper.
Asparagus and Hearts of Palm	Stir together 1 cup thinly sliced raw asparagus, ½ cup chopped hearts of palm, 2 tablespoons minced shallots, 1 tablespoon minced pickled jalapeños, and ¼ teaspoon kosher salt. Leave to infuse for at least 2 hours. For added brightness, season with a bit of the pickling brine from the peppers or a squeeze of lemon.

TIPS
for Creating Your Own Salsas, Relishes, and Fresh Chopped Sauces

- Ingredients of similar size and shape will knit together better, so take extra care in chopping and dicing. Diced tomatoes will toss best with diced mango. Julienned carrots tangle better with scallion greens sliced into long threads.

- Serve fresh raw sauces chilled or at room temperature, not icy cold. Aromatics will vaporize and enzymes will become more active at room temperature.

- Some salsas and relishes can be served warm.

- There is no reason why every ingredient must be fresh or raw. Mix in lightly cooked, pickled, or preserved ingredients.

- Olive bars and salad bars can be handy resources when you want a small quantity of something or are pinched for time.

- Finely mince very intense ingredients so they will be evenly integrated and distributed. Fresh habaneros are more palatable if they are small enough to deliver tiny bursts of heat throughout the sauce rather than one or two mouth-numbing surprises.

- Consistency improves cohesion, but contrast adds interest. Add a scattering of crunchy tidbits to soft salsas or something slightly chewy or slick to crisp mixtures.

- Consistency will change as a sauce matures. Consider each evolution as different, not better or worse.

- Remember that these are sauces, not salads—season them boldly.

SAUCE ON
THE SIDE

This seems like a good place to address the store-bought, ready-made sauce issue. There are more commercial sauce options every day. They are right there, looming from the store shelves while you pick out your pasta or lettuce. Some of them taste pretty great. So you might need another reminder of why you should make sauces when you can just buy them.

I think people should cook more. I think food tastes best when it starts with fresh ingredients and is enjoyed with people you care about. But I'm also a realist. I have a stash of backup sauces myself. My husband is brilliant at doctoring up a jar of simple tomato-basil pasta sauce, but if all he sees in the cupboard are onions, garlic, and canned tomatoes, he's more likely to call for a pizza than cook dinner from scratch. I'd be crazy not to keep jars of pasta sauce on hand.

I don't make my own mustard. I've tried several times, but my attempts have never been an improvement over the jarred stuff. I don't use a lot of mayo, so I'm certainly not going to make a batch every time I want a sandwich.

But you *can* make most sauces, and when you do, you will be pleased with your accomplishment. I can't even tell you how impressed guests are when you pull out a jar of your own homemade ketchup while the burgers are sizzling on the grill. The same is true for salad dressings, barbecue sauces, and fiery-hot chile blends.

Yes, you can buy all of these sauces, but when you feel inspired to try making them from scratch, you will be surprised not just by how easy they are, but by how much better they taste.

DRESSINGS

Anything that coats or tops foods is, in theory, dressing it. Vinaigrettes and creamy dressings are common, but you can also dress foods with thin tangy purees, reductions, and even syrups. They should all have intensity, a certain acidic brightness, and a consistency that will cover foods thinly and evenly.

SIMPLE EMULSIONS—GETTING OIL AND VINEGAR TO PLAY NICE

Oil and water molecules are fundamentally different. Water molecules are small, fast-moving, and magnetic. They are attracted to other molecules that have a similar polar nature. Oil molecules are long slow chains and are drawn to similar long molecules that lack a polar charge. Oil and water will never bond, but they can mingle as interspersed droplets, and when they do, the mixture is called an emulsion.

The science of emulsion is extremely complicated. I won't even pretend to understand all the intricacies and specifics, so let's stick with stirring oil and vinegar together. What I do understand about emulsions is that they have both continuous and dispersed phases: The continuous phase is the base. The dispersed phase is the distributed droplets held within that base. The volume of the dispersed phase can actually be larger than the continuous phase. Homemade sauces usually

have a continuous phase of water and a dispersed phase of oil, even when the quantity of oil is much greater than the water. This explains why it is easier to pull together a dressing when you gradually whisk or blend the oil into the vinegar rather than the other way around.

When blended oil or vinegar droplets find their own kind, they cling together. The bigger the drops become, the faster they collect others, and soon your vinaigrette has separated again. Mixtures that are very well blended have smaller droplets, so they take longer to separate. Vinaigrettes made in a blender are more stable than those just given a shake in the bottle or stirred together with a fork, because the droplets are smaller and better dispersed.

In addition to changing the size and distribution of the droplets, you can better control how quickly the oil and water molecules segregate by introducing an emulsifier. When I was working on this chapter, my sister voiced a concern. She reminded me that as a mother she tries to avoid buying foods with additives like stabilizers and emulsifiers. This made me laugh. I assured her that while some emulsifiers are made in labs by food manufacturers, not all are. My favorites are made by chickens and cows. Egg yolks are rich with lecithin, a wonderful natural emulsifier. Milk and cream are natural emulsions made stable with the protein casein.

I think of emulsifiers as ambassadors or mediators. They can attach comfortably to both partisans and help oil and water get along. When you add egg yolks to the vinegar and flavorings and then gradually add the oil, a vinaigrette can become as stable as mayonnaise. Caesar salad dressing is essentially a vinaigrette that has been enriched and stabilized with the naturally emulsifying properties of eggs.

1:3 VINAIGRETTE

Vinaigrette, while often overlooked as sauce, is actually so important that the recipe is sometimes listed alongside or in place of hollandaise among the mother sauces (see page 315). Vinaigrettes are most often made with a ratio of 1 part acid to 3 parts oil. They are easily whisked together at the last minute, but the flavors will continue to infuse and mellow overnight. If you avoid very perishable ingredients like fresh herbs, they will hold for a couple of weeks. That means that any salad dressings stored in your fridge should be your own.

Vinaigrettes don't always need to be paired with lettuce. They make great marinades. I often toss ingredients destined for the grill in a simple vinaigrette to both add flavor and prevent the food from sticking. If you do this, don't use vinaigrettes made with very good oils, as the flavor will be destroyed by the high heat. Many of the ingredients in this recipe are listed as optional because vinaigrette can be made with just vinegar or lemon juice, oil, salt, and pepper.

YIELD: 1 CUP

1 tablespoon finely minced shallot

1 small clove garlic, finely minced or pressed (optional)

½ teaspoon kosher salt, or to taste

½ teaspoon Dijon mustard or ¼ teaspoon dry mustard (optional)

Freshly ground black pepper

¼ cup freshly squeezed lemon juice or vinegar, such as red wine vinegar

¾ cup oil, such as olive or grape seed

> Stir together the shallot, garlic, if using, salt, mustard, if using, and plenty of pepper in a small bowl. Add the lemon juice and whisk to mix. Continue to whisk the base while gradually adding the oil in a thin stream. Taste for seasoning and adjust it to suit your dish.

> Alternatively, to make the vinaigrette in a blender or food processor, combine the shallot, garlic, salt, mustard, plenty of pepper, and the lemon juice in the jar or bowl and blend to mix. Gradually add the oil in a thin stream. Taste and adjust the seasoning. This will remain emulsified for longer than a hand-whisked dressing.

> If the vinaigrette separates, whisk or blend it again before serving.

> If storing, cover and refrigerate for up to 2 weeks.

WAYS TO CUSTOMIZE
1:3 VINAIGRETTE

The variations in the table below are all adaptations of the 1:3 Vinaigrette (page 255). They are examples of how a dressing can be customized by simply mixing and matching oils and vinegars and maybe adding a few stir-ins. I regularly scrabble through the cupboards and fridge and make dressing out of whatever strikes my fancy, but I am always starting with a 1:3 base. Since contemporary cooks have so many more options than just lemon juice, wine vinegar, and olive oil, though, the ratio can be fudged a bit. There are aged balsamic vinegars so smooth that they are labeled "drinking vinegar" and oils that are kept under lock and key at my local gourmet store. Start with the basic ratio and adjust it as you become more familiar with your ingredients.

Balsamic Rosemary	Use balsamic vinegar and olive oil. Add a pinch of red chile flakes. Stir ½ teaspoon chopped fresh rosemary into the finished dressing.
Honey Mustard	Use lemon juice, white wine vinegar, or unseasoned rice vinegar and a light oil, such as canola or light olive oil. Use Dijon, whole-grain, or spicy brown mustard and increase the amount to 3 tablespoons. Add 2 tablespoons honey and a pinch of cayenne.
Rice Vinegar, Scallion, and Sesame	Use unseasoned rice vinegar and canola, peanut, or vegetable oil. Substitute thinly sliced scallions for the shallot. Use dry mustard. Add ½ teaspoon minced or grated fresh ginger and ½ teaspoon sesame oil. Add a drop of honey or sugar for a sweeter dressing. Stir in a teaspoon of toasted sesame seeds if desired.
Roasted Red Pepper	Add ⅓ cup chopped roasted red peppers and ¼ teaspoon smoked paprika and puree until smooth.
Beet	Use apple cider vinegar. Add ½ cup grated or chopped cooked or pickled beets and a teaspoon of brown sugar. Puree until smooth.
Parmesan	Use extra-virgin olive oil. Add ¼ cup finely grated Parmesan or similar dry aged cheese, a pinch of cayenne, and (optional) ¼ teaspoon dried oregano.

Feta	Use lemon juice and extra-virgin olive oil. Double the garlic. Omit the mustard. Add ¼ cup (1 oz/28 g) crumbled feta cheese and ½ teaspoon dried oregano.
Taco	Use lime juice or white wine vinegar and a relatively flavorless oil, like canola or corn oil. Omit the mustard, salt, and pepper. Add 1 tablespoon taco seasoning. Taste and adjust with more salt, pepper, and/or seasoning mix if necessary. Blend with 2 teaspoons of tomato paste if desired.
Steak Sauce	Use red wine vinegar or balsamic vinegar. Increase the mustard to 1 tablespoon; use spicy brown or whole-grain mustard, if you prefer. Add 2 tablespoons of your favorite steak sauce and a good dash of Worcestershire. If desired, add 1 to 2 tablespoons caramelized onions or shallots for more texture.
Provençal	Use red wine vinegar and extra-virgin olive oil. Add 1 teaspoon tomato paste and 2 mashed anchovies while blending. Stir 2 tablespoons chopped capers and ½ teaspoon herbes de Provence into the finished dressing.
Pesto or Green Sauce	Use lemon juice or white wine vinegar. Omit the shallot, garlic, and mustard. Stir in 3 tablespoons Pesto (page 194, or see the table on page 196), Power Pesto (page 198), Hara Masala (page 206), or Mint Chutney (page 202).
Sherry, Orange, and Almond	Use sherry vinegar and extra-virgin olive oil. Blend in 2 tablespoons almond butter, 1 tablespoon frozen orange juice concentrate, ¼ teaspoon smoked paprika. Add ½ teaspoon finely grated orange zest if desired.
Apple, Walnut, and Thyme	Use apple cider vinegar and canola or grape seed oil. Substitute walnut oil for 2 tablespoons of the oil for more flavor. Add 2 tablespoons finely chopped walnuts, 1 tablespoon brown sugar, barley syrup, or frozen apple juice concentrate, ¼ teaspoon minced fresh thyme or a pinch of crumbled dried thyme, and a pinch of cayenne.

continues

Bacon	Use malt vinegar or apple cider vinegar. Increase the mustard to 2 teaspoons; use coarse or spicy brown mustard if you prefer. Stir ¼ cup finely chopped cooked bacon into the finished dressing. For the best flavor, leave to infuse for several hours in the fridge. Residual bacon fat will float to the surface and congeal when chilled; simply spoon it off and leave the dressing to warm to room temperature before using.
Lemon Tahini	Use lemon juice and extra-virgin olive oil. Add 2 tablespoons tahini, 1 teaspoon honey, and ½ teaspoon finely grated lemon zest. Blend until smooth. If desired, stir in 1 teaspoon za'atar.
Calamansi (Sweet Lime)	Use calamansi (sweet lime) juice and a very light oil, such as canola or avocado. Use chopped scallions in place of the shallot. Omit the mustard. Add 2 teaspoons grated palm sugar or honey, 1 teaspoon fish sauce, and (optional), a finely minced Thai bird chile. Frozen packets of calamansi juice are often sold in Filipino and other Asian markets.

TIPS
for Creating Original Vinaigrettes

- Start with a ratio of 1 part acid to 3 parts oil. People who prefer the taste and characteristics of oil more than acidity can use a ratio of 1:4.

- Salt really helps to balance extremes of acid and oil. I was taught that when a well-made vinaigrette tastes too much of oil, it should be fixed not with more acidity, but with more salt. It doesn't seem intuitive, but it works.

- Vary your choice of oils as well as vinegars. Sometimes a very light, thin, virtually flavorless oil is the right choice. If you don't like canola or vegetable oil, try light olive, avocado, or grape seed oil. Treat yourself now and then to a really good bottle of olive or nut oil. A tablespoon or two of toasted almond, pumpkin seed, or pistachio oil added to the dressing can make a very simple salad sing with flavor. Don't become a collector. Use the bottles up and then buy more. Store opened containers of oil in the refrigerator to maintain freshness.

- Vinaigrettes and dressings are a great way to use orphaned ingredients like the last olive, a squeeze of tomato paste, a couple of chives, or a tablespoon of leftover fruit or vegetable puree or pesto.

- Vinaigrettes should be well mixed so the flavors are evenly distributed. Use a whisk, or put all the ingredients in a sealed container and give them a good shake. Or use a blender, immersion blender, or food processor.

ADDING EMULSIFIERS— EGG YOLKS AND LIQUID SOY LECITHIN

I don't mind if my vinaigrettes separate and must be rewhisked before using, but if you find the division of oil and vinegar to be unpalatable, you can add an egg yolk to virtually any vinaigrette to make it both richer and more stable. The lecithin in egg yolks is a natural emulsifier. Although mayonnaise has a much higher oil-to-vinegar ratio than a vinaigrette, it is held stable thanks to egg yolks and their lecithin. Drop a raw or coddled egg yolk into the vinegar and aromatics and gradually blend in the oil. If you are cooking for someone with a compromised immune system, you can use a cooked egg yolk: press the cooked yolk through a fine sieve before adding it to the vinegar. The dressing won't be quite as creamy, but it will be safer. Egg whites don't have lecithin. They can add a bit of extra viscosity and lightness, but they aren't a great addition to most dressings.

If you prefer emulsified dressings, adding a bit of liquid soy lecithin is another option. It is a very thick, sticky liquid available at specialty health food stores. It is eggless and dairy-free. Liquid lecithin is oil soluble, so you need to stir it into the oil, not the vinegar. A few drops, no more than ¼ teaspoon, will turn 1 cup of 1:3 Vinaigrette (page 255) into a creamy-looking, stabilized emulsion, as long as it is thoroughly mixed. Add a tablespoon, and the vinaigrette will be so stable it can even be warmed gently without breaking. Soy lecithin is often sold in huge bottles, so share it with friends unless you make a *lot* of vinaigrettes. Powdered lecithin, an ingredient often used to make avant-garde foams, is not a substitute.

CLASSIC CAESAR SALAD DRESSING

Caesar salad dressing is an example of how the lecithin in egg yolks works as an emulsifier to keep oil and water droplets from separating. Heating, or "coddling," the whole egg gently alters its texture and flavor, removing some of the raw taste. Adding a coddled egg to most any vinaigrette will enrich the dressing and prevent it from separating.

YIELD: ABOUT 1 CUP

1 large egg

2 cloves garlic, chopped

2 salt or oil-packed anchovy fillets, soaked in water for 3 to 4 minutes and drained (or substitute 1 teaspoon anchovy paste)

¾ cup olive oil

3 tablespoons freshly squeezed lemon juice

2 or 3 dashes Worcestershire sauce

¾ teaspoon kosher salt, or to taste

Freshly ground black pepper

Pinch of cayenne pepper or dash of Tabasco sauce

> Put the egg (in the shell) in a bowl, pour boiling water over it to cover, and let it coddle for 10 minutes to lightly cook and thicken the yolk. (Please note that raw or undercooked egg yolks are a potential health hazard and should not be consumed by anyone with a compromised immune system.)

> Break the egg into a blender or food processor and add the garlic and anchovies. Turn the blender on and very gradually add the oil in a thin stream—when the dressing gets very thick, add the lemon juice to thin it, then continue to add the remaining oil. Season with the Worcestershire sauce, salt, plenty of pepper, and the cayenne.

> If storing, cover and refrigerate for up to 5 days.

SANBAIZU—THIN VINEGAR SOY DRESSING

This is sort of an all-purpose dressing from Japan. Splash it onto sliced cucumbers, cooked spinach, cold soba noodles, or anything you feel needs a quick hit of umami, salt, and acidity. It is particularly good with cold sliced octopus and scallions.

YIELD: ⅓ CUP

3 tablespoons unseasoned rice
    vinegar

1 tablespoon sugar

2 teaspoons light soy sauce

> Stir together and serve at any temperature. If storing, cover and refrigerate for up to 2 weeks.

GINGER MISO DRESSING

This is a virtually fat-free dressing with a lot of flavor and intensity. Use good fresh miso, or, if you have access to it, try shoyu koji, a live cultured soy seasoning. Mirin adds sweetness and cuts through some of the inherent saltiness of the other ingredients. Add a tablespoon of honey for an even sweeter dressing. This is great with broiled tofu or fish. It also makes a good spinach salad dressing and goes well with cold buckwheat noodles.

YIELD: ⅔ CUP

¼ cup miso (any color) or shoyu koji (see headnote)

¼ cup unseasoned rice vinegar

¼ cup water or Mock Stock, such as Carrot, Ginger Honey and Citrus, or Roasted Barley Tea (see the table on page 93).

2 tablespoons finely grated fresh ginger

2 tablespoons thinly sliced scallion greens

1 tablespoon mirin (sweet Japanese rice wine)

Freshly ground black pepper

A few drops of sesame oil (optional)

> Put the miso in a small bowl. Gradually whisk in the rice vinegar and water until smooth. Stir in the ginger, scallions, and mirin. Season with pepper to taste and the sesame oil, if using. The dressing will be very salty from the miso, so no salt should be necessary.

> Serve immediately, or cover and leave to infuse overnight in the refrigerator.

> The dressing can be refrigerated for up to 5 days.

SWEET PEANUT DRESSING

On a drive down the California coast, I stopped in San Francisco's Mission District and stumbled upon Boogaloos. It's a funky spot that specializes in breakfast with a Southwestern flair, but I was hungry for some greens and ordered the warm tofu salad. I'm so glad I did. Crunchy lettuce was topped with grated carrots, lightly sautéed red cabbage, green apples, and warm seared tofu. The whole thing was smothered with a sweet, tangy peanut dressing. On my last visit, I pestered the kitchen for a recipe, but all I got was an ingredient list. This is my re-creation. If you like it spicy, add a dollop of sambal oelek or a squeeze of sriracha (homemade, page 302, or store-bought).

YIELD: ⅓ CUP

3 tablespoons all-natural chunky peanut butter

3 tablespoons honey, or to taste

1 teaspoon finely grated fresh ginger

3 tablespoons unseasoned rice vinegar

¼ cup peanut oil or vegetable oil

A few drops of sesame oil

¼ teaspoon kosher salt, or to taste

Pinch of cayenne pepper (optional)

> Combine the peanut butter, honey, ginger, and rice vinegar in a blender and puree to a smooth paste. Gradually add the peanut oil, blending until it is completely mixed and emulsified, and then the sesame oil. Season with the salt and cayenne pepper, if using. To serve, heat gently over low heat.

> If storing, cover and refrigerate for up to 5 days.

TANGY CREAM DRESSING

Some people think a dressing isn't a dressing unless it's creamy: blue cheese, Thousand Island, buttermilk, and, of course, America's beloved ranch dressing. The balance of fat and acidity comes from tangy natural emulsions like buttermilk, sour cream, or mayonnaise, so there is little or no risk of separation. Consider this simple recipe to be a blank canvas, ripe for adaptation and experimentation. (See the table of variations on page 266.) It is quite thick, so it can be used as a dip or spread. Thin it as needed to suit your dish. The more delicate the greens, the thinner the dressing should be. Crunchy, sturdy lettuces like romaine, iceberg, and some endives can stand up to thick, creamy dressings, but tiny tender mixed greens or wisps of butter lettuce can be overpowered by a thick coating.

YIELD: 1 CUP

½ cup Mayonnaise (page 382) or Eggless Mayo (page 384)

⅓ cup sour cream or Vegan Cashew Sour Cream (page 273)

1 tablespoon freshly squeezed lemon juice or vinegar

1 small clove garlic, minced or pressed (optional)

½ teaspoon kosher salt

Freshly ground black pepper

Pinch of cayenne or dash of Tabasco sauce

1 to 2 tablespoons milk, buttermilk, or nondairy milk, or as needed

> Whisk together the mayonnaise, sour cream, lemon juice, garlic, salt, pepper to taste, and cayenne in a bowl. Thin to the desired consistency with the milk.

> If storing, cover and refrigerate for up to 5 days.

POPULAR CREAMY DRESSINGS AND DIPS

All of the recipes in this table begin with the Tangy Cream Dressing (page 265). The base is flavorful but not overly assertive or distracting—the fun part is jazzing it up. Many of these dressing variations are classics. They are thick, so they can be served as dips and spreads or thinned to delicately enhance wispy salad greens.

Old-Fashioned Buttermilk	Substitute buttermilk for the sour cream.
Roquefort/Blue Cheese	Stir in ¼ cup (1 oz/28 g) crumbled Roquefort or other blue cheese. Add a dash of Worcestershire sauce.
Thousand Island	Stir in ⅓ cup ketchup, 2 tablespoons finely minced shallots or onion, 1 tablespoon minced sweet or dill pickle, a dash of Worcestershire, and a good dash of Tabasco. Add a touch of prepared horseradish if you like a bit more pungency.
Ranch	Add 2 minced garlic cloves, 1 tablespoon chopped fresh chives, 1 tablespoon chopped fresh parsley, 1 teaspoon Dijon mustard, and ¼ teaspoon crumbled dried tarragon. This is best when made the day before and left to infuse overnight in the refrigerator.
Green Goddess with Avocado	Start with the Ranch Dressing Variation above: Add ½ cup mashed avocado (about ½ medium), 1 tablespoon minced onion or shallot, an additional tablespoon of lemon juice, and (optional) 1 mashed anchovy or ¼ teaspoon anchovy paste. Puree until smooth.
Dill	Add 2 tablespoons chopped fresh dill and (optional) a splash of dill pickle brine.
Mustard and Tarragon	Stir in 4 teaspoons Dijon mustard and 1 tablespoon chopped fresh tarragon or 1 teaspoon crumbled dried tarragon. Leave to infuse for at least 1 hour, or, preferably, overnight in the refrigerator.

Fennel	Stir in 2 tablespoons finely minced or grated fresh fennel and a teaspoon of finely chopped fennel fronds. If desired, add 1 tablespoon of pastis, such as Ricard.
Pesto or Green Sauce	Stir in ¼ cup Pesto (page 194, or see the table on page 196), Power Pesto (page 198), Hara Masala (page 206), or Mint Chutney (page 202).
Edamame and Wasabi	Omit the sour cream and use rice vinegar in place of the lemon juice. Boil ½ cup shelled edamame until tender. Cool. Add the edamame and 1 tablespoon prepared wasabi to the dressing and puree until smooth. Thin with additional rice vinegar as needed. Ideally, use Japanese Kewpie-Style Mayo (page 383).
Queso, Chipotle, and Lime	Use lime juice in place of the lemon juice. Stir in ¼ cup (1 oz/28 g) finely grated or crumbled Cotija cheese, 1 tablespoon finely minced canned chipotle chiles in adobo (about 2), and ½ teaspoon finely grated lime zest.

COOLING CONDIMENTS

In many regions, yogurt is a cooling, tangy accompaniment to savory meals rather than a sweet treat. Sauces and condiments made with yogurt go particularly well with yeasty flatbreads, fatty meats and fish, fried foods, and spicy dishes. *Especially* spicy dishes. Capsaicin, the component that makes chiles hot, is fat soluble, so cool, creamy sauces seem to wash them away and quickly dampen the fire.

CUCUMBER AND HERB YOGURT

Tzatziki may be the most familiar cucumber and yogurt sauce, but the combination is not exclusively Greek. *Khiyar bi laban* is the Lebanese version. Look for *masto khiar* in Turkey and Iran. *Snezhanka* is a Bulgarian variation. In India and Pakistan, you will find several types of yogurt raita. In each region, there are cooks who swear theirs is only way to make it properly. I prefer it thick, so I either use Greek yogurt or take a few minutes to drain plain yogurt in a strainer lined with a coffee filter before stirring it with the cucumbers. If you want it thinner and more fluid, use plain yogurt straight from the tub.

YIELD: 2 CUPS

1 medium cucumber

½ teaspoon kosher salt, plus more
  to taste

1½ cups plain Greek yogurt (or
  substitute plain yogurt; see
  headnote)

2 tablespoons extra-virgin olive oil
  (optional)

1 tablespoon chopped fresh mint,
  dill, and/or parsley

1 tablespoon freshly squeezed
  lemon juice or red wine vinegar

2 cloves garlic, minced or pressed

Freshly ground black pepper

> Peel the cucumber and slice it in half lengthwise. Use a spoon to scoop out the seeds and discard them. Grate the cucumber on the largest holes of a box grater.

> Combine the grated cucumber and salt in a bowl and leave for at least 5 minutes. The salt will pull water from the cucumber cells. Drain the salted cucumber, gently squeeze it dry, and return it to the bowl.

> Stir the yogurt into the cucumber. Stir in the olive oil, if using, chopped herbs, lemon juice, and garlic. Season with additional salt to taste and plenty of black pepper. The sauce can be served immediately, but the flavor will improve if you let it infuse, covered, for a few hours in the refrigerator. The sauce can be refrigerated for up to 3 days.

GOAT'S-MILK-YOGURT FALAFEL SAUCE

I call this falafel sauce because it is particularly good drizzled over the crispy fritters, but there are plenty of other ways to enjoy it. In fact, if you keep a squeeze bottle of this sauce in your fridge, you may soon find you can't live without it. It's lovely with grilled lamb, fish, and sliced tomatoes. Use it as a dressing or dip. It's a nice change from mayonnaise in tuna or egg salad.

I like the intensity of goat's-milk yogurt, but plain cow's-milk yogurt works as well. Draining the yogurt makes a thicker sauce—even 5 minutes will make a difference. Strain the yogurt overnight, and the sauce can be made into a spread.

YIELD: ½ CUP

¾ cup plain goat's-milk yogurt (or substitute plain cow's-milk yogurt)

1 clove garlic, minced or pressed

½ teaspoon dried mint, crumbled (optional)

Pinch of kosher salt

Freshly ground black pepper

> Set a sieve over a bowl and line it with a paper coffee filter or two layers of dampened cheese-cloth. Spoon the yogurt into the strainer and leave to drain for at least 5 minutes. Stir together the drained yogurt, garlic, and mint in a bowl. Season with the salt and pepper to taste.

> This can be served immediately, but the sauce will improve if the flavors have a chance to infuse. Cover and refrigerate for up to 5 days.

WHITE RADISH RAITA

Yogurt and frothy glasses of buttermilk are cooling accompaniments often served with Indian curries. This is a recipe from one of Madhur Jaffrey's earliest books, *World of the East Vegetarian Cooking* (Alfred A. Knopf, 1981). If you are a curious cook and don't know about Madhur Jaffrey, look her up. She is brilliant. This dish has heat, saltiness, tang, and a touch of sweetness from the cooked radish. In addition to being a lovely condiment, it is a good sauce for salmon and makes a tangy, intriguing spread for veggie burgers or sandwiches. Black mustard seeds are available at specialty markets.

YIELD: 2 CUPS

1 cup plain yogurt

1 tablespoon vegetable oil or
    coconut oil

1 teaspoon black mustard seeds

1 cup grated peeled white radish
    (daikon)

1 teaspoon minced green chile,
    such as serrano, jalapeño, or
    Thai bird, or to taste

½ teaspoon kosher salt, or to taste

2 tablespoons chopped fresh
    cilantro

> Set a strainer over a bowl and line it with a paper coffee filter or two layers of dampened cheesecloth. Spoon the yogurt into the sieve and leave to drain while you prepare the other ingredients.

> Heat a sauté pan over medium-high heat. Add the oil, then sprinkle in the mustard seeds and cook until the seeds start to pop. Add the radish, chile, and salt and cook, stirring often, until most of the moisture has evaporated and the radish is tender but not browned, about 4 minutes. Cool slightly.

> Transfer the yogurt to a bowl and stir in the cooked radish mixture. Add the cilantro and season with additional salt to taste if necessary.

> If storing, cover and refrigerate for up to 5 days.

VEGAN CASHEW SOUR CREAM

Raw cashews make a wonderfully rich, smooth white cream when they are softened and blended. They have long been used to thicken and enrich Indian curries but are now becoming more mainstream as an alternative to dairy creams. To mimic sour cream, the cashew cream is made quite thick, with the added tang of lemon juice. If you want a plain cream, omit the lemon juice and add an additional ⅓ cup water. Use less water to make a thick spread. Cashew cream is quite heat stable—it will thicken dramatically but not shatter when it is gently warmed.

Whole cashews tend to have more natural moisture and so blend up smoother than pieces. A high-speed blender works best for this, but I'm happy with the results I get with my standard home blender.

YIELD: 2 CUPS

1 cup (5 oz/140 g) whole raw cashews

⅔ to 1 cup water

2 tablespoons freshly squeezed lemon juice

Pinch of kosher salt (optional)

> Soak the cashews in plenty of cold water for at least 8 hours, or, preferably, overnight. If you are in a rush, you can soak the nuts in hot water for 4 hours, or until they are very soft and creamy feeling.

> Drain the softened nuts, rinse, and put in a blender. Add ⅔ cup water and puree to a fine cream, scraping down the sides of the jar regularly until completely smooth. If the cream seems at all gritty, press it through a fine sieve.

> Blend in the lemon juice and salt, if using. Thin with additional water if you want a thinner cream. It will thicken slightly when chilled.

> If storing, cover and refrigerate for up to 5 days.

DAIRY-FREE AVOCADO LIME CREAM

The next time you make tacos or tostadas, try drizzling them with this smooth, bright avocado cream. Ripe avocados are blended with a nondairy milk; lime and a good pinch of chile powder add punch. For variation, substitute diced ripe papaya for the avocado or add a tablespoon of honey or agave syrup to make this an interesting sauce for sweet corn tamales or desserts.

YIELD: ½ CUP

1 large ripe avocado, halved, pitted, and peeled

½ cup plain unsweetened nondairy milk, such as almond, oat, rice, or hemp milk, or as needed

½ teaspoon finely grated lime zest

2 tablespoons freshly squeezed lime juice

½ teaspoon kosher salt

Pinch of cayenne or chipotle chile powder or dash of Tapatío or Tabasco Sauce (optional)

> Combine the avocado, milk, lime zest, and lime juice in a blender and puree until smooth. Season to taste with the salt and chile powder. Add additional milk to make a more fluid sauce, if desired.

> If storing, cover and refrigerate for up to 3 days. The sauce will gradually discolor, but the acidity of the lime juice keeps it pretty green.

TABLE SAUCES

The assortment of condiments that seem to multiply when left alone in a dark fridge or cupboard are often overlooked as members of the sauce family. While it may be unreasonable to think you can create complicated seasoning sauces like soy, Worcestershire, or Tabasco, many of the items you buy off the store shelves are very simple to make.

HONEY-SWEETENED KETCHUP

This ketchup is comfortingly familiar. It is tangy, thick, sweet, spiced, and full of tomato flavor. I've found many homemade ketchup recipes to be not quite good enough to go to the trouble, but this is the exception, especially in late summer when the tomatoes are sweet and the grill is in almost constant use.

YIELD: 2 CUPS

1 tablespoon vegetable oil or grape seed oil

2 tablespoons minced yellow onion

1 tablespoon minced celery

1 clove garlic, chopped

1 cup diced ripe tomatoes

One 6 oz/170 g can tomato paste

½ cup water

¼ cup honey, or substitute packed brown sugar or apple juice sweetener

2 tablespoons white wine vinegar or unseasoned rice vinegar

3 or 4 whole allspice berries

3 whole cloves

½ cinnamon stick (about 1 inch/2.5 cm), cracked with the side of a knife

> Heat the oil in a medium saucepan over medium heat. Add the onion, celery, and garlic and cook until the vegetables are soft but not browned, about 4 minutes. Stir in the diced tomatoes, increase the heat to medium-high, cover, and cook until the tomatoes have softened and are juicy, 3 to 4 minutes.

> Stir in the tomato paste, water, honey, and vinegar, add the allspice, clove, cinnamon, peppercorns, and salt, and simmer, half-covered, over low heat until the sauce is thick and aromatic, 13 to 15 minutes. To prevent scorching, make sure the heat is low enough to maintain just a few simmering bubbles, and stir often. Cool slightly.

> Press the ketchup through a sieve into a bowl until all that is left is dry tomato skins, seeds, and spices; discard the solids.

> Cover and refrigerate for up to 2 weeks.

CHIPOTLE KETCHUP

> Stir in 1 tablespoon chopped canned chipotles in adobo with the diced tomatoes.

continues

5 or 6 black peppercorns

½ teaspoon kosher salt

Pinch of cayenne pepper
(optional)

CURRY KETCHUP

> Stir 1 to 2 tablespoons hot curry powder into the softened onion mixture. Cook for 15 seconds, then add the diced tomatoes.

NUOC CHAM—VIETNAMESE DIPPING SAUCE AND DRESSING

If you have ever enjoyed a Vietnamese meal, you're probably familiar with nuoc cham. It is the clear dipping sauce or dressing that is served alongside many dishes, including crispy spring rolls, grilled skewers, and rice crepes. It's fish sauce doctored up with garlic, chiles, sugar, and lime juice to the cook's taste. Strong mixes are used for bolder flavors like grilled beef or pork. Water is added to make thinner dressings for cold noodles, rice, and salads. I was introduced to Phú Quốc fish sauce by my stylist, Lynn. It has a strong, well-rounded flavor but a very delicate aroma. Although it's more expensive than many, it's well worth it.

YIELD: ¼ CUP

6 tablespoons freshly squeezed lime juice

¼ cup fish sauce

¼ cup sugar

2 to 3 tablespoons water

2 cloves garlic, minced

1 to 2 Thai bird chiles, very thinly sliced

> Stir together all of the ingredients in a bowl until the sugar is dissolved.

> To make a milder sauce or dressing for rice noodles and salads, add up to ¼ cup more water.

> Serve at room temperature.

> If storing, cover and refrigerate for up to 2 days.

TENTSUYU—TEMPURA DIPPING SAUCE

Anyone who has enjoyed tempura knows how good crispy, light-as-air battered shrimp and fried vegetables are when dipped into this thin, salty sauce. I don't make tempura at home very often, but I make this sauce all the time. I use it to simmer diced kabocha squash or sweet potatoes and to moisten sautéed shiitake mushrooms. Thin it with an additional ½ cup water, and it becomes a light broth that is excellent for soup noodles. The sauce is sometimes served with a bit of grated daikon radish in it.

YIELD: 1½ CUPS

1 cup Dashi (page 96) or Vegan Shiitake Dashi (page 97)

¼ cup mirin (sweet Japanese rice wine)

¼ cup light soy sauce

1 teaspoon sugar (optional)

> Combine all of the ingredients in a small saucepan and bring just up to the boil.

> Serve warm or cool.

> If storing, cover and refrigerate for up to 3 days.

KOLKATA-STYLE THIN FRESH FRUIT CHUTNEY

At a cooking class in Kolkata, India, the lovely Bandanas Gupta taught me how to make a quick fresh chutney by simply simmering fruits with spices and sugar syrup. It takes only minutes and can be made with virtually any fruit you have on hand. In many Bengali homes, chutney is considered a course in itself rather than just a condiment. I think a seasonal fruit chutney and crispy lentil papadums are a nice teatime alternative to pastries and a welcome change from chips and dip. Of course, chutney is also a pleasing contrast with a plate of spicy curry. I always have a bowl of this chutney and some plain rice and flatbread on hand when I serve curries to a crowd. It can seem like sanctuary for young people and those with sensitive palates who are leery of the "weird" stuff.

Panch pharon is a Bengali five-spice mixture made of equal quantities of whole cumin, black mustard, fennel, fenugreek, and kalonji (nigella) seeds. See the recipe below.

YIELD: 3 CUPS

⅓ cup sugar

⅓ cup water

2 to 3 cups diced fresh fruit, such as pineapple, peeled peaches, green tomatoes, pears, or apples, or virtually any seasonal fruit

1 teaspoon Panch Pharon (recipe follows), cracked in a mortar

Good pinch of kosher salt

> Combine the sugar and water in a medium saucepan and heat over medium heat until the sugar dissolves (see Preventing Crystallization, page 408). Bring to a boil and boil for 2 to 3 minutes. Add the fruit and panch pharon and simmer, stirring occasionally, until the fruit is just cooked through.

> Serve at room temperature.

> If storing, cover and refrigerate for up to a week.

Panch Pharon

1 teaspoon cumin seeds

1 teaspoon black mustard seeds

1 teaspoon fennel seeds

1 teaspoon fenugreek seeds

continues

1 teaspoon kalonji (nigella) seeds (sometimes erroneously called onion seeds)

> Combine the spices in a small dry skillet and toast over medium heat until they start to pop and are aromatic. Cool.

> Store in a sealed container in a cool dark location for up to 3 months.

TKEMALI—GEORGIAN PLUM "KETCHUP"

I discovered this sauce at a Russian market. I'll admit that I bought it mainly because the bottle was pretty, but the idea of plum ketchup intrigued me—there is no shortage of plums in the Northwest, and I'm always looking for new ways to use them. This Georgian condiment is like tomato ketchup in many ways. It's a fruit-based puree; it's sweet, tangy, and deeply flavored with onions and spices; and it goes with pretty much anything. I especially like it as a late-summer condiment for smoked sausages or grilled meats or chicken, but it can also be mopped up with potatoes, even French fries. It can be made with green, red, or purple plums, but they should be slightly unripe for added acidity.

YIELD: ABOUT 2 CUPS

12 oz/340 g slightly unripe fresh plums

2 teaspoons sugar

1 teaspoon chopped garlic

1 teaspoon hot paprika

1 teaspoon ground coriander

¾ teaspoon kosher salt

1 tablespoon chopped fresh dill

1 tablespoon chopped fresh mint

> Put the whole plums in a saucepan, cover with water, and bring the water to a boil, then reduce the heat and simmer until the skins are starting to burst and the plums have softened slightly, about 5 minutes. Drain the plums and cool until they can be comfortably handled.

> Cut up the plums, discarding the pits but not the loose skins. Put the plums, plum skins, sugar, garlic, paprika, coriander, and salt in a blender or food processor and puree until smooth.

> Return the mixture to the saucepan and simmer, stirring often, until it has darkened and is the consistency of ketchup, about 12 minutes. Stir in the dill and mint and let cool.

> Cover and refrigerate for up to 2 weeks.

QUICK STIR-TOGETHER CONDIMENTS

I cringe when I see some of the prepared sauces sold on store shelves. Why would anyone buy another bottle or jar when a similar and often superior mix can be stirred together with ingredients that are usually on hand?

Cocktail Sauce	Stir together ½ cup ketchup, 2 to 3 tablespoons prepared horseradish, and 1 to 2 tablespoons freshly squeezed lemon juice.
Horseradish Cream	Stir together equal quantities of prepared horseradish and sour cream.
Purple Horseradish Sauce	Stir together equal quantities of prepared horseradish and grated cooked or pickled beets.
Honey Mustard Sauce	Stir together equal quantities of Dijon, spicy brown, or Chinese hot mustard and honey.
Fry Sauce	Stir together ½ cup mayo, 3 tablespoons ketchup, 1 teaspoon vinegar, and a dash of Tabasco.
"Bulldog" Style Steak Sauce	Stir together equal quantities of hoisin sauce and Worcestershire sauce.
Soy Vinegar	Stir together 1 part soy sauce and 3 parts balsamic, rice, or Chinese black vinegar. Garnish with a few very fine slivers of scallion greens or fresh ginger.
Quick Ponzu Sauce	Stir together equal parts freshly squeezed lime juice and soy sauce. If desired, add a pinch of sugar.
Sesame and Lemon Honey Sauce	Stir together ¼ cup honey, 2 tablespoons freshly squeezed lemon juice, and 1 tablespoon sesame seeds. Microwave or heat until just warm.

Delores's Sweet-and-Sour Meatball Sauce	Stir together equal quantities barbeque sauce and grape jelly. Microwave or heat until the jelly is melted.
Sweet Lemon Cream Sauce	Stir together equal quantities of frozen lemonade concentrate and sweetened condensed milk. Use orange, limeade, or cranberry juice concentrate for variation. Serve with ripe strawberries or cake or cookies.

BARBECUE SAUCES

Wherever there is food and fire, there is also sauce. Most global barbecue sauces are made with a good amount of salt, spice, and acidity to stand up to the char and smoke and cut through residual fat. Few sauces instill more passion than regional American barbecue sauces. The topic has become a culinary war zone. I can practically hear readers aligning themselves into battle formation, ready to defend their favorites. Because the Northwest is known more for planked salmon than pulled pork, I stand on pretty neutral ground. I tend to proclaim undying loyalty to whichever regional sauce I'm licking from my fingertips. I love them all.

INFINITELY ADAPTABLE ALL-PURPOSE SWEET-AND-SPICY AMERICAN BBQ SAUCE BASE

I couldn't pick and choose between all of the wonderful regional American barbecue sauces, so I created a very basic all-purpose sauce base in the hope that you will mess with it and make it your own. It is intentionally "normal"—made with standard cupboard staples, including powdered garlic and onion. That's because I wanted a sauce that could be stirred together in virtually any American kitchen, even those with mostly ornamental spice racks. Substitute fresh garlic and onion if you prefer.

Regional barbecue sauces have as many similarities as they do differences. Add more sugar, acidity, or heat if that's how you like it. Intensify the flavors with a spoonful of molasses, a dollop of spicy mustard, or a good pinch of chipotle or ancho chile powder. Spike it with a few glugs of bourbon, a splash of cheap beer, or a smidgen of liquid smoke. Simmer it with grated apples, minced mango, sautéed bacon, or a heap of onions until it is dark and thick. Or leave it thin and use it as a mop or glaze. It's a decent sauce as is, but I'm sure you can make it even better.

YIELD: ¾ CUP

½ cup ketchup

3 tablespoons apple cider vinegar, rice vinegar, red wine vinegar, or freshly squeezed lemon juice

3 tablespoons granulated or brown sugar, or honey

2 tablespoons Worcestershire sauce

1 teaspoon onion powder or 1 tablespoon minced yellow onion

½ teaspoon kosher salt

½ teaspoon paprika

> Stir all the ingredients together. Use as is, or simmer to cook into a thicker syrup or a paste.

> If storing, cover and refrigerate for up to 2 weeks.

¼ teaspoon cayenne pepper or red chile flakes

¼ teaspoon garlic powder or 1 clove garlic, minced

Tabasco or other hot sauce to taste

EAST CAROLINA VINEGAR SAUCE

Carolina barbecue is all about pulled pork. For me, and much of the world, pit-cooked pork needs little more than salt, vinegar, a touch of sweetness, and a bit of heat to cut through the richness. This is the simplest of three fiercely contested Carolina barbecue sauces. It's more of a bright dressing than a traditional sauce, and it takes about two minutes to stir together, though if you make it ahead of time, the flavors will have a better chance to infuse. If you have any extra, you may find yourself sprinkling it on shrimp, sautéed greens, or even sweet potato fries.

YIELD: ½ CUP

½ cup white vinegar or apple cider vinegar

2 tablespoons brown sugar

1 teaspoon kosher salt

½ teaspoon red chile flakes

Plenty of freshly ground black pepper

> Stir all of the ingredients together in a small bowl or shake in a sealed jar until the sugar is dissolved.

> Serve.

> If storing, cover and refrigerate for up to 2 weeks.

HOISIN BARBECUE SAUCE

My mouth starts to water just thinking about the crispy mahogany ducks and roasted pork hanging from hooks in the front windows of Chinese barbecue joints. When I am inspired and have the time, I make those labor-intensive dishes from scratch. When I don't, this quick sauce sates my cravings. In addition to being a good marinade for pork destined for the smoker or barbecue, it is an excellent basting sauce for barbecued chicken or mushroom and onion skewers. Warm it and serve it alongside seared duck breast or drizzle some on steamed bok choy. You can even toss it with chewy noodles and sliced scallions for a side dish.

Hoisin sauce is available at most good supermarkets. Chinese 5-spice is a blend of cinnamon, star anise, fennel seeds, cloves, and Sichuan pepper. It adds a very distinct flavor and pungency, but I only use it in this recipe about half the time.

YIELD: ¼ CUP

½ cup hoisin sauce

¼ cup unseasoned rice vinegar

3 tablespoons soy sauce

1 tablespoon Shaoxing wine or medium-dry sherry

1 teaspoon finely grated fresh ginger

¼ teaspoon Chinese 5-spice powder (optional)

> Stir together all the ingredients in a bowl.

> If storing, cover and refrigerate for up to 5 days.

3-INGREDIENT TERIYAKI SAUCE

Every neighborhood in and around Seattle has multiple teriyaki joints that serve up big, cheap portions of steamed rice and heaps of grilled or broiled chicken, beef, pork, or tofu drenched in teriyaki sauce. It's Northwest comfort food. A former coworker let me in on the sauce secret. It takes only three ingredients: soy, sugar, and mirin, in a ratio of 4:2:1. It's supersweet, but that's part of the appeal. It gets sticky and caramelized when it's grilled or seared, but still has the salty, savory taste of soy. Use this as a marinade or a basting sauce, or just pour some over a bowl of rice. If you prefer a more complicated sauce, I've suggested a few optional additions that will give it more zip.

Mirin is a very sweet Japanese rice wine available at most good supermarkets and Asian markets.

YIELD: ½ CUP

½ cup soy sauce

¼ cup sugar

2 tablespoons mirin (sweet
  Japanese rice wine)

OPTIONAL ADDITIONS

1 clove garlic, minced or pressed

1 teaspoon finely grated fresh
  ginger

2 tablespoons thinly sliced
  scallions (white and green parts)

2 teaspoons Thai red curry paste,
  Korean chile paste (gochujang),
  or Vietnamese chile lemongrass
  paste

A few drops of sesame oil

> Combine the ingredients in a saucepan and heat, stirring, until the sugar is dissolved.

> If storing, cover and refrigerate for up to 2 weeks.

KOREAN PEAR BULGOGI SAUCE

I love Korean food. It's always an adventure in flavor and texture. As with most people, my introduction to Korean food started with barbecue: bulgogi beef, marinated in a blend of soy, garlic, and sesame. The seared meat is wrapped in lettuce leaves with a smear of chile paste. It's presently a dish in heavy rotation at our house during grilling season. Pears are often used instead of sugar in bulgogi marinades. I use pureed canned pears here for convenience, but for a really good sauce, use freshly extracted Asian pear juice boiled to double concentration.

Use the recipe as a marinade for up to 3 lbs/1.4 kg of kalbi-style beef short ribs, a jointed chicken, or up to 2 lbs/900 g pork or boneless chicken. You can also simmer the sauce until it is syrupy and use it as you would teriyaki sauce or to top rice bowls. Korean red chile powder is a brilliant red. It has a lot of flavor as well as heat. If you can't find it, substitute ½ teaspoon red chile flakes or ½ teaspoon cayenne pepper.

YIELD: 1½ CUPS

1 cup pear puree (made by pureeing canned pears in thin syrup or by reducing 2 cups pear juice)

½ cup soy sauce

2 tablespoons minced or pressed garlic

2 tablespoons toasted sesame seeds

1 teaspoon Korean red chile powder (gochu karu)

½ teaspoon freshly ground black pepper

1 teaspoon sesame oil

> Stir all the ingredients together and use as a marinade, or simmer in a saucepan until the garlic is softened and the sauce is syrupy, 3 to 5 minutes. Cool.

> If storing, cover and refrigerate for up to 1 week.

TAMI'S BRAZILIAN BARBECUE MOP

Brazilian barbecues are often all-day affairs. The grill is loaded and emptied repeatedly for family and friends. My neighbor, Tami, showed me how her grandfather in Saõ Paolo does things. We gathered on a summer evening, shared stories, strummed on guitars, and took turns watching baby Doyle while chunks of salt-rubbed beef were grilled over hot coals. As the beef cooked, Tami brushed it generously with a bunch of fresh cilantro dipped in this sauce. Drips and splashes that land on the coals are encouraged; the aromatic sizzle adds flavor. Apparently the sauce isn't right unless you add Tempero Sazón seasoning powder (available online). It is a wildly popular ingredient in Brazil that on close inspection looks a lot like a blend of MSG, garlic powder, and paprika. I'm fine with MSG. I like the umami and authenticity it adds to many recipes. But if you prefer, just add some extra salt, a little garlic powder, and a tiny pinch of paprika. In addition to beef, this mop can be used for fish, chicken, pork, and vegetables.

YIELD: 1½ CUPS

½ cup minced yellow onion

3 tablespoons chopped fresh cilantro, plus an entire bunch to use as a basting brush

2 or 3 cloves garlic, minced or pressed

3 tablespoons olive oil

¾ cup beer, such as PBR or other inexpensive American-style lager

½ teaspoon kosher salt

Freshly ground black pepper

½ teaspoon Tempero Sazón seasoning blend (optional; see headnote)

> Stir together the onion, chopped cilantro, and garlic in a small bowl. Add the olive oil and stir to mix. Gradually stir in the beer; The mixture will resemble a very thin, wet salsa. Season with the salt, plenty of pepper, and the Tempero Sazón, if using.

> Use the bunch of cilantro as a brush to generously mop the sauce onto simply seasoned ingredients on a hot grill. The juice will drop onto the coals and give the grilled food an aromatic dark char and flavor.

CUBAN MOJO

Throughout Latin America, barbecued and grilled foods are usually accompanied by piquant mixes of oil, aromatics, and a good measure of fresh citrus or vinegar, which are particularly good at cutting the richness of slow-roasted pork. Some of the most famous of these are the *mojos* of Cuba. Use this super-garlicky mix to marinate meats or poultry; mop it onto whole fish, shrimp, or spiny lobsters as they grill; or serve it as a stand-alone sauce or dip. Bitter oranges are traditional. Since they aren't available in the Northwest, I substitute a blend of fresh citrus juices or cheat and use the less-than-pure bottles of bitter orange juice sold at Latin markets.

YIELD: 1½ CUPS

8 to 10 cloves garlic

1½ teaspoons kosher salt

½ teaspoon dried oregano

½ teaspoon freshly ground black pepper

¼ teaspoon ground cumin (optional)

1 cup bitter orange juice (or substitute a mix of ½ cup freshly squeezed orange juice, ¼ cup freshly squeezed lime juice, and ¼ cup freshly squeezed lemon juice)

½ cup olive oil, or to taste

> Mash the garlic, salt, oregano, pepper, and cumin to a paste in a mortar. Mix the paste with the juice in a bowl, and whisk in the olive oil to taste. Alternatively, use a blender.

> The flavors meld and intensify if the mojo is left to infuse for at least 1 hour, and is even better when refrigerated overnight.

> If storing, cover and refrigerate for up to 5 days.

CHILE SAUCES

NOT JUST HOT

've never been chile shy. I remember my dad offering me a drop of Tabasco sauce on a well-dressed cracker when I was barely as tall as the kitchen table. I liked it immediately, but my life took on a whole new kind of spice when I met my husband. He consumed Tabasco sauce as if it was a beverage. At restaurants that offered their dishes with graduating heat levels, he would ask for an extra star. Finally, he met his match. A demure server at a local Thai restaurant beamed at his request. "You like it spicy? I do too. I order mine with ten stars. Do you want ten stars?" Definitely! By the end of the meal, he had learned some valuable lessons. First, what one person considers hot is mere child's play to another. Second, there is a point when chiles stop enhancing a dish and start to kill the flavors you set out to enjoy. The food becomes more like an extreme sport than an actual meal.

The burn of chiles is not technically a taste, it is the stimulation of tiny pain sensors on the palate. It's a pain that much of the world can't imagine living without. I don't add chiles just for the burn but to enhance the oral experience, to add complexity and depth. Now and then it's good to channel your inner dragon and breathe a little bit of fire, but this chapter focuses on the flavorful and textural elements of chiles, not just the heat.

TIPS
for Handling Chiles

- Wear disposable gloves. One eye rub or sniffle, even after you've rinsed your hands, is all it takes to learn your lesson. Years ago, someone told me that you can also neutralize the acids in chiles by washing your hands with baking soda. I've since learned that the acids aren't the problem, but when I live dangerously and forgo the gloves, I often scrub my hands with baking soda before washing them. It makes me feel better.

- Remove and discard the stems. Whole fresh chiles can be dropped into blended mixtures, but only to reduce the prep time. I can't think of a single place where a pepper stem will improve the flavor of a sauce.

- The heat is concentrated in the seeds and soft ribs inside the chiles. They don't always have to be removed, but they should be if you want a seedless sauce or a flavor that is more fruit than fire.

- To remove the seeds from fresh chiles, slice them lengthwise in half and cut or scrape the seeds out with a knife.

- To remove the seeds from dried chiles, shake them out if they are loose, or snip the chile lengthwise and nudge, pat, or scrape the seeds out.

- To remove the skin from a fresh chile pepper, evenly char the outside until it blackens and bubbles. I usually do this by rolling the whole pepper on a hot burner and finishing the crevices and stubborn spots with a blowtorch. You can also use a broiler or hot grill. Let the charred pepper steam a bit, in a covered bowl or a paper bag, to help loosen the skins. Then use coarse salt or a dry paper towel to help rub the skin off. Some cooks rinse the peppers to remove any black specks. I don't mind these and I prefer the taste when the peppers aren't rinsed.

- Dried chiles have not been cooked, so they benefit from a bit of toasting. You can warm small dried chiles in a dry skillet or oven until they darken slightly and smell toasted. For larger chiles, I usually hold them over a hot burner with tongs. They soften at first, then crisp up and start to crackle. Be careful not to burn them.

- To reconstitute dried chiles, soak or simmer them in water until they are fleshy and tender. If the soaking water has a flavor that is appealing, it can also be used as an ingredient.

- Remember that the surface you have prepared the chiles on will have chile oil on it. Give it a scrub with soapy water, not just a rinse.

FUCHSIA DUNLOP'S CHINESE CHILE OIL

Fuchsia Dunlop is one of my very favorite food writers. I keep a jar of her chile oil on hand at all times. This recipe is adapted from her wonderful book *Land of Plenty: Authentic Sichuan Recipes Personally Gathered in the Chinese Province of Sichuan* (W. W. Norton, 2003). It is especially good with dumplings, green vegetables, and steamed fish. It can also be added to stir-fry sauces and marinades.

YIELD: 1 CUP

¼ cup red chile flakes, preferably from Chinese chiles

1 cup peanut or corn oil

A coin of fresh ginger

> Put the chile flakes in a heatproof canning jar.

> Combine the oil and ginger in a small saucepan and cook over high heat until all of the moisture has cooked out of the ginger and it is shriveled but not burnt. Dunlop suggests that the oil be 225° to 250°F /107° to 120°C. If it is much hotter, there is a risk of burning the chiles and even shattering the jar.

> Remove the pan from the heat and discard the ginger. Carefully pour the hot oil over the chile flakes in the jar. They will fizz and crackle. That is to be expected from good fresh chile flakes that have a bit of residual moisture. Stir carefully and then leave to infuse at room temperature.

> When cool, seal and use as needed. The flavor will improve after a few days.

SWEET GARLIC AND PICKLED CHILE DIPPING SAUCE

This is a homemade version of the sweet, spicy, and garlicky sauce that is often served as a dip alongside fried Thai appetizers. It is so popular now that it is sold in big bottles at my local supermarket. I see it often as an alternative to Buffalo sauce on chicken wings and recently had it tossed with roasted Brussels sprouts.

As with ketchup, the commercial versions may be good, but homemade is better. Once you find a source for little red pickled peppers, you can simmer up a batch in minutes. The pickled peppers are a handy recipe alternative to fresh Thai bird chiles. But if you can't find them, minced fresh hot red chiles work fine. The sauces on store shelves maintain an even suspension of garlic and chile flake particles thanks to modern thickeners. You can mimic this by adding a tiny bit of xanthan gum (see page 180), but I think it is better to just give it a shake or stir when the particles settle.

YIELD: 1½ CUPS

1 cup sugar

½ cup water

3 tablespoons chopped garlic

3 tablespoons thinly sliced Thai or Vietnamese pickled red chiles (about 12) or minced fresh red serrano or Fresno chiles

3 to 4 tablespoons white vinegar or unseasoned rice vinegar, or to taste

1 teaspoon kosher salt

> Combine the sugar and water in a small saucepan and heat over medium heat until the sugar dissolves (see Preventing Crystallization, page 408). When the syrup is clear, increase the heat to medium-high and boil for 5 minutes.

> Remove the pan from the heat and stir in the garlic, chiles, and salt. Cool to room temperature, then add the vinegar.

> This is best left to infuse overnight, refrigerated, before serving.

> If storing, cover and refrigerate for up to 1 month.

HOMEMADE SRIRACHA

Big plastic bottles of this chile garlic sauce have become almost as ubiquitous on restaurant table-tops as ketchup and Tabasco. It is surprisingly easy to make. Sriracha chiles are rarely available fresh here, so you will probably have to make do with whatever fresh red chile peppers you can find. Long hot Korean red chiles and fresh cayenne peppers work particularly well, but in the off season, try a mix of red serrano, Fresno, red jalapeño, and habanero chiles. In the summer, the chile selection at my farmers' market is almost dizzying. I ask the sellers for a mix that hovers at around 50,000 to 70,000 Scoville units.

The heat of the fresh chiles is dramatically reduced by the blanching. If you want a really hot sauce, use really fiery peppers. If you prefer a sweeter, milder sauce, substitute a red baby bell for one or two of the hot peppers. The finished sauce has a lovely balance of flavors with not too much bite, so it can be used with a heavy hand, not just a drip or drizzle.

YIELD: 1 CUP

8 oz/225 g hot red chiles, such as fresh cayenne or Korean red chiles

3 tablespoons chopped garlic

2 tablespoons unseasoned rice vinegar or white vinegar

1 tablespoon kosher salt

1 teaspoon sugar

> Wearing gloves, remove the stems and seeds from the chiles and chop them into ½-inch/1.25 cm pieces (see Tips for Handling Chiles, page 298); if you have a high proportion of very small, fussy chiles, simply stem and chop them whole, then strain the seeds out after the sauce has been blended.

> Put the chiles in a saucepan with enough water to cover, bring the water just to a boil over high heat, and then drain; return the chiles to the pan.

> Add the garlic, vinegar, salt, and sugar to the saucepan with the chiles and stir well. Cover the pan, and simmer over medium-low heat, until the chiles are tender. For soft, meaty chiles, this will take about 15 minutes; for tougher chiles, it may take 20 minutes or more. Simmering with the lid on should let the mixture retain enough moisture for blending, but if the ingredients seem to be getting dry, add 1 to 2 tablespoons water.

> When the chiles are tender, cool the mixture slightly and then transfer it to a blender. Pulse the mixture until it is smooth, turning off the blender and scraping the sides as needed. Add a tablespoon or two of water if needed to make the sauce more liquid and easier to blend. The finished sauce should be just a bit thicker than ketchup.

> If there are residual skins or seeds in the puree that you find unpleasant, press the sauce through a fine sieve. I store this in a squeeze bottle.

> Cover and refrigerate for several months or freeze for up to a year.

TOMATO AND CHILE MOMO DUNK

I had my first plate of momos at a roadside stand when I was headed from Kolkata to Darjeeling. These simple boiled dumplings, often stuffed just with cabbage and onions, may have seemed unremarkable to some travelers, but I found them to be habit-forming. Many plates of momos followed that first one, and they were all accompanied by a fresh-tasting red chile sauce that carried a bit of heat but never overpowered the dumplings. Back home, I experimented with simply thinning several types of chile sauces and pastes, but they never had the balance of flavor I was looking for. Finally I landed on this incredibly simple blend of grated fresh tomato and sambal oelek, the commercially prepared chile and garlic sauce. Try it the next time you boil up some frozen pot stickers. Spoon any leftover sauce onto a bowl of rice topped with a scrambled or poached egg.

YIELD: 1 CUP

2 ripe Roma (plum) tomatoes

2 tablespoons sambal oelek or similar thick chile and garlic sauce

⅓ cup water

¼ teaspoon kosher salt

> Cut the tomatoes in half and squeeze them gently to remove the seeds. Grate the tomato pulp with a box grater by pressing the cut sides of the tomato against the large holes of the grater. With gentle pressure, the pulp should pass through, leaving the tough skin intact. Discard the skin. You should have about ¼ cup fresh tomato pulp.

> Stir together the tomato pulp, chile paste, water, and salt in a bowl.

> Serve.

> If storing, cover and refrigerate for up to 2 days.

SPICY SESAME DIPPING SAUCE

I'm slightly obsessed with Sichuan dumplings and fried scallion pancakes, but I'm pretty sure it's actually the spicy sesame and soy dipping sauce often served alongside that fuels my passion. This is my own version, stirred together from a mixture of ingredients that have become household staples ever since I fell in love with Fuchsia Dunlop's books. I urge you to collect and use the more exotic ingredients like the roasted sesame paste and black vinegar, but I understand how difficult it can be to hunt down specialty items outside of big cities and so have offered alternatives.

YIELD: ⅔ CUP

¼ cup Fuchsia Dunlop's Chinese Chile Oil (page 300) or store-bought hot chile oil

¼ cup peanut oil

2 tablespoons soy sauce

1 tablespoon Sichuan bean paste (optional, but recommended)

2 tablespoons Chinese black vinegar (or substitute balsamic vinegar)

2 teaspoons Chinese roasted sesame paste (*zhi ma jiang*); or substitute almond butter, smooth peanut butter, or tahini

½ teaspoon sesame oil

½ teaspoon sugar (optional)

A few fine slivers of fresh ginger or scallion for garnish (optional)

> Combine all of the ingredients except the optional ginger in a small bowl and whisk until smooth and evenly blended. Serve the sauce in small shallow bowls, garnished with the slivers of ginger or scallion.

> If storing, cover and refrigerate for up to 1 week.

ALL-PURPOSE HOT SAUCE

This sauce was created as a chile catchall. Make it with whatever mix of fresh peppers you have access to, hot or mild, and think of it as an alternative to salsa. It's great on many foods, but it is particularly good with corn, grits or polenta, tamales, or nachos. The citric acid is suggested to add a bit of tang without thinning the texture or flavors; omit it if you prefer a sauce with less acidity.

YIELD: 1¼ CUPS

4 oz/115 g hot chiles, stemmed, seeded, and chopped (about 1 cup chopped)

1 cup water

⅓ cup minced yellow onion

¼ cup grated carrot

1 tablespoon minced garlic

2 teaspoons kosher salt

½ teaspoon dried oregano

⅛ teaspoon ground cumin

⅛ teaspoon citric acid (optional)

> Combine the ingredients in a saucepan and bring the mixture to a boil over high heat, then reduce the heat to a gentle simmer, cover the pan, and cook until the chiles and onions are soft, about 15 minutes. Cool slightly.

> Transfer the chile mix to a blender or food processor and puree until smooth. I store this in a squeeze bottle.

> Refrigerate for up to 1 month.

HARISSA

For much of the world, harissa is the first ingredient cooks reach for when they want to add the kick of chiles. It is a sauce with Tunisian roots, but variations are common throughout the Mediterranean and Europe. Paula Wolfert introduced the sauce to many Americans through her wonderful books. Many households consider it a staple, almost as vital as bread and olive oil. Harissa is almost obligatory with couscous, but it is also nice stirred into soups, stews, and many different sauces. Use it in the Harissa Broth (page 142) or mix a bit into plain yogurt or mayonnaise as a dip for breadsticks or steamed artichoke leaves.

YIELD: 1 CUP

2 oz/60 g dried hot Tunisian chiles (or substitute chiles de árbol or other relatively indistinct hot dried chile)

2 to 3 cups boiling water

1 teaspoon coriander seeds

½ teaspoon caraway seeds

½ teaspoon fennel seeds

1 teaspoon kosher salt, or to taste

1 teaspoon dried mint

½ cup olive oil

3 or 4 cloves garlic (optional)

½ teaspoon finely grated lemon zest, or to taste

¼ teaspoon ground turmeric (optional)

> Remove the stems from the chiles and shake out the seeds. Put the chiles in a bowl and cover with the boiling water. Leave to soften, about 20 minutes.

> While the chiles are softening, toast the coriander, caraway, and fennel seeds in a small dry skillet over medium heat, shaking the pan regularly, until the fennel seeds just start to pop, about 3 minutes.

> Combine the toasted spices with the salt and dried mint in a spice grinder or coffee mill and grind to a fine powder. (Adding the salt to the grinder helps to make a finer, more even powder.)

> Drain the chiles and transfer them to a blender. Add the olive oil, garlic, powdered spices, lemon zest, and turmeric, if using, and puree to a smooth paste, stopping to scrape down the sides of the blender as needed.

continues

> Taste the harissa for seasoning—it will be very hot, but it should also taste spicy, salty, and well balanced. Add more salt, chiles, or lemon as needed.

> Cover and refrigerate for up to 1 month. The flavor will improve as the harissa infuses.

AJÍ AMARILLO SAUCE—PERUVIAN YELLOW PEPPER SAUCE

I heard about this gorgeous and flavorful pepper sauce from Peru and started on a recipe hunt. I found countless variations: mild, sweet, spicy. Some are made with cheese and spicy pepper paste, others with bread and mild roasted peppers. I've been served versions that look more like mayonnaise than pepper sauce.

My friend Kathy Casey fell pretty hard for ají amarillo sauce when she visited Peru on a consulting trip. She took photos of different sauces and brought home packets to freeze. She worked alongside a Peruvian chef who made a version she especially liked and she passed the technique along to me. Finding Peruvian yellow peppers can be a trick, so I made this version with yellow bell peppers and the added kick of serrano or habanero chiles. It isn't really meant to be spicy, more of a creamy condiment, but I like more heat.

Two slightly more authentic recipe variations are given below. One is made with Costa Peruana organic ají amarillo chile paste. In addition to convenience, it offers a concentrated intensity I really like. Another version is made with cheese.

Spoon the sauce over cold potatoes or hard-cooked eggs. It's also great with chicken and any dish you might slather salsa on. You may find yourself pouring it on everything.

YIELD: 2 CUPS

½ cup lightly packed torn soft white bread (crusts removed)

¼ cup milk, or as needed

3 tablespoons olive oil

2 cups minced Peruvian ají amarillo, or substitute yellow bell peppers (about 2 peppers)

½ cup minced yellow or red onion

1 tablespoon minced seeded red serrano or yellow habanero chile, or to taste

> Put the bread in a bowl and sprinkle it with the milk. Leave to soften while you prepare the remaining ingredients.

> Heat a medium saucepan over medium-high heat. Add the oil, then stir in the peppers, onion, chile, garlic, and half the salt. Cover and simmer, stirring often, until the vegetables are completely soft but not browned, about 15 minutes.

> Transfer the cooked pepper mixture to a blender or food processor, add the soaked bread and the remaining salt, and puree until smooth. The sauce should be just thick enough to coat a spoon; thin with a tablespoon more milk or water if needed. The sauce will thicken slightly as it cools.

continues

2 cloves garlic, chopped

1 teaspoon kosher salt

> Serve warm or at room temperature.

> If storing, cover and refrigerate for up to 1 week.

AJÍ AMARILLO SAUCE MADE WITH YELLOW PEPPER PASTE

> Reduce the yellow bell peppers to 1 cup. When the vegetables are tender, stir in ½ cup Costa Peruana brand organic ají amarillo chile paste and cook for 1 minute more. Proceed with the recipe.

AJÍ AMARILLO SAUCE MADE WITH CHEESE

> Omit the bread and milk. Add ½ cup (3 oz/85 g) crumbled queso fresco cheese with the peppers when blending. Thin with additional water if necessary.

TIPS
for Creating Your Own Chile Sauces

- Chiles are a fruit. In addition to heat, they can add sweetness, pulp, and pectin. Green chiles, which ripen into red chiles, have more of a fresh, almost herbal brightness. Red chiles have more natural sugars and tend to have a more rounded, deeper flavors.

- The bite of chiles is concentrated in the seeds and the tender tissues holding the seeds. If you remove them, the chile will be milder.

- Capsaicin, the chemical that makes chiles hot, is oil soluble. That's why a glass of milk or dollop of creamy condiment tames the flame better than a glass of water.

- There are so many chile varieties that some chile farmers I've met can barely keep track of them. I can find varieties like Anaheim, jalapeño, Fresno, poblano, habanero, and Thai bird chiles year-round without any trouble, so I've suggested them throughout this book. It's nice to experiment when you find new varieties. I tend to ask a lot of questions of shop owners and other customers.

- Chile sauces need more salt than many other sauces to seem balanced. Since the intense sauces tend to be served in small quantities, the amount of salt per serving is not excessive.

- If you make your sauce hotter than you can stand, your only choice may be to use less or stretch it by adding bulkier ingredients like a cooked carrot, potato, or onion puree.

RESPECT YOUR MOTHER

UPDATING THE
CLASSIC FRENCH
MOTHER SAUCES

The French mother sauces have long been considered the foundation of all classic sauce variations. Chef Antonin Carême (1744–1833) was one of the first great documentarians of French cuisine and technique. It was he who first classified sauces into categories rooted in an adaptable base, or "mother sauce." These base recipes could be embellished and transformed into the innumerable variations known as derivative sauces. Carême's original list is commonly accepted as béchamel, allemande, velouté, and espagnole. They were white to dark brown sauces thickened with roux and variously enriched with cream, eggs, and butter. Whether or not today's incarnations would instantly be recognized as his mother sauces is questionable. Carême's sauces have evolved and been simplified over the years.

Chef Auguste Escoffier (1847–1935) updated and expanded Carême's original list and lessons. Because he had an international profile and established global standards for sauce making, he is often credited as the creator of the mother sauces. Modern culinary students are still taught Escoffier's five mother sauces: béchamel, velouté, espagnole, tomato, and emulsified. Béchamel is a white sauce thickened with a barely cooked white roux. Velouté is made with a golden or blond roux. "Espagnole" has become an umbrella term for brown meat and vegetable stock thickened with a dark brown roux. Tomato sauces are relatively self-explanatory, but the family now often encompasses pureed sauces and sometimes those thickened with integral ingredients. Emulsified sauces are linked to vinaigrettes but most often refer to egg-based sauces like mayonnaise and hollandaise. These five classic sauces and techniques remain canonical. Once you understand how to make and adapt these sauces, you will be able to confidently make virtually any European sauce variation. They are an example of how understanding and mastering foundations is liberating rather than restrictive.

I believe in keeping culinary traditions alive. I'm an advocate of slow foods and artisans. I think there is still room in today's world for authentic, historically important sauces that are elaborate, expensive, and time-consuming, but I also think it's vital to respect how food and cooking evolves. As important as the historic sauces are, tools, knowledge, and tastes change. So should sauces. This section embraces the importance of roux and French traditions without corralling the recipes into isolated pens. Roux is roux.

Traditionalists may shriek at the idea of making a béchamel sauce with tofu and soy milk or mocking hollandaise by omitting the eggs and butter and adding corn and nutritional yeast flakes. I urge them to continue enjoying their beloved classics. I will remind them of all the magnificent fine-dining establishments that still make sauces with veal knuckles, chicken feet, whipping cream, and mountains of butter. As for true authenticity, I've read very old recipes for béchamel that call for a mixture of minced veal and heavy cream to be passed through a fine horsehair sieve. I don't know any modern culinary students who have been taught that "traditional" variation. The sauce has been updated many times since then. Why not now?

Contemporary sauces remain true to Carême's original idea of recipe bases as well as Escoffier's more global perspective. They are just more reliant on electricity, refrigeration, and a better understanding of food safety and nutrition. It's also past time to acknowledge that long before the French were refining their roux and egg sauces, chefs around the world were doing some pretty great things with kudzu root, tapioca, and agar-agar. These are not new or lesser ingredients, they were just shadowed for a while by the empire of pedigreed French sauces.

DEMYSTIFYING ROUX

Without question, the most vexing word for me as a young cook was *roux*. I'd march into the kitchen with optimism and enthusiasm, determined to make a refined French dish like cream of asparagus soup or a cheese soufflé, foods that I felt were sorely lacking on our family dinner menus, and I would become flummoxed at the first step: *"Make a roux with the butter and flour."* How was I supposed to know when the melted butter and flour had transformed into an unpronounceable French thing? Such magic must surely involve rhythmic whisking or special temperature gradations. So, for anyone who ever wondered: *Roux* is just a fancy French term for melted butter with some flour stirred into it! Phew, the twelve-year-old in me feels vindicated.

That's the thing about roux. It's so incredibly simple it can seem wrong. It seems as if there should be more. Why should a couple of basic kitchen staples stirred together in a pot warrant a foreign word with a silent x? The answer is that roux is inextricably linked to French culinary history. Manipulating the texture of sauces, soups, and stews with refined white flour was a ground-breaking technique. Stocks could be turned into silky sauces without the subtle grit of coarse grains, bread crumbs, or nut pastes. Sauces could be held and reheated without the tem-

peramental fuss of egg yolks, butter, or other slightly less universally appealing animal products, like organ meats and blood. Thick sauces could have body and even binding properties without endless pounding, mashing, and straining repeatedly through finer and finer mesh. French chefs and techniques refined and elevated global cuisine. Roux rocked the world. That's why we use the tiny, delicate French word instead of a more descriptive Anglicized version like "butter paste" or "floured butter."

Here's a simplified version of how roux works: The fat helps to coat, lubricate, and separate the wheat granules. It also adds a bit of flavor. Mixing and stirring disperse the fat and flour evenly so there are no globs and lumps. When liquid is added, the starch granules absorb water, swell, and become stickier. As they are heated, bits of starch peel off from the granules and tangle together to form shrub-like groups that interfere with the movement of the water and fat molecules. That makes the sauce thicker and more stable, but it remains tender, smooth, and velvety. The flavor alterations tend to be complementary rather than distracting, with the exception of the mild flavor masking that comes with the addition of starch.

After stock making, roux variations are the traditional starting point in sauce education. When the founding fathers of European gastronomy proclaimed that there were only a handful of sauces in the world that actually mattered, most of them started with roux. The three roux-based mother sauces, béchamel, velouté, and espagnole, are primarily differentiated by how long the flour is cooked. Barely cooked white roux works best with mild light or white liquids. If you keep it on the stove a bit longer, the roux picks up a golden color and toasted aroma that is well matched with slightly darker and more intensely flavored stocks. Cook the roux until it is brown, and it will add a deep, nutty flavor and complexity to rich, meaty sauces. Béchamel sauce is made with a white roux, velouté sauce with a golden toasted roux, and espagnole sauce with brown roux. Very dark, chestnut-brown roux like those used for gumbo are used primarily as a flavoring because the flour granules harden and lose thickening power.

As a culinary student, I loved the language, subtleties, elegance, and history of food and cooking. When you first understand and can skillfully execute the French mother sauces, and then see how they can be adapted, it is revelatory. But one day it hit me: When I was a kid, desperate to class up the joint with French refinement, my mother was absently throwing together another "boring" white sauce. She would drop a blob of margarine into a pot, shake in some flour, and stir it all together until it was bubbly. Then she would glug in some milk straight

from the carton and cook it for a while. She'd fancy it up with a little of this and that, and we'd eat it with biscuits for dinner. Surely that wasn't Antonin Carême's *sauce béchamel*? Her Thanksgiving gravy made with pan drippings, sizzled flour, and giblet stock couldn't possibly be a variation of velouté, could it? It took years before I linked the famous roux in rustic Louisiana gumbos and the elegant and expensive brown sauces served in high-class restaurants. As my culinary world expanded, my reverence for roux diminished: it's so incredibly simple.

Now, rather than dividing the exciting world of sauce making into gradient colors of toasted flour, I tend to sort of lump all roux-thickened sauces together. Both Holiday Gravy (page 330) and New Mexican Red Chile Sauce (page 339) are made with a roux that is toasted, but they are not obvious descendents of velouté sauce. Many spectacular sauces, not just those with fancy French names, are made with a base of flour and fat. Roux is one of the many ways you can thicken a sauce with starch. It just happens to be magnificent.

STARCH MASKS FLAVOR

Starch interferes with flavor. It can coat the palate and muddy the taste receptors. It can bind with flavor molecules so they slide away before your taste buds ever get a chance to meet them. Starch especially diminishes the taste of salt. If you pour bland gravy over pasty biscuits or toss a heap of pasta with a weak or watery sauce, you'd better hope the kitchen smells good, because that's about all the flavor you're going to get.

So, not only do you have to adjust the seasoning of your sauce to compensate for the starch levels in the foods it is served with, you need to consider the effect of starch when you use it to thicken a sauce. You are essentially adding a very bland component to alter the movement of water molecules. The sauce will be thicker, but the key flavors will be diminished.

There is a subtle taste of flour in sauces made with roux, especially those that are toasted or browned. Cornstarch has a very distinctive flavor that can virtually destroy a sauce when too much is used or it is under-cooked. Refer to the table of Texturizers on page 48 to determine which thickening option might be right for your own original sauces.

WHITE SAUCE DONE RIGHT (BÉCHAMEL)

White sauce, or béchamel, is one of the five French mother sauces. That essentially means that it is a building block for innumerable other sauces. Béchamel can also be used as an ingredient in soufflés, fritters, fillings, and casseroles. Best of all, white sauce is about the easiest way to learn how roux, a paste of fat and starch, can alter the texture of a liquid. Unfortunately, the simplicity of this preparation can also diminish its potential for greatness. A sloppily made white sauce can taste pasty, bland, and utterly uninteresting. Make it right by infusing the milk with savory flavors, carefully preparing the roux, and seasoning the sauce skillfully, and you will understand why it is a French classic.

This version is quite thin and fluid. It will thicken as it simmers and reduces and when it cools. For a thick, binding sauce, make the roux with 3 tablespoons butter and 3 tablespoons flour. Pepper is considered optional, because while the taste is complementary, black specks are not always welcome in a white sauce. Using finely ground white pepper is another option. Some cooks consider nutmeg a must, but I think it can be distracting. I most often add it when I will be mixing the sauce with spinach or hearty greens, or when I want a hint of spice in Italian or Greek casserole dishes.

YIELD: 1½ CUPS

2 cups whole milk

Infusing ingredients (choose 1 to 3), such as a bit of onion or shallot, 4 or 5 black peppercorns, a bay leaf, 1 or 2 parsley stems, a slice of carrot, clove of garlic, and/or a mushroom stem

2 tablespoons butter

2 tablespoons all-purpose flour

½ teaspoon kosher salt, or to taste

> Combine the milk and your choice of infusing ingredients in a medium saucepan and heat over medium-high heat until the milk begins to steam and small bubbles form at the edges of the pan. Remove the pan from the heat and set the milk aside to infuse. If you prefer, you can infuse the milk by combining the ingredients in a microwave-safe container and cooking on high for about 45 seconds.

> Heat a medium saucepan over medium-high heat and add the butter. When it bubbles, remove the pan from the heat and sprinkle the flour evenly over the melted butter. Stir until the butter and flour are a smooth paste. Return the pan to the heat and cook the roux, stirring often, until the raw aroma is cooked out and it is bubbly but not brown, about 1 minute. Strain half of the infused milk into the

continues

Very finely ground black pepper
(optional)

A few gratings of fresh nutmeg
(optional)

roux and whisk vigorously until it is smooth. Add the remaining (strained) milk and stir well. Bring the sauce to a boil, then reduce the heat to a simmer, season with the salt, and simmer, stirring often, for 8 to 10 minutes to make sure there is no raw flour taste and to give the starch particles a chance to swell and thicken the sauce. Season with additional salt to taste if desired and add the pepper and nutmeg if using.

> If you are not using the sauce right away, put a piece of buttered parchment, a butter wrapper, or piece of plastic wrap directly on the surface of the sauce to prevent a skin from forming, cover, and refrigerate for up to 3 days.

GLUTEN-FREE WHITE SAUCE
> Substitute rice flour for the wheat flour.

GOAT'S-MILK WHITE SAUCE
> Substitute goat's milk for cow's milk.

HOW TO FANCY UP A WHITE SAUCE

I was a child of à la king. For those of you who may not be familiar with this term, it's pretty much a fancied-up cream sauce. Originally it was a made with chicken. My mom preferred a mix of shrimp, peas, and sliced hard-boiled eggs. Creamed entrées can be dreadful when they are made carelessly—just ask old soldiers. But I think they are due for a renaissance. Use White Sauce Done Right (page 321) as a base and stir in your choice of the suggestions below. You can also use more contemporary white sauce variations like the Gluten-Free or Goat's Milk versions (page 322) or Vegan Soy Cream Sauce (page 328). Serve the sauce over toasted thick slabs of rustic bread, fluffy biscuits, or steamed red potatoes.

Leek and Tomato	Sauté 1 cup sliced leeks in 1 tablespoon butter until just tender. Stir into the sauce along with ½ cup peeled, diced, and well-drained tomatoes.
Spring Vegetable	Stir in 2 cups assorted cooked spring vegetables, such as baby carrots, baby turnips, asparagus, and pearl onions. Add 1 tablespoon chopped mixed tender fresh herbs, such as parsley, chives, and chervil.
Spinach and Portobello Mushroom	Blanch or steam 4 cups spinach, squeeze it dry, and chop. Sauté 1 chopped portobello mushroom and 1 chopped garlic clove in 1 to 2 tablespoons butter until brown and dry, about 6 minutes. Stir the spinach and mushrooms into the white sauce. Use the nutmeg.
Sausage Gravy	Brown 10 to 12 oz/285 to 340 g bulk (no casings) country or breakfast sausage in a skillet. Use the drippings to make the roux and then continue as written. Season with plenty of black pepper and a dash of Tabasco.
Mild Sweet Curry	Stir 2 tablespoons mild curry powder into the roux before adding the milk. Add ¼ cup Major Grey's chutney.
Mom's Creamed Shrimp and Peas	Stir in 6 oz/170 g cooked baby shrimp, 2 sliced hard-boiled eggs, and ½ cup thawed frozen peas. If desired, add ¼ cup chopped sweet onion and/or a teaspoon of chopped fresh dill.

continues

Smoked Turkey and Red Grapes	Stir in 8 oz/225 g diced smoked turkey, 1 cup halved red grapes, and 1 to 2 tablespoons dry sherry. Add 1 teaspoon chopped fresh tarragon or some crumbled blue cheese if you like.
Radicchio, Bresaola, and Parmesan	Sear 1 thickly sliced head of radicchio in 2 tablespoons olive oil in a hot skillet. Stir in 1 oz/28 g slivered bresaola (or spicy capicola or salami) and 1 minced or pressed garlic clove. Pour in the white sauce and warm gently. Finish with 2 tablespoons thinly sliced fresh basil and 2 tablespoons finely grated Parmesan cheese.
Caramelized Onion and Roasted Garlic	Sauté 1 chopped medium onion in 1 tablespoon butter or oil until brown and tender. Stir into the sauce along with 1 tablespoon roasted garlic (see the recipe on page 174), ½ teaspoon chopped fresh thyme, plenty of black pepper, and a dash of Tabasco.

THICK MUSHROOM CASSEROLE CREAM

This recipe mimics the cans of concentrated cream of mushroom soup that were once the foundation for classic American casseroles. To turn a basic béchamel sauce into a thick, binding cream, you increase the proportion of roux. Here I suggest 3 tablespoons each of butter and flour for 2 cups of milk, but for very binding sauces, increase the amounts to 4 tablespoons each. Seasoning will be muted by any starchy casserole ingredients like noodles or rice, so the sauce should be well seasoned, even slightly salty. I like to infuse the milk with dried mushrooms for added flavor. The sauce ingredients can be customized to your own tastes and dietary preferences by adapting the roux, the milk, and the flavorings. Several variations follow.

The sauce will thicken as it simmers and cools, so don't worry too much if it looks a bit thin at first. Cream of mushroom soup thins when you warm it too. Porcini powder can be made by simply grinding dried porcini mushrooms into a fine powder in a spice or coffee mill.

YIELD: 1¾ CUPS

2 cups whole milk

2 or 3 dried mushrooms, such as shiitake or forest, morels, or porcini slices, crumbled

Infusing ingredients (choose 1 to 3), such as a bit of onion or shallot, 4 or 5 black peppercorns, a bay leaf, 1 or 2 parsley stems, a carrot slice, and/or a clove of garlic

3 tablespoons butter

1 cup finely chopped mushrooms (any type)

1 tablespoon minced yellow onion

> Combine the milk, dried mushrooms, and your choice of infusing ingredients in a medium saucepan and heat over medium-high heat until the milk begins to steam and small bubbles form at the edges of the pan. Remove the milk from the heat and set aside to infuse. Or, if you prefer, combine the ingredients in a microwave-safe container and cook on high for about 45 seconds.

> Heat a medium saucepan over medium-high heat and add 1 tablespoon of the butter. When it bubbles, stir in the chopped mushrooms, onion, and celery and cook, stirring often, until the vegetables are soft but not browned, 4 to 5 minutes. Add the remaining 2 tablespoons butter, remove the pan from the heat, sprinkle the flour evenly over the mixture, and stir to combine. The roux will not be smooth because of the vegetables, but mix the flour in until there are no lumps. Return the pan to the

continues

1 tablespoon minced celery

3 tablespoons all-purpose flour

1 teaspoon kosher salt, or to taste

Very finely ground black pepper

1 teaspoon ground porcini powder
or a few drops of truffle oil
(optional)

1 tablespoon medium-dry sherry
(optional)

heat and cook the roux for another minute, stirring constantly. Strain half of the infused milk into the roux and stir to mix. Add the remaining (strained) milk and stir well. Add the salt and pepper to taste. For a more intense mushroom flavor, stir some of the sauce into the dried porcini powder until it is smooth, then return it to the pan. (If using truffle oil, stir it into the finished sauce.)

> Bring the sauce to a boil, then reduce the heat to a simmer and cook until the vegetables are completely tender and the flavors have infused, at least 10 to 12 minutes. The sauce will be thick, so stir it often to prevent it from scorching. Season the sauce with additional salt and pepper as necessary. Finish with the sherry if you choose.

> If you are not using the sauce right away, put a piece of plastic wrap or buttered parchment paper pressed directly on the surface of the sauce to prevent a skin from forming, cover, and refrigerate for up to 3 days.

CHEESY CASSEROLE CREAM

> Omit the mushrooms. Once the sauce is cooked, stir in 1 to 2 cups grated Gruyère cheese or any of the cheese suggestions in the table of Cheese Sauce Variations on page 359.

CELERY CASSEROLE CREAM

> Omit the mushrooms. Infuse the milk with a slice of onion, 3 or 4 slices of celery, and a pinch of celery seeds. Increase the minced celery in the sauce to ¼ cup. Puree or press the sauce through a sieve if you prefer a smooth texture.

CHICKEN CASSEROLE CREAM

> Omit the mushrooms. Substitute 1 cup Really Good Chicken Stock (page 114) for 1 cup of the milk. Stir in ½ cup minced cooked chicken with the seasonings.

GLUTEN-FREE CASSEROLE CREAM

> Substitute rice flour for the all-purpose flour.

DAIRY-FREE CASSEROLE CREAM

> Use a nondairy butter alternative or oil and substitute soy milk for the whole milk.

VEGAN SOY CREAM SAUCE

This all-soy recipe is an adaptable white sauce for those who prefer nondairy foods. It's smooth, thick, and creamy. Unlike béchamel, it has a clean finish and slight astringency. Make sure you buy unsweetened, unflavored soy milk. For a fresher taste, soak the tofu in boiling water for 4 to 5 minutes and drain well before blending. I like to add miso for a touch of umami and more depth. A tablespoon of nutritional yeast flakes also works. A thick casserole cream can be made by reducing the amount of milk to ⅔ cup.

YIELD: 2 CUPS

1 cup unflavored unsweetened soy milk

Infusing ingredients (choose 1 to 3), such as a sliver of onion, 3 or 4 black peppercorns, a bay leaf, 1 or 2 parsley stems, a slice of carrot, and/or a clove of garlic

8 oz/225 g soft tofu, drained

1 tablespoon white (shiro) miso

½ teaspoon kosher salt

Very finely ground black pepper

Pinch of cayenne pepper (optional)

> Combine the soy milk and your choice of infusing ingredients in a medium saucepan and heat over medium-high heat until steam rises and small bubbles form at the edges of the pan. Remove from the heat, cover, and let infuse for 5 minutes.

> Combine the tofu and miso in a blender, or the tall cup for an immersion blender, and puree to a smooth paste. Strain the soy milk and gradually add to the tofu, blending to make a creamy sauce.

> Pour the sauce into a clean saucepan, season with salt, pepper, and cayenne, if desired, and reheat. The sauce will thicken slightly as it simmers.

> Serve warm.

> If storing, cover and refrigerate for up to 3 days.

AROMATIC COCONUT CREAM SAUCE

Theoretically, you can make a nondairy version of béchamel simply by stirring coconut milk into a roux made with a butter substitute, but I think a much more intriguing coconut cream sauce is made with the techniques and aromatic ingredients used in Thai curries (see page 224). Some of the creamy coconut milk is simmered to concentrate the flavor and texture and carry the aroma of the ginger, garlic, and shallot, then the rest of the milk is added and the sauce is simmered to the ideal consistency. If you like, add some shaved fresh lemongrass with the shallots.

YIELD: 1½ CUPS

One 14 oz/414 ml can
   unsweetened coconut milk

1 tablespoon chopped shallot

1 clove garlic, minced

1 teaspoon minced fresh ginger

Pinch of red chile flakes

½ teaspoon kosher salt or 1
   teaspoon fish sauce

> Scoop the creamy top part of the coconut milk into a medium saucepan, add the shallot, garlic, ginger, red pepper flakes, and a pinch of the salt and cook over medium-high heat, stirring often, until the vegetables are tender and aromatic and the coconut milk is very thick and bubbly.

> Whisk in the remaining coconut milk, season with the remaining salt, and heat until hot. Strain or puree if you want a smooth sauce.

> Serve warm or cold.

> If storing, cover and refrigerate for up to 3 days. The sauce may separate slightly, but it will come together with gentle heat and stirring.

HOLIDAY GRAVY

I've heard rumors that gravy is just another weekday sauce in some households. For me, gravy means it's a holiday. Dinners that included both roasts and potatoes were few and far between when I was growing up. Gravy was a celebratory indulgence that usually meant that grandparents were in the vicinity. *Real gravy*, holiday gravy, requires a big chunk of roasted meat and that's something I rarely serve, so I still enjoy it only a few times a year. Mashed potatoes and gravy remain my favorite part of traditional holiday meals.

Holiday gravy should always be made from scratch and served by the boatload. It should carry the primal flavors of slowly cooked meat and fire. When there is plenty of good gravy, it's easier to overlook dry turkey, pasty stuffing, or potatoes with an "interesting" consistency.

This is a traditional roux-thickened gravy made with pan drippings. Nothing flavors gravy like the savory roasted bits and concentrated residue left in the pan after the entrée has cooked. Gravy liquefies those flavors and puts them back in play. Roasted vegetables and a really good vegetable stock can also work if meat is out of the question. Double or even triple this recipe if you are serving a crowd.

YIELD: 2 CUPS

2 tablespoons drippings and residue left in the pan used to roast chicken, turkey, beef, pork, lamb, or even root vegetables

Butter or vegetable oil if needed

2 tablespoons all-purpose flour

2 cups flavorful stock, such as Really Good Turkey or Chicken Stock (page 114) or Brown Bone Stock (page 117), heated

> Drain off all but 2 tablespoons of the drippings from the roasting pan. If there aren't 2 tablespoons of drippings left, add butter or oil as necessary. Sprinkle the flour into the roasting pan and stir until it combines with the drippings into a thin, lump-free paste. There will be brown bits mixed into the roux, but they can be strained out later.

> Put the roasting pan on a burner set at medium heat; if the pan is very large pan, use two burners. Cook the roux, stirring, until it is bubbly and golden brown, 2 to 3 minutes, doing your best to gently soften and dissolve the brown bits into the fat and flour mixture to capture the flavors. Move the roasting pan around as the roux cooks so it doesn't cook only in one spot.

Kosher salt and freshly ground
black pepper

Additional seasonings such as
lemon juice, chopped fresh
herbs, a few dashes of Tabasco
and/or a dash of Worcestershire
or fish sauce (optional)

> Remove the pan from the heat, pour in half of the
stock, and whisk it into the roux until smooth. Add
the remaining stock and a pinch each of salt and
pepper, return the pan to the heat, and simmer,
whisking often, until the gravy has thickened and
the raw taste of flour is completely gone, at least 5
minutes. If you want the sauce to simmer longer
for a smoother, slightly richer texture and flavor,
transfer the gravy to a saucepan, half-cover it, and
simmer, stirring often, until it reaches the desired
consistency.

> Taste and season with additional salt and pepper.
Strain if necessary. If desired, add a touch of lemon
juice, herbs, Tabasco, and/or an umami-rich sauce
for freshness or savory depth. Serve warm.

> If storing, cover and refrigerate for 4 days or freeze
for up to 4 months.

OIL SLICKS—HOW TO GET RID OF UNWANTED GREASE

No one should have to tip and maneuver a gravy boat to avoid a top layer of grease. There are two common scenarios that result in greasy gravy.

First, the ratio of fat to flour is off—too much fat was used. Drippings add flavor to gravy, but it is the savory brown residue at the bottom of the roasting pan that really counts. If you're not comfortable eyeballing things yet, pour all of the liquid from the pan into a measuring cup and do the math: 1 tablespoon fat mixed with 1 tablespoon flour will thicken 1 cup liquid to gravy consistency. Decide how much stock you plan to thicken and then return the appropriate amount of drippings to the roasting pan.

The second common mistake is to use greasy stock. Start with clear, fat-free stock whenever you can. My grandmother and mother always started their turkey gravy by simmering the turkey giblets and an onion in a pot of water while the turkey roasted. Once the giblets were tender, the neck meat was pulled off the bone and it and the other bits were chopped and stirred into the gravy. It was wonderful. But if the meal was rushed and the deep layer of fat wasn't carefully spooned off the giblet stock, the gravy would end up greasy. Grandma sometimes "fixed" this by dropping a handful of ice cubes into the gravy. The fat would congeal around the ice and she would just lift it off the surface. This was quite brilliant, and I tried it myself a few times. Unfortunately, the melting ice dilutes the gravy and the flavor suffers. If you have time, you can pour the strained, greasy stock into a shallow container and freeze it until the fat solidifies, but it takes a few hours. A better solution is to use a fat separator, a measuring cup with an offset spout. Leave the liquid to settle and separate, then pour the good stuff from the bottom; stop pouring once the fat starts to flow.

I'm also a fan of a gadget called a fat or grease mop. It is a ridiculous-looking wand of floppy synthetic fibers similar to those used to clean up ocean spills. Drag it over the surface of stock, soup, or gravy, and it will suck up excess grease like magic. Then throw it in the dishwasher.

GRAMMA BOBBI'S 'MATER GRAVY

I first heard about tomato gravy from my friend Bobbi Levins, aka Gramma Bobbi. She's one of those magical Southern cooks who makes everything taste good. When you ask her about her recipes, she just shrugs her shoulders and says, "That's just how my mamma used to do it." One of her family's favorites is 'mater gravy—tomatoes simmered in drippings—poured over piping-hot biscuits. I'd always assumed 'mater gravy was an exclusively Southern thing until my mother-in-law was over during a recipe test. One taste, and she starting reminiscing about the gravy her mother made when she was a child in North Dakota.

This particular recipe is a combination of both gravies. It is marvelous on biscuits or corn grits, but it's also good with meat loaf, chicken, pork chops, and even spaghetti squash. You can add a little chopped onion, garlic, or minced green pepper if you like. I added the bacon as a treat, but it's just as good without it. Warming the milk helps to prevent it from "shattering" when it is stirred in. Bacon and canned tomatoes vary in salt content, so trust your own taste when adding salt.

YIELD: 3 CUPS

3 strips thick-sliced bacon, finely chopped (if you prefer a sauce made without bacon, make the roux with 2 tablespoons butter instead)

2 tablespoons all-purpose flour

One 14½ oz/411 g can diced tomatoes

About ½ teaspoon kosher salt, or to taste

Freshly ground black pepper

1½ cups milk, or as needed, warmed

Pinch of cayenne pepper or a dash of Tabasco sauce

> Fry the bacon in a skillet until it is crisp. Using a slotted spoon, lift the pieces of bacon from the pan, leaving the bacon fat. Save the crisp bacon for later. (Or, if you choose not to use bacon, melt the butter in a skillet over medium heat until it bubbles.)

> Remove the pan from the heat, sprinkle in the flour, and stir to make a smooth, even paste. Return the pan to the heat and cook, stirring constantly, until the flour is a toast-colored brown, about 3 minutes. Stir in the tomatoes and mix well, breaking up any large pieces with a spoon. Season with a bit of the salt and some pepper and simmer until the mixture is thick, 2 to 3 minutes.

> Gradually stir in the warm milk, then continue to simmer until the gravy comes together and thickens, about 5 minutes. Simmer it for longer if you like it very thick, or add a bit more milk if you want

continues

to thin it slightly. Season with the remaining salt, pepper to taste, and the cayenne.

> Serve hot, with the crisp bacon stirred in or sprinkled on top as a garnish.

> If storing, cover and refrigerate for up to 3 days; refrigerate the bacon separately and add before serving.

GLUTEN-FREE TOMATO CREAM GRAVY

> Use rice flour in place of the wheat flour. Or, omit the roux altogether and simply simmer the canned tomatoes until they are thick; use only 1 cup warm milk. There is a higher risk that the milk will "shatter" when the roux is omitted.

ARKANSAS CHOCOLATE GRAVY

This is an old Ozarks mountain-country favorite meant to be served on biscuits for breakfast. All of the fundamentals of a roux-thickened sauce are here, but there is none of the pomp and circumstance of the French classics. Kids love it, and since it is made with milk, I can pour it over their waffles or French toast and still convince myself I am serving them something kind of nourishing. (Aunt standards for diet and nutrition tend to be similar to indulgent grandparents' rules.) They just mumble "chocolate sauce" in between oversized mouthfuls.

This sauce may have rustic roots, but when you serve it in a pretty bowl, in a sun-kissed gazebo, with a baguette and summer strawberries for dipping, it seems very elegant and refined. The ratio of butter to flour is higher here than in most roux-thickened sauces, purely as an indulgence. You can drop the butter down to as little as 2 tablespoons if you prefer.

YIELD: 3 CUPS

6 tablespoons butter

½ cup sugar

2 tablespoons all-purpose flour

¼ cup unsweetened cocoa powder, sifted to remove any lumps

2½ cups milk, warmed, or more as desired

Pinch of kosher salt

½ teaspoon vanilla extract

> Heat a medium saucepan over medium heat and add the butter. Stir in the sugar until it dissolves, about 1 minute. Remove the pan from the heat, sprinkle the flour evenly over the melted butter, and stir until the butter and flour are a smooth paste. Return the pan to the heat and cook the roux, stirring often, until the raw aroma is cooked out and it is bubbly but not brown, about 1 minute. Stir in the cocoa powder. Add half of the milk and whisk until smooth. Add the remaining milk and stir well. Bring the sauce to a boil, then reduce the heat to a simmer, season with the salt, and cook, stirring often, for 5 minutes, to make sure there is no raw taste and to give the starch particles a chance to swell and thicken the sauce. For a thinner gravy, add more milk.

> Stir in the vanilla and serve. This is also quite good cold.

> If you aren't going to enjoy the sauce immediately, put a butter wrapper, oiled piece of parchment, or

continues

plastic wrap directly on the surface of the slightly cooled sauce to pre-vent a skin from forming, cover, and refrigerate for up to 3 days. The cold gravy will be thick and look a little lumpy, but it will smooth out with heat and a little whisking.

SHELLEY'S LEMON SAUCE FOR FISH (VELOUTÉ)

My sister, Shelley, isn't much of a cook or eater. She is perfectly capable of making good food when she chooses to, but since food is rarely a priority, she tends to grab whatever is convenient when she realizes how ridiculously long it's been since her last meal. Every now and then, though, she will crave fresh seafood and green vegetables and eat with the zeal of a starving python. When that button is triggered, this is one of the recipes she reaches for. It is the first thing I ever made for her when I came home from cooking school.

I never told her that it was a variation of velouté sauce, made with a toasted golden roux, the juices from some oven-poached fish fillets, and lots of fresh lemon. She doesn't care a whit about that stuff. She just knows it's fast and good. She's likely to use store-bought clam nectar or a cube of fish bouillon and a chunk of halibut. Sometimes she'll even settle for breaded frozen fish fillets and a side of microwaved broccoli. I'm okay with that. If she felt any pressure to make a fancy dish, she'd probably skip it altogether and have a blueberry muffin for dinner. Cooking is a better option. If you are using store-bought clam nectar, reduce or omit the salt.

YIELD: 1¾ CUPS

1 cup milk

Infusing ingredients (choose 2 or 3) such as a sliver of onion, 3 or 4 black peppercorns, a bay leaf, a few parsley stems, a slice of carrot, and/or a clove of garlic

2 tablespoons butter

2 tablespoons all-purpose flour

1 cup Fish Stock (page 122) or Clam Nectar (page 140)

1 teaspoon finely grated lemon zest

½ teaspoon kosher salt, or to taste

> Combine the milk and your choice of infusing ingredients in a medium saucepan and heat over medium-high heat until steam rises and small bubbles form at the edges of the pan. Remove from the heat and set aside to infuse.

> Heat a medium saucepan over medium heat and add the butter. When it is bubbling, remove the pan from the heat and stir in the flour until it becomes a smooth paste. Return the pan to the heat and cook, stirring constantly, until the flour is golden brown and smells of toast, 2 to 3 minutes.

> Strain the milk into the pan and stir or whisk until smooth. Add the stock, half of the lemon zest, and the salt. Bring the sauce to a boil, then reduce the heat to a gentle simmer and cook, stirring often, until the sauce has thickened and become velvety,

continues

2 tablespoons freshly squeezed
   lemon juice

2 tablespoons chopped capers and/
   or 1 tablespoon chopped mild
   fresh herbs, such as parsley,
   chives, or dill (optional)

6 to 8 minutes. Add the lemon juice, and capers and/or herbs. Stir in the remaining lemon zest. Serve warm.

> If storing, cover and refrigerate for up to 2 days.

NEW MEXICAN RED CHILE SAUCE

I was surprised when I learned that many of the New Mexican chile sauces I have fallen deeply in love with start with roux. It may not be historically accurate, or even necessary, but it is pretty common, and I like the textural control and toasty flavor. I was unimpressed with most red chile sauces until my friend Jamie taught me how his family toasts the chiles before softening them and then fries the chile puree a bit before adding any liquid. The greater complexity and depth of flavor is remarkable.

This sauce it is great on tamales and enchiladas. I often substitute one or two guajillo or other chiles for a darker, smokier taste. The sauce improves with time, so make it a day ahead if you can.

YIELD: 2 CUPS

2 oz/60 g dried New Mexican chiles (8 to 10)—substitute a few guajillo or pasilla chiles if you prefer

½ cup chopped yellow or white onion

2 cloves garlic

About 3½ cups water

2 tablespoons vegetable oil

2 tablespoons all-purpose flour

1 teaspoon kosher salt, plus more to taste

½ teaspoon ground cumin

½ teaspoon dried oregano

> Using kitchen shears, remove the stems from the chiles and split them lengthwise in half. Shake out the seeds and flatten the chiles. Toast them by holding them one at a time with tongs over a hot burner. The chile will first soften slightly and then darken, blister, and crackle a bit; flip to make sure both sides are browned. Repeat until all of the chiles are toasted. Or, if you prefer, you can put the chiles in a large dry skillet over medium-high heat and flip them regularly until they have darkened and started to crackle or smoke slightly.

> Put the toasted chiles, onion, and garlic in a saucepan with enough water to cover, cover the pot, and simmer over medium heat until the chiles are soft, about 20 minutes.

> Drain the chiles in a sieve set over a bowl. Measure out ½ cup of the cooking water (or 1½ cups if you want to use the liquid instead of the stock). Put the solids in a blender and puree until smooth, stopping to scrape the sides often and adding a tablespoon or two of the reserved cooking water if necessary to make a smooth paste.

continues

1 cup Brown Bone Stock (page 117), Really Good Chicken Stock (page 114), Vegetable Stock (page 106), Light Tomato or Sofrito Vegetable Stock (see the table on page 108), or the strained liquid from simmering the chiles

> Heat the oil in a saucepan over medium high heat. Remove the pan from the burner and stir in the flour to make a smooth paste. Return the pan to the heat and cook, stirring often, until the roux has the color and aroma of dark toast, about 3 minutes. Remove the pan from the heat and add the chile puree—it will spatter and bubble. Stir to mix completely and season with the salt, cumin, and oregano.

> Return the pan to the heat and cook for 1 minute, stirring constantly. Whisk in the stock and the reserved ½ cup chile cooking water, cover, and simmer, stirring occasionally, until the sauce has mellowed and thickened slightly, 15 to 20 minutes.

> Season with additional salt to taste—to get this sauce really dialed in, you will probably need more salt than you expect.

> Serve warm.

> If storing, cover and refrigerate for up to a week or freeze for up to 3 months.

CREOLE SAUCE MADE WITH DARK BROWN ROUX

In Louisiana, a dark brown roux is not just a thickener—it can be a benchmark for who you are as a person. It takes mettle to keep the roux on the stove until the very last minute. The flour must be just this side of burnt, yet with nary a hint of scorching. I will take the pan off the stove repeatedly, thinking I've done it, only to grimace and put it back on for just a tiny bit longer. I'm a babe in the woods when it comes to authentic Cajun and Creole cooking, but I have an appreciation for the unique toasted taste of dishes made with really dark, slow-cooked roux.

This sauce improves after a day or two and freezes well, so keep some on hand to serve as a dollop alongside a fried catfish fillet, to smother a sausage in a bun like a Cajun hot dog, or to simmer with virtually any mix of meats and seafood for a hearty meal with rice.

This version does not call for gumbo filé, powdered sassafras, a natural thickener with a unique slippery texture, because I'm not a fan. Stir a bit in at the end if you like. I usually make my own Cajun spice mix, but to simplify things, here I suggest using a good commercial blend.

YIELD: 3 CUPS

¼ cup vegetable oil

¼ cup all-purpose flour

1 cup chopped yellow onion

1 cup chopped green bell pepper

¼ cup chopped celery

4 cloves garlic, chopped

2 tablespoons good-quality Cajun spice mix

> Heat the oil in a large heavy-bottomed saucepan over medium heat. Remove the pan from the heat and stir in the flour until it is smooth. Return the pan to the burner and cook the roux, stirring constantly, until it is chestnut brown. For really big pots of gumbo, cooking the roux can take almost an hour; for a small batch of sauce like this, it will be closer to 10 minutes. You may find yourself taking the roux off the heat, checking the color, and then returning it to cook just a little longer; I do this a lot.

> Add the onion, bell pepper, celery, garlic, and Cajun spice mix, stir and cook for 1 minute. Add the stock, tomatoes, and salt and simmer, partly covered, for about 1 hour, until the sauce has thickened and the flavors have stewed together.

continues

2 cups Vegetable Stock (page 106, or see the table on page 108), Quick Shrimp Shell Stock (page 120), or Really Good Chicken Stock (page 114)

One 14½ oz/411 g can diced tomatoes

1 teaspoon kosher salt, or to taste

1 tablespoon freshly squeezed lemon juice

1 teaspoon Tabasco or Crystal pepper sauce, or more to taste

2 tablespoons chopped fresh parsley

> Season the sauce with the lemon juice, hot sauce, and salt to taste if needed. Stir in the parsley just before serving.

> Serve hot or refrigerate overnight for the flavors to develop even more.

> If storing, cover and refrigerate for 5 days or freeze for up to 3 months.

TIPS
for Creating Roux-Thickened Sauces

- Butter is the most commonly used fat because it adds richness and flavor. (It is also the most commonly used fat because the technique is French and they make great butter there.) Any heat-tolerant fat works. The best gravies are made with the drippings in the bottom of the roasting pan.

- Wheat flour is the preferred starch because it is easy to use, and inexpensive, and it can create a silky, smooth texture without much flavor interference. Finely milled rice or sweet rice flour also works, but the sauces can separate and get slightly grainy when chilled.

- Roux is most commonly made with equal quantities of fat and flour by volume, but occasionally a recipe will call for a different ratio (see Arkansas Chocolate Gravy, page 335). The main consideration is that the flour blend smoothly into the fat and the roux remain liquid rather than doughy. Ideally, a roux should spread in the pan as it cooks but be thick enough to form distinct channels as it is stirred.

- The longer you cook a roux, the browner and more flavorful it becomes. Subtle sauces are best thickened with very pale, mild roux. Robust and spicy sauces can benefit from the dark-toast taste of brown roux.

- The darker the roux, the less thickening potential it has. It can take 2 tablespoons of dark roux to get the same texture as a sauce made with 1 tablespoon light roux.

- Some culinary schools teach the mantra of "hot roux, cold liquid" for making lump-free soups and sauces. I disagree. Adding a cold liquid can offer a bit more control when making recipes in industrial-sized pots, but for home cooking, I prefer using warm liquids. Adding liquids straight from the fridge can make the butter or drippings congeal. They will eventually melt, but these solids can be disconcerting. Obviously, both techniques work—the important point is to make a perfectly smooth roux before adding liquid and whisking the sauce well as the liquid is being introduced.

- The darker the roux, the longer the sauce should cook.

EXPANDING ON ROUX

Gluten-Free Roux

A gluten-free roux can be made just by using a different kind of flour. I prefer finely milled rice flour. Brown rice flour, if you can find it, also works well. In certain applications I like quinoa flour and masa harina; they add a certain rustic appeal and very specific flavor, and they take a little extra simmering. But sometimes different is good. I don't recommend gluten-free flour mixes meant for baking. They are often high in garbanzo bean flour and xanthan gum. Both of these ingredients can be used to thicken sauces, but they don't work well in roux, especially in what are unknown ratios. I've never had luck with sorghum flour, although I've seen gluten-free websites that tout it.

Gluten-free roux often don't have quite the pleasing silkiness of wheat-flour roux. They also don't store as well and can become grainy and separated. Gluten-free pure starch slurries like potato starch and kudzu root may be preferable in some applications.

Dairy-Free or Vegan Roux

Roux can be successfully made with virtually any heat-tolerant liquid fat. Vegetable oil, coconut oil, and butter substitutes can be used with various stocks to make sauces that are kosher, vegan, and allergy-free. Some margarines and butter substitutes have a very high water content. If they start to splatter and separate when heated,

they can make the roux slightly sticky and doughy rather than smooth and even. Try not to overstir the roux in these cases.

Cold Roux

Roux can be made in large batches and stored. In large restaurants and institutions, buckets of cold roux are sometimes kept on hand as both a time-saving technique and a quick remedy for thin sauces, soups, and stews. To make roux ahead of time, simply proceed as you normally would, cooking the fat and flour to the desired color, then scrape the warm roux into a container and chill until you are ready to use it. Two tablespoons of cold roux will have roughly the same thickening power as a mix of 2 tablespoons flour and 2 tablespoons fat. Gradually melt spoonfuls of the cold roux into a simmering soup or sauce, stirring until it reaches the texture you want.

Kneaded Butter (Beurre Manié)

I love kneaded butter (*beurre manié* is the French term). It is a paste of softened butter mashed with flour that can be melted into simmering liquids to both thicken and enrich them. I use it for rich stews, braised meaty dishes, or pan sauces that have wonderfully flavorful cooking liquids but in a quantity I can't accurately estimate at the start of cooking. For these, I prefer to cook the ingredients to perfection, taste the juices, and then judge the best way to thicken them.

I was taught to make kneaded butter

with a ratio of 2 parts butter to 1 part flour. It's more common these days to use 1:1, but I like the way a higher-fat-content mix melts and blends into sauces that need just a finishing enhancement, so I often split the difference and use 1½ tablespoons of butter to each tablespoon of all-purpose flour. Mash the flour into the softened butter with the back of a fork until evenly combined. Scoop up some of the kneaded butter and melt it into the sauce. The best way to do this is to rub the kneaded butter against the side of the hot pan at the waterline and stir it as it melts into the sauce. Continue to add more until you have reached the desired consistency. Be sure to simmer the liquid for at least 3 to 5 minutes to remove any raw flour taste.

If you do not consume dairy products, refer to the table of Texturizers on page 48 for an alternative. Margarine does not work well as kneaded butter. I've had luck with solid coconut oil when it is added slowly and thoroughly whisked in before adding more, but it adds a distinctive flavor. Relatively stable nondairy butters like Earth Balance can also work, but they are finicky and prone to separation. There are better options.

Wondra (Modified Wheat Flour)

Wheat flour thickens sauces when the granules are hydrated to the point that the starch particles start to peel off into clinging strings and bushes. This transformation is called gelatinization. Wondra is a General Mills product often touted as superfine or gravy flour. It is wheat flour that has been cooked and partially hydrated—enough to become gelatinized—then dried and milled back into a powder. It thickens almost instantly, is less likely to clump, and doesn't have the raw taste of wheat because it has already been cooked. It's a handy product.

Apparently it is meant to be stirred into water and used as a slurry (see Slurries, page 367). But I reach for Wondra when I want a really quick fix for a rustic dish. I shake, stir, and then repeat until I reach the consistency I'm looking for. Wondra can even be added to uncooked sauces that need thickening, although it is not my first choice there. The main drawback is that it takes a lot more Wondra than all-purpose flour to thicken a liquid. That can dramatically mute the flavors and create an odd slightly pasty and gritty consistency. Be sure to boost your seasonings accordingly.

THE MIGHTY DEMI-GLACE

WHAT'S THE DIFFERENCE BETWEEN A DEMI-GLACE, A "DEMI," AND A MEAT REDUCTION?

The terms "demi-glace," "demi," and "reduction" are often used interchangeably. They all refer to a shiny, intense, often quite clear brown gravy. Semantics don't alter how they taste, but in case you've ever wondered, there is actually a difference.

True demi-glace is a traditional French sauce made of half meat glace and half brown roux-thickened sauce (espagnole). Demi-glaces may be more popular than ever, but few are actually made the way they once were. Some chefs will use a brown roux to thicken concentrated meat stocks, but few go to the trouble of making two labor-intensive sauces and mixing them, even if it is more traditional and economical.

That is part of the reason that the term "demi" shows up so often. It is an abbreviation of demi-glace that takes some of the formality, as well as some of the obligatory authenticity, away. These days "demi" tends to be the term of choice to describe virtually any concentrated brown sauce.

A meat reduction is made by simmering and concentrating a meaty stock, sometimes with other flavorful ingredients like wine, until it's syrupy and sauce-like. Meat Glace (page 158) is a superconcentrated meat

reduction. There is no added thickener: the texture is derived from the concentration of dissolved proteins. Reductions like these have become the most coveted of demis. They are clear, pure, concentrated meat flavor with a pleasing natural body. They are also very expensive.

DEMI-GLACE "CHEATS"

I debated the inclusion of a classic demi-glace in this book for a long time. I wrote out and tested several variations. In the end, they all seemed like the sort of recipes I had originally set out to avoid: expensive, time-consuming, resource-heavy, and tinged with pretention in the name of tradition. But leaving demi-glace out entirely seemed like a glaring omission. I had to do a bit of soul searching. In the end, I felt it was important to include a recipe for Meat Glace (page 158) because it is unmatched as an intense, meaty sauce as well as an ingredient. It is technically a reduction, not a demi-glace, because there is no brown roux. I suggest that curious meat-loving cooks try making it at least once in their life. But anybody who is willing to go through the routine every time they want to serve lamb chops is a much more devoted cook than I am. The solution to my demi-glace quandary was to admit this.

On the very rare occasions I serve a

demi at home, I "cheat." I start with a good-quality commercially prepared product and customize it to my taste and menu. The longer I pondered it, the more I realized that it wasn't really a cheat at all. *No one* I know makes demi-glace from scratch anymore. Even the people who raise urban chickens, nurture rustic bread starters, and obsess for days over smoking pits of meat—don't make demi-glace. Why keep that a secret? If you are the exception, I tip my hat to your dedication to the craft of sauce making.

Demis made from store-bought bases are convenient and affordable and can be remarkably good. Restaurants use them. They often have thickeners and flavorings added, but so does traditional French demi-glace.

Rather than just reconstituting the sauce base with water as the package says, I suggest you treat the base as you would a meat glace. Build a sauce from aromatics, wine, and good, gelatin-rich stock and simply intensify it with the demi-glace base.

The best sources are restaurants or butchers in your town that sell their own meat reductions, demi bases, and stocks. The resurgence of craft butchers has made this a much more viable option than it was even a few years ago. D'Artagnan brand Veal Demi Glace and Duck and Veal Demi are good products that are used in many restaurants. They can be ordered online and found in the freezers of good gourmet supermarkets. More than Gourmet brand products are much more common—I've found them in some pretty remote locations—so that's what I call for in the demi-glace recipe and table that follow.

As for stock, few commercial beef or veal stocks sold off store shelves have the depth of flavor, high gelatin content, and delicate seasoning balance that is best for making demis. Remember that you can whip up a batch of Pressure-Cooker Brown Bone Stock (page 119) enhanced with gelatin-rich oxtails in just a few hours. If that isn't an option, I suggest you use a good frozen product. I'm fond of Stock Options, a boutique product from Portland, Oregon, and Perfect Addition brand.

DEMI-GLACE MADE FROM STORE-BOUGHT BASE

As an experiment I made both this sauce and a pure meat reduction from scratch and served them side by side. The homemade reduction was clear and glossy with a cleaner, pure meat flavor tinged with wine and herbs, but the "cheater" demi held its own better than I could have imagined. You can certainly make this using the Meat Glace on page 158, but for an adaptable sauce that takes minutes rather than days, the choice is simple. Use this sauce for the very best cuts of meat, like tender lamb chops and boutique steaks .

YIELD: ⅔ CUP

1 teaspoon olive or grape seed oil

3 tablespoons minced shallots

3 tablespoons red wine vinegar or sherry vinegar

3 or 4 black peppercorns

½ cup robust red wine

1 package (1.5oz/42.5 g) More than Gourmet demi-glace base or similar product

1 cup gelatin-rich stock, such as Pressure-Cooker Brown Bone Stock (page 119) or good-quality frozen beef or veal stock, such as Stock Options or Perfect Addition brand

1 bouquet garni (1 large sprig fresh thyme, 1 bay leaf, and 3 or 4 bruised parsley sprigs, tied in a bundle; see page 103)

Kosher salt

> Heat the oil in a medium saucepan over medium heat. Add the shallots and cook until softened but not browned, about 2 minutes. Add the vinegar and peppercorns and simmer until the liquid has reduced to a film but the shallots have not browned. Add the wine, increase the temperature slightly, and simmer until the wine has reduced by half.

> Stir in the demi-glace base until melted. Add the stock, bouquet garni, and a pinch of salt, cover the pot, leaving the lid slightly tilted so some of the steam can escape, and simmer over low heat, stirring occasionally, until the flavors have married and the sauce is thick and glossy, about 30 minutes.

> Set a sieve over a clean saucepan and line it with dampened cheesecloth. Strain the sauce, pressing very lightly on the solids to remove as much liquid as possible; discard the solids. Reheat the sauce over medium heat. Taste for seasoning. Remember that the sauce is meant to be very intense. (At this point, the sauce can be refrigerated or frozen.)

continues

2 tablespoons cold unsalted butter, cut into small cubes (optional)

1 teaspoon very finely chopped fresh herbs, such as parsley, chives, thyme, and/or tarragon (optional)

1 to 2 teaspoons Cognac (optional)

> To finish the sauce with butter, whisk the cubes of cold butter into the simmering sauce until just melted. Add the herbs and Cognac if using. Serve.

> Do not refrigerate or boil the sauce after the butter has been added.

ELEGANT EMBELLISHMENTS FOR DEMI-GLACE MADE FROM STORE-BOUGHT BASE

Use the recipe for Demi-Glace Made from Store-Bought Base (page 349) as the foundation for the following variations. I have included recipes that call for a poultry demi base as well as a vegetarian version. More than Gourmet demi-glace bases come in several varieties.

Green Peppercorns and Cream	Once the sauce has been strained, stir in 1 tablespoon chopped drained green peppercorns in brine and 2 tablespoons heavy cream. The sauce will become very peppery as it infuses. Serve with cuts of tender beef, such as tournedos or fillet.
Cumberland Sauce (Red Currant and Juniper)	Add 5 to 7 crushed juniper berries along with the shallots. Use orange juice in place of the vinegar. Simmer the sauce with a strip of orange zest. Melt ¼ cup well-stirred red currant jelly into the sauce before straining. Excellent with venison or pheasant.
Guajillo Chile	Stem, seed, and toast 1 guajillo chile and slice or crumble. Add 1 tablespoon of the chile with 2 tablespoons minced carrot and a minced garlic clove to the shallots. Use ¾ cup stock and ½ cup tomato juice. Omit the bouquet garni and Cognac. Season with extra salt.
Mustard and Orange	Add 1 teaspoon yellow or brown mustard seeds along with the shallots. Use orange juice in place of the wine. Use a poultry, duck, or game demi-glace base. Use Really Good Chicken Stock (page 114) in place of the beef or veal stock. Finish with 1 to 2 tablespoons orange marmalade when a sweeter sauce is appropriate. Serve with seared duck breasts.
Coq au Vin	Use a poultry, duck, or game demi-glace base. While the sauce is simmering, fry ½ cup (2 oz/60 g) minced bacon with ½ cup halved pearl onions and ½ cup chopped mushrooms until browned; drain off excess fat. Strain the simmered sauce into the pan with the bacon, onions, and mushrooms. Finish with 2 teaspoons very finely chopped fresh parsley and a pinch of chopped fresh thyme.

continues

Quince and Sage	Add ½ cup minced quince to the shallots. Use cider in place of the wine. Use a poultry or duck demi-glace base. Use Really Good Chicken Stock (page 114) or a very good frozen stock. Finish with 1 teaspoon chopped fresh sage. Excellent with turkey or pork roast.
Vegetarian Mushroom and Amaro	Add ½ cup minced cremini or shiitake mushrooms and 2 tablespoons minced carrots along with shallots and sauté until they are browned and dry. Use a roasted vegetable demi-glace base and mushroom stock or Fresh Mushroom Jus (page 138). Finish with 1 to 2 tablespoons Amaro Averna or similar bitter amaro liqueur in place of the Cognac. Because there is no gelatin, this sauce will not have quite the same viscosity as the others.

Chile sauces (clockwise from top left: Homemade Sriracha, Tomato and Chile Momo Dunk, Sweet Garlic and Pickled Chile Dipping Sauce, Harissa, All-Purpose Hot Sauce, Fuchsia Dunlop's Chinese Chile Oil), from *Sauce on the Side*, pages 302, 304, 301, 307, 306, and 300.

Andouille sausage sandwich smothered in
Creole Sauce Made with Dark Brown Roux,
from *Respect Your Mother*, page 341

Shrimp and baby bok choy with Endlessly Adaptable
Stir-Fry Sauce—Salted/Fermented Black Beans Variation,
from *Respect Your Mother*, pages 369 and 370.

Cauliflower steaks and Coconut
"Butter" with South Indian Flavors,
from *Respect Your Mother*, page 399

Pound cake with Lemon Clove Syrup,
from *Syrups and Sweet Sauces*, page 409.

Remedies for Faltering Sauces (clockwise from top: immersion blender, fresh herbs, whisk, lemon, fine sieve, cheesecloth, egg, fat mop, salt, olive oil, nutritional yeast), page 446.

Waffles and bananas with Arkansas Chocolate Gravy, from *Respect Your Mother*, page 335.

TIPS

for Creating Original Demi-Glace Variations from Store-Bought Base

- Aromatics like shallots and the bouquet garni can be considered optional since both the demi-glace base and the stock will have depth from assorted vegetables and herbs, but every added flavor increases complexity.

- Use as little fat as possible to soften and cook the aromatics. The fat can float to the surface and alter the perceived purity of the finished sauce. Softening the aromatics in oil or butter helps to sweeten them and distribute the flavors, but you can also just simmer the shallots in the vinegar for a slightly more pungent bite.

- The acid from the vinegar helps cut through some of the salty, umami intensity. Be sure to reduce the vinegar until the pan is almost dry to retain the acidity and flavor but remove unnecessary water. You want to use a vinegar that tastes good, like a quallity red wine or sherry vinegar, but there is no need to use very expensive vinegars with subtle nuances. Those are best saved for fresh foods.

- Concentration is key: not only should the glace be intense, but the flavors and liquid ingredients that are added should be strong. Adding wine straight from the bottle without reducing it a bit can dilute the sauce more than enhance it.

- It is possible to overreduce a demi-glace. The sauce is meant to be dark, intense, and slightly sticky, but never scorched or burnt (see Can a Sauce Be Overreduced?, page 161). Swirl the pan and give it a stir to see how the sauce coats a spoon. Don't just look at it, smell and taste it too. It will thicken as it cools.

- It can be tricky to judge the seasoning of a demi-glace because of its intensity. A taste can seem jarring when there is no vehicle to carry the flavors and add perspective. Use a tuft of bread, or even dilute a bit of the sauce with a tablespoon or two of water, to better judge the balance of salt, sweet, acid, and bitter without burning out your sense of taste. The sauce will become livelier with a finish of fresh herbs, butter, and/or a bit of Cognac, but the seasoning should be dialed in before those ingredients are added.

continues

- The time and expense invested in demi-glace is deserving of a really special entrée. Buy the best cuts, prepare them well, and use the sauce as an embellishment, not a cover-up. A little goes a long way.

- Demi-glace is a sticky sauce and every transfer you make will reduce the yield. Scrape saucepans and other containers well with a silicone spatula. Let the sauce drain very well in the sieve, but don't press on it too firmly. Every drop is precious.

- Rarely is there any leftover demi-glace, but if there is, remember that the cold sauce will get solid and rubbery. That's good—it means there is a lot of natural gelatin. Any butter will rise and solidify on the surface. Scrape as much of this butter off as possible before reheating the sauce, thin the sauce with a bit of water or stock if needed, and add fresh butter.

CHEESE SAUCES

Few Western sauces have the universal appeal of a gooey, rich cheese sauce. Unfortunately, homemade cheese sauce is often a disappointment to many home cooks. It's too milky, it's not cheesy enough, it's stringy, greasy, or gritty. Believe me, I've been there. Don't despair! Help is on the way.

I think the most important consideration when making cheese sauce, or Mornay, as it's known in traditional sauce-making circles, is to remember that it is a white sauce flavored with cheese. It is not melted cheese in sauce form. To get the best flavor and texture, you need start with a stellar white sauce (see White Sauce Done Right, page 321). Infuse the milk with savory tidbits like a sliver of onion, a garlic clove, and a few peppercorns. Make a smooth, bubbly roux and cook it until you can smell a whiff of buttered toast. Simmer and season the white sauce and then add the cheese. If you want your sauce to have a strong cheese flavor and smooth melted texture, use cheeses that have those characteristics. Cheap, flavorless "Cheddar" cheese might turn a sauce orange, but it won't magically develop more flavor in

the pan. Gruyère is used in traditional Mornay sauce because it's sharp and nutty and it melts well. Cheeses that break and separate when they get hot will get greasy, gritty, and stringy when they are overheated in a sauce too. That's why you should never boil a cheese sauce after the cheese is added. Once you put these common-sense techniques into play, you may find yourself customizing the recipes with various cheeses in every possible combination.

If what you really want is not a classic Mornay sauce but gooey, bright orange, liquid cheese, skip to page 363. That takes an entirely different set of ingredients and techniques.

The dairy-free Vegan Cashew "Cheese" Sauce (page 365) should not be dismissed as a sad substitute for those with specialty diets. It's really good, especially on tacos and vegetables. My neighbor Chris is a cheese fanatic with very particular tastes. I gave him a sample without telling him what it was. He kept tasting it, trying to place the variety. He was very surprised when I told him it was actually cheese-free.

CLASSIC CHEESE SAUCE (MORNAY)

Mornay is a white sauce flavored and enriched with melted cheese. It is especially good in gratinéed dishes that are baked or broiled until they bubble and brown on top. Mornay sauces are also lovely binders for vegetables in cannelloni or crepes. As a young cook, I was often frustrated because my cheese sauces never turned out as smooth and flavorful as I wanted. Now I understand that to make a great cheese sauce you need to start by making a really good white sauce and then melt in some quality cheese. Heaps of bland cheese stirred into a pasty, weak sauce will not magically develop more flavor in the pan. Gruyère is the cheese used in classic Mornay because it is nutty and sharp and melts well. A tablespoon of nutritional yeast flakes can intensify the savory umami flavors without adding more sodium.

YIELD: 3 CUPS

2 cups whole milk

Infusing ingredients (choose 1 to 3) such as a bit of onion, black peppercorns, a bay leaf, a few parsley stems, a slice of carrot, and/or a clove of garlic

2 tablespoons butter

2 tablespoons all-purpose flour

¼ teaspoon kosher salt, or to taste

¼ teaspoon dry mustard

Pinch of cayenne pepper

4 to 5 oz/115 to 140 g Gruyère, sharp Cheddar, or a combination, grated (1½ to 2 cups)

Dash of Worcestershire sauce (optional)

> Combine the milk and your choice of infusing ingredients in a saucepan and heat over medium-high heat until the milk begins to steam and small bubbles form at the edges of the pan. Remove the pan from the heat and leave the milk to infuse while you prepare the roux. Or, if you prefer, combine the ingredients in a microwave-safe container and cook on high for about 45 seconds.

> Heat a medium saucepan over medium-high heat and add the butter. When it bubbles, remove the pan from the heat, sprinkle the flour evenly over the melted butter, and stir until the butter and flour are a smooth paste. Return the pan to the heat and cook over medium heat until the raw aroma is cooked out and the roux starts to smell of very light toast, about 30 seconds. Strain half of the infused milk into the roux and whisk vigorously until smooth. Add the rest of the (strained) milk and the salt. Sprinkle in the mustard and cayenne and stir to mix. Bring the sauce to a boil, then reduce the heat to a simmer and cook, stirring often, for at least 5

continues

minutes to make sure there is no raw flour taste and to give the starch particles a chance to swell and thicken.

> Stir in the grated cheese. Season with additional salt and the Worcestershire if you choose. Heat gently until the cheese melts, but don't boil the sauce after the cheese is added, or it can get gritty or stringy. Serve warm.

> If you are not using the sauce right away, put a piece of buttered parchment, a butter wrapper, or plastic wrap directly on the surface of the sauce to prevent a skin from forming, cover, and refrigerate for up to 3 days.

CHEESE SAUCE VARIATIONS

Adapt the taste and texture of Classic Cheese Sauce (page 357) by using different cheese varieties. Sauces made with Parmesan, feta, or Fontina are very nice in lasagna, moussaka, or stuffed pasta dishes. A Camembert and herb sauce can be tucked into crepes with thin slices of ham. A Cheddar and ale sauce can be a pub-style alternative in scalloped potatoes. All can be baked to a bubbly brown gratinée.

Cheddar and Ale	Use only 1½ cups milk. Stir ½ cup amber ale into the roux before adding the strained milk. Use extra-sharp Cheddar in place of the Gruyère. Add 1 tablespoon spicy brown mustard, ¼ teaspoon smoked paprika, and a dash of Worcestershire.
Tomato Goat	Use 4 oz/115 g crumbled chèvre or grated Bûcheron in place of the Gruyère. Stir ½ cup peeled, seeded, and diced tomatoes and 1 minced or pressed garlic clove and add a tablespoon of chopped fresh basil. This is particularly good made with goat's milk.
Feta and Garlic	Use 4 oz/115 g crumbled feta cheese in place of the Gruyère. Stir in 2 minced or pressed garlic cloves, ½ teaspoon crumbled dried oregano, and a dash of Tabasco. For a smoother sauce, puree with an immersion blender.
Camembert and Herbs	Use 8 oz/225 g chopped Camembert in place of the Gruyère. If the rind is tender, it should melt; if it is tough or rubbery or you find it unappealing, remove it. Add 1 tablespoon chopped fresh parsley, 2 teaspoons minced fresh chives, and ½ teaspoon chopped fresh thyme.
Gjetost and Green Apple	Use 8 oz/225 g grated Gjetost in place of the Gruyère. Sauté 1 cup minced peeled Granny Smith apple in 1 tablespoon butter until just tender and gently stir into the warm sauce. If desired, add a tablespoon of applejack or apple brandy before serving.
Blue	Use 2 oz/60 g grated Gruyère and 3 oz/85 g crumbled blue cheese. Add an extra dash of Worcestershire.

continues

Asiago and Fontina	Use 4 oz/115 g grated Fontina and 2 oz/60 g grated Asiago in place of the Gruyère.
American and Chipotle	Use 8 oz/225 g chopped or grated American cheese in place of the Gruyère. Stir 2 tablespoons finely minced canned chipotle in adobo into the warm sauce.
Smoked Gouda and Bacon	Use 5 oz/140 g grated smoked Gouda in place of the Gruyère. Stir in ⅓ cup crisp bacon bits.

TIPS
for Creating Your Own Cheese Sauces

- Start by making a really good, intensely flavored white sauce (see White Sauce Done Right, page 321). If the sauce is going to be used as a base or served with starchy or bland ingredients, boost the seasoning even more with dry mustard and a pinch of cayenne pepper. Add some umami with a few drops of Worcestershire sauce, liquid amino acids, nutritional yeast flakes, or a touch of miso.

- Choose an appropriate cheese. The stronger the cheese, the cheesier the sauce will be. Cheeses that melt smoothly will make sauces that are velvety. Aged Parmesan and feta cheese make wonderful cheese sauces, but they won't be as uniformly smooth and drippy as sauces made with Gruyère or Fontina. Combine cheeses for a balance of flavor and consistency: Monterey Jack and chèvre, Emmentaler and Roquefort, aged and young Goudas. If you want the flavor of sharp Cheddar but the comforting characteristics of processed cheese, add both.

- Don't boil the sauce after the cheese has been added. Cheeses are emulsions, and they can break when they are overheated. The starch in roux helps to stabilize the emulsions, but it doesn't make them indestructible.

- Mornay sauce can be intensely cheesy and gooey, but it will never have the characteristics of a pure liquefied cheese such as fondue or nacho cheese sauce. For that, you need to add commercial "melting salts" like sodium citrate. See Gooey Orange Nacho Cheese Sauce, page 363.

- Cheese sauces usually store and reheat well when refrigerated but can get gritty if frozen.

GRATINÉE—TURNING CHEESE SAUCE INTO A BROWN AND BUBBLY TOPPING

To bake a dish until it bubbles and browns is to gratinée it, or to serve it au gratin. Shallow heatproof oval or round dishes called gratin dishes expose plenty of surface area and create a higher ratio of appealing top crust. The crust can be made with grated cheese, bread crumbs, or just extended cooking time, but I think the best gratinéed dishes are made with a top layer of cheese sauce. Drizzle a cheesy sauce over a dish and bake it to bubbly, brown perfection, and even picky eaters gobble up unfamiliar vegetables like Belgian endive, cannelloni stuffed with chard, or eggplant casseroles. Layer potatoes, pasta, or popular vegetables like broccoli with a cheese sauce, and you better make extra, because these dishes vanish in a flash. The most successful gratinéed dishes are made with cheese sauces that are bold-flavored and thick enough to drape over the ingredients, showing contour but not running straight to the bottom of the dish.

The sauce needs to be uncovered to brown. It takes about 15 to 20 minutes for a cheese sauce to become brown and bubbly in a moderately hot oven. You can also gratinée dishes by broiling them. I often sprinkle a touch of additional grated cheese and bread crumbs over the top of the cheese sauce to add a bit of crunch. The bread crumbs also absorb any oil that may seep from overheated cheese.

GOOEY ORANGE NACHO CHEESE SAUCE

Gooey orange processed cheese is one of my guilty pleasures. That doesn't mean I don't adore aromatic aged ripe cheeses, I just crave the "fake" stuff every now and then. Luckily, Nathan Myhrvold, the founder of *Modernist Cuisine* and The Cooking Lab, feels the same way. He and his team showed me how to turn top-notch cheeses into slices and melted spoonfuls that have the pleasing texture of processed cheese. You get all the drippy, salty nacho cheese sauce goodness, plus the confidence of knowing exactly what went into it. The trick is sodium citrate, a salty, slightly sour powder derived from citric acid. It is a "melting salt" similar to the ones James L. Kraft first added to cheese to make it more shelf-stable. Sodium citrate is not a grocery store item—you will have to order it online. Be sure you buy a food-grade product.

To make this sauce, you need an immersion blender and a power source close enough to the stove that you can blend the sauce right in the saucepan. Unlike traditional cheese sauces, it's important that you boil this sauce; it won't come together otherwise. The sodium citrate stabilizes the emulsion so it doesn't turn to curds when it gets too hot. The sauce will seem slightly thin when it is boiling but will thicken as it cools. And it thickens very quickly—the sauce remains liquid only when it is warm. If it gets too cold or solid, simply reheat it. If you want to adapt this recipe to make melty macaroni and cheese, make a double batch of jalapeño-free sauce and mix it with 1 lb/450 g cooked macaroni.

The salt in the cheese plus the sodium citrate make this a very salty sauce.

YIELD: ABOUT 2 CUPS

1 cup milk, water, or an appropriate mock stock, such as Tomato or Corncob (see the table on page 93)

1¼ teaspoons food-grade sodium citrate (available online)

12 oz/340 g sharp Cheddar cheese, grated

2 tablespoons chopped pickled jalapeños or nacho slices (optional)

> Combine the milk and sodium citrate in a medium saucepan and bring to a boil over medium-high heat. (While you should avoid boiling a regular cheese sauce, a sauce made with sodium citrate must be boiling or at least simmering for the cheese to blend properly.) Use an immersion blender to gradually blend in the cheese, a handful at a time; this should take about 3 minutes. Make sure each addition of cheese is melted and thoroughly blended and the mixture has returned to a simmer before adding more. The sauce may look odd at first, a bit like a wet, separated mess, but if you keep boiling and blending, it will gradually come together and the finished sauce will be smooth and creamy.

continues

> Stir in the chopped jalapeños, if using, and serve.

> If storing, cover and refrigerate for up to a week. The sauce will thicken and congeal as it cools; remelt it when ready to serve.

VEGAN CASHEW "CHEESE" SAUCE

It may sound a bit dubious, but let me assure you this sauce tastes really good. Yes, it fits neatly into dairy-free diets and lifestyles, but that doesn't mean it should be dismissed as a recipe for health food freaks. Each creamy, savory bite tastes as decadent as other cheese sauces. Scoop it onto celery sticks. Slather it into tacos. Spread it on toast or just sneak a spoonful now and then. It is a "raw food," if that matters to you. It can also be heated to become very thick and spreadable. A high-speed blender makes the creamiest sauce, but I've had good luck with my standard household blender. If you live in a remote area, look for miso and nutritional yeast flakes at stores featuring natural and health foods; I can find everything at my local grocery store. Whole cashews have more moisture than cashew pieces, so they blend up smoother.

YIELD: 1 CUP

1 cup (5 oz/140 g) whole raw cashews

About 1 cup cold water

1 tablespoon miso (I prefer red [aka] miso)

1 tablespoon nutritional yeast flakes

½ teaspoon kosher salt, or sea salt to taste

Pinch of cayenne pepper

Pinch of dry mustard

> Soak the cashews in plenty of cold water for at least 6 hours, or, preferably, overnight. Drain.

> Put the softened cashews in a blender with ½ cup of the cold water and puree to a smooth paste. Add the miso, yeast, salt, cayenne, and mustard and blend until very smooth. Gradually add additional water to reach the saucy consistency that you like.

> Serve immediately, or serve chilled or gently warmed. When heated, the sauce will thicken dramatically and become stickier and more viscous, like a more traditional cheese sauce or dip; thin it with additional water if needed.

> If storing, cover and refrigerate for up to 5 days. It is easy to serve if transferred to a squeeze bottle.

NUTRITIONAL YEAST FLAKES . . . SERIOUSLY?

I'm going to guess that among all of the diverse ingredients called for in this book, my use of nutritional yeast flakes may inspire the most raised eyebrows. Let me explain. I use nutritional yeast flakes because I like the taste. I think if this ingredient had a more appealing name or zippy marketing campaign, you might even find it alongside the salt and pepper on restaurant tables. It is not the same thing as active yeast—it will not leaven bread. It is a seasoning that happens to have a lot of nutritional value; thus the unfortunate name. Yeast-derived seasonings are packed with umami, so they stimulate the same areas on your palate as roasted meats, tomato concentrates, and Parmesan cheese. A tablespoon stirred into a cup of hot water can mimic chicken broth. Many commercial chicken bases are mostly yeast concentrates. It is savory but vegan, salty but low sodium, and packed with enough nutritional benefits that it is often found in giant bulk bins at health food stores. I heartily recommend that even the most avid carnivore search it out. It's really good on hot buttered popcorn.

SLURRIES

POURABLE STARCH
THICKENERS

In culinary terms, a slurry is powdered starch stirred with enough cold water to make it smooth and pourable. It is a thickening agent ideal for sauces that are already simmering in the pot, for wheat- or fat-free recipes, and for some international sauces. Thickening a stir-fry sauce with roux would be preposterous. A slurry made with a touch of cornstarch, potato starch, or tapioca starch will bubble and thicken a liquid into a glaze in less than a minute.

A slurry needs to be perfectly smooth before it is added to a sauce. Many of us learned how clumps of dry powder can form in a liquid when we made our own chocolate milk as kids. I used to do it intentionally because I liked the sweet powdery pockets, but pure starch doesn't have the same appeal. To make a slurry, put the starch in a small bowl or measuring cup and gradually stir in the cold liquid. You need to use cold liquid, because heat can make it sticky and lumpy. The starch will quickly settle to the bottom, so make sure you give it another stir before you add it to the sauce. You can also combine the wet and the dry in a jar and shake them together.

Years ago, I was invited to Thanksgiving with a dear friend's extended family. As always, I couldn't help but poke my head into the kitchen. Everyone was in a flutter because the "gravy cup" was missing. Apparently the person in charge of holiday gravy had a particular lidded plastic cup that had magical properties. It was required for shaking up the slurry. After a hullabaloo, the cup was located and everyone breathed a sigh of relief. There would be gravy after all. In hindsight, I think the cup must have had marks indicating how much flour and water were needed to thicken a certain volume of stock. I had never really considered thickening turkey gravy with slurry until then, but clearly it is the-way-things-are-done in some households.

While slurries are very easy to make, I can see how getting the ratio right might seem a little tricky. Slurries can be made of different starches and all of them taste and thicken differently. (For tips, go to the table of Texturizers on page 48.) Some can get quite unappealing in excess and be a distraction rather than enhancement. That's why I tend to be lighthanded, almost overcautious, when it comes to adding a slurry. I don't use wheat-flour slurries much because if the recipe is wheat-friendly, I prefer to use a roux or kneaded butter. I reserve slurries for thinner quick-cooking sauces. In particular, I like them for barely clinging stir-fry sauces, juicy fruit sauces, and, occasionally, gravies for guests with special diets. And I don't just dump it into the sauce—I add the well-stirred slurry by the drizzle and splash, stir, wait, and watch what happens before adding more.

ENDLESSLY ADAPTABLE STIR-FRY SAUCE

I probably make this sauce more than any other in the book. When I was in culinary school, we were lucky enough to spend a week learning from Yan Kit So, a wonderful cookbook writer and teacher of traditional Chinese recipes and techniques. I have always loved to cook Chinese food—I made my first dim sum feast at age fourteen. From Yan Kit So, I learned to have a better appreciation of simplicity and how good stir-fry technique can add almost as much flavor as sauce.

Since I don't have room to spell out the entire technique in detail, I'll remind you of the key points here: Prep your ingredients carefully and keep them separate. Use a hot wok and be ready to shake and rock it. Infuse your hot cooking oil with aromatics, but don't let them burn. The aromatics you use will greatly influence the taste of the finished dish. Don't assume that everything will take the same amount of time to cook. Don't overcrowd the pan. Err on the side of thin sauces rather than thick.

This recipe is a simple base that can be easily adapted. I use it as written with delicate fresh-tasting vegetables like snow peas, bok choy, or pea shoots. When I want a bolder sauce, I boost it with a dollop of black bean paste or chile sauce. Cornstarch works well as the thickener, but I prefer potato starch because it seems less gluey and the flavor is quite indistinct. Both starches must reach the boiling point, or they will remain opaque and taste raw and starchy.

YIELD: ABOUT ½ CUP

½ teaspoon potato starch or cornstarch

½ cup Really Good Chicken Stock (page 114), Vegetable Stock (page 106, or see the table on page 108) or an appropriate Mock Stock such as Mock Chicken, Dried Shrimp, or Mushroom (see the table on page 93), or as needed

½ teaspoon soy sauce

¼ teaspoon sugar

Freshly ground black pepper or a pinch of finely ground white pepper (if black specks seem inappropriate for the dish)

> Put the starch in a small bowl and gradually stir in the remaining ingredients until smooth.

> When your stir-fry ingredients are just cooked, stir the sauce again and pour it into the pan: Pull the food to one side and tilt the pan to make sure the sauce comes to a boil, thickens, and clears. If it seems too sticky, add a bit more stock or water. Toss the ingredients together with the sauce until they are glazed and serve.

STIR-FRY SAUCE VARIATIONS

Let me clarify right up front that using a universal sauce base is not the way to make authentic stir-fried dishes, but it's a great place to start. In my opinion, the most common mistake people make when creating their own stir-fry sauce is to add too much soy sauce. Think of soy sauce as a seasoning, not a condiment. The primary flavors in your dish should come from the aromatics and the fresh foods you are cooking. I inevitably start my stir-fries by infusing the hot oil with chopped garlic, coins of fresh ginger, and a pinch of chile flakes or a whole dried chile. Little more is needed, but there are plenty of really great Asian condiments that you can buy and add generously. An almost embarrassing amount of the real estate in my fridge is devoted to Chinese sauces and condiments. Start with the Endlessly Adaptable Stir-Fry Sauce (page 369) and stir in a spoonful of whatever seems right for the night. Here are a few of my favorites.

Oyster Sauce	Stir in 2 tablespoons oyster sauce.
Hoisin Sauce	Stir in 2 tablespoons hoisin sauce.
Sweet-and-Sour	Add 3 tablespoons brown sugar, 2 tablespoons rice or white wine vinegar, and (optional) a drop of red food coloring. Infuse the cooking oil with an extra coin of ginger.
Salted/Fermented Black Beans	Mash 1 teaspoon fermented salted black beans with a pinch of sugar and stir into the sauce. Or add 2 tablespoons prepared black bean and garlic or black bean and chile sauce. Finish the dish with plenty of sliced scallion greens or torn fresh Thai basil leaves.
General Tso's (Sweet Garlic and Black Pepper)	Add 3 or 4 small dried red chiles and 2 sliced garlic cloves to the aromatics used to infuse the cooking oil. Increase soy sauce to 1 tablespoon. Increase the sugar to 2 tablespoons and use brown sugar. Add 2 tablespoons Shaoxing wine or medium-dry sherry, 1 tablespoon hoisin sauce, 1 tablespoon rice vinegar, and ½ teaspoon black pepper.
Kung Pao	Add 1 to 2 tablespoons prepared chile garlic sauce or sambal oelek, 1 teaspoon prepared oyster sauce, and (optional) an additional tablespoon of sugar to the base. Add 2 or 3 dried small whole chiles to the aromatics used to infuse the cooking oil. Add roasted peanuts to the stir-fry ingredients. Finish the dish with a few drops of sesame oil.

Thai Basil and Bird's-Eye Chile	Add 2 tablespoons oyster sauce or 1 tablespoon prepared black bean sauce to the basic sauce mix. Add 2 to 5 sliced Thai bird chiles, depending on how spicy you like it, to the aromatics used to infuse the cooking oil. Finish the stir-fry by tossing in 1 cup loosely packed fresh Thai basil leaves just before serving.
Thai Red Curry Paste	Add 1 to 2 teaspoons Thai red curry paste. Increase the sugar to ½ teaspoon, or more to taste. Once the sauce has thickened in the pan, stir in 1 teaspoon fish sauce, a squeeze of fresh lime juice, and (optional) a splash of Lemongrass and Lime Leaf Extract (page 99).
Vietnamese Lemongrass and Chile	Add 1 to 2 tablespoon of sambal oelek or similar hot red chile paste to the sauce. Add a sliced shallot, 1 tablespoon very thinly sliced or shaved lemongrass, and 3 garlic cloves to the aromatics used to infuse the cooking oil. Once the sauce has thickened in the pan, add 1 teaspoon fish sauce and a squeeze of fresh lime juice.
Orange and Honey	Add 2 tablespoons honey and 2 tablespoons frozen orange juice concentrate to the sauce base. Add 2 coins fresh ginger, a piece of star anise, and (optional) a small dried chile to the aromatics used to infuse the cooking oil. Finish the dish with sliced scallion greens and toasted sesame seeds.
Sweet Korean Chile Sauce	Omit the starch. Increase the sugar to 2 tablespoons, and stir in 3 tablespoons Korean chile paste (gochujang) and 1 tablespoon rice vinegar. Corn syrup is sometimes added for a sweeter, stickier texture. Finish the dish with plenty of sliced scallions and a few drops of toasted sesame oil.
Sichuan Bean Paste	Add a pinch of Sichuan peppercorns to the aromatics used to infuse the cooking oil. Add 1 tablespoon Sichuan bean paste to the wok and cook for a minute before adding the sauce. Finish the dish with a few drops of sesame oil.

continues

Ketchup and Tamarind	Omit the starch. Substitute Tamarind Water (page 91) for the stock. Increase the sugar to 2 teaspoons, or to taste. Stir in ¼ cup ketchup. Add 1 to 3 sliced Thai bird chiles and 2 to 3 chopped garlic cloves to the aromatics used to infuse the cooking oil. Once the sauce has thickened in the pan, stir in 1 teaspoon fish sauce and 1 teaspoon freshly squeezed lime juice. Garnish the dish with plenty of coarsely chopped fresh cilantro and sliced scallions.
Mild Curry	Stir in 1 tablespoon mild curry powder and (optional) 1 tablespoon honey.

TIPS
for Creating Your Own Stir-Fry Sauces

- The aromatics, such as ginger, garlic, chiles, and onions, that are infused into the hot cooking oil play an important part in developing and balancing sauce flavor.

- Use a sauce base liquid that is more flavorful than plain water. Use chicken or vegetable stock or look at the table of Mock Stocks and Simple Infusions (page 93) for ideas.

- Remember that soy sauce is best used as a seasoning, not as a sauce itself. A teaspoon or two is often enough unless you are looking for a distinctive soy sauce flavor.

- Few stir-fry sauces need more than 1 teaspoon of cornstarch or potato starch per cup of liquid. A thinner sauce is usually preferable to a thicker one. If the finished sauce doesn't seem thick enough, you can always simmer it longer to thicken it through reduction or add a touch more slurry.

- Adding thick and pasty ingredients like Korean chile paste (gochujang), Sichuan bean paste, or thick hoisin sauce will also help thicken the sauce.

- If your sauce doesn't taste quite intense enough at the end, consider finishing the dish with a touch of fish sauce, soy sauce, vinegar, or sesame oil, or a drizzle of hoisin sauce, oyster sauce, or Fuchsia Dunlop's Chinese Chile Oil (page 300). A scattering of sliced scallions and chopped fresh cilantro can also help.

- To coat about 1 lb/450 g stir-fried rice noodles or fresh egg noodles, triple the sauce recipe of your choice from the table on page 370.

CHERRY WINE SAUCE

For fruit sauces that need a touch of thickening, I reach for tapioca. Tapioca has a rather distinct flavor, but it seems appropriate for fruit sauces. It is an ingredient used in a lot of pie fillings. It cooks quickly and continues to thicken quite a bit after it cools, so you don't need much. I buy tapioca starch at Asian markets. If you have trouble finding it, you can grind tapioca pearls to a fine powder in a coffee or spice grinder and then sift the powder through a very fine sieve.

This recipe tastes a bit like cherries in mulled wine. You can use fresh, frozen, or even drained jarred cherries. If the cherries are very sweet and you want a bit of extra brightness, finish the sauce with a tablespoon of fresh lemon juice or ⅛ teaspoon powdered citric acid. Serve it with roasted duck, almond cake, or cheesecake.

YIELD: 1½ CUPS

1 cup pitted cherries

½ cup fruity red wine (for a nonalcoholic version, substitute cherry, pomegranate, or cranberry juice and reduce the amount of sugar accordingly), or as needed

2 tablespoons sugar

1 cinnamon stick

1 teaspoon tapioca starch, mixed with 1 tablespoon cold water

Tiny pinch of kosher salt

> Combine the cherries, wine, sugar, and cinnamon stick in a small heavy-bottomed saucepan and bring to a simmer over medium-high heat. Stir the tapioca slurry thoroughly and pour into the sauce. It will thicken almost immediately, but bring it to a boil so it becomes clear and shiny and to remove any raw taste. Stir in the salt and remove from the heat.

> Thin with additional wine or juice if the sauce seems too thick. Remove the cinnamon stick. Serve warm or cool.

> If storing, cover and refrigerate for up to 3 days.

COLD THICKENERS

There are all sorts of intriguing textures you can get when you expand your larder to include scientific powders and commercial food additives. Too many, if you ask me. I like knowing how to create saucy consistencies with alternative ingredients, but many modernist texturizers are difficult to source, can be expensive, and require a better understanding of organic chemistry than I ever really want to have. If you want to experiment with alternative textures for fresh sauces, I suggest starting with two relatively common ingredients—xanthan gum and agar-agar. They are particularly well suited for turning raw fresh ingredients into unexpected sauces and both are readily available at natural food markets.

FRESH MELON-TINI SAUCE THICKENED WITH XANTHAN GUM

Sometimes a silly, boozy, bright green fruit sauce is just what your party needs. This sauce is simply flavored fresh fruit and vodka with a bit of xanthan gum to hold it together. An almost minuscule quantity of xanthan gum will help to pull a watery or weepy sauce together. A bit more works as a thickener. Add too much, and liquids become unpleasantly slimy.

Serve this sauce with angel food cake or coconut desserts, or for an intriguing bright flash of color and flavor on more elaborate presentations. Because the sauce is uncooked, it remains very high in alcohol.

YIELD: ABOUT 1 CUP

1 teaspoon sugar, or to taste (depending on the sweetness of the melon)

⅛ teaspoon powdered citric acid (optional)

Tiny pinch of xanthan gum (just what will fit on the tip of a small paring knife; see Xanthan Gum, page 180)

1 cup peeled ripe honeydew melon chunks

¼ cup Midori or other green melon liqueur

2 tablespoons vodka

> Stir together the sugar, citric acid, if using, and xanthan gum in a small bowl.

> Put the melon in a blender and puree until smooth. It will get foamy. Add the Midori and vodka. Pulse a few times. Sprinkle on the sugar mixture and blend until well mixed and just thickened. Add more sugar to taste if necessary. If you like, pass the sauce through a fine sieve for a smoother texture.

> If storing, cover and refrigerate for up to 3 days.

BOOZY STRAWBERRY WATERMELON SAUCE

> Substitute a mixture of watermelon and strawberries for the honeydew. Substitute a red or pink tart liqueur such as Dekuyper watermelon or Berry Fusion schnapps for the Midori.

FRESH CITRUS SAUCE THICKENED WITH AGAR-AGAR

This sauce is a fluid gel. Fluid gels are very modernist sauces. The first time I came across the term was in the books of English superstar chef Heston Blumenthal. The concept baffled me at first. Why go to all the trouble of gelling a liquid if all you're going to do is liquefy it again at the end? Chef Maxime Bilet, founder of the Hungry Owl Innovation Group and former head of the *Modernist Cuisine* Cooking Lab, explained to me that fluid gels are best used to texturize liquids that are ideally served pure and untouched by heat. It's hard to thicken wines or fresh juices into clinging sauces without boiling them or adulterating the flavors with a lot of added ingredients. Fluid gels are a great solution.

Chefs like Blumenthal use advanced math, chemistry, and laboratory-grade ingredients to make some really incredible fluid gels. For the home cook, I suggest using gelatin or agar-agar.

Agar-agar is a vegetarian gelling agent made from seaweed. It has been used internationally for centuries. I find Eden brand agar-agar flakes to be the easiest to use. I have also broken up and then ground strips of agar-agar into a powder in my spice mill. Large pieces take longer to melt, and it is preferable to heat the juice as little as possible. Agar-agar does have a unique taste that is too pronounced for fine wines or subtle liquids.

This bright citrus sauce is especially good with light, elegant desserts such as parfaits and mousses.

YIELD: 2 CUPS

1½ cups mixed freshly squeezed citrus juice, such as orange, grapefruit, and tangerine, plus more as needed

1 tablespoon agar-agar flakes (preferably Eden brand)

2 tablespoons freshly squeezed lime juice, or to taste

1 tablespoon honey or agave syrup (optional)

Pinch of kosher salt (optional)

> Stir together ½ cup of the juice and the agar-agar in a very small saucepan and gradually bring the mixture to a simmer, stirring constantly. Continue to cook and stir until the agar is completely melted. It may take several minutes until there are no tiny beads of agar that cling to your spoon or the bottom of the pan. Remove from the heat and cool for 5 minutes so you don't overheat the fresh juice.

> Stir the remaining 1 cup juice into the agar-agar mixture. Transfer to a shallow dish and refrigerate until set firmly, about 1 hour. (Agar-agar sets more quickly than gelatin.)

> Scoop the gel into a blender, add the lime juice, and puree until smooth. Bubbles will become trapped in

the gel, but that is to be expected. Thin the sauce with additional juice as needed to reach the consistency you like. Add more lime juice if the sauce seems too sweet, or, if it is very tart, add the honey. Add the salt if you are serving the sauce with a savory dish. The sauce should be loose, fluid, and clinging, with just enough body to gently pool but not run on a plate.

> Chilling the sauce will cause it to gradually firm up again. Blend to liquefy.

FRESH BLACKBERRY PORT SAUCE THICKENED WITH AGAR-AGAR

> Substitute 1 cup of blackberry juice (pressed from about 4 cups of fresh blackberries) and ½ cup port for the citrus juices. Melt the agar-agar in ½ cup of the blackberry juice with 2 tablespoons sugar. Cool and stir in the remaining juice and the port. Refrigerate until set. Blend or stir into a smooth sauce, adding more port as needed to reach a fluid but clinging consistency.

EMULSIFIED EGG SAUCES AND THEIR MODERN ALTERNATIVES

Mayonnaise and hollandaise may be the most familiar emulsified egg sauces, but if you look back in culinary history, you will find eggs added to sauces everywhere. In the great houses of Europe, practically all elegant dishes were stuffed, bound, glazed, or garnished with eggs. Egg-based emulsified sauces were so valued they were included in the list of fundamental French mother sauces, those preparations that were, and still are, considered essential foundations for sauce mastery (see page 312).

Rich, buttery hollandaise seems to be losing favor these days, but mayonnaise remains a global favorite. It may seem strange to refer to that familiar jar in the fridge as sauce, but it is. You should consider making it from scratch now and then. Not only will that result in a better, fresher product, it will help you understand a classic sauce-making technique, and the more you know, the more your skills will improve.

Egg yolks contain lecithin, a natural emulsifier that helps to thicken oil and water mixtures and make them more stable (see Adding Emulsifiers—Egg Yolks and Liquid Soy Lecithin, page 260). The emulsifying properties of lecithin means that egg-based sauces can contain a much higher percentage of fat. The real trick is introducing that fat, whether oil or melted butter, slowly enough that the oil and water droplets stay mixed instead of separating.

Way back when I was in culinary school, we had to make our first batches of mayonnaise with a wooden spoon. We coaxed the oil into the egg yolk one drop at a time. I'm not sure I ever got it done under the 5-minute time limit. (For hollandaise, we were allowed a whisk.) I love telling this story, not because it has any relevance in modern life—you would have to be pretty passionate about understanding emulsions to give it a try—but because it is another reminder of how brilliant chefs must have been to figure out how to make these dishes without electricity. I can only imagine what Carême might have created if he had access to an immersion blender.

Egg yolks can also thicken sauces by delicately gelling them. The natural gelling properties of eggs are used mainly in custard sauces and to add a rich finish. (See Finishing and Enriching Sauces with Egg Yolks, page 433.) Gradually stir some of the warm sauce into the egg yolks to blend and gently heat them without cooking, then stir this tempered mixture back into the rest of the sauce and heat it gently until it thickens. Do not boil the sauce, or the egg yolks will curdle.

MAYONNAISE

Mayonnaise is a lesson in ingredient diplomacy. The oil needs to be introduced to the egg yolks very slowly at first, and on their terms. Once the two clearly start to unite, things can proceed with more enthusiasm and informality. When you make your own mayonnaise, you have complete control of the quality of ingredients and balance of flavors. Use eggs fresh from your urban coop and juice squeezed from the fruit of your own lemon tree. Use sherry vinegar and a touch of walnut oil. Reduce the salt for a low-sodium version. I don't suggest making mayo entirely with extra-virgin olive oil, because it becomes pasty and dense, especially when refrigerated.

Once you get a feel for it, a batch of fresh mayonnaise will take about 3 minutes to make. I think an immersion blender is the most efficient tool for making mayonnaise, so that's what I call for here.

Fresh mayonnaise does not have the extended shelf life of a commercial product, so don't expect it to keep for more than a few days. And do not serve sauces made with raw or undercooked eggs to anyone with a compromised immune system.

YIELD: 1 CUP

3 large egg yolks

¼ teaspoon dry mustard

Pinch of cayenne pepper

1 cup vegetable or light olive oil

3 to 4 tablespoons freshly squeezed lemon juice, white wine vinegar, or unseasoned rice vinegar

1 teaspoon kosher salt

> Put the egg yolks, mustard, and cayenne in the cup that came with your immersion blender, another tall cylindrical container, or a large liquid measuring cup. Hold the blades of the immersion blender over the yolks and turn it on. Slowly drizzle in the oil a few drips at a time, blending until the egg yolks become creamy and even and it is clear that the ingredients are mixing together smoothly, then start adding the oil more quickly, in a thin stream, gradually lifting and moving the blender around as the volume increases. When the mixture gets too thick to maneuver easily, add some of the lemon juice. If at any time the egg yolks and oil don't seem to be blending or look greasy and curd-like, stop blending, clean the blades, and start over in a clean container with fresh egg yolks, gradually adding the broken mayo as you did the oil. Continue adding oil, gradually increasing the stream, until all of it is incorporated.

> Blend in the remaining lemon juice and the salt.

> Cover and refrigerate for up to 5 days.

JAPANESE KEWPIE-STYLE MAYO

> Use a very light oil, such as canola. Substitute rice vinegar for the lemon juice. Season with ¾ teaspoon kosher salt, ¼ teaspoon MSG, and a pinch of sugar.

EGGLESS MAYO

You don't have to eat eggs to enjoy mayo. Stir this eggless version into potato salad and dressings or add a smear to a sandwich. Xanthan gum is crucial here because it helps to bind the ingredients and adds more viscosity and a slightly gelled consistency that mimics real mayo. Feel free to substitute another oil if you prefer.

YIELD: 2 CUPS

4 oz/115 g silken tofu (a piece roughly the size of a stick of butter), drained

3 to 4 tablespoons freshly squeezed lemon juice, wine vinegar, or unseasoned rice vinegar

¼ teaspoon dry mustard

Pinch of cayenne pepper

¼ teaspoon xanthan gum (see page 180)

1 cup vegetable oil, light olive oil, or other rather neutral oil

1 teaspoon kosher salt, or to taste

¼ teaspoon finely ground black pepper (optional)

> Crumble the tofu into a blender. Add 2 tablespoons of the lemon juice, the mustard, and cayenne. Sprinkle the xanthan gum over the top and pulse the blender until the ingredients are evenly combined, scraping down the sides of the jar with a rubber spatula as needed. The mixture will not be smooth, but it should be well mixed.

> Gradually add the oil, pouring it in a thin stream. Stop the blender to scrape down the sides and give the mayo a stir with the spatula now and then. Remember that this will not behave the same way as a traditional mayonnaise. The mayo is going to be really ugly at some points, looking lumpy, gritty, and greasy. The xanthan gum will eventually pull it all together. Continue blending until you have used all of the oil.

> Add more lemon juice to taste and season with the salt and pepper.

> Cover and refrigerate for up to 1 week.

INTERNATIONAL SAUCES THAT START WITH A CUP OF MAYO

I grew up thinking that mayo was a true American food because there was always a jar in the fridge. It was stirred into tuna and spread on turkey sandwiches, but that was about it. Gradually I came to realize that the word itself was French. When I moved to England as a teenager, I first saw mayonnaise served as an actual sauce. It was made smooth and liquid and draped generously over halved hard-boiled eggs. Now I know that mayo is a global favorite. No doubt kids in Spain, Peru, and Japan are growing up thinking it is from their own country.

All of these sauces start with 1 cup of mayo unless otherwise specified. You can use homemade (page 382), eggless (page 384), or even your favorite store brand, but I suggest you stay away from sweet salad-dressing-style mayonnaise blends.

Aioli	Blend or stir in 1 tablespoon finely chopped or pressed garlic, an additional 1 tablespoon lemon juice, and an extra pinch of cayenne or a dash of Tabasco. Some recipes for aioli also include ¼ cup cold cooked, peeled potato or soft, white bread crumbs, blended in. Serve alongside simply prepared vegetables and seafood or use as a dip for fried foods like French fries or calamari, or as a dressing for egg or potato salads.
Rouille	Puree with ⅓ cup soft white bread crumbs, ¼ cup chopped roasted red peppers, 2 chopped garlic cloves, and 1 teaspoon harissa. If desired, add a few threads of saffron soaked in 1 teaspoon warm water. This is traditionally served with bouillabaisse. It is also good with seafood or as part of a Mediterranean vegetable or meze platter, with grilled eggplant and zucchini, green beans, and sliced tomatoes.
Tartar Sauce	Stir in 2 tablespoons finely minced onion or shallots, 2 tablespoons freshly squeezed lemon juice, 1 tablespoon minced fresh dill or sweet pickle, plenty of black pepper, a dash of Tabasco, and (optional) some chopped fresh parsley or dill. Serve with fried fish and seafood.
Kimchee Tartar Sauce	Kewpie-Style Mayo is preferable here. Blend or stir in ⅓ cup finely chopped kimchee, with its juice, 1 minced garlic clove, and 1 tablespoon rice vinegar. Use as you would traditional tartar sauce.

continues

Creole Remoulade	Stir in 2 tablespoons ketchup, 2 tablespoons minced red bell pepper, 2 tablespoons sliced scallions, 1 minced or pressed garlic clove, 1 tablespoon red wine vinegar, 2 teaspoons prepared horseradish, 2 teaspoons coarse mustard, ½ teaspoon Tabasco or Crystal hot sauce, and a dash of Worcestershire. Use with fried catfish, shrimp, or croquettes or as a sandwich spread.
Mock Romesco	Puree with ¼ cup soft white bread crumbs, 2 tablespoons almond butter, 1 tablespoon sherry vinegar or freshly squeezed lemon juice, 1 tablespoon chopped pimentos, 2 minced or pressed garlic cloves, 2 teaspoons tomato paste, and a good pinch of cayenne.
Chinese Honey Shrimp Sauce	Stir ½ cup mayo together with ¼ cup freshly squeezed lemon juice, 3 tablespoons sweetened condensed milk, and 2 tablespoons honey. Traditionally used to dress crispy fried shrimp and walnuts; also good on fruit salads.
Miso	Kewpie-Style Mayo is preferable here. Stir in ⅓ cup white miso, ¼ cup mirin, 2 tablespoons sake, and 2 teaspoons sugar. Use as a marinade for grilled tofu or fish fillets or to dress salad greens.
Berbere	Stir in 1 to 2 tablespoons African berbere chile powder. Use as a spread in chicken or other sandwiches or as a condiment for grilled meat, seafood, or vegetable skewers.
Scallion and Wasabi	Kewpie-Style Mayo is preferable here. Stir in 3 tablespoons minced scallions and 1 tablespoon prepared wasabi.
Sushi-Bar Hot Sauce	Kewpie-Style Mayo is preferable here. Stir in ¼ cup sriracha and 1 tablespoon unseasoned rice vinegar. Use in or over sushi rolls, as a tempura dip, stir into chicken salad, or serve as a variation on tartar sauce.
Blue Cheese and Dry Sherry	Stir in ¼ cup (1 oz/28 g) crumbled blue cheese and 3 tablespoons dry sherry. Serve alongside cold ham, smoked turkey, or asparagus. Use as a chicken salad dressing.

Tonnato (Tuna)	Puree with one 5 oz/140 g can drained tuna, 2 tablespoons freshly squeezed lemon juice, 2 cloves garlic, 1 mashed anchovy or 1 teaspoon anchovy paste, a pinch of cayenne, and plenty of black pepper. Stir 2 tablespoons chopped capers into the smooth sauce. Traditionally served with cold sliced veal, but also good with chicken, fish, or potatoes.
Motoyaki (Tobiko and Miso)	Use ½ cup Kewpie-Style Mayo. Stir in 1 tablespoon tobiko (flying fish roe), 1 tablespoon white miso, 2 teaspoons finely sliced scallions or fresh chives, and (optional) 1 teaspoon sugar. Spread generously over oysters or scallops in the shell and broil until bubbly and brown.
Lobster	Reduce 2 cups Lobster Shell Stock (page 121) to 3 tablespoons. Cool, and stir into the mayonnaise, along with 1 teaspoon minced fresh chives if desired. Season with 1 tablespoon additional lemon juice for a brighter sauce. Use with seafood or cold beef or as a dip or dressing for artichokes or asparagus.
Fines Herbes	Stir in 1 teaspoon chopped fresh parsley or chervil, 1 teaspoon chopped fresh tarragon, and 1 teaspoon chopped fresh chives. Use to dress peas, endive, spring vegetables, or chilled seafood.
Super-Green	Use eggless mayo. Puree with ½ cup chopped blanched greens, such as kale, spinach, or nettles, 1 clove garlic, 2 tablespoons freshly squeezed lemon juice, and a few gratings of nutmeg. Use in lettuce wraps, as a dressing for whole-grain salads, or as a vegetable dip.
Lime and Cotija Cheese	Stir in ½ cup finely grated or crumbled Cotija cheese, 2 tablespoons freshly squeezed lime juice, and ¼ teaspoon chile powder. Add a dollop of crema or sour cream if you like. Serve with grilled corn or use as a summer chicken or potato salad dressing.

EASY IMMERSION-BLENDER HOLLANDAISE

Hollandaise is essentially mayonnaise made with warm butter instead of oil. The same principles apply. You need to introduce the fat into the egg yolks very slowly at first. Once they seem to be getting along, you can proceed more quickly. When I was in cooking school, there were always stories of great French chefs who would squeeze cold butter between their warm hands and whisk in the softened bits as they gradually dropped into the sauce. I found that image to be picturesque and tempting, but since I don't much like thick hollandaise sauce, I can't see being that patient and methodical. In fact, I've even abandoned the whisk. Melting the butter and whizzing it all up with an immersion blender might make a classical chef cringe, but it's quick, fresh, and remarkably goof-proof. You will never again be tempted by the inferior, overstabilized packets and tubs of hollandaise that have been showing up on store shelves recently.

YIELD: 1 CUP

4 large egg yolks

Pinch of dry mustard

2 sticks (8 oz/225 g) unsalted butter, melted

2 tablespoons freshly squeezed lemon juice, or to taste

½ teaspoon kosher salt

Pinch of cayenne pepper or dash of Tabasco (optional)

> Combine the egg yolks and mustard in the cup that came with your immersion blender or other tall cylindrical container, or in a 2-cup liquid measuring cup. Place the blender directly on the egg yolks and blend on medium. Very gradually add the melted butter: Start with just a few drips to warm the eggs but not cook them. Then, as the butter is incorporated and the mixture looks creamy and even, pour in the butter a bit faster. Mix, raising the immersion blender as needed, until you have added all of the butter and the sauce is lemon colored and smooth.

> Season with the lemon juice, salt, and cayenne, if using. If you prefer a thinner sauce, stir in a tablespoon of warm water.

> Serve immediately. Or keep warm in a double boiler over gentle heat or a thermal carafe.

VEGAN CORN "HOLLANDAISE"

The friends I have introduced this sauce to—even die-hard carnivores and butter lovers—claim to prefer this vegan version to classic hollandaise. The creamy yellow sauce mimics the texture of hollandaise without relying on eggs and butter. It is not as cloying, it's heat stable, it's tasty enough to be slurped up by the spoonful, and there is little or no guilt afterward. You will need a few specialty ingredients: miso, nutritional yeast flakes, and arrowroot. These are available at some supermarkets and at natural foods markets. Arrowroot is added for stability and gentle thickening; kudzu root (available at health foods markets) can also be used.

YIELD: ABOUT 1½ CUPS

1½ cups water, Corn Stock (see the table on page 109), or Corncob Mock Stock (see the table on page 94)

1 cup fresh or thawed frozen yellow corn kernels

⅓ cup (1.5 oz/45 g) whole raw cashews

1 tablespoon white (shiro) miso

1 teaspoon nutritional yeast flakes

½ teaspoon arrowroot

1 to 2 teaspoons freshly squeezed lemon juice

½ teaspoon kosher salt

Pinch of cayenne pepper or dash of Tabasco

> Combine the water, corn kernels, and cashews in a saucepan, cover, and simmer until the cashews are tender and the corn is very soft, about 20 minutes. Cool slightly.

> Transfer the cashew mixture to a blender, add the miso, yeast, and arrowroot, and puree until very smooth. Strain back into the saucepan, pressing the solids against the sides of the strainer to extract as much smooth pulp and liquid as possible. Heat the sauce over medium heat, stirring constantly, until it is just simmering and has thickened. Season with the lemon juice, salt, and cayenne. Serve warm.

> Unlike hollandaise, this sauce can be refrigerated and reheated. Cover and refrigerate for up to 5 days.

SOUS VIDE AND SAUCE MAKING

Sous-vide cooking refers to a type of controlled low-temperature cooking. Foods are cooked by putting them in an airless environment, like a vacuum-sealed bag, and sinking them into a tank of preheated circulating water. It is a remarkable technique that results in textures and moisture levels that are impossible to achieve with more traditional methods.

Sauce making and sous-vide cooking are complementary techniques. Sous-vide-cooked meats need embellishment. They are often underseasoned, because salt can affect the texture of long-cooked foods, making them seem more cured than succulent. The cooking temperatures are too low to create the brown colors and flavors of roasted or seared meat. That can be remedied with a high-temperature blast in a deep fryer, on a very hot grill, or even with a blowtorch, but there are no cooking juices or integral sauces like those you get with cooking techniques such as braising and sautéing. That means creative, complementary sauces are vital.

The technique of cooking sous vide can also be used to prepare ingredients for sauces. Stock ingredients and cold water can be sealed in a large zipper-top bag, with as much air removed as possible, and then cooked at gentle temperatures until the flavors are thoroughly infused. Fresh fruits and vegetables can be sealed on their own and cooked until meltingly tender without drying out, caramelizing, or leaching their flavors and nutrients into water. Puree these pure-tasting ingredients with flavorful liquids like reduced wines, broths, or juices, and you have elegant and innovative sauce purees.

Sous vide is particularly good for making warm egg-based sauces like hollandaise and custards. You can seal the egg yolks and cook them until they are just thickened but still liquid. Then they are stable enough that you can add plenty of softened butter or cream with little risk of separating. You can also stir egg yolks, cream, and sugar together in a bag, seal, and slowly cook at the precise temperature to set into a creamy gel, avoiding the risk of curdling the sauce on the stovetop.

A controlled-temperature water bath is also a good tool for keeping delicate sauces warm. You can make your butter or egg-enriched sauces ahead of time and keep them at a safe temperature for half an hour or so instead of whisking them up in a frenzy while the asparagus cools.

BUTTER... WITH RESTRAINT

Butter with *restraint*? I have friends who have actually shrieked at the mere suggestion. Let me explain. My tendency to use a light hand with butter has little to do with health or ethics. Butter is just *so* good as a simple sauce and embellishment that it can become a crutch. You don't think you have the skill or time to pull together a sauce? Melt some butter. Your sauce seems thin or doesn't taste quite right? Add more butter. You want the texture of your sauce to be more velvety or clinging, or maybe you just want more volume? Whisk in cold butter. All of these are tried-and-true sauce making methods, but when you consciously try to limit your use of butter, to use it with a lighter hand, you will find yourself thinking more creatively. You will come up with intriguing alternatives, enhanced flavors, and ways to manipulate texture without reaching for a quick high-fat fix. In the end, I think you will become a better cook.

When I use a lot of butter, I feel like I'm cheating. I feel as if I'm sneaking hidden fat and calories into my unwitting guests' dinners or trying to compensate for the fact that my food isn't quite as good as it should be. I've known restaurant chefs to put more butter into a single pasta sauce than I eat in a month—some don't even include butter in the menu description. It seems like a cover-up. You can do better. If you take the time to build flavors in your sauce, to season carefully and manipulate texture thoughtfully, and then add a touch of butter to enrich what is an already great sauce, it will soar to new heights. (see Finishing and Enriching Sauces with Suspended Melted Butter, page 431.) Less can be more.

A tablespoon of melted or browned butter is perhaps the simplest of sauces. You can enhance that plain butter by infusing it or stirring additional flavors into it. But as part of a sauce, when added carefully, butter will blend evenly into a warm liquid (even water) and flavor, enrich, and thicken every drop. Perhaps the most treasured of suspended-butter sauces is White Wine Butter Sauce (Beurre Blanc; page 314).

BUTTER VOCABULARY

Butter has a vocabulary all its own. Here are some of the most common terms.

- **Unsalted:** Unsalted butter is best for cooking and baking because it tastes fresher and you have control over the exact amount of salt you add to your dish. Salt quantities vary from brand to brand. Once you taste a butter sauce made with unsalted butter alongside one that was made with salted butter, you will never question the reasoning again. The unsalted-butter sauce is silky, where the other seems almost briny.

- **Salted:** Salt is added to butter for flavor and preservation. While not ideal for sauce making (see above), salted butter is a must for warm toast.

- **Cultured:** Cultured butter is made from milk that had live cultures introduced before churning. It has a faint yogurt quality, tang, and complexity. Cultured butters are quite expensive. They are particularly popular in dairy-rich European countries, but they are showing up more often in specialty markets here.

- **Softened:** Softened butter can be stirred or whipped but is not at all melted or oily. To soften cold butter, cut it into grape-sized cubes. Separate them so they don't touch. They will become soft quite quickly, with no risk of getting oily.

- **Compound:** Compound butters have flavorful ingredients stirred into them (see page 395). Chilled compound butters can be simply sliced into pats and melted on hot foods to make almost instant sauces.

- **Melted:** Melted butter has been heated to the point of fluidity. When carefully melted, the butter will maintain a cohesive creaminess. If it is heated to over 140°F/60°C, the butterfat and water will separate, the emulsion will break, and the butterfat will float to the surface. Butter that has broken and separated will never have the same emulsifying properties as butter that hasn't been melted.

- **Clarified:** Clarified butter is clean, melted butterfat. To clarify butter, it is brought to a boil so the emulsion fully breaks and then left to settle into distinct layers. The foam and impurities are skimmed from the top and the clear pure melted butterfat is care-

continues

fully poured off, or strained through cheesecloth, leaving behind the cloudy milk solids. Clarified butter has a higher heat tolerance, so it can be used to sear foods.

- **Brown Butter (beurre noisette):** Brown butter is butter that has been cooked until the emulsion breaks and the milk solids that settle to the bottom are toasted, brown, and nutty.

- **Black Butter (beurre noir):** Black butter is a French sauce made with butter that is cooked until the emulsion breaks and the milk solids are just past nutty brown but not burnt. Lemon juice or vinegar and a few seasonings are traditionally stirred in before serving.

- **Ghee:** Ghee is a clarified butter that is a popular cooking oil and flavoring in India. It is a bit like a hybrid of clarified and brown butter. It is cooked for longer and at a lower heat than regular clarified butter, often for 20 minutes or more over medium-low heat. The milk solids turn golden but should never brown; the aroma is more buttered popcorn than toast. Ghee is more shelf stable than whole butter.

- **Suspended Melted Butter (mounted butter/beurre monté):** Butter that is barely melted and still emulsified is especially treasured in classic sauce making. To "mount a sauce with butter" means to stir pieces of cold butter into a warm sauce until they become liquid and the sauce is gently thickened. *Monter au beurre* is the French term. Mounted butter or beurre monté can be as simple as butter whisked into simmering water to dress fresh vegetables without making them greasy. (See Finishing and Enriching Sauces with Suspended Melted Butter, page 431.)

COMPOUND BUTTERS

Butter that is softened and mixed with other ingredients to make a unique ingredient or sauce goes by the rather utilitarian, almost pharmaceutical, title of "compound butter." Seasonal vegetables, a seared chicken breast, or even a warm roll can be transformed with a smear of soft compound butter. Compound butters can also be used to finish and enrich sauces or to make intriguing variations of the White Wine Butter Sauce (Beurre Blanc; page 314).

WASABI BUTTER

The richness of butter with the zip of wasabi is an intriguing flavor enhancement for classic dishes like grilled salmon, shrimp, or even steak. Or make a side dish of spicy wasabi peas by melting the butter over garden-fresh English or sugar snap peas. If you are lucky enough to live in a region where you can get fresh shiso leaves, use 1 tablespoon chopped fresh leaves in place of the scallions for a slightly peppery, minty flavor.

YIELD: ½ CUP

1 stick (4 oz/115 g) unsalted butter, softened

1 tablespoon prepared wasabi

1 tablespoon thinly sliced scallions (white and green parts)

¼ teaspoon kosher salt, or to taste

> Stir the ingredients together until they are well blended. Pack the butter into an airtight container or scoop it onto a piece of plastic wrap or parchment paper, form it into a log, and wrap tightly.

> Refrigerate for up to 3 weeks or freeze for up to 3 months. Let the butter, or pats of butter, warm to room temperature before using so it melts quickly.

SCANDINAVIAN FISH ROE AND DILL BUTTER

This butter was inspired by the many tubes and containers of fish roe paste that are popular condiments and sandwich spreads in Scandinavian countries. While I have used anchovies for years, I hadn't considered fish roe to be a similarly adaptable, salty, and savory ingredient. If you have a source for it, you can mix in some prepared Scandinavian fish roe paste into butter, but I suggest using small pink roe such as capelin, tobiko/flying fish roe, or even Greek tarama. Avoid dyed black roe, which will make the butter an unpleasant color. This is particularly good melted over boiled potatoes or white fish. You can also spread it on rye crackers.

YIELD: ½ CUP

1 stick (4 oz/115 g) unsalted butter, softened

2 tablespoons pink fish roe, such as capelin, tobiko, or tarama

1 tablespoon chopped fresh dill

Salt to taste (depending on how salty the roe is)

> Stir the ingredients together until they are well blended.

> Pack the butter into an airtight container or scoop it onto a piece of plastic wrap or parchment paper, form it into a log, and wrap tightly.

> Refrigerate for up to 1 week or freeze for up to 3 months. Let the butter, or pats of butter, warm to room temperature before using so it melts quickly.

DRIED FRUIT AND BRANDY BUTTER

This is a lovely butter to have on hand during the holidays. It is a treat when melted on sweet potatoes or seared chicken or spread on crusty bread. My friends Hailey and Renate were inspired and served it as a sauce on fresh goat cheese ravioli with wilted arugula. For a more savory butter, add a tablespoon of minced caramelized shallots and some chopped fresh parsley.

YIELD: ½ CUP

2 tablespoons minced dried fruit, such as apricots, dates, figs, pears, golden raisins, and/or cranberries

2 tablespoons brandy (substitute orange juice or apple cider if you prefer a nonalcoholic alternative)

1 stick (4 oz/115 g) unsalted butter, softened

½ teaspoon kosher salt, or to taste

¼ teaspoon ground ginger

A few gratings of nutmeg (optional)

> Soak the chopped fruit in the brandy until it absorbs the liquid and becomes soft, at least 15 minutes.

> Stir the ingredients together until they are well blended. Pack the butter into an airtight container or scoop it onto a piece of plastic wrap or parchment paper, form it into a log, and wrap it tightly.

> Refrigerate for up to 3 weeks or freeze for up to 3 months. Let the butter, or pats of butter, warm to room temperature before using so it melts quickly.

COCONUT "BUTTER" WITH SOUTH INDIAN FLAVORS

In South India, coconut oil is the cooking oil of choice. Many dishes are garnished with a drizzle of coconut oil, popped black mustard seeds, crispy fried curry leaves, and frizzled small red onions. I like to stir these wonderful ingredients together like a compound butter and spread or melt it on various foods as the whim strikes: on savory pancakes, pilafs, or grilled whole fish.

Curry leaves come from a small tropical plant. They have a complicated taste and fragrance that can be redolent of mixed spices. (Curry powder is not made from curry leaves.) They are commonly fried until crisp and used as a crunchy garnish or added to simmered dishes for an herbal depth. Fresh curry leaves can be found at specialty markets. I often have some stored in the freezer. If your climate allows, try growing a plant of your own.

YIELD: ABOUT 1½ CUPS

¾ cup pure coconut oil

1 tablespoon black mustard seeds

2 teaspoons cumin seeds

1 cup thinly sliced shallots (about 4 large shallots)

¼ cup fresh curry leaves, torn into pieces (optional)

½ teaspoon kosher salt

¼ teaspoon hot Indian chile powder, cayenne, or similar hot red chile powder (optional)

⅛ teaspoon ground turmeric

> Heat 3 tablespoons of the coconut oil in a sauté pan or skillet over medium-high heat. Add the mustard and cumin seeds and cook until the mustard seeds pop. Add the shallots and curry leaves, if you have them, and cook until the shallots are brown and the curry leaves have turned dark and crisp, about 6 minutes.

> Put the remaining coconut oil in a bowl. Add the cooked shallot mixture, the salt, chile powder, and turmeric and stir together. Serve.

> Cover and refrigerate for up to 1 week. The chilled mixture will look grainy, but it will melt evenly when heated.

IDEAS FOR FLAVORING A STICK OF BUTTER

Butter is an especially good vehicle for carrying other flavors. Use unsalted butter so you have more control over the seasoning. Use the following ingredients for 1 stick (4 oz/115 g) softened unsalted butter; 1 tablespoon per person is a good serving size. Pack the butter into a bowl or shape it into a log, wrap tightly, and chill or freeze until ready to use. You can also pack the soft butter into decorative molds. Let the butter warm to room temperature before you serve it so it doesn't chill the food it is meant to enhance.

Garlic and Parsley ("Snail Butter")	Stir in 2 tablespoons minced fresh herbs, such as parsley, chives, tarragon and/or chervil, 1 tablespoon finely minced shallot, 2 finely minced or pressed garlic cloves, ½ teaspoon finely grated lemon zest, and ½ teaspoon kosher salt. Use on escargots, mussels, or potatoes or for garlic bread.
Green Olive and Caper	Stir in 2 tablespoons chopped pimento-stuffed green olives and 2 tablespoons chopped drained capers; do not add any salt. Use on fish, shellfish, bread, or grilled tomatoes.
Toasted Coconut, Habanero, and Lime	Stir in 2 tablespoons toasted coconut flakes, 1 minced habanero pepper, 2 teaspoons finely grated lime zest, ½ teaspoon kosher salt, and (optional) a pinch of ground allspice. Use on shrimp, lobster, or corn cakes.
Cashews, Golden Raisins, and Curry Powder	Stir in 3 tablespoons finely chopped roasted salted cashews, 2 tablespoons finely chopped golden raisins, and 2 teaspoons hot curry powder. Taste before adding salt, because the saltiness of the nuts can vary greatly, then season accordingly. Serve with chicken, pork scallopini, cauliflower or spread on warm flatbreads.
Walnut and Horseradish	Stir in 3 tablespoons chopped toasted walnuts, 2 tablespoons prepared horseradish, 1 tablespoon chopped fresh parsley, ¼ teaspoon chopped fresh thyme, ½ teaspoon kosher salt, and plenty of freshly ground black pepper. Serve with steaks, salmon fillets, or roasted beets.

New Mexico Christmas (Green and Red Chile)	Stir in 2 tablespoons finely minced roasted green chiles, 1 tablespoon finely minced or grated onion, 1 teaspoon New Mexican red or chipotle chile powder, and ¼ teaspoon kosher salt. Serve on pork chops, eggs, or corn on the cob.
Anchovy	Soak 6 salt-packed anchovy fillets in a few tablespoons of water or milk for 2 minutes; drain. Or use 6 oil-packed anchovy fillets. Mash the anchovies with a fork. Stir in the mashed anchovies, 1 teaspoon very finely chopped fresh parsley, and a pinch of red chile flakes. Taste before adding any salt to gauge the saltiness of the anchovies, then season accordingly. Serve with steaks or stir into warm pasta.
Hazelnut and Thyme	Stir in 3 tablespoons finely chopped roasted hazelnuts, 2 teaspoons finely grated orange zest, ½ teaspoon chopped fresh thyme, ½ teaspoon kosher salt, and a pinch of red chile flakes. Serve with chicken, game birds, carrots, sweet potatoes, or other root vegetables.
Lemon Tarragon	Stir in 1 tablespoon finely grated lemon zest, 1 tablespoon finely chopped fresh tarragon, and ½ teaspoon kosher salt. Serve with steamed mussels or clams, mild white fish, asparagus, or braised Belgian endive.
Porcini and Truffle	Stir in 1 tablespoon finely ground dried porcini mushrooms, ½ teaspoon kosher salt, and 6 to 8 drops of truffle oil. Serve with steak, eggs, cheese-stuffed pastas, or baked potatoes.
Pub (Roasted Garlic and Barley Syrup)	Stir in 2 tablespoons mashed roasted garlic (see the recipe on page 174), 1 tablespoon barley malt syrup, 1 tablespoon finely chopped fresh parsley, and 1 teaspoon nutritional yeast flakes. Taste before adding any salt, because the yeast adds saltiness. Hop oil or essence is available at brewers supply stores or online—add a few drops if you like a greener "hoppy" beer flavor. Serve with steaks, pork chops, or grilled oysters on the half-shell. Spread on dark bread or warm rolls.
Arlene's Lavender and Honey	Grind or pulverize 1 teaspoon food-grade dried lavender into a coarse powder in a spice or coffee mill and stir it in with 3 tablespoons honey. Serve on roasted chicken, steamed red potatoes, crepes, or scones.

TIPS
for Creating and Using Compound Butters

- To soften cold butter, cut it into pieces, separate them, and leave them at room temperature while you prepare the other ingredients. Don't soften butter in the microwave—it is too easy to melt it.

- The flavorings can be mashed into the soft butter with a fork, stirred in with a spoon, or whipped in with a mixer.

- If the ingredients are wet or you are introducing a liquid, a higher mixing speed is best so the liquid doesn't get trapped in the cold butter as beads.

- Particles should be small enough that they can be evenly dispersed.

- Compound butters improve as the flavors infuse. Well wrapped, they will keep in the refrigerator for weeks and the freezer for months.

- Compound butters are often rolled into logs for easy cutting and serving, but if you find it more convenient, you can scoop it from a ramekin or bowl. You can also roll it into butter balls or press the butter into individual decorative molds.

- Let cold compound butter return to room temperature while you prepare the food you are going to serve it with. If the butter is very cold, it will not melt well and will cool the hot food.

- If your butter is not melting, blast it quickly with a blowtorch, or pop it under a hot broiler for a moment, but slightly undermelted butter that is still softening on the food is preferable to greasy melted butter pools on the bottom of the plate or platter.

WHITE WINE BUTTER SAUCE (BEURRE BLANC)

A sauce of liquid but not fully melted butter made tangy with shallot-infused wine is a classic French sauce for vegetables and fish. It is just a smidge less rich than hollandaise. I included this recipe because it is easy to dress up by using a compound butter rather than plain unsalted butter. Even though it is a bit butter heavy for my preference, it's a good Plan B sauce that can be whipped up in minutes if your other recipes go awry.

YIELD: ½ CUP

1 tablespoon finely minced shallot

2 tablespoons white wine vinegar

¼ cup bright dry white wine, such as Fumet Blanc or Viognier

1 stick (4 oz/115 g) cold unsalted butter or compound butter (see the table on page 400), cut into cranberry-sized cubes

Kosher salt

> Combine the shallot and vinegar in a small saucepan and simmer until the vinegar has almost completely evaporated. The shallots should just be moist, but not browned. Add the wine and simmer until the wine has reduced to 1 tablespoon. Reduce the temperature to medium-low and gradually whisk in the cold butter a few pieces at a time, waiting until they are just melted before adding more. Do not overheat the butter. If you want a smooth butter sauce, you can strain it to remove the shallots, but do not strain if you are using a compound butter. Compound butter will already be salted, so taste and season accordingly.

> Serve warm. The sauce cannot be reheated if it is chilled.

SYRUPS
AND SWEET
SAUCES

Throughout this book, I often suggest you cook savory sauces such as reductions, gravies, and purees to a syrupy, slightly sticky consistency. Syrupy is an appealing texture because it clings but still runs freely and pools on the plate. Perhaps the quickest way to make sauces syrupy is just to add sugar. Sugar dramatically tilts the seasoning balance, of course, but that's not always unwelcome. American cuisine is known for pairing sweet and fruity flavors with savory tastes more than in many other countries. We like ketchup on burgers, sweet barbecue sauces on smoked and grilled meats, cranberry sauce with roasted turkey, and pineapple glaze or honey mustard on baked ham. Many of the syrups and fruit sauces in this chapter can enhance appetizers and savory dishes as well as desserts.

You can add sugar to fresh ingredients to make them syrupy, or make a plain sugar syrup and infuse it with flavors. You can also use naturally syrupy ingredients like honey, agave syrup, molasses, and superconcentrated apple or grape juice to modify the texture and taste of sauces.

For many people, the first thing that comes to mind as syrup is warm maple syrup dripping off a stack of pancakes or filling the cavities of crunchy waffles. Bright-colored syrups rich with natural fruits like Sweet Ginger Peach Sauce (page 414) are also marvelous on pancakes. The same is true for intriguing homemade syrup infusions and syrupy blends. Syrups can be customized with savory elements, acidity, saltiness, or herbal perfumes. They can be used both straight, as an ingredient, or as artsy dots and squiggles on plated presentations.

SIMPLE SYRUP

It's always nice to have this syrup on hand for sweetening iced tea, shaking up with cocktails, or finishing desserts, as well as for sauces. See the table on page 410 for some suggestions for simple, elegant infusions.

YIELD: 1½ CUPS

1 cup water

1 cup superfine or granulated sugar

> Combine the water and sugar in a saucepan and heat gently over medium heat, swirling the pan, until the sugar has completely dissolved. Increase the heat and boil for 5 minutes. Remove from the heat and cool.

> Cover and refrigerate for up to 1 month.

THICK SIMPLE SYRUP
> Increase the sugar to 2 cups.

PREVENTING CRYSTALLIZATION

Crystals can quickly grow on other crystals, so to make clear, liquid syrups you need to be sure that every trace of solid sugar is fully dissolved into the water. If you are a candy maker, you know this already. If you have time, soak the sugar in the water for a while to soften it. Stir sugar syrups minimally, if at all, especially while there are still granules visible. I don't stir thin sugar syrups, I just shake the pan and swirl it a bit as the sugar dissolves. Enthusiastic stirring or whisking tends to leave whole sugar crystals at the waterline. They can lurk there until you think all is clear and then get washed into the mixture to wreak havoc. Don't bring the syrup to a boil until the sugar is completely dissolved and the liquid is clear. Candy makers often cover the pan for the first few minutes of boiling so the steam dissolves any sneaky waterline crystals. You can also dab them with a wet pastry brush until they dissolve.

LEMON CLOVE SYRUP

This is particularly good with butter cakes and fresh fruit such as apricots or poached pears. It can also be used to drench classic desserts like *babas*, trifle, and phyllo pastries. Cracked cardamom pods can be used in place of cloves as a variation.

YIELD: 1½ CUPS

1 cup water

1 cup granulated sugar

8 whole cloves

4 slices lemon

> Combine the water, sugar, and cloves in a saucepan and heat gently over medium heat until the sugar has completely dissolved. Increase the heat and boil for 5 minutes. Remove from the heat, add the lemon slices, cover, and leave to steep for 5 minutes.

> Strain and serve at room temperature.

> If storing, cover and refrigerate for up to 1 month.

ELEGANT AND UNEXPECTED SIMPLE SYRUP INFUSIONS

At the beginning of this book, I urged you to create quick savory teas and infusions. The same tips apply to creating innovative syrups. When you have ingredients that you can't quite figure out how to introduce as solids to your sauce, try infusing them. These syrup recipes can be used for both savory and sweet dishes. Infused syrups store well, so you can keep a few on hand to add to vinaigrettes or pan sauces. Add a drizzle as a complement to a fresh relish or spiced sauce puree. Splash some on fresh fruit or drench cakes in the syrup. You can even shake them up with cocktails. When using fresh flora, take extra care to ensure they are free of sprays and pesticides and they are safe to consume.

Hibiscus	Add ¼ cup crumbled dried hibiscus flowers (*flor de jamaica*) before boiling the syrup. Cover and leave to steep until cool. Strain.
Rosemary	Add 2 sprigs fresh rosemary to the hot syrup. Cover and leave to infuse for 5 minutes. Strain.
Bay Leaf	Add 6 or 7 fresh bay leaves to the hot syrup. (Dried bay leaves are not recommended because they don't have the same fresh aroma and spiciness.) Cover and leave to infuse for 5 minutes. Strain.
Earl Grey Tea or Black Tea	Stir 2 tablespoons loose Earl Grey tea and a slice of lemon into the hot syrup. Cover and leave to infuse for 3 minutes. Strain. Strong black teas also work well. My favorite for syrup is Batik brand Ukrainian tea.
Lavender	Add 3 sprigs fresh food-grade lavender to the warm syrup. Cover and leave to steep for 5 minutes. Strain. If fresh is unavailable, use 1½ teaspoons of food-grade dried lavender blossoms.
Spruce Tips or Douglas Fir	Add ¾ cup freshly picked unsprayed, non-chemically treated spruce tips (only available in the early spring) or a 6-inch/15 cm young, flexible sprig of Douglas fir to the hot syrup. Cover and leave to steep until cool. Strain.
Rose Hip	Add ¼ cup cracked dried rose hips to the syrup before boiling. Leave to steep until cool. Strain.

Maple Bacon	Cook 2 strips of bacon until very crisp. Drain well and break in half. Warm 1 cup pure maple syrup over medium heat. Drop the bacon into the warm syrup, but do not stir. Cover and leave to steep for 5 minutes. Remove the bacon and strain the syrup through cheesecloth.
Anise	Add 1 tablespoon cracked fennel seeds to the syrup before boiling. Leave to steep until cool. Strain. Alternatively, add ¼ cup minced fresh fennel to the hot syrup. Cover, and steep for 5 minutes. Strain.
Li Hing (Salty Plum)	Stir ¼ cup li hing powder (available where Hawaiian foods are sold and online) into ½ cup simple syrup, or add 3 or 4 whole salted plums to the syrup before boiling. Leave to infuse for at least 30 minutes. Strain.

COCONUT SYRUP

Like simple syrup, this recipe is just two ingredients boiled together. The syrup is thick, sweet, and creamy but not as pasty or processed tasting as the canned sweetened coconut cream sold for cocktails. Serve it alongside dark chocolate or fresh fruit desserts. Drizzle it over tropical fruit, sorbets, or even shaved ice. The finished consistency depends on how much you choose to reduce syrup. A thin, milky sauce will takes only 3 to 4 minutes; a thick, sticky cream can take closer to 10. The texture can also vary according to how much fat is in the coconut cream to start. Very-high-fat creams will take less time than light creams. The syrup may gradually separate, but it comes together with a quick stir or shake.

YIELD: 2 CUPS

One 14 oz/414 ml can
    unsweetened coconut milk

½ cup sugar

> Combine the coconut milk and sugar in a saucepan and gradually heat until the sugar is dissolved. Bring to a boil and simmer until syrupy, about 8 minutes. As it thickens, check the consistency regularly by lifting the pan from the stove and swirling the syrup in the pan. When it clings to the sides and bottom of the pan like warm honey, it is done. If you're not sure, remove the pan from the heat and drizzle a few drops of sauce on a cold plate. If the syrup runs like water, it needs more time; if it collects in dots before running, it is done. It will thicken as it cools.

> Cover and refrigerate for up to 2 weeks. The syrup may separate, but it will stir together easily.

FRESH MINT SYRUP

If you want to garnish a dessert plate with something a little bit more intriguing than a simple mint sprig, consider a few drops or squiggles of this fresh mint syrup. It's also good with savory dishes like roasted lamb and spiced grilled chicken. The mint leaves are quickly blanched so they maintain their brilliant green color. If you don't blanch the leaves, the flavor is more intense, but the syrup darkens quickly. You can also make this with lemon balm or organic scented geranium leaves.

YIELD: ½ CUP

2 cups lightly packed fresh mint leaves

½ cup Simple Syrup (page 407), or as needed

> Bring a pot of water to a boil. Set an ice bath nearby.

> Drop all of the mint leaves into the boiling water, stir once, and immediately drain. Plunge the blanched mint into the ice water to stop the cooking.

> Drain the mint and squeeze out the water. Put the mint into a blender and blend, gradually pouring in the syrup, until smooth. Press the syrup through a fine sieve and add additional simple syrup if you like a thinner sauce. Serve.

> If storing, cover and refrigerate for up to 1 day.

SWEET GINGER PEACH SAUCE

This recipe can be adapted for almost any soft fruit. It is halfway between a puree and a syrup, with a flowing consistency but some natural body. Simmer it for a few minutes longer if you want a thicker sauce. Don't bother to remove the peach skins before you make it—they add flavor and can be strained out after the sauce is pureed. You can also use an infused simple syrup here—a few tablespoons of Black Tea Syrup (see the table page 410) is lovely in this.

YIELD: 1 CUP

1 cup diced fresh or frozen peaches

½ cup Simple Syrup (page 407)

2 coins fresh ginger

Pinch of citric acid for added tartness (optional)

> Combine the ingredients in a saucepan and bring to a boil over high heat, then reduce the heat and simmer until the peaches are tender, about 5 minutes. Cool slightly.

> Fish out the ginger and discard. Transfer the mixture to a blender and puree until smooth. Press the sauce through a sieve to even the texture and remove any bits of skin.

> Serve warm or cool.

> If storing, cover and refrigerate for up to 3 days.

SEASONAL DESSERT SAUCES

These are the sweet sister sauces to the savory vegetable and fruit sauce purees on page 177. The bright colors and fresh flavors can really liven up a plate. Choose inviting seasonal ingredients and simmer them with Simple Syrup (page 407) or a sweet juice until they are tender. The texture can vary from thick and chunky to thin and velvety, depending on how much you choose to process the cooked sauce. If you prefer a very simple fresh fruit sauce, you can puree fresh fruit like berries and cherries with cold sugar syrup and strain. Some uncooked fruit sauces will discolor without a bit of added acidity like lemon juice or citric acid.

Rhubarb	Combine 1 cup sliced fresh or frozen rhubarb with ½ cup Simple Syrup (page 407) or sweet fruit juice such as cherry, black currant, pomegranate, or cranberry in a saucepan and simmer until the rhubarb is tender, about 8 minutes. Stir to mix, or puree and press through a fine sieve for smoother sauce.
Stone Fruits (Cherry, Plum, Apricot, or Nectarine)	Combine 1 cup pitted cherries or unpeeled fresh chunks of stone fruits with ½ cup Simple Syrup (page 407) in a saucepan and simmer until soft. Puree. Press through a sieve if needed to remove any skin.
Berry	Combine 1 cup fresh berries and ⅓ cup Simple Syrup (page 407) in a saucepan and simmer, uncovered, until syrupy. Simply stir for a rustic sauce, or press through a sieve. Fresh uncooked berries can also be blended with cold simple syrup and strained for a fresh flavor.
Tomato	Combine 1 cup diced tomatoes with ½ cup Simple Syrup (page 407) in a saucepan and simmer, uncovered, until the tomatoes are juicy and the sauce is slightly thickened. Puree and press through a sieve. Serve with soufflés and cheese dishes.
Carrot Orange	Combine 1 cup diced carrots, 1 cup orange juice, and ¼ cup sugar in a saucepan and warm gently until the sugar has dissolved, then raise the heat and simmer, uncovered, for 5 minutes. Puree or press through a sieve for a smoother sauce.

continues

Blueberry	Combine 1 cup fresh or frozen blueberries with 1 cup blueberry juice blend, black currant, or grape juice and ¼ cup sugar in a saucepan and warm gently until the sugar has dissolved, then raise the heat and simmer, uncovered, for 5 minutes. Leave the berries whole or puree until smooth. Press through a sieve for a smooth sauce.
Mango Chipotle	Combine 1 cup diced fresh or frozen mango with ¾ cup margarita mix or Simple Syrup (page 407) and 1 chopped canned chipotle chile in adobo in a saucepan and bring to a boil, then reduce the heat and simmer, covered, until the mango is soft, about 4 minutes. Puree and strain. Season with a pinch of salt and freshly squeezed lime juice to taste.
Spiced Pineapple	Combine 1 cup diced fresh or frozen pineapple, 1 cup water, ¼ cup lightly packed dark brown sugar, 1 teaspoon minced fresh ginger, 1 cracked cinnamon stick, 6 whole cloves, and a 1-inch/2.5 cm piece of vanilla bean in a saucepan and warm until the sugar is completely dissolved, then increase the heat to a simmer and cook, covered, until the pineapple is completely tender, about 5 minutes. Fish out and discard the cinnamon, cloves, and vanilla bean. Puree. Press through a sieve for a thinner, smoother sauce.

TIPS

for Creating Your Own Syrups and Seasonal Dessert Sauces

- Syrup made with cane sugar tends to boil up clearer than beet sugar because there are fewer impurities.

- You can add flavorings before or after the syrup boils, depending on the ingredients and preferred concentration. Fresh flavors tend to be best added later rather than earlier.

- Evaporated cane juice, brown sugar, grated palm sugar, or Demerara can be used in the same ratio to make flavorful syrups, but clarity and color will be altered.

- Molasses, treacle, maple syrup, corn syrup, cane syrup, and agave nectar can be warmed and infused with flavorings. You will need to add water to dilute the intensity and thickness.

- Sugar-free sweeteners like aspartame or stevia will not make sauces syrupy.

5-MINUTE DARK CHOCOLATE SAUCE

There is always a place for good, simple chocolate sauce, especially one that can be thrown together in minutes. This isn't fancy. It's quite thin in texture but loaded with chocolate flavor. Since it is made with cocoa, you can add just as much sweetness as you like. The liquid used can be water, milk, cream, coconut milk, or even orange juice.

½ cup unsweetened cocoa powder, sifted to remove any lumps

½ cup sugar

1 cup water (see headnote)

A few drops of vanilla extract (optional)

Tiny pinch of kosher salt

> Put the cocoa and sugar in a saucepan and stir to mix. Gradually whisk in half the water to make a smooth paste, then stir in the rest. Bring to a boil and simmer for 2 minutes, stirring constantly to prevent the sauce from burning on the bottom; it will thicken quickly after it boils. Season with the vanilla, if using, and salt.

> Serve warm or cold.

> If storing, cover and refrigerate for up to 2 weeks.

FLAVORINGS FOR 5-MINUTE CHOCOLATE SAUCE

There are probably a zillion different ways you can flavor a chocolate sauce. As a rule, I change the base liquid, add infusions, or stir in a little something extra once the sauce cools. Sometimes I do all three. At the moment, I'm experimenting with a black licorice chocolate sauce, but it's not quite there yet.

Extra-Rich	Substitute half-and-half or heavy cream for the water.
Orange	Substitute orange juice for the water. If desired, add a few drops of pure orange oil or a tablespoon of orange liqueur after the sauce has cooled slightly.
Raspberry	Stir ¼ cup seedless or strained raspberry preserves into the warm sauce. Add 2 tablespoons raspberry liqueur once the sauce has cooled slightly.
Coconut	Use 1 cup unsweetened coconut milk in place of the water. Stir in 1 tablespoon rum once the sauce has cooled slightly if you like.
Mocha	Substitute strong black coffee for the water. Stir in 2 tablespoons coffee liqueur after the sauce has cooled slightly.
Mexican Coffee	Stir ½ teaspoon ground cinnamon into the cocoa and sugar. Substitute strong black coffee for the water. Stir 2 tablespoons almond butter into the hot sauce. Add 1 to 2 tablespoons rum or coffee liqueur and a few extra drops of vanilla extract once the sauce has cooled slightly.
Ancho Chile	Stir ⅛ to ¼ teaspoon ancho chile powder into the sugar and cocoa mix.
Black Forest	Substitute the strained juice from Montmorency or similar jarred cherries for the water and stir in ⅓ cup diced pitted cherries. Add 1 tablespoon kirsch and a few drops of pure almond oil or extract once the sauce has cooled slightly.
Fresh Mint	Stir 2 or 3 sprigs fresh mint into the hot sauce, cover, and leave to infuse for 5 minutes. Strain.

CARAMEL SAUCE

A bowl of homemade caramel sauce can be a problem—I often lose all control and end up pouring the sauce on absolutely everything, or slurping it up by the spoonful. I'm not a huge fan of superrich sauces, but this one gets me every time. You must use the heaviest cream to prevent the sauce from "shattering." Look for creams that are 36 to 40% butterfat. Follow the tips on page 408 to prevent the sugar syrup from crystallizing, and cook the caramel until it is very dark. The slight bitterness adds depth and complexity. The flavor improves overnight, so make this ahead if possible.

YIELD: 1⅓ CUPS

½ cup sugar

¼ cup water

1 cup heavy cream, brought to
    room temperature

Pinch of kosher salt

A few drops of vanilla extract

> Combine the sugar and water in a heavy saucepan and heat over medium heat, swirling the pan now and then, until the sugar is completely dissolved. Increase the heat and boil until the sugar starts to caramelize. Watch it very closely, and remove it from the stove when it is the color of strong tea. Averting your face and protecting your hands from the steam, immediately but gradually pour the cream into the caramel, stirring to mix. The caramel will steam and boil violently. Cool slightly, then stir in the salt and vanilla.

> If storing, cover and refrigerate for up to 5 days. The sauce may separate a bit, but it will stir together.

SALTED CARAMEL SAUCE

> Increase the salt to ½ teaspoon.

CARAMEL COLORING

> Caramelize the sugar to a dark mahogany brown. Remove from the heat and gradually add ½ cup warm water, taking care to avert your face and protect hands from the steam. Stir to mix. Cover and store in a cool, dark spot for up to 1 month.

SWEET-AND-SPICY BUTTER PECAN SAUCE

This sweet, boozy, buttery sauce can be served with entrées as well as desserts. Drizzle it over fried chicken or pork chops or use as a glaze on sweet potatoes or acorn squash—or just pour it over ice cream.

YIELD: 1 CUP

⅓ cup granulated sugar

3 tablespoons light or dark brown sugar

¼ cup water

⅔ cup (3 oz/85 g) pecan halves

3 tablespoons bourbon or whiskey (for a nonalcoholic version, use additional orange juice)

3 tablespoons orange juice

3 tablespoons cold butter, diced

Good pinch of cayenne pepper or chipotle chile pepper (optional)

> Stir together the sugars and water in a heavy saucepan, and gently warm until the sugar is completely dissolved. Bring the syrup to a boil over medium-high heat, add the pecans, reduce the heat, and simmer until the syrup is thick and sticky and the pecans are toasted through, 5 to 6 minutes. Turn the pecans as needed, using the tip of a sharp knife or a skewer rather than a spoon to prevent globs of sugar from sticking to your stirring tool.

> Remove the pan from the heat. Averting your face and protecting your hands from the steam, add the bourbon and orange juice and stir to mix. Whisk in the cold butter a bit at a time, stirring until each piece is melted before adding more. Season with the salt and cayenne.

> Serve warm or at room temperature.

> If storing, cover and refrigerate for up to 3 days. The butter will congeal on the top and the pecans will soften, but this is not meant to be a fully emulsified sauce and will be appealing when warmed.

ENGLISH POURING CUSTARD (CRÈME ANGLAISE)

I feel lucky to have learned about pouring custard from skilled English cooks. It was only later that I realized it was the same thing as fancy crème anglaise. This sauce is like melted ice cream. In fact, it is the base for many classic frozen custards and rich ice creams. Pour it over warm apple pie, fresh fruit, or dense, sticky spice cakes.

Arrowroot can make dairy-based sauces oddly slippery, so use it only if you are new to making custard or heat-sensitive sauces—it helps to gently stabilize the sauce so it is less likely to curdle. It is not failsafe; you can still curdle custards made with arrowroot, but it adds a bit of security until you get a feel for how egg-thickened sauces respond to heat. See the table on page 424 for flavoring ideas.

YIELD: 1½ CUPS

1½ cups milk, preferably whole milk

¼ cup sugar (add a tablespoon or two more if you like sweeter custard)

1-inch/2.5 cm piece of vanilla bean (or substitute ¼ teaspoon vanilla extract)

3 large egg yolks

½ teaspoon arrowroot (optional)

Pinch of kosher salt

> Stir together the milk and sugar in a medium heavy saucepan. Split the vanilla bean open and scrape out the seeds. Add the seeds and bean to the milk and sugar. (If you are using vanilla extract, add it after the custard has cooked.) Heat the milk until steam rises and bubbles form around the edges of the pan. Remove the pan from the heat, cover, and set aside.

> Stir together the egg yolks, arrowroot, if using, and salt in a medium bowl. Temper the egg yolks by gradually pouring in ½ cup of the warm milk, stirring constantly so the egg yolks warm slightly but don't cook. Gradually pour the tempered egg yolks into the pan with the remaining milk, stirring constantly (you don't need to remove the vanilla bean yet).

> Heat the sauce over medium heat, stirring constantly with a wooden spoon or silicone spatula, scraping the bottom of the pan with each stir—you need to make sure that the custard doesn't cook or thicken too quickly at the bottom of the pan. If it does seem to be thickening on the bottom, remove

the pan from the heat and stir well, then reduce the temperature to medium-low, and begin to cook again. The custard will thicken very gradually. When the tiny bubbles and foam at the surface start to clear, you are nearly there. The custard should be the consistency of very heavy cream and just coat the back of the spoon. (That means when you turn the spoon over, the custard should glaze the spoon and when you run your finger through it a clear channel should form and hold.) The custard will thicken slightly as it cools. If at any time the custard seems to "break" and turn gritty, immediately pour it into a cold container, add a chip of ice, and whisk or blend it quickly. It will never be as silky as an unbroken sauce, but it can be rescued.

> Strain the custard through a fine sieve. Add the vanilla extract, if using.

> Serve warm or cold.

> If not using right away, press a butter wrapper, piece of parchment paper, or plastic wrap directly against the surface to prevent a skin from forming, cover, and refrigerate for up to 3 days.

FLAVORED CUSTARD SAUCES

Pouring custard is essentially liquid ice cream and can be similarly flavored.

Coffee	Add ¼ cup whole or cracked dark-roast coffee beans to the milk before heating it. Leave the coffee in the custard while it cooks, then strain the finished sauce. Alternatively, simply stir 2 teaspoons instant espresso powder mixed with 2 teaspoons water or 2 tablespoons coffee liqueur into the finished sauce.
Hazelnut	Stir ¼ cup finely chopped roasted hazelnuts and 1 tablespoon hazelnut liqueur into the finished sauce. Or, for a very lightly flavored custard, infuse the milk with ½ cup cracked roasted hazelnuts, then strain.
Chocolate Chip	Stir 3 tablespoons (1 oz/28 g) shaved or finely chopped bittersweet chocolate into the chilled sauce. Serve cool, or the chocolate pieces will melt. The chocolate will settle to the bottom, so stir before serving.
Malt	Substitute 3 tablespoons barley malt syrup for the sugar or stir ¼ cup malted milk powder into the warm sauce. Add malt to the chocolate chip or berry sauces for variation.
Berry	Stir a few tablespoons of the warm custard into ¼ cup seedless berry jam until smooth, then pour the jam mixture back into the sauce and stir until mixed. Finish with a tablespoon of berry liqueur if you like.
Honey	Substitute a dark natural honey for the sugar. If desired, add a few drops of almond extract or a tablespoon of amaretto.
Nougat (Honey, Pistachio, and Candied Fruit)	Substitute a dark natural honey for the sugar. Stir in 3 tablespoons (1 oz/28 g) chopped roasted pistachios, 1 teaspoon finely minced candied citron, and 1 teaspoon finely minced glacé cherries into the warm sauce.
Cinnamon	Infuse the milk with 2 broken cinnamon sticks.

Pumpkin	Infuse the milk with 1 cinnamon stick, 2 or 3 coins of fresh ginger, and 3 or 4 whole cloves. Stir ½ cup canned pumpkin puree into the egg yolks until smooth. Finish the sauce with a few gratings of nutmeg. Or, if you prefer, omit the whole spices and nutmeg and stir ½ teaspoon pumpkin pie spice into the pumpkin and egg mixture.
Green Tea (Matcha)	Omit the vanilla. Stir 2 teaspoons powdered green tea (matcha) into 1 to 2 tablespoons of the cold milk until smooth. Add the green tea mixture to the remaining milk and proceed with the recipe.

PULLING IT ALL TOGETHER

MAKING SAUCES LIKE A PRO

I f you've made it to this point in the book, you should understand most of the foundations of sauce making. You may have tried some new recipes and even thrown together a few customized alternatives. Now it's time to try making sauces like a chef—spontaneously, creatively, and confidently.

The next pages will remind you of the basics; suggest ways to incorporate sauces into your menus, and to enrich and finish sauces; describe how to customize sauces for guests with special diets; and offer ideas for rescuing sauces that don't quite meet your expectations.

BRUSHING UP ON THE BASICS

Try to remember that great sauces are not magically conjured; they are constructed. Here is a "cheat sheet" if you need a quick reminder of the key principles.

- Choose good ingredients (see Maximize Flavor, page 35).

- Consider every drop of liquid, because you can't pick out the bad ones (see Maximize Flavor, page 35).

- Treat fats as if they are precious materials—don't kill their flavors or use them wastefully (see Maximize Flavor, page 35).

- Altering the movement of water molecules will change the texture of a sauce (see Manipulate Texture, page 39).

- Taste. Think. Act. Repeat (see Season Confidently, page 72).

- Think about how your palate "feels" when creating balance (see Season Confidently, page 72).

- Trust your own taste (see Season Confidently, page 72).

- Clean your palate when it becomes confused: rinse your mouth, have a cracker, get some fresh air (see Season Confidently, page 72).

- Different is not always bad.

- Sauces are not served alone. Consider what they are going to be served with and adjust the seasonings accordingly.

- Remember that starch masks flavor (see Starch Masks Flavor, page 319). If you are going to serve a sauce with a starchy food, make sure it is especially flavorful.

- Don't panic. Cook smart. If your sauce isn't burnt, curdled beyond repair, or spoiled, you should be able to figure out a way to salvage it (see the table of Remedies for Faltering Sauces, page 446).

COOKING FOODS IN SAUCE

Many of the world's greatest sauces are not made to be served alongside an entrée but are a crucial part of the entire preparation—there is no clear delineation between where the dish stops and the sauce begins. These are sometimes called "integral sauces."

Including only independent sauces in *Mastering Sauces* was a conscious decision. Authenticity may be compromised here and there, but it means the recipes are more adaptable and accessible. It doesn't take much to turn a sauce into a unified dish or entrée. Learn to make a good Tikka Masala Sauce (page 222), and adding chicken is no big deal. You can also use the same basic sauce for paneer, vegetables, shrimp, or lamb. The broths, purees, tomato sauces, white sauces, and gravies all can be used as delicious integral sauces by simmering them with entrée ingredients.

You can build a sauce around a featured ingredient or simmer ingredients in a finished sauce. For instance, if you sear chicken quarters in a pan before you start the process of making Quick Mole Sauce (see the table on page 185), you have the beginnings of a feast. Try smothering mahi mahi fillets in Tomatillo and Pumpkin Seed Sauce (page 214) and baking or simmering it until the fish is cooked through. Or drop shrimp, slices of spicy sausage, or vegetables into a simmering pot of Creole Sauce Made with Dark Brown Roux (page 341) to make a quick, rich stew.

Flavors will meld, evolve, and marry as they infuse. When making a dish with an integral sauce, think about staggering the addition of the other ingredients to ensure they are cooked properly. Brown tough cuts and simmer them for hours in sauce. Add quick-cooking vegetables near the end and fresh, floral herbs right before serving.

Define your ideal texture for each sauce and take the necessary steps to get it there—thin it with a flavorful liquid, reduce and concentrate it, blend it, emulsify it, add a thickener. If you want to alter the texture of the sauce but don't want to interfere with the main ingredient—i.e., by breaking up tender potatoes or boiling seafood that is already cooked to perfection—lift the solids out, adjust the texture of the sauce, and then reintroduce the other components.

Season to taste. The balance of seasoning will change depending on the amount and characteristics of the ingredients you add. If the added components have very distinctive tastes, make them part of the overall balance. Remember to season all of the ingredients, the whole dish, not just the sauce. Expand your seasoning choices to complement the melded ingredients. A splash of fish sauce may be more appropriate than another pinch of salt. A finish of dried green mango powder may add a sweet-tart taste to your curry that will be more interesting than a squeeze of lime.

FINAL FLAIR—FINISHING AND ENRICHING SAUCES

Throughout this book, I have referred to finishing and enriching sauces. Many classical European sauces, especially those from royal courts and elegant houses, were not served until they were almost as rich as the guests themselves. I don't see the point of serving each guest a stick of butter or a cup of whipping cream when you can get a stronger base flavor and similar sense of richness with much, much less, but there are times when nothing pushes a sauce towards heaven more than a barely melted swirl of butter or a splash of heavy cream.

Finishing and Enriching Sauces with Suspended Melted Butter

Perhaps the most prized characteristic of butter in sauce making is the almost magical way it blends and becomes suspended in warm liquids. It remains as silky, smooth, and fluid as the cream it was made from. Even simmering water becomes something elegant on vegetables when bits of cold butter are gradually stirred into it. The French call this *beurre monté*—literally, "mounted butter." In English, the process is often referred to as mounting or finishing a sauce with butter. It is one of the most popular ways to enrich a sauce and the foundation of classic sauces like White Wine Butter Sauce (page 403) and Hollandaise (page 388). The technique can also be used to enhance reductions, purees, and fruit syrups and is great with pan sauces. In addition to added flavor, the texture becomes melt-in-your-mouth heavenly.

Scientifically, it is also quite an amazing transformation. Very simply, fresh cream is a water-based emulsion with dispersed fat droplets. The butter that is made from that cream has been churned into an oil-based emulsion with dispersed water droplets. With careful temperature control and whisking, you can disperse those butter fat droplets back into water to create a texture similar to the original cream, but in a liquid more flavorful than plain milk: wine, for example; or demi-glace.

The sauce must be hot and the butter cold. Cut the butter into pieces about the size of a cranberry or grape. Warm the sauce to a trembling simmer and whisk in a piece of butter until it barely melts, then add another and repeat. It's not difficult. You can add a few more pieces at a time as you get a feel for it—you will soon understand how quickly or slowly you need to add the butter. It must be slow enough so that you don't chill the sauce, quick enough so it doesn't overheat and break the emulsion.

If you need to keep a butter sauce warm for longer than just a few minutes, you can hold it in a container resting in a warm water bath or in a thermos to keep it at a controlled temperature. At about 140°F/60°C, the emulsion will start to fail. Take care that serving dishes and ingredients are not so hot that the butter-enriched sauces will break on contact.

Finishing and Enriching Sauces with Great Oils

You can gradually add good oils to sauces to enrich them. The texture will be altered with the addition of rich and flavorful fat. Some sauces can even be slightly thickened, others will separate—but not always in an unappealing way. A splash of fruity olive oil brightens the Spicy Charred Eggplant Sauce Puree (see the table on page 177). Roasted pumpkin seed oil adds a toasty richness to the Butternut Squash and Piquillo Pepper Salsa (page 239).

Finishing Sauces with Nondairy and Vegan Butter Alternatives

Don't do it: real butter can be melted into an emulsified suspension, but oils and nondairy butter alternatives really cannot. Theoretically, it's possible, and I've managed it a few times. I've even tried blending warm oils with liquid soy lecithin, but the result doesn't seem worth the effort. If what you want is a butter sauce, use butter.

Finishing and Enriching Sauces with Dairy Products

Even a few tablespoons of heavy cream will make almost any sauce thicker and silkier. But there is a caveat: cream and dairy products are natural emulsions, so they need to be added with extra care. In many recipes, you are warned to never boil the sauce or soup after the dairy product has been added because there is a chance the emulsion will break. When that happens, your creamy, uniform sauce becomes dotted with tiny white beads or grains of butterfat. But just when you are convinced that you can never boil another creamy preparation, you come across a recipe like the Condensed Coffee Cream (see the table on page 152) that is boiled and concentrated. What's the deal? I wish I could set in stone the answers of when and how to add cream to any recipe, but the truth is that I'm still slightly baffled by it all.

Shocking changes in temperature and acidity can cause dairy products to break. Introduce them gradually. Warm the milk, or stir a bit of the hot sauce into sour cream or yogurt before adding it to the sauce. The higher the fat content of the cream, the more stable it is when heated. It may seem counterintuitive, but very heavy whipping cream (at least 36-percent butterfat) will hold together better than half-and-half or whole milk when it is heated or boiled. Starch also adds stability. Warmed milk thickened with roux—i.e., béchamel sauce—can be practically bulletproof. Sour cream and crème fraîche do not act the same way, because sour cream is thickened with additives and crème fraîche is thickened with natural cultures. Crème fraîche is actually more heat tolerant. If you're not sure about how the dairy product you are using will behave, don't boil it.

Finishing and Enriching Sauces with Egg Yolks

Egg yolks are very rich, silky, and full of fat and flavor. Thickening sauces with egg yolks is an ancient technique. Eggs can thicken warm sauces by trapping water in a mesh of proteins that develops with gentle heat and time. Rather than just whisking them into the sauce, temper egg yolks by stirring a bit of warm sauce into them and then gradually pouring the mixture back into the rest of the warm, but not simmering, sauce. Continue to heat the sauce gently, stirring constantly, until it begins to thicken. If the sauce boils, the eggs will cook and the sauce will have tiny bits of scrambled eggs throughout. Maintain a low, gentle temperature and stir often. You can also use a double boiler as a safety net.

IT'S-BEEN-A-LONG-DAMN-DAY-WINE-FROM-YOUR-GLASS PAN SAUCE

You don't actually have to sacrifice wine from your glass to make this sauce. The point is that with an understanding of the fundamentals, you can cook a great meal from fresh ingredients in less time than it takes to get a pizza delivered.

> **PREP** (see Maximize Flavor, page 35)
Choose a quick-cooking entrée like boneless chicken, fish fillets, shrimp, or mushrooms. Pat dry.

> **SEAR** (see the Maillard Reaction, page 110)
Heat a large skillet over medium-high heat. Swirl in a bit of oil and let it heat up, then sear your entrée until it is browned on one side. Flip it and sear the other side, then cook until the food is just cooked through. Transfer the food to a plate or platter.

> **DEGLAZE** (see Deglazing a Pan, page 111)
Pour in enough wine, savory tea, stock, broth, or juice to just coat the bottom of the pan. Even water works if you have enough good brown residue. Lift the pan from the burner and give it a swirl. The liquid should instantly bubble, dissolve the brown sticky bits, and then mostly evaporate. Add a bit more liquid if the pan dries out or there are stubborn tidbits that need additional softening. In the end, you want about 1 tablespoon reduced wine or other liquid per person in the pan. At this point, you can season the sauce and serve, or customize it with a little extra "oomph."

> **EMBELLISH** (optional)
If you want something a bit more interesting than reduced wine with savory brown flavors, consider stirring a little something extra into the pan sauce. You don't need much—maybe some chopped fresh herbs, a spoonful of hot pepper jelly, a diced tomato, or a glug of barbecue sauce.

> **FINISH** (see Final Flair—Finishing and Enriching Sauces, page 431)
If you feel you need richness after your long damn day, whisk about a teaspoon of cold butter per person into the simmering sauce until it is just melted. Or use another rich or creamy ingredient like some well-stirred plain yogurt or drizzle of really good olive oil. Taste and adjust the seasoning. Pour the sauce over your entrée. Grab some hot potatoes from the microwave, rinse off a handful of baby spinach, and refill your glass. You deserve it.

I'VE GOT CHICKEN, I NEED A SAUCE—RIGHT NOW!

It's dinnertime and you are faced, once again, with naked chicken breasts desperate for adornment. We've all been there. Many of the sauces in this book will go with chicken. But here are a few good starting points.

A FEW EXCELLENT SAUCES FOR CHICKEN

continues

A FEW EXCELLENT SAUCES FOR VEGETABLES

A FEW EXCELLENT SAUCES FOR FISH

Tamarind Coriander Broth (page 130)

Carrot Caraway Broth (page 132)

Bloody Mary Cocktail Sauce Reduction (table, page 151)

Green Pea and Thai Basil Sauce and variations (page 169)

Spicy Charred Eggplant Sauce Puree (table, page 177)

Grilled Scallion and Dashi Puree (table, page 178)

Warm Parsley and Bacon Pesto (table, page 197)

Power Pesto (page 198)

Tomatillo and Pumpkin Seed Sauce (page 214)

Apricot Fennel Relish (table, page 245)

Green Goddess Dressing with Avocado (table, page 266)

Mustard and Tarragon Dressing (table, page 266)

Cucumber and Herb Yogurt (page 270)

Nuoc Cham (page 279)

3-Ingredient Teriyaki Sauce (page 292)

Leek and Tomato White Sauce (table, page 323)

Shelley's Lemon Sauce for Fish (page 337)

Rouille (table, page 385)

Kimchee Tartar Sauce (table, page 385)

Sushi-Bar Hot Sauce (table, page 386)

Vegan Corn "Hollandaise" (page 389)

A FEW EXCELLENT SAUCES FOR SHELLFISH

A FEW EXCELLENT SAUCES FOR BEEF

Beefy Beet Broth (page 134)

Fresh Mushroom Jus (page 138)

Balsamic Vinegar Reduction (page 149)

Onion and Ale Reduction (table, page 150)

Carrot Reduction with Sriracha (table, page 150)

Celery Juice Reduction with Horseradish (page 153)

Roasted Cauliflower–Parmesan Sauce (page 172)

Celeriac, Shallot, and Mustard Sauce Puree (table, page 177)

Ranchero Sauce (table, page 186)

Bagnet Verd—Piedmontese Green Sauce (page 200)

Chinese Crackling Scallion and Garlic Sauce (page 203)

Stir-Together Peanut Butter–Hoisin Dipping Sauce (page 211)

Pistachio and Preserved Lemon Gremolata (page 216)

Fiery Island Curry Sauce (page 226)

Steak Sauce Vinaigrette (table, page 257)

Classic Caesar Salad Dressing (page 261)

Tkemali—Georgian Plum "Ketchup" (page 283)

"Bulldog" Style Steak Sauce (table, page 284)

Delores's Sweet-and-Sour Meatball Sauce (table, page 285)

Korean Pear Bulgogi Sauce (page 293)

Tami's Brazilian Barbecue Mop (page 294)

Demi-Glace and Variations (page 349; table, page 351)

Blue Cheese Sauce (table, page 359)

Pub Butter (table, page 401)

A FEW EXCELLENT SAUCES FOR PORK

A FEW EXCELLENT SAUCES FOR HAM, SAUSAGES, AND CURED MEATS

Tomato and Old Bay Clam Nectar (page 141)

Pomegranate Reduction (page 149)

Red Cabbage and Vinegar Reduction (table, page 150)

Spicy Thai Pineapple Reduction (table, page 150)

Apple and Onion Redeye Gravy (page 155)

Date Gastrique (page 156)

Parsnip and Parsley Sauce Puree (table, page 178)

Cranberry Apple Sauce Puree (table, page 179)

Mint Chutney (page 202)

Butternut Squash and Piquillo Pepper Salsa (page 239)

Fresh Pear, Cranberry, and Kumquat Relish (page 240)

Last-Minute Cherry Tomato and Olive-Bar Antipasto Relish (page 241)

Mango and Peppadew Peppers Salsa (table, page 245)

Roasted Red Pepper Vinaigrette (table, page 256)

Beet Vinaigrette (table, page 256)

Tkemali—Georgian Plum "Ketchup" (page 283)

Horseradish Cream (table, page 284)

Honey Mustard Sauce (table, page 284)

Creole Sauce Made with Dark Brown Roux (page 341)

Blue Cheese and Dry Sherry Sauce (table, page 386)

Sweet Ginger Peach Sauce (page 414)

Carrot Orange Syrup (table, page 415)

A FEW EXCELLENT SAUCES FOR DESSERTS

Rose-Scented Almond Milk (page 98)

Strong Red Bush (Rooibos) Tea with Honey (page 129)

Balsamic Vinegar Reduction (page 149)

Port Reduction (page 149)

Cherry Juice Reduction (table, page 151)

Pear, Chardonnay, and Cardamom Reduction (table, page 151)

Cream Sherry Reduction (table, page 151)

Black Currant and Pastis Reduction (table, page 151)

Condensed Coffee Cream (table, page 152)

Coffee-Banana Rum Sauce (page 176)

Pear and Campari Sauce Puree (table, page 179)

Holiday Persimmon Sauce Puree (table, page 179)

Sweet Lemon Cream Sauce (table, page 285)

Arkansas Chocolate Gravy (page 335)

Cherry Wine Sauce (page 374)

Fresh Melon-tini Sauce Thickened with Xanthan Gum (page 377)

Fresh Citrus Sauce Thickened with Agar-Agar (page 378)

Fresh Blackberry Port Sauce Thickened with Agar-Agar (page 379)

Lemon Clove Syrup (page 409)

Earl Grey Tea Syrup (table, page 410)

Fresh Mint Syrup (page 413)

5-Minute Dark Chocolate Coconut Sauce (table, page 419)

Nougat English Pouring Custard (table, page 424)

CREATIVE MIXING AND MATCHING

Understanding the three fundamentals of sauce making frees you to experiment and come up with your own original preparations. Here are some of my favorites:

- Deglaze a skillet (see Deglazing a Pan, page 111) with Tamarind Coriander Broth (page 130).

- Reduce Rich and Savory Meatless (Vegan) Brown Stock (page 112) into a concentrated broth, stir in a bit of Vegan Cashew Sour Cream (page 273), and make a vegan stroganoff. Do not boil.

- Toss pasta with Grilled Artichoke Salsa (page 237) or Last-Minute Cherry Tomato and Olive-Bar Antipasto Relish (page 241).

- Use Carrot Caraway Broth (page 132) to make gravy.

- Stir Hara Masala (page 206), Mint Chutney (page 202), or Harissa (page 307) into plain yogurt and use it as a sauce, dip, dressing, or marinade.

- Dress a bean salad with Tomato and Chile Momo Dunk (page 304).

- Glaze grilled chicken skewers with Sweet Peanut Dressing (page 264).

- Use Lemon Clove Syrup (page 409) to poach pears.

SAUCE MAKING FOR SPECIAL DIETS

You can customize a sauce for virtually any diet. Here are some tips.

Vegetarian

The majority of the sauces in the book are vegetarian. Substitute an alternative stock for those made with chicken, meat, fish, shrimp shells, or dashi. Ask your guests about eggs and where they stand on seasonings such as fish sauce and Worcestershire, before adding them.

Gluten-Free

Many of the sauces in the book are gluten-free, and some of the traditional recipes offer gluten-free alternatives. In addition to many flours, be sure to avoid soy sauce, malt syrup, beer and ales, Marmite, Worcestershire sauce, miso, some commercial stocks and soup bases, and many prepared Asian condiments and sauces, like hoisin sauce.

Vegan

Many of the sauces in the book are, or can easily be made, completely animal-free. Customize your own sauces by using vegetable stocks, vegan shiitake dashi, and dairy-free alternatives, such as soy or almond milk. Use oils in place of butter. Use vegan Worcestershire sauce. Some vegans avoid honey.

Low-Sodium

Making sauces from scratch, from fresh ingredients, will dramatically lower sodium content. Make sauces with infusions, fresh stocks, seasonal produce, and your own mayonnaise. By volume, kosher salt is lower in sodium than table salt. Be aware of hidden sources of sodium, such as commercially made stocks and soup bases, cheese, soy sauce, fish sauce, miso, MSG, sodium citrate, dashi, and some prepared condiments. Nutritional yeast flakes taste salty but are very low in sodium.

The Big 8—The Most Common and Dangerous Food Allergies

Many of the recipes in this book are suitable for allergy sufferers, but please don't minimize the severity of allergies, especially to the eight most dangerous allergens—eggs, soy, peanuts, tree nuts, milk, fish, shellfish, and wheat. Remember that cross-contamination is always a concern, and allergens can lurk on tools such as cutting boards, wooden spoons, sieves, and blenders.

Diabetes

Making your own sauces offers more control over ingredients for the cook and diner. Season with sweeteners in moderation; substituting artificial sweeteners is not recommended for these recipes. Monitor carbohydrates, such as sweet fruit and vegetable purees, as well. Keep an eye on portion size.

REMEDIES FOR FALTERING SAUCES

Skilled cooks can often rescue foods when things take a nasty turn. I'm not going to suggest that every sauce can be resuscitated, but with some quick thinking and a little action, you'll be surprised at what you can achieve.

It's Too Thin	Are you sure? Thin sauces tend to be preferable to sauces that are too thick. Is there a chance it might thicken as it cools slightly?
	Is it a heat-tolerant sauce? Simmer it for longer to evaporate excess water and concentrate the texturizing elements, or add a thickener that you can stir right into the pot and cook quickly such as kneaded butter, slurry, or a starchy puree.
	Is it a heat-sensitive sauce, like those made with eggs or butter? Enrich it by gradually adding another egg yolk. Or, if it is a warm sauce, gradually add another tablespoon or two of butter or a tablespoon of heavy cream or crème fraîche. A tiny bit of xanthan gum can also help make the sauce more viscous, but it needs to be stirred or blended in well, and that may damage the structure of set egg gels like custards.
	Is the sauce uncooked? Can you drain off some of the excess liquid, as with salsas or purees that have settled? If the juices are an important part of the flavor, you may be able to thicken them separately and return them to the sauce. If it is a chunky sauce, consider adding more solids, or giving the sauce a few pulses with an immersion blender so the liquid has more particulates.
	Is it the flavor and not the texture that is thin? Change the ratio of flavorful and flavorless particles.
	Rethink the presentation—perhaps serving the sauce tableside from a pitcher or ladle or serving the dish in shallow bowls.

It's Too Thick	Is it cold? Bring the sauce to room temperature or warm it.
	Has it cooked down too long and become overconcentrated due to evaporation? For example, does your tomato sauce seem more like tomato paste? If the taste is also too intense, simply thin the sauce with water. If the taste is good, thin the sauce with a complementary liquid such as infused water, stock, broth, juice, or wine.
	Is it too thick because there are too many starches or added thickeners? For instance, is it a white sauce that seems pasty? Or a stir-fry sauce that is gummy? Try gradually stirring in more liquid. Try blending it with more liquid in a blender or with an immersion blender. It may look knobby at first but should eventually thin, because many thickeners lose their strength when cut or broken up. (This will not work with xanthan gum.)
	Is it too thick because there are too many particulates or solids? For example, is it a sweet potato sauce that seems like more of a side dish gone wrong? Thin it with additional flavorful liquids, press it through a fine-mesh strainer, or blend it to break up the mesh of starches or proteins that are interrupting the movement of water.
	Is it too thick but there are textural elements that won't be as appealing when stirred or blended (for example, a curry with tender vegetables)? Strain off the sauce from the solids, alter the texture of the strained liquid, and then reintroduce it to the solids.
There's Not Enough	Do you have the time and ingredients to quickly throw together another batch?
	Can you bulk up what you have with an appropriate ingredient like minced fruit or vegetable, a vegetable puree, a can of tomatoes, a dollop of sour cream, extra butter, or flavorful oil?

continues

	Consider serving the sauce with a second quick and simple sauce or condiment that will complement it. Whip up a stir-together condiment from the table on page 284, a salsa made with chopped fresh produce, a mayo or yogurt sauce, or an instant puree made from well-seasoned canned fruits or vegetables such as peaches or pimentos.
	Serve the meal plated rather than family-style so you can control the portioning of the sauce.
It's Curdled/ Broken/ Shattered	Is it an egg-yolk-enriched dressing, such as mayo? Add 1 or 2 fresh egg yolks to the clean blender jar and gradually add the broken mayo to the yolks as you would the oil.
	Is it a warm egg emulsion like Hollandaise? At the first sign of trouble, remove the sauce from the heat, transfer it to a cool container, and whisk or blend like crazy. Try putting 1 or 2 fresh egg yolks into a clean bowl or blender and gradually adding the warm sauce, as you would the butter. Or, if the emulsion has broken because the eggs have been overheated and have cooked, you may be able to blend it smooth at high speed, though the texture will never be as refined or smooth as it was meant to be.
	Is it a gelled egg sauce such as English Pouring Custard (page 422) or a sauce that was finished and enriched with an egg yolk? Pull it off the heat immediately, transfer to a cool container, and add a few small ice chips if possible, and whisk or blend like crazy. The cooked egg is irreversible, but you may be able to blend the particles so they are small enough to be acceptable. Even if you strain the sauce, you will have to settle for a slightly coarse and gritty texture. If you still can't get the sauce to pull together evenly with this, you will have to turn to a Plan B sauce.
	Is it a creamy sauce? Creamy ingredients are usually natural emulsions that are irreversible once broken. There's not much you can do other than try blending the sauce at high speed until it is as smooth as possible; tiny beads will still remain. Many nondairy milks like almond and hemp milks break when they are overheated. Again, they can't be recovered.

	Is it a nut sauce? Try stirring or blending a bit more. You can stir separated natural peanut or almond butter together, so keep it up! If it looks gritty, add a bit of extra liquid.
The Solids Sink or Float	Give the sauce a stir before you serve it. It may be a natural characteristic that doesn't need to be fixed.
	Is there a chance that the body of the sauce is too thin? Consider adding something from the table of Texturizers (page 48).
It Seems Greasy/The Fat Is Rising to the Top of the Sauce	Is it a simple vinaigrette? Whisk or blend it together.
	Did you finish or enrich the sauce with a flavorful oil? It should be tasty, so enjoy it. Just stir it again before you serve it.
	Is it a butter sauce that is meant to be melted, like a compound butter? It's probably fine. If the food seems to be swimming in an excess of greasy-looking melted butter, pour some off.
	Is it a sauce that is meant to be emulsified or suspended or have a creamy, buttery finish? You have a problem. The emulsion has broken and you will not be able to resuscitate it, especially if the sauce is meant to be served right away. If you have the time, remove as much of the melted butter as you can—pour or spoon it off the top. Ideally, chill the sauce completely and lift the remaining butter solids from the top. Once you have removed as much butter as possible, you may be able to introduce fresh cold butter. If, though, after the first few pieces the butter is clearly separating again, you will have to go to a Plan B sauce. That might be the melted butter you removed, infused with herbs, garlic, or another flavoring.

continues

	Is it gravy? Spoon, mop (use a fat mop; see page 27), or pour off the unwanted fat. Or pour the gravy into a fat separator so you can pour the good stuff into a gravy boat from the bottom and leave the fat in the cup. Or chill the gravy completely, lift the congealed fat from the surface, and reheat. Refer to Oil Slicks—How to Get Rid of Unwanted Grease (page 332) to see how to prevent it from happening again.
	Is it a spice-rich curry or coconut milk sauce? Small pools of spiced oil are a sign that the cook cares about flavor. Serve it with pride.
	Did you add too much oil at the beginning, to soften the onions and garlic? Or did you neglect to drain the sausage before starting the pasta sauce? These are tricky. Do what you can to spoon off as much fat as possible. Or use a fat mop (see page 27). Or chill the sauce completely, lift off any congealed fat, and reheat the sauce.
	Is it a chunky sauce or salsa? Consider draining off the liquid from the solids, removing the fat using any of the techniques described above or creating an emulsion, and then reintroducing it. Or discard the liquid and add fresh liquid.
It's Lumpy	Did the lumps show up once a thickener was added? Chances are the thickener was not evenly dispersed or was not smoothly blended before it was introduced. That can be hard to fix. If it is a smooth sauce, consider straining it. You may be able to blend it, but chances are you will break up the thickening structure and it will become thin again. In that case, try to rethicken it and add more flavor and seasonings as needed. If the sauce is highly textured, as with a "fancied-up" white sauce (see the table on page 323), there's not much you can do. You could pick out the noticeable lumps one by one, but it might be best just to serve it. Next time you'll be more careful.
	Are there just unblended solids or hard brown bits from the bottom of a roasting pan that may not have dissolved? Strain the sauce.
	Is it an emulsified sauce? Has it broken into lumps, beads, or curds? Review the remedies for curdled/broken/shattered sauces on page 448.

	Consider adding additional, more appealing lumps as camouflage: stir in some chopped olives, sliced scallions, minced tomatoes, or coarsely chopped fresh herbs.
It's Grainy	Was there an emulsion that might have broken? Is the grit actually cooked egg or separated solids from overheated cheese or dairy products? Refer to the curdled/broken/shattered remedies on page 448.
	Are the particles simply too large? Try reducing the particle size by blending the sauce at high speed, or pressing the sauce through a sieve, or straining it through a few layers of dampened cheesecloth. If you are using cheesecloth, gather up the edges to make a parcel and gradually tighten and squeeze to remove as much liquid as possible. The quantity will be reduced and the sauce will be thinner, but it will be smooth.
	Are there undercooked elements, as with, for example, the Roasted Cauliflower–Parmesan Sauce (page 172)? Simmer the sauce for longer and reblend it, or strain it and cook only the harder bits, then reintroduce them.
It's Gooey	Is it too cold? Try warming the sauce slightly.
	Thin it with a flavorful and/or slightly acidic liquid.
	Cornstarch and potato or tapioca starch will gradually break down when heated or blended. Try cooking the sauce longer or whizzing it up a bit with an immersion blender.
	Arrowroot can make milky mixtures slimy. Too much xanthan gum can make sauces unpleasantly gooey. These aren't errors that can really be remedied. Kudzu can give sauces an odd texture when chilled, but it should go away when they are warmed.

continues

	If the gooey sauce is blended with ingredients that shouldn't be heated or overly agitated, consider straining or even rinsing the sauce off the solids. Repair the sauce, make a fresh batch of the same sauce, or make a new quick-to-fix sauce and reintroduce the solids.	
It's Congealed	Is it a meaty sauce, like demi-glace or gravy? Stocks and sauces with a lot of natural gelatin will solidify when chilled. Has the fat congealed, as with a gravy or butter sauce that is too cold? Try gently warming the sauce to make it more liquid.	
	Is it a meatless reduction or puree? Warm it slightly, or thin it with a flavorful liquid until it becomes liquid again.	
	Was the sauce made with a lot of oil or butter? Many oils solidify when chilled. Mayo made with extra-virgin olive oil will seem pasty when chilled. Sauces made with melted or suspended butter should never be chilled, because they cannot be easily rewarmed.	
	Sauces thickened with starches can seem pasty, gooey, or congealed when cool. They will loosen when they are heated, or you can simply add more flavorful liquid to thin the sauce to the desired consistency.	
	Sauces thickened with kudzu root have an unusual congealed texture when they are cold but it will melt away when they are warmed.	
	Sauces with a high nut or seed content can seize up, especially when they are heated. Gradually whisk in some additional liquid.	
	Cheese sauces made with sodium citrate, like the Gooey Orange Nacho Cheese Sauce (page 363), will quickly congeal as they cool, but they can be remelted without a problem. They can also be melted and thinned with a bit of additional milk.	

It's Slimy	Is it old? A sauce that was once lovely and is now slippery should be thrown out.
	Did you add xanthan gum? If the sauce is just a touch slippery, try stirring in some additional flavorful liquid, but don't blend or whisk aggressively. If the texture has become unpleasant, throw it out.
	Some vinaigrettes will have an odd slightly slimy texture when they are very cold and the oil has congealed. Leave them to warm to room temperature and give them a good stir.
	Are there naturally mucilaginous ingredients? Okra, nopales (cactus paddles), and gumbo filé have textures that can make a sauce seem slimy. Add a bit of extra acidity like lime juice or vinegar. If that doesn't work, serve the sauce with the understanding that it is what it is. You will know better next time.
	Did you add arrowroot or kudzu root? Arrowroot can become slimy when used to thicken milky sauces. Kudzu root can get strangely slimy when used in excess.
It's Pasty	Was the sauce made with naturally starchy ingredients like potatoes? Thin it by gently stirring in more flavorful liquid. Press it through a sieve if necessary.
	Did you add a thickener such as roux or slurry? There was probably too much. Thin the sauce, boost the flavors back to where they should be, and season accordingly.
	Does "pasty" describe the taste more than the texture? The starch probably wasn't cooked for long enough—return the sauce to the stove. Always make sure pure starches reach the boiling point. Raw flour may need as long as 5 minutes of simmering to remove the raw taste. Bean flours can take 30 minutes to taste cooked.

continues

It's Ugly/It's an Unappealing Color	Is there another description on this table that may be more accurate? Is it lumpy? Separated? Refer to those remedies.
	Try blending, straining, or reducing the sauce to bring it together or make it look more cohesive and intentional.
	Stir in or scatter on some appropriate, appealing elements like sautéed mushrooms, diced tomatoes, crumbled bacon, grated cheese, or sliced scallion greens.
	Brighten dim or gray sauces with colorful ingredients, especially those with relatively unobtrusive flavors, like a touch of tomato paste, dash of paprika, bit of achiote paste, or tiny bit of turmeric.
	Darken and intensify brown sauces with soy sauce, Worcestershire, Marmite, Caramel Coloring (page 420), or even Meat Glace (page 158).
I Think It's Burnt	Is it bitter, smoky tasting, oddly dark, or dotted with black flecks? Throw it out.
	Did you catch it just in time? Do not stir! Quickly separate the good from the bad as best you can. If the bottom of the pot has just developed a noticeable crust but the sauce does not taste off or look too terrible, pour the sauce into a clean pot without agitating or scraping the bottom at all. You don't want any dark flakes or specks mixed into the sauce. If they are unavoidable, mask them with extra black pepper or minced herbs.
	Is it a reduction that has just gone a touch too far but has not actually caramelized? You may be able to brighten it up with some acidic ingredients like vinegar or lemon juice; pungent items like minced or grated fresh onion or a touch of horseradish or mustard; or a dollop of sour cream or yogurt.
	If you built your sauce around burnt ingredients like scorched garlic or crumbly black pan residue—you should know better!

It Doesn't Taste Right	Try to define "right." It can be tricky, but think about the sauce you meant to create and you will have a better chance at arriving at the solution.
	Refer to Maximize Flavor (page 35) and Season Confidently (page 72) for tips on boosting and balancing flavors.
	Is there a chance your ingredients are bad? When in doubt, throw it out!
	Ingredients and brands vary. You may have to compensate if you are using a new or unfamiliar product. Out-of-season produce can be virtually tasteless. It's a good idea to get into the habit of tasting and smelling ingredients before you add them.
	Different isn't always bad.
	Has it cooked or infused for long enough? Sometimes a sauce just needs a bit more time to marry, concentrate, or mellow. Step away from it for a while.
	Remember that the sauce is not meant to stand alone. Taste it with a bit of the food it is to be served with.
	Alternative versions will not taste exactly like traditional sauces. Don't expect Vegan Soy Cream Sauce (page 328) to taste the same as a traditional béchamel. Appreciate them for what they are. Seasoning or boosting the flavors to your taste can help.
It's Bland	Refer to Maximize Flavor (page 35), Season Confidently (page 72), and the Seasoning Alternatives (page 79).
	Did you add starch or serve the sauce with something starchy? Starch dims flavor. You will probably have to boost the seasoning quite a bit, especially the salt.

continues

	Since most flavors are oil soluble, a little bit of fat, like a few drops of good oil, a touch of butter, or a touch of cream or yogurt, can make more flavors available.
	Change the ratio of flavorful and flavorless particles (see page 38). Remove excess water through evaporation and reduction.
It Tasted Good in the Pot, but Now That It's on the Table, It's Nothing Special	That happens sometimes when you season just the sauce rather than consider the entire meal. Salt, pepper, lemon slices, and condiments are there to be used on restaurant tables, so why not yours?
	Try not to apologize. Consider the merits of "remembering" something that was "meant" to be added at the last minute—grated cheese, chopped fresh herbs, grated lemon zest, or a scattering of nuts. Pass some assorted items like unique salts, condiments, soy or fish sauce, and garnishes as though you had planned for guests to customize the dish to their own tastes.
	Perhaps serve a secondary element or special finish at the table, like plain yogurt, aged balsamic vinegar, spicy mustard, or very special oil or honey.
It's Too Salty	Remember that sauces are not meant to be served alone. Bland high-volume items like noodles are enhanced by salty sauces, not damaged.
	Can you dilute the sauce with additional liquid? Make sure you use unsalted liquids, not a salty stock, broth, or commercial product.
	Do what you can to add unseasoned bulk to the sauce, such as additional onions, some chopped apple or carrots, olive oil, nuts, or creamy ingredients. Try to avoid salty embellishments like olives, anchovies, and cheese.
	Try balancing the intensity with contrasting tastes. Add a bit more sugar or vinegar or some heat from fresh or dried chiles. Avoid adding umami-rich ingredients, since they tend to be perceived as salty.

	Creamy dairy foods and wheat flour can coat the tongue slightly and help to minimize the perception of salt. Wondra is a modified starch that doesn't have a pronounced raw taste so it can be added without cooking it. It will thicken the sauce and make it cloudy but dim some of the saltiness.
	Cut way back on the portion size. A few drops of soy is enough to flavor some dishes, so why not just a drizzle of super-intense red sauce or concentrated gravy? Change up the presentation and serve the sauce as a dollop or smear. A chef might rename the sauce "salted mango relish" or "savory chicken glaze" and make it seem intentional.
	Don't top the dish with any salty embellishments you may have intended to use, such as grated cheese, bacon bits, or pickled vegetables. Let guests serve themselves.
It's Too Sweet	You can't take the sweet away, but can you dilute the sauce or bulk it up with mild-flavored ingredients?
	Sometimes a bit of freshness can help. Add chopped herbs such as parsley or mint or some grated citrus zest. Add a bit of pungency from grated raw onion or a dollop of spicy mustard or chile sauce.
	Boost the bitter and umami elements with ingredients like aged cheese, Worcestershire sauce, chiles, or cocoa powder. These will "widen" how the sauce stimulates the palate.
	Sometimes it helps to add even more sweetness so the sauce seem intentionally sweet rather than just strangely off.
It's Sour	Stir the sauce well and taste it with some food rather than judging it on its own. Does it still seem sour?
	Change the taste balance by adding salt, sugar, or a bulkier base ingredient. Sweet-and-sour and hot-and-sour are popular taste combinations. Many popular condiments, such as pickles and mustards, are salty and sour.

continues

	Add more fat, like oil, butter, or cream.
	Pour, drain, or spoon off some of the liquid and replace it with a milder or more balanced flavor-appropriate ingredient, like stock, juice, or coconut cream.
	Does the sauce still have time to cook? Sometimes sour tastes will mellow with cooking or fade as other ingredients sweeten or intensify, as with acidic tomatoes and citrus juices. Tart wines, vinegars, and juices can sometimes sweeten as they reduce, but not always. Unsweetened rhubarb is sour no matter how much you cook it.
It's Too Spicy	Scoop out some of the sauce and bulk up what is left with unseasoned mild ingredients such as tomatoes, fresh or roasted sweet peppers, cooked onions, or a vegetable puree.
	Boost the salt, sweet, and umami tastes to make the sauce more intense overall and serve it in smaller portions, perhaps with a second mild or contrasting sauce.
	Are there visible pieces of chile that you can pick out?
	Fat carries capsaicin, so serving a cooling yogurt or dollop of sour cream alongside can help tame the fire.
	Serve the sauce with plenty of plain starchy foods like rice and noodles.

ACKNOWLEDGMENTS

I knew this was going to be a big project, but I had no idea what I was really taking on until right smack in the middle of it. I could never have done it without the love and unwavering support of Jeff Volland, Roy Fowler, Shelley Boyce, and Kris Latta. For twenty years my dear friend Cynthia Nims has led me in the right direction whenever I get lost. Her perspective, advice, and ability to listen have been invaluable.

I am very lucky to have had the guidance, support, and camaraderie of Maria Guarnaschelli. She trusted me, pushed me, and helped get things done right. It wasn't easy, but we seemed to "get" each other and laughed as often as possible. If only she were a Seahawks fan. Mitchell Kohles and Sophie Duvernoy deserve praise as well. Alison Fargis and Ellen Scordato at Stonesong meticulously took care of the business side of things and dealt with every unforeseen complication. The editing expertise of Judith Sutton and Wayt Gibbs is incomparable. Angie Norwood Browne and Patty Wittmann swooped in at the last minute and created images that were as artistic, warm, and inviting as they are themselves. Ryan Matthew Smith's brainstorms, generosity, flexibility, and love of good tavern burgers will always be appreciated. The book was inspired by the expertise of Nathan Myhrvold, Chris Young, Maxime Bilet, Grant Crilly, Johnny Zhu, and Anjana Shankar.

Thanks must also go to Desiree Volland, Susan Swift, Gwen Hayes, Colleen Farnham, Sierra Boyce, Colleen Merrill, Jody Everts, Anne Nagel, and Beverly Shortridge. If I could list everyone who played a part I would, but I'd end up writing another book.

Thank you all.

INDEX

Orange Chocolate Sauce, 419

Raspberry Chocolate Sauce, 419

chopping, 45

chopping and cutting tools, 22–23

chutneys:

Kolkata-Style Thin Fresh Fruit Chutney, 281–82

Mint Chutney, 202

cilantro:

Cilantro and Cotija Cheese Pesto, 196

Fiery Island Curry Sauce, 226–27

Hara Masala–Indian Green Spice Base, 206

Pico de Gallo, 244

Quick Diced Guacamole, 245

Spicy Pineapple Salsa, 245

Tami's Brazilian Barbecue Mop, 294

Tomatillo and Pumpkin Seed Sauce, 214–15

Trinidad Green Seasoning, 204–5

Cinnamon Custard Sauce, 424

Clam Nectar, 140–41

Meaty Clam Nectar, 141

Tomato and Old Bay Clam Nectar, 141

cloves:

Lemon Clove Syrup, 409

Pumpkin Custard Sauce, 425

Spiced Pineapple Sauce, 416

Cocktail Sauce, 284

coconut:

Coconut Stock, 109

Toasted Coconut, Habanero, and Lime Butter, 400

coconut milk:

Aromatic Coconut Cream Sauce, 329

Coconut Chocolate Sauce, 419

Coconut Stock, 109

Coconut Syrup, 412

Pranee's Thai Peanut Sauce, 209–10

Thai Coconut Curry Sauce, 224–25

coconut oil:

Coconut "Butter" with South Indian Flavors, 399

in dairy-free or vegan roux, 344

coffee:

Apple and Onion Redeye Gravy, 155

Coffee-Banana Rum Sauce, 176

Coffee Custard Sauce, 424

Condensed Coffee Cream Reduction, 152

Mexican Coffee Chocolate Sauce, 419

Mocha Chocolate Sauce, 419

colanders, 21

Cola Reduction, 152

cold thickeners, 375–79

collagen, 44, 102, 117, 157

condensed milk:

Chinese Honey Shrimp Sauce, 386

Sweet Lemon Cream Sauce, 285

condiments, 268–74

"Bulldog" Style Steak Sauce, 284

Cocktail Sauce, 284

Cucumber and Herb Yogurt, 270

Dairy-Free Avocado Lime Cream, 274

Delores's Sweet-and-Sour Meatball Sauce, 285

Fry Sauce, 284

Goat's-Milk-Yogurt Falafel Sauce, 271

Honey Mustard Sauce, 284

Honey-Sweetened Ketchup, 277–78

Horseradish Cream, 284

Kolkata-Style Thin Fresh Fruit Chutney, 281–82